"At last. A concise, scholarly, common-sense guide to eschatology that will serve as an inspiration to countless Bible students and a gentle corrective to those for whom end-times zeal has been misguided."

—Gary M. Burge
Professor of New Testament, Wheaton College and Graduate School

"Although no one will agree with every interpretation he defends, Schnabel does an admirable job of surveying the major views of the texts and then defending his conclusions. Irenic and firm, scholarly and accessible, careful and engaging, understandable for a broad audience without being simplistic, Schnabel interacts with a variety of biblical scholars, historians, and theologians as well as popular eschatology from several prominent pastors, novelists, and television preachers. This is an excellent resource and a model of evangelical biblical scholarship. Pastors, teachers, and students of the Scripture will find it a helpful tool and a useful source of information on these important questions."

—Glenn R. Kreider
Professor of Theological Studies, Dallas Theological Seminary

"This excellent and timely book provides clear, reasonable, and theologically sound answers to the questions that so many Christians have today about the last days. The book's great value lies in its interpretive approach. Professor Schnabel expertly explains every critical eschatological text in the Bible within its own historical and cultural context. He then shows how the original message of those texts should shape Christian thinking and practice today. In the process, he warns against the damage that badly informed and provincial readings can do to the life and witness of the church and issues a salutary plea for Christians to focus, undistracted, on the central eschatological concerns of the Bible."

—Frank Thielman
ᵔⁿ Divinity School

"Schnabel provides in this book m〈   〉wers to questions about the end times that every Chr〈   〉ost welcome and vital contribution because the quest〈   〉every generation. Those who do not have the sound bil〈   〉 will become easy prey to false prophets who have throughout the ages duped their devotees with outlandish predictions. Those who dismiss the issue of the end times as the domain of bizarre fanatics will grow slack in their vigilance and be both uninformed and unprepared. Again, every Christian should study and absorb this book."

—David E. Garland
Dean and William M. Hinson Professor of Christian Scriptures,
George W. Truett Theological Seminary, Baylor University

"Today, teachings about the end times are all over the map, ranging from serious, to sensational, to just plain silly. In his *40 Questions About the End Times*, Eckhard Schnabel brings to this cacophony the heart of a churchman, the careful analysis of one of our best New Testament

40 QUESTIONS ABOUT
The End Times

Eckhard Schnabel

Benjamin L. Merkle, Series Editor

40 Questions About the End Times
© 2011 Eckhard J. Schnabel

Published by Kregel Publications, a division of Kregel Inc., 2450 Oak Industrial Dr. NE, Grand Rapids, MI 49505.

This book is a title in the 40 Questions Series edited by Benjamin L. Merkle.

Library of Congress Cataloging-in-Publication Data
Schnabel, Eckhard J.
    40 questions about the end times / Eckhard Schnabel.
      p. cm.—(40 questions series)
    Includes bibliographical references (p. 321) and indexes.
    1. End of the world—Miscellanea. I. Title. II. Title: Forty questions about the end times.
    BT877.S36 2011
    236'.9—dc22

                            2011046564

ISBN 978-0-8254-3896-7

Printed in the United States of America

9 10 11 12 13 / 29 28 27 26 25 24 23 22 21

For Grant Osborne

Contents

Part 1: General Questions about the Future

A. The Future of the World

B. The Future of the Church

C. The Future of Israel

Part 2: The Return of Jesus Christ

A. Events before the Return of Jesus

Part 3: The Millennium and the Last Judgment

Part 4: Interpreting the End Times

Introduction

Jesus and the apostles spoke about the past—about Adam and Abraham, David and Solomon, and God's intervention in the history of Israel. They spoke about the present—the arrival of the kingdom of God, the new era of salvation, and the life, death, and resurrection of Jesus Christ. And sometimes they spoke about the future—the resurrection of the dead, the day of judgment, God's perfect new world, and about the time leading up to the end. Some of these passages, particularly those that speak about the time leading up to the end, raise a series of important questions. It is these questions that this book addresses.

It may be helpful at the outset to clarify the meaning of some terms that are used in discussions about the end times. The expression *the end times* is the modern equivalent for the scriptural expression *the last days*, which refers to the final period of history before *the last day*, which is the day of Jesus' second coming and the day of the last judgment. The term *eschatology* refers to the doctrine of "the last things" (from Greek, *eschatos*, "last"). Used in a strict sense, *eschatology* refers to prophecies, events, and developments that are close to, and connected with, the last period of history before the end. In a more general sense, the word is used to describe, for example, the fulfillment of the prophecies of the Old Testament prophets in the person, ministry, death, and resurrection of Jesus Christ and in the life and ministry of the church—the messianic period of the last days when Israel's Messiah has come and when his followers reach Jerusalem, Judea, Samaria, and all the nations with the gospel. The term *apocalyptic* describes events related more directly with the end of the world. The Greek term *apokalypsis* means "revelation" and has a general meaning not necessarily tied to the future, but the English term *apocalyptic* is usually used either for catastrophes of immense magnitude (e.g., the destruction of an entire city by an earthquake) and in the New Testament for texts and events that are connected with the end.

Regarding the basic approaches or "systems" of interpreting the end times, the following terms are often used in the discussion. *Amillennialism* (from Latin *mille*, "thousand," and *annus*, "year," with the letter *a* as negation) describes the position of interpreters who reject the view that there will be a literal thousand-year reign of Jesus in the future. They interpret Revelation 20:1–6, the one text in which the phrase "a thousand years" occurs in the

Bible (see questions 33–35), as referring to Christ's reign in and through the church in the present age. *Premillennialism* describes the view that Jesus will return before (Latin *prae*) the thousand-year reign, a "golden age" of peace in human history on earth which foreshadows the perfection of God's new world. *Postmillennialism* designates the view that Jesus will return in glory after (Latin *post*) a period of "millennial" conditions ushered in by the ministry of the church on earth before Jesus' return.

Dispensationalism describes the view that God intervenes in human history in different ways according to different periods or "dispensations" (or administrations). More specifically, the term describes a particular view of the end times initiated by John Nelson Darby in the nineteenth century, popularized by the *Scofield Reference Bible* and more recently by fictional depictions of the end times. Classical dispensationalism holds that (1) prophecies for Israel (the Jews) and prophecies for the church need to be strictly held apart, (2) the Old Testament prophecies for the Jewish people will be fulfilled for the Jewish people (in the future, if they have not been fulfilled already), (3) the church will be removed from the earth in a secret rapture before the great tribulation during which the Jewish people will come to faith in Jesus as their Messiah, (4) the appearance of the Antichrist will herald the beginning of the last phase of history, and (5) Jesus will return to earth and establish a thousand-year reign, before the eternal state of the new heavens and the new earth. Progressive dispensationalism acknowledges that (1) Jesus inaugurated the kingdom of God at this first coming which will be consummated at his second coming, (2) there is no sharp distinction between Israel and the church, and (3) Old Testament promises for Israel are at least in part fulfilled in the church, while insisting that national (ethnic) Israel has a future in God's plans for the world.

Discussions of the rapture (see question 10) use the terms *pretribulational* (the rapture takes place before the period of tribulation), *midtribulational* (the rapture happens in the middle of the tribulation period), and *posttribulational* (the rapture happens after the tribulation, a position that identifies the rapture with Jesus' return from heaven). The *preterist* position (Latin *praeteritus*, "past, by-gone, former") holds that the prophecies of Jesus in the Gospels and of John in the book of Revelation have already been fulfilled in the past, either in the events of A.D. 66–70 when Jerusalem was destroyed, and/or in events during John's lifetime in the first century or soon thereafter (up to the fall of the Roman Empire in A.D. 476). The *historicist* interpretation of Revelation holds that John's prophecies provide divine revelation for the entire church age, relating to past, present, and future historical events.

I will generally refrain from using these terms, not because they cannot be helpful in marking a position, but because labels are often used as "party terms" that tend to commit people to an entire system of belief regarding the end times. I am not interested in labels, nor in justifying a particular "systematic" approach to the interpretation of passages that speak about the end times. I will not compare eschatological systems with each other, such as classical dispensationalism, progressive dispensationalism, amillennialism, postmillennialism, premillennialism, or preterist positions (whether partial preterist or consistent preterist). I am interested in reading the relevant texts of the Old and New Testaments afresh. It is my hope that the readers of this volume will share this interest. If we are serious about our commitment to the authority of Scripture, and if we truly believe that Scripture is *norma normans* (i.e., the authority that provides the norm for what we believe and how we live), then a re-reading of the relevant passages about a particular topic, such as passages about the end times, is a continuing necessity and privilege. The following principles and convictions are basic for such a re-reading.

First, when Christians speak about the end times, it seems obvious that the primary "text" is God's revelation in the New Testament (i.e., what Jesus, Peter, Paul, and John say about the end times). In other words, the prophecies of the Old Testament must be integrated into the framework of New Testament prophecy. While the Old Testament remains the revealed word of God, it is the New Testament that informs Christians how to read the Old Testament. Regarding unfulfilled Old Testament prophecy, we need to be careful not to relate such prophecies automatically to the end times. If we do this, we are in the danger of detaching the prophet from his contemporaries and uprooting Old Testament prophecy from its historical context. As a result, we invite "sensationalistic and overly contemporized interpretation in the modern context in which the prophecy is transplanted."[1] When Old Testament prophecies seem unfulfilled,[2] we need to recognize that often God's statements of what he intends to do are conditional. That is, the realization of his intentions depends on (is contingent upon) the changed behavior of the people. Such conditions are sometimes stated explicitly (e.g., Isa. 1:19–20), "but more often they are unstated and implicit."[3] It is important to remember that "although the prophets never questioned Yahweh's power to fulfill what he had predicted, they often left room for a different outcome, especially if the conditions that had provoked the prophecy in the first place should change."[4]

Second, Jesus asserted repeatedly that nobody knows the date or the time of his return. Before his death, he stated that the disciples have not been given the right to know the "day and hour" of his return, which God has set

---

1. Robert B. Chisholm, "When Prophecy Appears to Fail, Check Your Hermeneutic," *JETS* 53 (2010): 561.
2. For example, Huldah's prophecy of Josiah's death (cf. 2 Kings 22:15–20 with 23:29–30), and the prophecy of Tyre's destruction by Nebuchadnezzar (cf. Ezek. 26:7–11 with 29:17–18).
3. Chisholm argues that Jeremiah 18:1–12 suggests that all unqualified prophecies are subject to implicit conditions, since repentance always has the potential of affecting prophecies of judgment ("When Prophecy Appears to Fail," 563).
4. Daniel I. Block, *The Book of Ezekiel*, NICOT (Grand Rapids: Eerdmans, 1998), 2:148.

in his authority (Matt. 24:36). After his resurrection he told the disciples, again, that "it is not for you to know the times or periods" which God has set by his own authority (Acts 1:7). And in the second part of the Olivet Discourse about the end times, Jesus repeatedly stressed that he will return unexpectedly and suddenly like a thief in the night (Matt. 24:36–25:30). These statements, which are not ambiguous but clear and decisive, need to be taken seriously. Any interpretation of end-time texts (or what some call "the prophetic word") that seeks to narrow down the nearness of Jesus' second return and to calculate the nearness of the end (or the rapture, or the Antichrist) ignores Jesus' assertion.

Third, the early Christians believed that the end times began with the coming of Jesus, Israel's Messiah, in particular with his death and resurrection (see question 1). This conviction needs to be taken seriously when we interpret texts that speak about the events related to the end times.

Fourth, the early Christians believed that Jesus *might* return during their lifetime (see questions 1, 4, 7). This means that the apostles interpreted biblical prophecy—what the Old Testament predicted and what Jesus prophesied—concerning the end times as either fulfilled or as about to be fulfilled in the near future. The apostles' convictions need to be taken seriously when we interpret the relevant Old Testament texts, Jesus' prophecy, and the apostles' exposition.

Fifth, the same principles of interpretation must be followed when we study texts about the end times that we use when we study other parts of Scripture. We take into account the genre (or text-type) of the book or the passage in question. We study the meaning of sentences, phrases, and words in order to establish as best as we can how the author of the text and his readers understood them in the historical, cultural, and linguistic context in which they lived (see the volume *40 Questions About Interpreting the Bible* by Robert L. Plummer). Some interpreters work with the principle that the language of prophecies should be interpreted literally as long as this can be reasonably followed. This is an illegitimate demand because it leaves the decision when to interpret literally and when to interpret symbolically up to the modern interpreter. It is the original author and his cultural and linguistic context that determine whether an expression or a statement should be interpreted literally or not.

For example, in the statement "those who are victorious I will make pillars in the temple of my God" (Rev. 3:12 NIV), even so-called literalists would want to take the phrase "pillars in the temple of my God" symbolically—although one could argue that as God turned Lot's wife into a pillar of salt (Gen. 19:26), he can turn the believers from Philadelphia (who are addressed in Rev. 3:7–13) into literal pillars in a literal temple. While this may sound strange, we need to remind ourselves that there are end-time "specialists" committed to a "literal" interpretation who argue that the two witnesses of Revelation 11, interpreted as two literal evangelists who are thought to appear in the second

half of the last seven years of history, will literally destroy the people who oppose them with fire coming from their mouth (Rev. 11:5).

It might be helpful to remind ourselves of the classical principle that we
proceed from clear passages and use them to shed light on unclear passages.
While there are many details in biblical prophecy that are disputed because
the meaning of particular expressions and statements is not immediately
clear, there is much that is beyond dispute. We need to move from the larger
picture to the details, not the other way round. It seems preposterous that
some end-time specialists wait for the Antichrist, or for terrible disasters to
happen, the timing of which in God's plan is disputed. Followers of Jesus wait
for Jesus' return, not for the Antichrist.

Regarding the book of Revelation, the most extensive New Testament text
about the end times, it is important to keep in mind the genre of the book.
Genre (or text-type) of a passage implies something like a contract between
the author and his or her readers. The genre of a text signals how a text should
be read. For example, Proverbs 21:21 ("He who pursues righteousness and
love finds life, prosperity and honor"; NIV) is not a prophecy but a general-
izing proverb that is often true but not always. There have been millions of
faithful Christian believers throughout the ages who pursued righteousness
and loved their families, friends, and even their enemies but never found life,
prosperity, and honor. On the contrary, many lost their lives in persecution,
had their possessions confiscated, and were shamed in public. A proverb
needs to be interpreted as a proverb, a legal text as a legal text, a hymn as a
poetic text, and a historical text as a historical text. In approaching the book
of Revelation, it is important to recognize that it is a mixed genre.

The book of Revelation is an apocalypse (Rev. 1:1). This means that it is
a book about the end times that uses many traditional images and symbols,
as apocalyptic texts generally do. The book of Revelation is also a prophecy
(Rev. 1:3). This means that it is a text in which a prophet conveys to his contemporaries new revelation that God has granted to him in visions, with the
purpose of encouraging and exhorting his readers. The prophets of the Bible
do not address readers living in the distant future, unconcerned about their
contemporaries. When they speak about the future, they always *also* address
their contemporaries. Prophecy is not only informative regarding future
events. Prophecy is admonition. The Old Testament prophets use a combination of prediction, warning, exhortation, and appeals to prompt God's people
to change their behavior. While the prophets of Scripture at times speak about
the distant future—the end of history, the future coming of the day of judgment, the second coming of Jesus—they do so in addressing readers whose
linguistic capabilities they know. This truth is stated in Revelation 22:10,
when the angel tells John, "Do not seal up the words of the prophecy of this
scroll, because the time is near" (NIV). This instruction is in explicit and direct
contrast to the instruction that Daniel received: "The vision of the evenings

and mornings that has been given you is true, but seal up the vision, for it concerns the distant future" (Dan. 8:26 NIV). Since John's visions concern the present and since the time of the end is near, he was asked to write the prophecy contained in the book of Revelation in such a way that his readers in the churches of Asia Minor would understand the meaning of the visions. The fact that the book of Revelation is also a letter—note the typical letter pre-script (Rev. 1:4–5) and the concluding benediction (Rev. 22:21)—reinforces the truth that John wrote for his contemporaries, expecting the believers in the first-century churches not only to hear but to understand and to take to heart what he wrote (Rev. 1:3).

The book of Revelation relates a series of visions, not a "systematic" account about the end times. A sequence of visions is not necessarily a chronological series of events. John records visions that he has received; he may or may not present them in the sequence in which he received the visions. Since he records the visions that he received serially, the possibility cannot be excluded that the content of visions which speak about real events in the future—such as the judgment on the world and Jesus' second coming—overlap. This would mean that the same events are described several times in several visions. The problem with some systems of eschatological interpretation is that a sequence of events is reconstructed by combining particular passages with each other, without a single biblical text describing such a sequence. While such reconstructions are not *a priori* impossible, they should not be dogmatically asserted as the only possible interpretation.

Several colleagues and friends have contributed to the writing of this book. I thank Ben Merkle for inviting me to contribute this volume to the 40 Questions Series. Doug Sweeney, my colleague at Trinity Evangelical Divinity School, and Ben Snyder, my teaching assistant, have kindly and competently read the entire manuscript; their questions, comments, and suggestions have made the manuscript a better book. Rick Cook and Scott Manetsch have discussed many of the forty questions with me during long runs along the Des Plaines River. Mirjam Schnabel has read a large part of the manuscript. Her comments on grammar, style, and content have been invaluable. I am grateful to them all. I also thank Bob Hansen for his invitation to present much of the material in the book to the Christian Perspectives class at The Orchard Evangelical Free Church at Arlington Heights and the members of the class for their willingness to listen and their eagerness to discuss. The book is dedicated to Grant Osborne, esteemed colleague in the New Testament Department at Trinity Evangelical Divinity School who has written an important commentary on the book of Revelation, with whom I have taught an Adult Bible Fellowship series on Revelation in the Village Church of Gurnee. His exegetical expertise, his willingness to seriously consider answers to questions that are different from his own, his love for the gospel, and his kindness are exemplary.

Abbreviations

AB	Anchor Bible
BBR	*Bulletin of Biblical Research*
BDAG	W. Bauer, F. W. Danker, W. F. Arndt, and F. W. Gingrich. *Greek-English Lexicon of the New Testament and Other Early Christian Literature.* 3rd ed. Chicago: University of Chicago Press, 2000.
BECNT	Baker Exegetical Commentary on the New Testament
BNTC	Black's New Testament Commentaries
CBQ	*Catholic Biblical Quarterly*
DJD	Discoveries in the Judean Desert
EBC	Expositor's Bible Commentary
HNTC	Harper's New Testament Commentaries
IEJ	*Israel Exploration Journal*
IVPNTC	IVP New Testament Commentary
JETS	*Journal of the Evangelical Theological Society*
JSNT	*Journal for the Study of the New Testament*
JSNTSup	Journal for the Study of the New Testament: Supplement Series
KEK	Kritisch-exegetischer Kommentar über das Neue Testament (Meyer-Kommentar)
MNTC	Moffatt New Testament Commentary
NAC	New American Commentary
NCBC	New Century Bible Commentary
NICNT	New International Commentary on the New Testament
NICOT	New International Commentary on the Old Testament
NIGTC	New International Greek Testament Commentary
NovT	*Novum Testamentum*
NovTSup	Supplements to Novum Testamentum
NSBT	New Studies in Biblical Theology
PNTC	Pillar New Testament Commentary
SNTSMS	Society for New Testament Studies Monograph Series
TynBul	*Tyndale Bulletin*
TrinJ	*Trinity Journal*
WBC	Word Biblical Commentary

PART 1

General Questions about the Future

The Future of the World

When Do the End Times Begin?

The apostles were convinced that they were living in the last days. In the Old Testament, the expression "the last days" refers to the future time of God's final intervention in Israel's history and in the history of the world.[1] The earliest Christians dated the beginning of the end times to the coming of Jesus, particularly his death and resurrection and the giving of the Holy Spirit, a complex of events that constitutes the fulfillment of God's promises of Israel's restoration and humanity's salvation.

The End Times Have Begun with Jesus' Coming: Acts 2:16–21

One important passage in the New Testament teaching that the end times began with Jesus' coming is found in Peter's speech given on the day of Pentecost. After clarifying for the Jews who had gathered from around the world that the speaking in unlearned languages by Jesus' followers is not the result of drunkenness (Acts 2:15), Peter asserts that the audiovisual phenomena of the sound from heaven, the tongues of fire, and the speaking in unlearnt languages (Acts 2:1–4) constitutes the fulfillment of prophecy. He provides a long quotation from the prophet Joel that begins with the assertion, "In the last days it will be, God declares, that I will pour out my Spirit upon all flesh, and your sons and your daughters shall prophesy, and your young men shall see visions, and your old men shall dream dreams" (Acts 2:17, quoting Joel 2:28). The rest of the Joel quotation and Peter's explanation shows that Peter links the beginning of the last days not merely with the coming of the Holy Spirit on Pentecost but with the entire ministry of Jesus, which includes the giving of the Spirit and the proclamation of salvation for all those who call on the name of the Lord (Acts 2:21, quoting Joel 2:32). The content of Joel 2:30–32,

---

1. See Isaiah 2:2; Jeremiah 23:20; Ezekiel 38:16; Daniel 11:20; Hosea 3:5; Micah 4:1. See KJV, NASB, NIV, NLT, and other versions. The NRSV translated the relevant Hebrew phrase "in the latter days" or "in the days to come."

which Peter regards as fulfilled, is used to explain more than just the Pentecost phenomena. It should be noted that the phrase "in the last days" (*en tais eschatais hēmerais*) in Acts 2:17 is an addition to the text of Joel, who begins this particular prophecy with the phrase "and afterward." Peter clarifies that what follows in Joel's prophecy relates to the last days of God's history of salvation: the end times as the new age that was ushered in by Jesus.

Joel's prophecy of "wonders and signs" was fulfilled in the miracles that Jesus performed, which were signs of the coming of the kingdom of God and of his role in this kingdom. Joel's prophecy was fulfilled in the events of Jesus' death, notably in the darkening of the sun, mentioned in Acts 2:20. The sequence of "wonders" in the sky followed by "signs" on earth corresponds to Luke's account of the darkening of the sun at the time of Jesus' crucifixion (Luke 23:45a), a "wonder" in the sky, followed by the rending of the curtain in the temple (v. 45b), a sign that took place on earth.[2] The earthquake that Matthew 27:51 reports for the day of Jesus' crucifixion—a sign on the earth— is not mentioned by Luke in Acts 2, but it would have been remembered by the people living in Jerusalem.

Joel's prophecy mentioning "blood and fire" and the turning of the "moon to blood" is more difficult to interpret. The description cannot easily be linked with Jesus' ministry or death. In Luke 22:20, we have a reference to Jesus' blood that is shed and that inaugurates the new covenant; other references to Jesus' blood in Acts occur in 5:28 and 20:28. However, none of these references link Jesus' blood with fire or smoke, or other signs on earth. Still, some scholars suggest that "there may be some typology in Jesus' death, as Luke 22:20 combined with the descriptions of Jesus' death might suggest."[3] The suggestion that Acts 2:19 refers to a lunar eclipse during which the moon assumes a dull, red color, which was visible in Jerusalem at Passover in A.D. 33,[4] is intriguing; however, it requires a later date for Jesus' crucifixion, which is more plausibly dated in the year A.D. 30. Joel's prophecy of "wonders in the sky" can be seen as having been fulfilled in the ascension of Jesus, who ascended in a cloud into heaven (Acts 1:9, 11).

The prophecy of "wonders in the sky" can also be linked with the manifestations on Pentecost that descended "from heaven" (Acts 2:2) and that Peter is in the process of explaining. The reference to "fire" can be linked with the visual phenomenon of the "tongues of fire that separated and came to rest on each of them" (v. 3 NIV). The "cloud of smoke" could refer to the cloud

---

2. In Matthew 27:51 and Mark 15:38, the rending of the curtain comes after the darkening of the sun and after Jesus' death.
3. Darrell L. Bock, *Acts*, BECNT (Grand Rapids: Baker Academic, 2007), 116.
4. Colin J. Humphreys and W. Graeme Waddington, "The Jewish Calendar, a Lunar Eclipse and the Date of Christ's Crucifixion," *TynBul* 43 (1992): 331–51.

behind which Jesus disappeared when he ascended to the Father (Acts 1:9).[5] Or it could refer to the "tongues," which looked like fire, appearing in the room in which the believers had assembled. Since Luke's description of the manifestations on the day of Pentecost in Acts 2:2–4 contains allusions to God's theophany on Mount Sinai, Joel's prophecy of a "cloud of smoke" may be taken to describe God's theophany at Pentecost with language reminiscent of God's appearance on Mount Sinai. Since the Jews celebrated the giving of the Law on Sinai during the Feast of Pentecost, this interpretation, while not explicitly indicated by the text, is certainly a possibility.

Peter ends his quotation from Joel's prophecy with the line, "Then everyone who calls on the name of the Lord shall be saved" (Acts 2:21, quoting Joel 2:32). Joel's prophecy of salvation is interpreted by Peter in the sense that "Lord" refers to Jesus (as his following explanations demonstrate) and that "everyone" refers to the Jews living in Jerusalem, the diaspora Jews who have returned to Jerusalem, the Jews who continue to live in the regions whose languages the apostles had spoken, and "all those who are far away" (Acts 2:39), that is, to all human beings, whether they are male or female, young or old, slaves or free (Acts 2:17–18). Joel's comment "for in Mount Zion and in Jerusalem there shall be those who escape" (Joel 2:32) is omitted by Peter since the salvation that God offers through Jesus, Israel's Messiah and Lord, moves beyond Jerusalem to Judea, Samaria, and even to the ends of the earth (Acts 1:8).

In sum, Joel's reference to "wonders in the sky above and signs on the earth below" (Acts 2:19 NASB) does not introduce a comment on the last day of judgment (whose arrival is described with similar language in several passages) separate from the present fulfillment of Joel's prophecy. The day of judgment was, for Peter, a future event that was not "fulfilled" in his day. Peter links all of Joel 2:28–32, quoted in Acts 2:17–21, with the assertion in Acts 2:16 that "this is what was spoken through the prophet Joel." The view that Peter regards Joel 2:28–29 as fulfilled, but not Joel 2:30–32, is hardly convincing: if Peter only wanted to quote a prophecy that he believed was fulfilled by the phenomena that he wants to explain to the crowd, he would not have needed Joel 2:30–32; Luke can quote Scripture with omissions, if necessary. Peter (and Luke) understood the "wonders and signs" performed by Jesus, as well as the events associated with Jesus' crucifixion and ascension and the events of Pentecost as representing varying degrees of fulfillment of Joel's prophecy: Joel speaks of the last days that have begun with Jesus and that will culminate in God's judgment. The connections of the "wonders" and "signs" of Joel's prophecy with Jesus' ministry and death provide the basis for Peter's subsequent arguments concerning the status and the significance of Jesus. The reference to the "last days" establishes how Peter reads the prophets: God has begun to fulfill his promises; the last days have arrived

---

5. It should be noted that Luke uses a different word for "cloud" in Acts 1:9 (*nephelē*) than in Acts 2:19 (*atmis*, denoting "moist vapor, steam").

with Jesus' ministry, death, resurrection, and ascension, and his bestowal of the Spirit.[6]

The Hour to Wake Up: Romans 13:11–12

In Romans 13:11–12, Paul appeals to the Christians in the city of Rome to understand "the present time" and explains that "the hour has already come for you to wake up from your slumber, because our salvation is nearer now than when we first believed. The night is nearly over; the day is almost here. So let us put aside the deeds of darkness and put on the armor of light" (NIV). The "night" is the present evil age (see Gal. 1:4); "the day" is the day of the Lord. Paul's assertion that "the day is almost here" (Rom. 13:12 NIV) means that the day when God will bring to an end human history as we know it is fast approaching. Paul is convinced that Jesus might return within a very short period of time. Paul does not seek to narrow down the time frame within which Jesus will return, nor does he base his exhortation on the assumption that Jesus' return would take place very soon. But he clearly believes that Jesus' return is the next event in God's plan. And this means that he is convinced that he lives in the last days and that the end times have begun.

The End Times and the Last Days
Hebrews 1:1–2; 9:26

The author to the Hebrews begins his homily with the assertion that God's revelation has taken a major turn in the recent past: while he had spoken to the Israelites and the Jewish people in the past through prophets "at many times and in various ways," he has now been speaking to his people through his Son (Heb. 1:1 NIV). The author dates God's speaking through Jesus his Son as having happened "in these last days" (*ep' eschatou tōn hēmerōn*, Heb. 1:2). The demonstrative pronoun (*toutōn*, "these") indicates that the last days have begun: "in these days which are the last days."[7] The entire period between Jesus' first coming and the future consummation of God's purposes constitutes "the last days." When the author asserts that Jesus Christ, our High Priest, did not have to suffer many times but appeared once for all "to do away with sin by the sacrifice of himself" (Heb. 9:26 NIV), he relates Jesus' appearance both to the "foundation the world," emphasizing the universal scope of Christ's work, and to "the end of the age" (*synteleia tōn aiōnōn*; lit. "the end of the ages"), emphasizing that Jesus' death had inaugurated the last days. The coming of the Messiah, and in particular his salvific death, marks the beginning of the end.

---

6. Contrary to some popular interpretations, the "last days" is not, for Peter, a period immediately before the final judgment (and thus still in the future). Rather, the expression "the last days" describes the time period that was inaugurated with Jesus' ministry, death, resurrection, and ascension.

7. Paul Ellingworth, *The Epistle to the Hebrew: A Commentary on the Greek Text*, NIGTC (Grand Rapids: Eerdmans, 1993), 93; for Hebrews 9:26, see ibid., 484.

The time that extends from Jesus' coming into the present (of the author) is the end time.

James 5:7–9

James' prophetic indictment of wealthy landowners (James 5:1–6) includes the charge that they "have hoarded wealth in the last days" (*en eschatais hēmerais*; v. 3 NIV). The statement is ironic: these wealthy people have piled up wealth as if they would live forever, not realizing that they live in the last days in which there may not be many more opportunities to repent and put their wealth to good use. They are "especially foolish because they ignore the many signs of the rapidly approaching judgment."[8] James exhorts the believers to patiently endure the trials of the present (James 5:7–11) "until the Lord's coming" (v. 7 NIV), that is, until Jesus' second coming. He grounds his exhortation in the statement that the Lord's "coming" (*hē parousia*) is "near" and that Jesus the Judge is "standing at the door!" (vv. 8–9 NIV). Both the verb "near" (*ēggiken*) and the image of a person standing at the door about to knock emphasize the nearness of Jesus' coming. Again, we see that the first Christians were convinced that the last days had arrived.

1 Peter 1:20

Peter asserts that Jesus was "destined before the foundation of the world, but was revealed at the end of the ages for your sake" (1 Peter 1:20). The phrase "at the end of the ages" (*ep' eschatou tōn chronōn*) reflects the early Christian conviction that the last period of history has been inaugurated. In Old Testament and Jewish texts about the end, the resurrection of the dead and a time of affliction are mentioned as anticipated events, among other expectations. Peter emphasizes both of these themes in the context of his assertion that the "revelation" of Jesus the Messiah (i.e., his coming) took place at the end of the ages: God raised Jesus from the dead (1 Peter 1:3, 21) and both Jesus and his followers suffer (vv. 2, 7, 11, 17, 19). The end times have begun with Jesus' suffering and resurrection, and they continue as God's people are suffering.

2 Peter 3:3; Jude 18

In 2 Peter 3:1–18, Peter insists that the "coming" (*parousia*) of the Lord Jesus (i.e., his second coming) will indeed happen despite scoffers who doubt

---

8. Douglas J. Moo, *The Letter of James*, PNTC (Grand Rapids: Eerdmans, 2000), 215. He refers to the translation in the REB: "you have piled up wealth in an age that is near its close." The interpretation that the wealthy store up wrath against future judgment misses the meaning of the plural "last days," which refers to the end times (so James Adamson, *The Epistle of James*, NICNT [Grand Rapids: Eerdmans, 1976], 185, with reference to Romans 2:5; thus also the NLT: "This treasure you have accumulated will stand as evidence against you on the day of judgment").

that there will be a major, climactic intervention of the Lord in history. He asserts that the arrival of such scoffers was prophesied: "First of all you must understand this, that in the last days scoffers will come, scoffing and indulging their own lusts" (2 Peter 3:3). The expression "in the last days" (*ep' eschatōn tōn hēmerōn*) describes the time when these false teachers have appeared, which is the present of Peter's own time. He makes the rather ironic point that the skepticism of the mockers concerning Jesus' second coming is precisely a sign that the last days have arrived and that the end is imminent.[9]

In a similar description of false teachers, Jude reminds his readers of a prophecy of the apostles who said, "In the last time there will be scoffers, indulging their own ungodly lusts" (Jude 18). Again, the phrase "in the last time" (*ep' eschatou tou chronou*) characterizes the present time of the Christian author in the first century. The end times are not a period in the (distant) future but a present reality since the (first) coming of Jesus.

1 John 2:18

John connects the enemies of the gospel, troublemakers and heretics who have left the Christian community (1 John 2:19), with the prophecy that the "antichrist [*antichristos*] is coming," which probably refers to Jesus' announcement that "false messiahs [*pseudochristoi*] and false prophets [*pseudoprophētai*]" will be coming (Matt. 24:24).[10] John asserts that since "it is the last hour" (NIV) many antichrists have come, which is how we know that "it is the last hour" (1 John 2:18). In other words, the appearance of antichrists, false teachers who cause trouble for Jesus' followers, proves that the "last hour" (*eschatē hōra*) is a present reality. The time of John's ministry in Asia Minor in the first century is the "end time."

How Does One Explain the Two-Thousand-Year (and Counting) Duration of the End Times?

If the apostles believed that the end times—the last days—began with Jesus' first coming, it seems difficult to understand that two thousand years later we are still waiting for Jesus' promised second coming. If "the end times" began in the first century A.D., why are we still waiting for the end? Can "the last days" really last for so long? The delay of Jesus' second coming was already perceived as a problem by some whom Peter calls "scoffers"—people who gleefully provoked the faithful Christians with the words, "Where is the promise of his coming? For ever since our ancestors died, all things continue as they were from the beginning of creation!" (2 Peter 3:4). Peter answers that these people ignore three facts. First, they forget that God, who created the world and then sent the great flood, will one day bring about the day of

---

9. Thomas R. Schreiner, *1, 2 Peter, Jude*, NAC 37 (Nashville: B&H, 2003), 371 with n. 16.

10. On Matthew 24, see question 3; on the Antichrist, see questions 17–21.

judgment when the present heavens and earth will be destroyed along with the godless (3:5–7). Second, they forget that for God, "one day is like a thousand years, and a thousand years are like one day" (v. 8). This means that God's time is unlike our human time, the latter being rather limited. Third, they forget that the delay of Jesus' second coming is due not to God being somehow negligent in fulfilling his promises but to God being patient. God does not want sinners to perish "but all to come to repentance" (v. 9). Then Peter reminds his readers that "the day of the Lord will come like a thief, and then the heavens will pass away with a loud noise, and the elements will be dissolved with fire, and the earth and everything that is done on it will be disclosed" (v. 10). The delay of Jesus' second coming—a delay of now two thousand years—must not diminish our watchfulness. Christians must be ready for Jesus' second coming, whenever it will happen.

Summary

The end times are a present reality since the first coming of Jesus. This is the conviction of Peter, Paul, John, Jude, and the author of the epistle to the Hebrews. The conviction that the present time is the "end time" derives from the belief of the apostles that Jesus is Israel's promised Messiah in whose person, ministry, death, and resurrection God has fulfilled his promises of salvation. As the earliest Christians were all Jewish believers who knew the prophecies of the Scriptures and who were familiar with Jewish texts that spoke of the end, they linked the appearance of the Messiah with the last days. The coming of Jesus, Israel's Messiah and Savior of humankind, inaugurated the end times. This is the reason why the early Christians prayed earnestly and regularly for the return of Jesus, with the prayer call *marana tha*, "Our Lord, come!" (1 Cor. 16:22; cf. Rev. 22:20). End-time "specialists" who describe the last days or the end times as a future period misunderstand the structure of New Testament eschatology. Jesus and the apostles taught that the end (*eschatos*) is near, the last days have begun, and the end times are now a present reality. As some of the passages have shown, this conviction was not a source of speculation about the nearness of the "last day" or the period of "last days." Rather, it was the cause of great concern that Christians make sure that their everyday lives conform to the truth of the gospel and to the holiness of God so that they are ready to hear the knock of the Lord who is standing at the door.

REFLECTION QUESTIONS

1. What has been your understanding of the "end time"?

2. How is the idea of the end times connected with Jesus' first coming?

3. What are some of the consequences of the apostles' conviction regarding the end times for us today?

4. How does the conviction that the end times is a present reality impact Christian living?

5. How does the conviction that the end times is a present reality challenge speculations about the imminence of Jesus' second coming?

What Is the Fullness of Time?

The question about the end times is connected with Jesus' proclamation about the fulfillment of "the time" and the coming of the kingdom of God, and with passages in the Epistles that speak about the fullness of time.

Jesus and the Fulfillment of Time

Mark 1:15

According to Mark, Jesus' message could be summarized with a sentence that contains two assertions and two commands: "The time is fulfilled, and the kingdom of God has come near; repent, and believe in the good news." The phrase "the time is fulfilled" (*peplērōtai ho kairos*) describes that the end of a line has been reached. The verb "fulfill" also refers to the prophetic hope for a time of deliverance (see Mark 1:1–3). Thus, the noun *kairos*, usually translated as "time," can be taken to denote a "span of time" that has come to an end and as the decisive moment that has now arrived in which this hope has become a reality. The expression refers "to the fulfillment of prophetic hope in the time of messianic deliverance."[1] The perfect tense of the verb (*peplērōtai*, "is fulfilled") indicates that Jesus does not announce a future event but the time of fulfillment as a present state of affairs. With the beginning of Jesus' ministry, a new era of God's history with the world has begun— the time of God's kingship when his promises of restoration and salvation for Israel are being fulfilled.

Luke 4:21

When Jesus preached for the first time in public, in the synagogue in Nazareth, he read a passage from the prophet Isaiah that spoke of the coming of God's new age of salvation: the Servant of the Lord who is anointed with God's Spirit proclaims good news to the poor, heals the blind, and proclaims

---

1. R. T. France, *The Gospel of Matthew*, NICNT (Grand Rapids: Eerdmans, 2007), 91.

the year of the Lord's favor (Isa. 61:1–2). Jesus began his explanation of the text by asserting that "today this Scripture is fulfilled in your hearing" (Luke 4:21). The term "today" refers to the immediate present when fulfillment is a reality, and the perfect tense of the verb (*peplērōtai*, "is fulfilled") describes an existing state of fulfillment. Jesus thus announced that "the time that all people faithful to God have been waiting for is now here and it is found in me."[2]

Matthew 24

When Jesus answered the disciples' question about "the sign of your coming and of the end of the age" (Matt. 24:3), he spoke about events that would take place before the climactic sign of the destruction of Jerusalem (vv. 2, 15–22) and before the end of history when he will return (vv. 29–31). This means that the time before A.D. 70, the date of the destruction of Jerusalem, already belongs to the last days before the end. This means that the time between Jesus' first coming and Jesus' second coming is the end time.

Jesus' First Coming Has Brought About the Fullness of Time
Galatians 4:4–5

Several passages in Paul's letters make the point that Jesus' coming into the world happened at the time when God brought about the fulfillment of his promises. In Galatians 4:4–5, Paul explains that "when the fullness of time had come, God sent his Son, born of a woman, born under the law, in order to redeem those who were under the law, so that we might receive adoption as children" (NRSV). The redemption of those "under the law" is the redemption of those under "the curse of the law" (Gal. 3:13), a curse that pronounces the death penalty against sinners. Paul asserts that this redemption became a reality when God sent his son Jesus, Israel's Messiah, into the world in "the fullness of time" (*to plērōma tou chronou*; NIV: "when the set time had fully come"). The fullness of time is the particular point in time at which God fulfills his promises of redemption by sending the Messiah—"the nodal point of salvation-history" that constitutes "the divinely ordained epoch for the people of God to enter into their inheritance."[3] Jesus' coming into the world ushers in the era of the fulfillment of God's promises to his people.

Ephesians 1:10

Paul's summary of the gospel in Ephesians 1:7–10 includes a similar statement. He asserts that in Jesus Christ "we have redemption through his blood, the forgiveness of our trespasses, according to the riches of his grace that he lavished on us. With all wisdom and insight he has made known

---

2. Darrell L. Bock, *Luke*, 2 vols., BECNT (Grand Rapids: Baker Academic, 1995–96), 1:413.
3. F. F. Bruce, *Commentary on Galatians*, NIGTC (Grand Rapids: Eerdmans, 1982), 194.

to us the mystery of his will, according to his good pleasure that he set forth in Christ, as a plan for the fullness of time, to gather up all things in him, things in heaven and things on earth" (Eph. 1:7–10). The "fullness of time" (*tou plērōmatos tōn kairōn*; lit. "the fullness of the times") refers to the completion of the outworking of God's saving purposes that brings the sequence of the various periods of salvation history to their climactic consummation. This final implementation of God's plan is not a matter merely of the future: the revelation of the divine plan through Jesus' saving work has already happened (Eph. 1:7–9), which means that "significant steps have already been taken to set in motion the achievement of this goal."[4] And this means, since Jesus is Israel's Messiah ("Christ"), that the last days before the end have begun.

1 Corinthians 10:11

When Paul refers to events during Israel's exodus from Egypt as he warns the Corinthian Christians not to take the sin of idolatry lightly, he insists that "these things happened to them as an example and were written down for our instruction, on whom the ends of the ages has come" (1 Cor. 10:11 NRSV). As regards the expression "the ends of the ages " (*ta telē tōn aiōnōn*), it has been suggested that the plural of the noun translated as "the ends" (*ta telē*) should be taken literally in the sense that Paul refers to two "ends" of two ages: the end point of the old age and the beginning of the new age; it is suggested that Paul describes the coming together of the two ages during his own lifetime, and emphasizes here the fact that the Corinthian Christians live in the new dispensation. While attractive, this interpretation requires an unnatural meaning for the Greek term *telos* in the sense of "beginning." Another interpretation suggests that the plural *ta telē* derives from the plural "ages" or that both plural nouns represent a Hebrew idiom that uses plural nouns when a singular noun is used in English: Paul speaks of "the end of the age" (NLT). Since Paul believes that the old age and the new age overlap, it is more likely that he asserts here that successive periods of God's intervention in the history of Israel and in the history of humankind have reached their respective ends. This means that the plural *ta telē* has the same meaning as "end" in the

---

4. P. T. O'Brien, *The Letter to the Ephesians*, PNTC (Grand Rapids: Eerdmans, 1999), 113–14. Harold W. Hoehner links the "fullness of time" with the future earthly messianic kingdom, which is not explicitly indicated in the text and thus should not be taken as the meaning intended by Paul (*Ephesians: An Exegetical Commentary* [Grand Rapids: Baker Academic, 2002], 219). Te-Li Lau explains the meaning of Ephesians 1:10 in the context of Paul's concern in the letter: "The existence of a united church then is a reminder to the cosmic powers that their power over humanity has been decisively broken and that their final defeat is imminent" (*The Politics of Peace: Ephesians, Dio Chrysostom, and the Confucian Four Books*, NovTSup 133 [Leiden: Brill, 2010], 293).

singular.[5] Whether or not we interpret the plural *aiōn* as referring to multiple periods of salvation-historical eras, such as the old dispensation and the new dispensation (translation with "ages"), or to the one era of human history (translation with "age"), Paul's point is clear: the coming of Jesus has ushered in the last period of history, the last days, the end times.

Summary

The end times are a present reality that can be described with the expression "the last days." Jesus' coming, death, and resurrection constitute "the fullness of time" (i.e., the last era of God's history of salvation in which Scripture's prophecies about the time of messianic deliverance are fulfilled). The conviction that Jesus' first coming constitutes the fulfillment of the Old Testament prophecies of Israel's deliverance and restoration was initiated by Jesus' proclamation of the dawn of God's kingdom. Thus, the conviction of the early Christians—that the period of the last days, expected by the prophets for the future, is a present reality—is grounded in Jesus himself and his message.

REFLECTION QUESTIONS

1. What did Jesus say about the expectations of the Old Testament prophets?

2. What is the significance of Jesus' proclamation of the coming of the kingdom of God?

3. How is the "fullness of time" related to Jesus' death and resurrection?

4. In what way is the "fullness of time" related to our own time?

5. In what way is the "end of the ages" connected with Jesus?

---

5. Walter Bauer, Frederick William Danker, William F. Arndt, and F. Wilbur Gingrich, *A Greek-English Lexicon of the New Testament and Other Early Christian Literature* [BDAG], 3rd ed., rev. and ed. Frederick William Danker (Chicago: University of Chicago Press, 2000), 32 (*aiōn* 2b).

What Are the Signs of the End (Matt. 24)?

Jesus spoke about the end times and the last judgment during the last week of his earthly ministry.[1] All three Synoptic Gospels relate Jesus' eschatological discourse (Matt. 24–25; Mark 13; Luke 21). Since Christian views about the end times must be informed by Jesus' explanations regarding the period leading up to the end,[2] a study of these texts is of fundamental significance. The reports of Matthew, Mark, and Luke about Jesus' discourse on the end times are in essential agreement; the passage in Matthew is the most extensive and provides fuller details, especially about the last judgment. Therefore, the following discussion will follow Matthew's presentation; we will refer to material that only Mark and Luke present where necessary. The following table presents the content in a necessarily abbreviated manner.[3]

---

1. For a defense that the discourses presented by Matthew, Mark, and Luke derive from a discourse given by Jesus, see David Wenham, *The Rediscovery of Jesus' Eschatological Discourse, Gospel Perspectives 4* (Sheffield: JSOT Press, 1984).
2. While the term "the end times" refers to the entire period between Jesus' first and second coming (see question 1), I use the term "the end" as a reference to Jesus' second coming and the last judgment.
3. For the structure of Jesus' eschatological discourse, see question 4.

THE SIGNS OF THE END		
JESUS' PREDICTION OF THE DESTRUCTION OF THE TEMPLE AND THE DISCIPLES' QUESTION		
MATTHEW 24:2–3	MARK 13:2–4	LUKE 21:6–7
Prediction of the destruction of the temple in Jerusalem	Prediction of the destruction of the temple in Jerusalem	Prediction of the destruction of the temple in Jerusalem
Question of the disciples: When will Jerusalem be destroyed? What will be the sign of Jesus' return and the end of the age?	Question of the disciples: When will Jerusalem be destroyed? What will be sign of Jesus' return and the end of the age?	Question of the disciples: When will Jerusalem be destroyed? What will be the sign of Jesus' return and the end of the age?
THE TIME UNTIL THE END—TRIBULATION		
MATTHEW 24:4–28	MARK 13:5–23	LUKE 21:8–24
1. seduction, messianic pretenders	1. seduction, messianic pretenders	1. seduction, messianic pretenders
2. wars, rumors of war; international unrest	2. wars, rumors of war; international unrest	2. wars, rumors of wars international unrest
3. famine	3. earthquakes	3. earthquakes
4. earthquakes	4. famine	4. famine: plagues, horrible events, signs in the sky
5. persecution	5. persecution	5. persecution
6. false prophets		
7. injustice, lack of love		
8. universal proclamation of the gospel	proclamation of the gospel to all nations	
9. A SPECIFIC EVENT OF DIVINE JUDGMENT: THE DESTRUCTION OF JERUSALEM		
MATT. 24:15–22	MARK 13:14–20	LUKE 21:20–24
(a) desolating sacrilege	(a) desolating sacrilege	(a) desolation of the city
(b) escape to the mountains	(b) escape to the mountains	(b) escape to the mountains
(c) people save their bare lives	(c) people save their bare lives	
(d) pregnant and nursing women are in peril	(d) pregnant and nursing women are in peril	(d) pregnant and nursing women are in peril
(e) horrific tribulation	(e) horrific tribulation	(e) great tribulation: casualties, captivity, dispersion, pagans control Jerusalem

(f) shortening of time	(f) shortening of time	
10. messianic pretenders, false prophets	10. messianic pretenders, false prophets	10. messianic pretenders, false prophets
11. THE RETURN OF JESUS		
MATT. 24:29–31	**MARK 13:24–27**	**LUKE 21:25–28**
(a) sun becomes dark	(a) sun becomes dark	(a) sign in the sun
(b) moon becomes dark	(b) moon becomes dark	(b) sign in the moon
(c) stars fall from the sky	(c) stars fall from the sky	(c) sign in the stars
(d) powers of sky shaken	(d) powers of the sky shaken	
(e) sign of the Son in heaven; Son comes on the clouds	(e) Son comes on the clouds	(e) Son comes on the clouds
(f) sending of angels; trumpet sound; gathering of the elect	(f) sending of angels; gathering of the elect	

The Signs of the End

Jesus mentions ten signs that herald the end of the age and the event of his return. The first four signs are related to world affairs: (1) seduction of many people by messianic pretenders who claim to have royal dignity and the ability to redeem Israel; (2) wars and rumors of war; (3) famine; and (4) earthquakes (order of last two signs reversed in Mark and Luke). The next four signs are related to Jesus' followers: (5) persecution, which includes torture, martyrdom, and apostasy; (6) false prophets who deceive people in the community of Jesus' followers; (7) injustice and lack of love among believers; and (8) the worldwide proclamation of the gospel. The next sign is (9) a specific event that relates the destruction of Jerusalem and of the temple. Jesus here mentions six elements: (a) the "desolating sacrilege" (or "abomination of desolation"), a term that explicitly alludes to the book of Daniel (Dan. 8:13; 9:27; 11:31; 12:11), predicts an event that ritually pollutes the temple in Jerusalem; (b) people escape from Jerusalem and from the entire province of Judea to the mountains; (c) people save their lives as they flee without their possessions; (d) pregnant and nursing women are in peril; (e) the tribulation of these events is horrific (Luke speaks of casualties by killing with the sword, of prisoners led into captivity, of Jews being led into dispersion among the Gentiles, and of pagans controlling Jerusalem); and (f) God will cut this time of great suffering short so that the elect will survive. The sign following next (10) predicts and warns again about the coming of messianic claimants and of false prophets who perform miracles and who intend to deceive Jesus' followers with predictions of Jesus' return.

The last element of Jesus' prophecy consists of (11) a series of events that accompany Jesus' return.

Sign 1 speaks of the seduction of many people by messianic pretenders: people who say "I am the Messiah" are Jewish would-be leaders who claim to have royal dignity and the ability to redeem Israel. Since Christians believe that Jesus is the Messiah who has already come, Jesus refers here to Jewish leaders with messianic aspirations (the claim to be Jesus the Messiah at his return is hardly in view). This prediction was fulfilled in the first century and through history since then. Josephus mentions messianic pretenders for the years leading up to the crisis of A.D. 66–70 in Judea, among them a Samaritan, Theudas, Judas of Galilee, and a Jew from Egypt.[4] Simon bar Kokhba, the leader of the second Jewish revolt in A.D. 132–135 that ended in catastrophe, had messianic aspirations.[5] Sabbatai Zevi (1626–1676), a rabbi who was born in Smyrna in modern-day Turkey, claimed to be the Messiah at age twenty-two. He visited Salonica, Cairo, and Jerusalem and converted to Islam in Constantinople in 1666. He still has followers in Turkey today.[6] Rabbi Menachem Mendel Schneerson (1902–1994) inspired such devotion among his followers, the Lubavitch community, that some believed he was the Messiah; when he died at the age of ninety-two in June 1994, some continued to celebrate him as "King Moshiach" (King Messiah).[7]

Sign 2 speaks of wars and rumors of war. Although the period from A.D. 30–60 was relatively peaceful in territories controlled by the Roman Empire, there were armed conflicts and civil disturbances in the East:

33	Disturbances in Armenia caused by the Parthian king Artabanos
36	War between Rome and Parthia (A.D. 36)
	War between Herod Antipas, the ruler of Galilee, and the Nabatean king Aretas IV
39/40	Large demonstrations in Ptolemais and Tiberias of Jews who protest against the Roman legate in Syria who had moved two Roman legions to Judea
42	Rebellion in Mauretania

---

4. Josephus, *Jewish Antiquities* 18.85–87; 20.97–99, 102, 169–72, 160–61, 167–68, 188. For Theudas, see Acts 5:36 (four hundred followers); for the Egyptian, see Acts 21:38 (four thousand followers).
5. See Hanan Eshel, "The Bar Kochba Revolt, 132–135," in *The Cambridge History of Judaism,* vol. 4: *The Late Roman-Rabbinic Period*, ed. Steven T. Katz (Cambridge: Cambridge University Press, 2006), 105–27.
6. See Gershom Scholem, *Sabbatai Sevi: The Mystical Messiah, 1626–1676* (Princeton, NJ: Princeton University Press, 1973).
7. See M. Avrum Ehrlich, *The Messiah of Brooklyn: Understanding Lubavitch Hasidism Past and Present* (Jersey City, NJ: KTAV, 2004).

43   Invasion of Britain by the Roman general Aulus Plautius and the emperor Claudius

48   Unrest in Jerusalem and Judea resulting from the provocative behavior of Roman soldiers; twenty thousand Jewish citizens killed

57   Armed conflict between the Roman legate in Moesia and tribes from the North; one hundred thousand resettled people in Moesia

58   Conquest of Armenia by the Roman general Domitius Corbulo

61   Adiabene is attacked by the Armenian king Tigranes V; Syria is threatened by the Parthians

62   The Roman general Caesennius Paetus arrives in Cappadocia with the task to annex Armenia; he forces the Parthian king Vologaeses I to capitulate

66   Beginning of the Jewish revolt against the Romans

      Galilee conquered by the Roman legate Cestius Gallus; defeat of the Roman army in an ambush at Beth Horon by the Jewish insurgents

67   Galilee reconquered by the Roman army under General Vespasian

68   Jewish resistance in the north is crushed by Vespasian

      Civil war between the fanatical Zealots and Jews who advocated surrender in Jerusalem

68/69 Civil war between the supporters of the "four emperors" Galba, Otho, Vitellius, and Vespasian

69   Vespasian becomes emperor; his son Titus finishes the war against the Jews in Judea

70   Siege and destruction of Jerusalem; according to Josephus, 1.1 million Jews were killed and ninety-seven thousand were enslaved

After the first century, wars and military conflicts continued to characterize history. The number of people killed in wars throughout history increased as population numbers grew larger and as warfare affected not only the combatants but directly and indirectly (through plagues or diseases) also civilians. The following gruesome statistics are particularly frightening when we see beyond the numbers the fate of individual people and their families:[8]

1206–1227 Mongol conquests under Genghis Khan; perhaps 40 million dead

1492–1900 European colonization of South and North America; about 20 million dead

---

8. See the unedifying work of Micheal Clodfelter, *Warfare and Armed Conflicts: A Statistical Encyclopedia of Casualty and Other Figures, 1494–2007*, 3rd ed. (Jefferson, NC: McFarland, 2008).

1500–1870	Atlantic slave trade; about 18 million dead
1618–1644	Manchu conquest of China, defeat of the Ming Dynasty; perhaps 25 million dead
1618–1648	Thirty Years War in Europe; 7 million dead
1803–1815	Napoleonic wars in Europe; 4 million dead
1850–1864	Taiping rebellion in China; 20 million dead
1914–1918	First World War; 15 million dead
1917–1922	Civil war in Russia; 9 million dead
1924–1953	Terror regime of Joseph Stalin; about 20 million dead
1939–1945	Second World War; 55 million dead

Sign 3 (famine; Luke adds plagues, horrible events, and signs in the sky) could be observed in Judea less than ten years after Jesus' prophecy, when there was a severe famine (A.D. 44–46).[9] In A.D. 51, there were famines in various regions of the Roman Empire.[10] Famines continue to characterize the conditions of human existence. The famine in India under British occupation during the nineteenth century cost 17 million lives, and the famine caused by Mao Tse-tung's industrialization program called "Great Leap Forward" cost perhaps 40 million people their lives.

Sign 4 could be observed in Judea as well. There was a serious earthquake in Palestine some time before A.D. 60,[11] and there were earthquakes in Asia Minor in A.D. 61, in Rome in A.D. 67,[12] on Cyprus in A.D. 76, and in Pompeii in A.D. 79. Josephus described the earthquake in Judea of 31 B.C. as "such as had not happened at any time," and Pliny called the earthquake in Asia Minor of A.D. 17 that devastated Sardis the "greatest" in human memory.[13] Earthquakes continue to be part of the human experience in many parts of the world, including the Middle East. It should be noted that Jesus does not predict that there was an increase in earthquakes, as some end-time "specialists" sometimes claim.[14]

---

9. See Acts 11:28; Josephus, *Jewish Antiquities* 3.320; 20.51–53, 101.
10. See Peter Garnsey, *Famine and Food Supply in the Graeco-Roman World: Responses to Risk and Crisis* (Cambridge: Cambridge University Press, 1988); Bruce W. Winter, "Acts and Food Shortages," in *The Book of Acts in Its Graeco-Roman Setting*, ed. David W. J. Gill and Conrad Gempf, *The Book of Acts in Its First-Century Setting*, vol. 2 (Exeter: Paternoster, 1994), 59–78.
11. Josephus, *Jewish War* 3.286–287. See D. H. K. Amiran, E. Arieh, and T. Turcotte, "Earthquakes in Israel and Adjacent Areas: Macroseismic Observations since 100 B.C.E.," *IEJ* 44 (1994): 260–305.
12. Pliny, *Natural History* 2.84.
13. Josephus, *Jewish Antiquities* 15.121; Pliny, *Natural History* 2.86.
14. While the number of casualties in modern earthquakes is sometimes distressingly high, this is not due to an increase in the number of earthquakes but to the higher population

These four signs relate to world affairs and represent false alarms.[15] The appearance of messianic pretenders, new wars and rumors of war, and famines and earthquakes "must take place" and can be observed and connected with Jesus' prophecy, "but the end is not yet" (Matt. 24:6). Such events are all "but the beginning of the birth pangs" (v. 8). They characterize the distress of the messianic era that the prophets had predicted,[16] which may be a protracted period until the end (*to telos*) finally comes. These labor pains include specifically the suffering of the people living in Jerusalem, which will be besieged and destroyed (vv. 15–22). They describe the suffering that characterizes human history between Jesus' first and second coming.

Sign 5, which predicts persecution (Matt. 24:9), could be observed soon after Jesus' own arrest, torture, and crucifixion, when Peter and John and the Twelve were repeatedly arrested (Acts 4:3; 5:18; 12:3), when Stephen and the apostle James were killed (Acts 7:58–60; 12:1–2), and when Jerusalem believers and missionaries such as Paul were repeatedly put into prison.[17] Christians continued to be persecuted, even more severely, in the second, third, and fourth centuries and since then again and again, particularly in the twentieth century in Communist regimes and in Islamic countries.[18] The pre-

---

density in areas prone to experience earthquakes. Geologists state that the number of earthquakes has not increased during the twentieth century. An article on the website of the U.S. Geological Survey, under the heading "Are Earthquakes Really on the Increase?" begins with the sentence: "We continue to be asked by many people throughout the world if earthquakes are on the increase. Although it may seem that we are having more earthquakes, earthquakes of magnitude 7.0 or greater have remained fairly constant" (http://earthquake.usgs.gov/learn/topics/increase_in_earthquakes.php [accessed May 28, 2010]).

15. R. T. France, *The Gospel of Matthew*, NICNT (Grand Rapids: Eerdmans, 2007), 902. France limits these signs to occurrences before the destruction of Jerusalem in A.D. 70.

16. See Isaiah 13:8; 26:17–18; Jeremiah 4:31; 6:24; 22:23; Micah 4:9–10; *2 Baruch* 27–29. In rabbinic literature, "labor pain of the Messiah" is almost a technical term for the period of distress before the coming of the Messiah (see [b. Šabb.] 118a).

17. See W. H. C. Frend, "Persecutions: Genesis and Legacy," in *Origins to Constantine*, ed. Margaret M. Mitchell and Frances M. Young, *Cambridge History of Christianity*, vol. 1 (Cambridge: Cambridge University Press, 2006), 503–23.

18. Barrett and Johnson give the following statistics: in the 200s, about 409,000 Christians were killed; in the 300s, 2.7 million; in the 400s, 513,000; later in the 1600s, 11 million; in the 1800s, 1.5 million; and in the 1900s, 41 million. In 1214, Genghis Khan was responsible for the death of 4 million Christians; in 1358, Tamerlane killed 4 million Nestorian Christians; in 1630, all 400 Tibetan Christians were wiped out; from 1921 to 1950, about 15 million Christians died in Soviet prison camps; from 1929 to 1937, 14.5 million Orthodox Christians were killed under Stalin; and from 1950 to 1980, another 5 million Christians died in Soviet prison camps (David B. Barrett and Todd M. Johnson, eds., *World Christian Trends AD 30–AD 2200: Interpreting the Annual Christian Megacensus* [Pasadena, CA: William Carey Library, 2001], 399). Also see David H. Adeney, "The Church and Persecution," in *The Church in the Bible and the World: An International Study*, ed. D. A. Carson (1987; repr., Grand Rapids: Baker Academic; Carlisle: Paternoster, 1993), 275–302, 348.

diction of persecution begins with a reference to "tribulation" (*thlipsis*, Matt. 24:9), thus the translation of RSV, ESV (NRSV translates "they will hand you over to be tortured," and NIV has "you will be handed over to be persecuted"). The prediction that Jesus' followers will be "hated by all nations" on account of their allegiance to Jesus reflects the missionary expansion of the church beyond Jerusalem and Judea (see sign 8).

Sign 6, which speaks of false prophets who deceive people in the community of Jesus' followers (Matt. 24:10–11), is similar to sign 1 but focuses more specifically on impostors who seek to deceive the Christian community. Paul warned the elders of the church in Ephesus of "savage wolves" (Acts 20:29–30); his letters are evidence of the appearance of false teachers in the early church of the first century. The history of the church continues to be full of examples of heretics and heretical teachings.

Sign 7, which predicts injustice and lack of love among believers (Matt. 24:12–13), could be observed in the early church (e.g., in the church in Ephesus toward the end of the first century, Rev. 2:4–5). Despite wonderful examples of Christian charity and love, even to non-Christians,[19] the history of the church has been, unfortunately and tragically, more often than not a history of harsh, sometimes violent attacks against dissenters and unbelievers.

Sign 8, the worldwide proclamation of the gospel (Matt. 24:14), was impressively fulfilled already in the first century as the ends of the earth in the south (Ethiopia), west (Spain), north (Scythia), and east (India) were reached with the gospel.[20] Once the gospel has been proclaimed throughout the world, the end can come. Since the first century, the gospel has been taken to all regions and all nations of the earth.[21]

Sign 9, which predicts the siege and the destruction of Jerusalem (Matt. 24:15–22), was fulfilled from A.D. 66 to 70. Jesus mentions five developments.

(a) The reference to "desolating sacrilege" (*bdelygma tēs erēmōseōs;* RSV, NRSV) or "abomination of desolation" (KJV, NASB, NET, ESV; see NIV "the abomination that causes desolation") predicts an event that ritually pollutes the temple in Jerusalem. Jesus (in Matthew) explicitly alludes to Daniel (Dan. 8:13; 9:27; 11:31; 12:11). The prophecy of Daniel 11:31 was fulfilled when Antiochus IV Epiphanes desecrated the temple in Jerusalem by erecting an altar for pagan sacrifices in 168 B.C., which stood in the temple for three years. Interestingly, the author of 1 Maccabees 1:54 describes this altar with

19. On the Christians' response to epidemics, see Rodney Stark, *The Rise of Christianity* (San Francisco: HarperCollins, 1997), 73–94.

20. See Eckhard J. Schnabel, *Early Christian Mission* (Downers Grove, IL: InterVarsity Press, 2004), 1:373–76, 469–98.

21. See Barrett and Johnson, *World Christian Trends*; Martin I. Klauber and Scott M. Manetsch, eds., *The Great Commission: Evangelicals and the History of World Missions* (Nashville: B&H, 2008).

the same expression (*bdelygma erēmōseōs*).[22] Because Daniel's prophecy was fulfilled in the past, the readers are alerted to the fact that they need to "understand" (Matt. 24:15). This suggests that something will happen that "is in recognizable continuity with the devastating pollution set up by Antiochus, but just what form it will take is left to the imagination."[23] Jesus' prophecy must refer to the temple that he and his disciples see as they sit on the Mount of Olives (Matt. 24:3). The interpretive view that Jesus predicts an event shortly before the end (i.e., in the twenty-first century or in a later century) is impossible if we assume that Jesus' prophecy in Matthew 24 was given to the disciples in the spring of A.D. 33 and meant to be understood by the disciples.[24] Some relate the prophecy to the order given by Emperor Gaius Caligula in A.D. 40 to set up a statue of himself in the temple in Jerusalem, an order that caused disturbances among the Jews. This plan was averted only because Gaius was assassinated in A.D. 41. Others relate the prophecy to the events of A.D. 67–68 when the Zealots took over the temple "with polluted feet," setting up their headquarters in the temple and murdering people in the temple precincts.[25] Others relate Jesus' prediction to the events of A.D. 70 when Roman troops broke through to the temple mount, setting up their idolatrous standards and sacrificing to them[26] (by then it would have been too late to flee from Jerusalem). In Luke, the prophecy of the desolation is linked with "Jerusalem being surrounded by armies" (Luke 21:20) and thus seems to link the pollution (abomination) with the military standards of the Roman army.

(b) People escape from Jerusalem and from the entire province of Judea to the mountains. (c) People should save their lives, fleeing without their possessions. (d) Pregnant and nursing women are in peril. These instructions in Matthew 24:16–19 are very specific; they must refer to a specific historical event, specifically to the Jewish War from A.D. 66 to 70. Eusebius relates that the

---

22. See Josephus, *Jewish Antiquities* 12.320, who uses the verb *erēmoō* when he describes the sacrilegious effects of the pagan altar.
23. France, *Gospel of Matthew*, 912.
24. The end-time "specialists" who assert that Jesus predicts an event during the last seven years of history have to assume that Jesus prophesies "across" the events of A.D. 66–70 and that he assumes that a third temple would be built after the destruction of the second temple in A.D. 70. None of this could have been known by the disciples, who in that case would have been misled—those who lived to witness the events of A.D. 66–70—by Jesus if this view were correct.
25. Josephus, *Jewish War* 4.150–57, 196–207; for the description "with polluted feet they invaded the sanctuary," see ibid., 4.150.
26. Ibid., 6.316. In *Jewish War* 3.123 and 5.48 he mentions the eagle: the eagle standard (aquila), common to all Roman legions, was supreme because of its association with Jupiter. See Graham Webster, *The Roman Imperial Army of the First and Second Centuries A.D.*, 3rd ed. (Norman: University of Oklahoma Press, 1998), 135.

Jerusalem Christians left the city and fled to Pella, about sixty-five miles northeast of Jerusalem, before Jerusalem was destroyed.[27]

(e) The tribulation of these events is horrific. (Luke speaks of casualties by killing with the sword, of prisoners led into captivity, of Jews being led into dispersion among the Gentiles, and of pagans controlling Jerusalem.) The language with which Matthew (as well as Mark and Luke) describes the crisis of the siege and destruction of Jerusalem compares with Josephus's grim description of the horrors of the siege.[28] Josephus relates that 1.1 million Jews were killed and ninety-seven thousand were enslaved; he asserts that in his opinion "the misfortunes of all nations since the world began fall short of those of the Jews."[29] This assessment corresponds to Jesus' prediction: "For at that time there will be great distress [*thlipsis megalē*], such as has not been from the beginning of the world until now" (Matt. 24:21, author's translation.).[30] The expression "great distress" (or "great tribulation," as in KJV, NASB, RSV, ESV) refers here to the period of extreme suffering that is connected with the siege and destruction of Jerusalem.[31] Readers of Matthew, Mark, and Luke at the end of the first century, without doubt, would regard Jesus' prophecy to have been fulfilled by the events connected with the destruction of Jerusalem in A.D. 70. Modern readers may well wonder whether more recent events could be interpreted as fulfillment. The siege of Leningrad by the German army between 1941 and 1944 was one of the longest and most devastating sieges in history: of 2.5 million trapped inhabitants, between 640,000 and 800,000 died, mostly of hunger.[32]

(f) God will cut "those days" of great suffering short so that the elect will survive. It seems most plausible to connect the expression "those days" (*hai hēmerai ekeinai*) in Matthew 24:22 with the same expression "in those days" (*en ekeinais tais hēmerais*) in 24:19. Jesus' prediction does not spare the "elect" (i.e., Jesus' followers from among the Jews living in Jerusalem and in Judea) from the horrors of the Roman invasion and the siege of Jerusalem, but he assures them that they will survive, physically, because this great tribulation will be curtailed by God. The Romans captured the city of Jerusalem after a siege of five months, cutting short the tribulation of the people who had remained

---

27. Eusebius, *Ecclesiastical History* 3.5.3. See Craig R. Koester, "The Origin and Significance of the Flight to Pella Tradition," *CBQ* 51 (1989): 90–106.
28. Josephus, *Jewish War* 5.424–38, 512–18, 567–72; 6.193–213.
29. Ibid., 1.12; for the casualty figures, see ibid., 6.420.
30. The continuation of the prophecy with the phrase "never to be equaled again," which is hyperbolic language, characterizes this period of tribulation as an event within history. If it is taken to refer to a future tribulation right before the end of the world (e.g., the tribulation of three and a half years that end-time "specialists" often speak of), the statement "there will be great distress . . . never to be equaled again" becomes nonsensical, because at the end there is no further history during which a tribulation could occur.
31. The same expression occurs in Revelation 7:14. See question 7.
32. See Michael Jones, *Leningrad: State of Siege* (New York: Basic Books, 2008).

in the city suffering severe famine. Others see a break between Matthew 24:21 and 24:22, linking verse 22 not with the siege of Jerusalem but with the entire period of the time between Jesus' first and second coming, of which 24:15–21—the siege of Jerusalem—is only a part.[33] If the expression "those days" in 24:22 is connected with "the distress [tribulation; *thlipsin*] of those days" in 24:29 (NIV) and thus with 24:9 where "distress/tribulation" (*thlipsin*) is mentioned for the first time, then the perspective of 24:22 is indeed greater than the "great distress" ("great tribulation"; *thlipsis megalē*) that characterizes the siege of Jerusalem.[34]

Sign 10 predicts the coming of messianic claimants and of false prophets who perform miracles and who intend to deceive Jesus' followers with predictions of Jesus' return (Matt. 24:23–25). Following after sign 1, which predicted messianic pretenders, and sign 6, which predicted false prophets, sign 10 speaks both of both messianic claimants and false prophets. This prophecy appears to assume a wider reference than interpreters allow who restrict the prediction to the last years or months of the crisis in Jerusalem between A.D. 66 and 70.[35] The adverb of time (the Greek term *tote*) at the beginning of 24:23, translated as "then" or "at that time," does not have to be restricted to the period described immediately before (24:15–22, the siege of Jerusalem), but generally "introduces that which follows in time"[36] and can thus indeed describe a subsequent phase of the end-time events.

Sign 11, the last element of Jesus' prophecy, consists of a series of events that accompany Jesus' return (Matt. 24:29–31). Jesus predicts the following: (a) the sun will become dark; (b) the moon will become dark; (c) stars fall from the sky; (d) the powers of the sky are shaken; (e) the sign of the Son of Man will become visible in heaven, and he will come on the clouds with power and glory; (f) the Son of Man will send out angels who will be accompanied by a loud trumpet call and who will gather the elect from all regions of the earth. The apocalyptic, cosmic language of the prophecy in 24:29 uses language from the Old Testament prophets who predict not the physical dissolution of the universe but, with symbolic language, catastrophic political

---

33. D. A. Carson, *Matthew*, EBC 8 (Grand Rapids: Zondervan, 1984), 502. This interpretation is not as implausible as France suggests (*Gospel of Matthew*, 916n70).

34. See Carson, *Matthew*, 504–5.

35. E.g., France sees the prophecy of messianic claimants fulfilled in the claims of Simon bar Giora, who was regarded as king (Josephus, *J.W.* 4.510), in the anonymous person mentioned in *Jewish War* 6.285–88, and in the signs and wonders that occurred, according to *Jewish War* 6.289–300 (see *Ant.* 20.168), in the period before the city was destroyed. If Jesus indeed describes in Matthew 24 the entire period between his first and second coming, with the siege and destruction of Jerusalem (24:15–22) being a series of events among many other development, these prophecies and the signs and wonders of A.D. 66–70 would be part of the fulfillment but not the complete and final fulfillment of Jesus' prophecy (France, *Gospel of Matthew*, 916–17).

36. BDAG, 1012 (*tote* 2).

events within history.[37] This does not prove, however, that the prophecy must be limited to the siege and destruction of Jerusalem in A.D. 70 (described both as a climactic act of judgment and as "the symbol of a new beginning, the heavenly enthronement of the Son of Man").[38] The language of this section is most naturally understood as a prophecy of Jesus' return: the celestial disturbances are linked with the coming of the Son of Man with the clouds of heaven, with power and great glory, with angels and a loud trumpet call, and with the gathering of the elect from all corners of the earth (24:30–31). The question of the disciples in 24:3 primed them (and Matthew's readers) for comments on Jesus' return and the end of the age. The description of the cosmic events could be meant metaphorically, symbolizing the dissolution of the first creation that will give way to the new heavens and the new earth.[39] But the description could also be meant literally, describing the collapse of the universe before the "renewal of all things" that will be initiated by the Son of Man when he is seated on the throne of his glory (Matt. 19:28).

Jesus' prophecy in signs 1–10 describes world history since the first century, with the siege and destruction of Jerusalem (sign 9) representing a particular event that happened in A.D. 70. With the exception of sign 8 (proclamation of the gospel) and Jesus' return, Jesus' prophecy characterizes world history since the fall. For end-time "specialists" such an interpretation is unexciting because it provides no opportunities for speculation about specific connections with their own time (see question 32 for a discussion of whether Jesus will return soon).

What would be so special about prophesying that history continues essentially unchanged? The answer to this question becomes obvious when we place it in the context of Jewish expectations about the Messiah. While there was no unified view of who the Messiah would be, what he would do, and what the consequences of his arrival would be for Israel and for the world, there was apparently an essential agreement that the Messiah, a Davidic king, would be a political savior who would liberate Israel from her enemies and subjugate the nations. Jesus' prophecy about the future of the world until the end when he would return was surprising and "exciting" for his disciples precisely because it contradicted their expectations. Jesus points out that there would be no cataclysmic defeat of Israel's enemies in the near future but that history would continue more or less as it had always been—a history of seduction and war and famine and earthquakes and injustice, with the destruction of Jerusalem as a low point for the disciples and for the Jewish people.

---

37. See Isaiah 13:10; 34:4; also Ezekiel 32:7–8; Amos 8:9; Joel 2:10, 30–31; 3:15. Matthew 24:30 alludes to Daniel 7:13–14.
38. France, *Gospel of Matthew*, 891, 921–23, quotation ibid., 928.
39. Mark 13:19 refers to the period from "the beginning of the creation that God created until now." Note that none of the Gospel writers refer to the "new creation."

One new factor included the proclamation of the gospel, a task for which he had called and trained the Twelve.

Summary

Jesus' answer to the disciples' question about the destruction of Jerusalem and the signs signaling the end of the age is a prophecy of ten signs, followed with a description of his return. The time between Jesus' present life and ministry (in the first century) and Jesus' return in glory is characterized by the activities of messianic pretenders and false prophets, by wars and rumors of war, by famines and earthquakes, by persecution of Christians and lack of love among believers, and by the worldwide proclamation of the gospel. The destruction of Jerusalem represents a series of climactic events (sign 9) that, however, do not constitute the end. Jesus' return will be public and universal (intimated in sign 10), as the cosmic events illustrate.

REFLECTION QUESTIONS

1. What do the disciples want to know from Jesus?

2. Does Jesus answer their question?

3. Which of the signs describe normal albeit tragic human affairs?

4. Which of the signs describe extraordinary, unique events?

5. Why does Jesus speak repeatedly of false prophets?

When Will the Signs
of the End Take Place?

When Jesus answered the disciples' question about the destruction of the temple in Jerusalem and his return and the end of the age, he prophesied events and developments that the disciples understood. The events of signs 1 through 8 and sign 10 (see question 3) describe realities in the first century as well as the history of the church from the first century until today. Sign 9, the siege and destruction of Jerusalem, happened in A.D. 70. That the reference of Jesus' prophecy in Matthew 24–25 (and Mark 13 / Luke 21) refers to the entire period between Jesus' first coming in the first century and his second coming emerges from a consideration of (1) the structure of Jesus' discourse on the end times, (2) Jesus' warnings and exhortations, and (3) Jesus' comments on the consequences of his prophecy for his followers.

The Structure of Jesus' Discourse on the End Times

Jesus' discourse on the end times follows his prediction of the destruction of the temple in Jerusalem and a question of the disciples. When the disciples admire the magnificent building of the temple and the surrounding colonnaded halls, built by Herod I, Jesus responds with a prophecy: "Truly I tell you, not one stone will be left here upon another; all will be thrown down" (Matt. 24:2). The disciples, evidently stunned by Jesus' prophecy, ask him the following question: "Tell us, when will this be, and what will be the sign of your coming and of the end of the age?" The question consists of two parts: (1) When will the temple be destroyed? (2) What will be the sign of Jesus' return and the end of the present world?

Some have argued that Jesus' eschatological discourse speaks only of the destruction of the temple.[1] It is possible to understand the apocalyptic

---

1. See N. T. Wright, *Jesus and the Victory of God, Christian Origins and the Question of God*, vol. 2 (Minneapolis: Fortress, 1996), 339–66.

language of Matthew 24:29–31 in a metaphorical sense. After all, allusions to Old Testament prophecies in which such cosmic language is used can be understood as symbolic depictions of political catastrophes within history, rather than as predictions of the physical dissolution of the universe. Such interpretations, however, play down signals in the text that Jesus moves from explaining his prophecy of the destruction of Jerusalem to explaining his return and the end of the ages. Also, such interpretations require the view that Jesus ignored the second part of the disciples' question.

The disciples' double question has led some interpreters to structure the following discourse in two main parts, corresponding to the two questions of the disciples: the subject of part one (Matt. 24:4–35) is the destruction of the temple and the subject of part two (Matt. 24:36–25:46) is Jesus' return and the end.[2] While this interpretation provides a neat structure of Jesus' discourse, it has to interpret Matthew 24:29–31 in a purely metaphorical sense, which is unlikely given the disciples' question about the end and which by definition has to be an event of cosmic proportions.

The disciples' question, formulated as a double question, was therefore meant as one single question. It seems that the disciples understood Jesus' prophecy of the destruction of the temple as a prophecy about the end, a series of events that includes the event of a third (and final) destruction of Jerusalem.[3] It is thus preferable to treat Jesus' discourse as an explanation of the signs of the end of the age (part 1), with the destruction of Jerusalem as one specific sign of a series of events that culminate in Jesus' return. Jesus follows his description of the signs for his return with an explanation of the consequences of his prophecy for his followers (part 2) before he concludes with a description of the last judgment (part 3).

The Starting Point of the Signs

When do the signs that signal the destruction of Jerusalem and of Jesus' return begin to appear? Since Jesus answers a question of his disciples, his answer must be relevant for his disciples (note in Matt. 24 that Jesus uses the second person plural, referring to the disciples to whom he speaks). This means that the signs that Jesus lists in his prophecy begin to appear, potentially at least, immediately. This is confirmed by the fact that Jesus' prophecy includes the prediction of the siege of Jerusalem, prompted by the Jewish

---

2. See R. T. France, *The Gospel of Matthew*, NICNT (Grand Rapids: Eerdmans, 2007), 890–94; see also Jeffrey A. Gibbs, *Jerusalem and Parousia: Jesus' Eschatological Discourse in Matthew's Gospel* (St. Louis: Concordia Academic Press, 2000), 170–74; Alistair I. Wilson, *When Will These Things Happen? A Study of Jesus as Judge in Matthew 21–25*, Paternoster Biblical Monographs (Carlisle: Paternoster, 2004), 133–35. For critical interaction, see Edward Adams, "The Coming of the Son of Man in Mark's Gospel," *TynBul* 56, no. 2 (2005): 39–61.

3. See D. A. Carson, *Matthew*, EBC 8 (Grand Rapids: Zondervan, 1984), 492–95.

revolt against the Romans in A.D. 66, and of the destruction of Jerusalem in the fall of A.D. 70. The starting point of the signs listed by Jesus in Matthew 24 is the time before A.D. 66. The church today is not waiting for these signs to begin to appear. They began in the first century, already observed by Jesus' disciples.

Warnings and Exhortations

Jesus' enumeration of signs begins, and is punctuated with, a series of warnings formulated with commands (imperatives): "beware that no one leads you astray" (Matt. 24:4), "see that you are not alarmed" (v. 6), "let the reader understand" (v. 15), "from the fig tree learn its lesson" (v. 32), "keep awake" (v. 42), "understand this" (v. 43), "you also must be ready" (v. 44), and "keep awake" (25:13).

The repeated declaration that nobody knows the date of Jesus' return, which will happen unexpectedly, does not allow speculation regarding how close we are to Jesus' return. Jesus emphasizes that "about that day and hour no one knows" (Matt. 24:36), "you do not know on what day your Lord is coming" (v. 42), "the Son of Man is coming at an unexpected hour" (v. 44), "the master of that slave will come on a day when he does not expect him and at an hour that he does not know" (v. 50), and "you know neither the day nor the hour" (25:13).

The fact that no one knows the date of Jesus' return or the date of the end of the age establishes the need for watchfulness. While Jesus' return might well be delayed for a considerable period of time, it may happen rather quickly (after the siege and destruction of Jerusalem, an event that could not possibly be missed). In a series of seven parables and analogies, Jesus exhorts his followers to always be ready for his return.

The parable of the fig tree (Matt. 24:32–35), whose new shoots are a harbinger of summer, teaches the disciples that once they witness the events described in the ten signs of the end (24:4–28), they may know that the end is near. Jesus asserts that it is "this generation" (*hē genea hautē*; v. 34) that will witness the signs that he predicted. As the disciples witnessed the events of signs 1 through 8 unfold during the time of their ministry, and as at least some of the disciples were still alive in A.D. 66–70 when Jerusalem was destroyed (sign 9), Jesus' assertion proved to be true.[4] Jesus goes on to assert that "about that day and hour no one knows, neither the angels of heaven, nor the Son, but only the Father" (v. 36). The day of Jesus' return and of the end of the age (24:3) is and will remain unknown to his followers.

---

4. Carson points out that "this does *not* mean that the distress must end within that time but only that 'all these things' must happen within it . . . [T]here is no *terminus ad quem* to this distress other than the Parousia itself" (*Matthew*, 507).

The analogy of Noah's generation (Matt. 24:37–39) teaches the disciples about the danger of being unprepared. Since the exact time of Jesus' return is unknown, it is possible to be caught unawares. As the flood described in Genesis 7:6–24, although announced beforehand, was sudden and universal, the event of Jesus' return will be sudden and universal. It will come without warning. Note the description of normal life at the time of Noah's flood—people eat and drink, marry and give in marriage (Matt. 24:38). Only those who are prepared will escape its judgment and destruction.

The analogy of everyday routines (Matt. 24:40–41)—men will work in the field; women will be grinding with a hand mill—underlines again the unexpected suddenness of Jesus' return and the danger of being unprepared. Jesus exhorts his followers, again, to keep watch because "you do not know on what day your Lord will come" (v. 42).

The parable of the thief in the night (Matt. 24:43)[5] underscores yet again the exhortation to watchfulness. Burglars depend on the element of surprise when they break into a house. Not even the most ingenious calculation can anticipate their arrival. Thus, house owners have to be constantly alert if they want to avoid being victims. Jesus exhorts his followers that they "must be ready, because the Son of Man will come at an hour when you do not expect him" (v. 44 NIV). Jesus can come back at any time, once the signs of the end described in Matthew 24:4–28 have taken place.

The parable of the slaves left in charge (Matt. 24:45–51) teaches Jesus' followers to be ready for the unexpected return of the master by doing the tasks that they have been given. They are warned of the serious consequences of not being ready for Jesus' return, which will happen "on a day when he does not expect him and at an hour he is not aware of" (v. 50 NIV).

The parable of wise and foolish virgins (Matt. 25:1–13), in which the arrival of the bridegroom is delayed for an extended period of time, teaches Jesus' followers yet again the need to be ready at any time for Jesus' return. People who think that they know when the bridegroom comes and that they have things under control will not be ready when he delays his arrival. They will miss the wedding feast. Readiness cannot be achieved by last-minute activities meant to correct calculations that turned out to be miscalculations. Followers of Jesus who really know Jesus and who are thus prepared for a long delay are ready for Jesus' return at any time.[6]

The parable of the slaves who were entrusted with money (Matt. 25:14–30) speaks again about a potentially extended absence of the master. Jesus teaches his disciples about the need to use the opportunity of the present time and the privileges that each has been given to continue to live and work for him, rather than wasting time by doing nothing (also see question 32).

---

5. See Luke 12:39; 1 Thessalonians 5:2, 4; 2 Peter 3:10; Revelation 3:3; 16:15.
6. Note Jesus' indictment of the foolish bridesmaids in Matthew 25:12.

Summary

The time of Jesus' return and of the end of the age is unknown. Only God the Father knows the date, and he has revealed it neither to Jesus nor to the angels, nor will he reveal it to Jesus' followers. The consequences of this fact are obvious: Christians must be ready for Jesus' return, which will happen suddenly and unexpectedly. It can happen any time, after the signs that Jesus described in Matthew 24:4–28 are being observed. Since the one specific event that Jesus prophesied—the siege and destruction of Jerusalem (Matt. 24:15–22)—took place in A.D. 70, and since the other signs of the end that Jesus listed could be observed even before A.D. 70, Jesus could return any time after A.D. 70.

Because the day of Jesus' return is (and will remain) unknown to his followers, speculations are not only fruitless and irrelevant but positively rebellious. The biggest mistake of some end-time "specialists" is the production of (ever new) prophecies of the date of Jesus' return. Followers of Jesus who acknowledge the divinely ordained ignorance regarding the time of Jesus' return are ready for that day when they live and work for Jesus.

REFLECTION QUESTIONS

1. What is the starting point of the signs of the end?

2. Who knows the time and day of Jesus' return?

3. What is the significance of the destruction of Jerusalem in A.D. 70?

4. Why must Christians be ready for Jesus' return?

5. What entails readiness for Jesus' return?

What Are the Seal, Trumpet, and Bowl Judgments (Rev. 6–16)?

John's visions in the Apocalypse, revealed to him by the exalted Jesus Christ (Rev. 1:1), relate three series of judgments: the seven seals, the seven trumpets, and the seven bowls. Note that John saw a fourth series of seven judgments—the seven thunders—but was asked not to write it down (Rev. 10:1–8). The following table summarizes the details of the seal, trumpet, and bowl judgments.

THE SEAL, TRUMPET, AND BOWL JUDGMENTS		
THE SEVEN SEALS REVELATION 6:1–17 + 8:1–5	THE SEVEN TRUMPETS REVELATION 8:6–9:21 + 11:15–19	THE SEVEN BOWLS REVELATION 15:1–16:21
1. wars of conquest	1. hail, fire, blood fall on the earth; a third of the vegetation is burned up	1. festering sores on the earth's inhabitants
2. international unrest; people kill each other	2. mountain thrown into sea; one third of the sea creatures die; one third of maritime commerce dies	2. sea turns to blood; all sea creatures die
	3. star falls from the sky on rivers; one third of the rivers and springs poisoned; many people die	3. rivers turn to blood

THE SEAL, TRUMPET, AND BOWL JUDGMENTS		
THE SEVEN SEALS REVELATION 6:1–17 + 8:1–5	THE SEVEN TRUMPETS REVELATION 8:6–9:21 + 11:15–19	THE SEVEN BOWLS REVELATION 15:1–16:21
	4. sun, moon, stars are struck; one third of the day becomes dark	4. sun scorches people
3. famine, hunger		
4. sword, famine, plague, wild animals; one-fourth of humankind killed		
5. persecution	5. sun and air darkened with locusts; locusts torment humankind	5. the beast's kingdom is darkened; agony on earth
	6. demonic cavalry, one third of humankind killed	6. river dries up to prepare way for armies for the final battle
6. earthquake (a) sun darkened (b) moon turns blood red (c) stars fall from the sky (d) sky recedes like a scroll		
7. silence (a) thunder (b) voices/rumblings (c) lightning (d) earthquake	7. announcement of God's reign (a) lightning (b) voices/rumblings (c) thunder (d) earthquake (e) great hailstorm	7. proclamation of the end (a) lightning (b) voices/rumblings (c) thunder (d) great earthquake: cities of the nations collapse; final judgment of Babylon; islands and mountains disappear (e) huge hailstones

Intensification of the Seal, Trumpet, and Bowl Judgments

Each subsequent series seems to represent an intensification of judgment. The seal judgments destroy a quarter of the earth (Rev. 6:8), the trumpet judgments affect a third of the earth (Rev. 8:7, 9, 10, 11, 12; 9:15), and the bowl judgments affect the whole earth: land, sea, inland waters, and the air (Rev. 16:1–21). The seal and trumpet judgments affect human beings indirectly, whereas the bowl judgments are poured out directly upon the earth dwellers.

What does this intensification mean? Some suggest that it means that life on planet earth will get progressively worse, until the end comes. This interpretation is difficult if the three series of seven judgments describe *all* of God's judgments between Jesus' first and second coming. Two answers are more plausible. First, John describes the seal, trumpet, and bowl judgments with intensifying language in order to increase the drama of his portrayal of God's judgments and thus to increase the intensity of the Christian readers' expectation of Jesus' return. Second, the intensification of the three series of judgments increases the urgency to stay faithful to the gospel and to be ready for the possibility of martyrdom.

The Interludes

John interrupts the three series of judgment in Revelation 7:1–17 between seal 6 and 7, in 10:1–11:13 between trumpet 6 and 7, and in 12:1–14:20 between the trumpet and the bowl judgments. These interludes provide information about the situation of the followers of the Lamb and about the conflict with the forces of God's enemy, emphasizing God's sovereign control over history until the consummation of his promises.

The first interlude, which interrupts the seven seals, answers the question at the end of the sixth seal, "Who is able to stand?" (Rev. 6:17): the people of God, who are the followers of the Lamb, will be able to stand as God's judgment comes upon the world, while the earth dwellers will not be able to stand. The first interlude clarifies the status of the Christians: they are God's possession and as such under God's protection. The interlude is a double vision: the vision of the 144,000 (Rev. 7:1–8) and the great multitude before God's throne (Rev. 7:9–17). The two groups are identical (for details see question 9). The "seal of the living God" (7:2) that is given to the people of God symbolizes the fact that they belong to God and that they are therefore protected from God's destructive wrath that is poured out on the world. The parallel with the martyrs that are mentioned in connection with the opening of the fifth seal (6:9–11) is important. The assurance of being God's possession and of being under God's protection applies already to the events of the previous seal judgments (6:1–7). The saints are saved from God's wrath of destruction as they are assured spiritual protection, but they are not protected from the wrath of the beast from the sea, God's demonic enemy. This explains why followers of the Lamb have died and will continue to die as martyrs. In this sense the double vision describes the promise of protection (the sealing in 7:1–8) and the fulfillment of the promise as the multitude of Jesus' followers celebrates in heaven (7:9–17).[1]

---

1. For the theme of protection, also see Revelation 3:10; 8:13; 9:4; 16:6.

The second interlude, which interrupts the seven trumpets, is also a double vision: the vision of the angel with the small scroll (Rev. 10:1–11) and vision of the two witnesses (Rev. 11:1–14). The interlude clarifies the role of the Christians: they are reminded of their task of prophetic witness. In the vision the angel commands John to eat a small scroll, which is an enactment of the commissioning of the prophet Ezekiel (see Ezek. 2:8–3:3). Thus, the readers are reminded of the sweetness of obedience and of the bitterness of rejection and suffering—a ministry to which the church is called. The scene in which John is directed to measure the temple of God and the altar (replicating the action of the prophet Ezekiel, see Ezek. 40:3–14) confirms the message of the first interlude: (1) the followers of the Lamb belong to God and are under his protection, and (2) God grants them spiritual protection even while the forces of God's enemy persecute and kill them.[2] The two witnesses are identified with two lampstands that stand before God (Rev. 11:4) and thus with the churches (see 1:12, 20). That is, not with two specific churches, but with the entire church whose task is to bear witness (the Law required truth to be established by two witnesses; see Deut. 17:6; 19:15). The role of the church is to witness to the truth of God and the Lamb of God in the midst of opposition and in view of the possibility of Christian witnesses being killed as martyrs (on the two witnesses, see question 25).

The third interlude is inserted between the trumpet and the bowl judgment series (Rev. 12:1–14:20). In a series of visions, John demonstrates how the calling described in the second interlude—the divine calling to missionary proclamation and suffering—is part of the great conflict between the people of God and the forces of evil that control the world (described as the evil triumvirate of dragon, beast, and false prophet). Whenever Satan "conquers" the people of God through persecution (Rev. 13:7), they "conquer" the forces of evil "by the blood of the Lamb and by the word of their testimony, for they did not cling to life even in the face of death" (12:11). That is, they conquer evil through their willingness to suffer as they rely on the reality of the effects of Jesus' death and as they bear witness to the truth.

The Purpose of the Three Series of Judgments

The meaning of the details of the seal, trumpet, and bowl judgments can be understood only if they are connected with the three interludes. The following emphases are central.[3] First, God punishes the earth and humankind

---

2. Grant R. Osborne combines the traditional options of interpretation: John conveys a prophecy about the final, future period of history (futurist perspective), while at the same time he conveys God's message of spiritual protection alongside the possibility of martyrdom to the church of his time (preterist perspective), and to the church of all historical periods (idealist perspective) (*Revelation*, BECNT [Grand Rapids: Baker Academic, 2002], 415).

3. Adapted from Osborne, *Revelation*, 270–71.

in specific acts of judgments, often by simply allowing evil to run its course with its intended and unintended consequences. Second, God's people are protected from these judgments, safe under divine spiritual protection (Rev. 3:10; 7:1–8; 9:4; 16:2) in the midst of persecution, during which some may die as martyrs. Third, God's sovereignty is never in doubt—even the demonic forces cannot operate without divine authorization (note the expression "it was given" or similar wording in Rev. 6:2, 4, 8; 8:2, 3; 9:1, 3, 5; 13:5, 7, 14, 15). Fourth, the depravity of humanity becomes evident in the refusal of the people to repent and worship the Lamb and in their preference to worship the very demonic forces that bring about their downfall (Rev. 9:20–21; 16:1, 11). Fifth, the mission of God's people continues to be the task of missionary witness in the world despite being hated and suffering martyrdom (Rev. 11:1–13). Sixth, God's judgments provide a final chance to repent, as God demonstrates the powerlessness of the gods and the (false) prophets that the earth dwellers worship and follow (Rev. 9:20; 14:6–7; 16:9, 11). Seventh, at the end God will dismantle his first creation (Rev. 6:12–14) in order to bring in the perfection of a new creation (Rev. 20:11; 21:1).

Summary

John describes the judgment that God will bring upon the earth in three series of seven judgments each. God's judgment falls on the earth as well as on humankind. That is, the entire fallen creation is affected by the destructive wrath of God. The description of God's judgments emphasizes the evil nature of the forces opposed to God, and it underlines the sovereignty of the almighty God whose power nothing and nobody can withstand. The description of God's judgment is accompanied by God's assurance for his people, who are safe since they belong to him, and by God's commission to witness to the truth of the gospel even in the midst of suffering, persecution, and martyrdom.[4]

REFLECTION QUESTIONS

1. How are the three series of the seal, trumpet, and bowl judgments connected with each other?

2. How do commentators interpret the details of the three series of judgments?

3. How should we understand the intensification of the three series of judgments?

---

4. The question whether we should understand the details of John's prophecy of a threefold series of judgments literally or symbolically, and the question when this threefold series of judgments takes place, will be addressed in questions 6 and 7.

4. What does John show in the interludes that interrupt the three series of judgments?

5. What is the purpose of the three series of judgments?

Should We Understand John's Visions Literally or Symbolically?

Interpreters of John's Apocalypse have struggled since earliest times with the language that he uses to describe the visions that the risen Jesus Christ granted him. How much of the detail of the three series of judgments, and of the later visions, does John want to be taken literally? How much is symbolic? Some of John's descriptions are easy to recognize as symbolic (or metaphorical). For example, when the risen Jesus promises to the Christians in Philadelphia, "If you conquer, I will make you a pillar in the temple of my God" (Rev. 3:12), even interpreters who want to explain the contents of the book of Revelation as literally as possible state that "this is of course a figure of speech."[1] Since the Reformation, the importance of a literal interpretation has been recognized and emphasized by evangelical interpreters of Scripture. However, the expression "literal interpretation" or, with the Latin phrase the Reformers used, finding the *sensus literalis* of Scripture, must be carefully defined. Not every word or expression in the Bible is to be understood "literally" in terms of the normal usage of the word or expression. When Jesus says, "I am the gate for the sheep" (John 10:7), neither the word "gate" nor the word "sheep" is meant to be understood in the normal usage of the words. In this context, the two words are used with a symbolic, metaphorical, or figurative meaning. If John, who relates Jesus' words, wanted his readers to understand the *words* "gate" and "sheep" as *symbols* for the significance of Jesus who provides access to God's presence and God's salvation ("gate") for God's people

---

1. John F. Walvoord, *The Revelation of Jesus* Christ (Chicago: Moody Press, 1966), 88. Robert L. Thomas concurs: "The language is clearly metaphorical" (*Revelation 1–7: An Exegetical Commentary* [Chicago: Moody, 1992], 292).

("sheep"),[2] such a symbolic reading is the intended reading. A "literal" or, rather, "literalist" reading leads in this case to nonsense, in other cases to misinterpretation. The main question is not how many of the words and expressions of the Bible we can interpret literally, but whether the author's intended meaning is literal or symbolic (or figurative).

The Symbolism of the Three Series of Judgments

An entirely symbolic interpretation of the book of Revelation is certainly not how John wanted his readers to understand the content of what he wrote. A consistently symbolic interpretation would reduce God's judgment over sinners at the end to a mere symbol. Since the descriptions of judgment serve as warnings to Jesus' followers to be unswerving and consistent in their loyalty to Jesus, even if this means suffering and martyrdom, the judgments that are depicted must have some form of historical reality. Mere symbols neither destroy nor hurt. If there is no "bite" of historical reality, rhetoric that is intended to warn is empty and quickly will be dismissed as irrelevant.

On the other hand, since many individual judgments of the three series would end civilization as John's readers knew it, in particular the bowl judgments,[3] John describes the content of the visions that he received with a certain amount of symbolism and hyperbole. He uses both Old Testament language and allusions to contemporary political, social, and military realities in the first century. And we need to remember that John wrote a prophecy (Rev. 1:3) that he was asked not to seal (22:10). Rather, it was to be sent as letter (see 1:4–6) that was to be read and understood by Christian readers in the first century.

We should note that a symbolic description of events does not mean that nothing ever happens. While John's language may be at times symbolic, he still may describe real events.

The Symbolism and Reality of the Seal, Trumpet, and Bowl Judgments

There is no space here to provide an interpretation of all seven elements of the seal, trumpet, and bowl judgments, twenty-one announcements of judgments in all.[4] We will limit ourselves to a discussion of the first element in the three series of judgments, demonstrating the main options for interpretation.

---

2. See Craig S. Keener, *The Gospel of John: A Commentary* (Peabody, MA: Hendrickson, 2003), 801, 810–11.
3. Grant R. Osborne, *Revelation*, BECNT (Grand Rapids: Baker Academic, 2002), 580. For example, the destruction of the sea in the second bowl judgment is tantamount to the destruction of Mediterranean society whose trade depended on maritime commerce, and the pollution of the rivers and springs makes human life impossible.
4. For details, see Osborne, *Revelation*, 272–300 (seals 1–6), 336–38 (seal 7), 349–89 (trumpets 1–6), 438–50 (trumpet 7), and 559–602 (bowls 1–7).

The First Seal Judgment

The first seal judgment depicts a rider on a white horse who has a bow and a crown and who conquers (Rev. 6:1–2). It is impossible to imagine that a literal rider on a literal horse with a literal bow will come from God's heavenly throne to earth and conquer the world, all by himself.

Scholars who interpret biblical prophecy as much as possible in a literal manner see in the rider "the world ruler of the tribulation" who is then identified with the first beast of the sea of Revelation 13.[5] A more cautious literal interpretation—"literal" in the sense of seeing the fulfillment in historical figures—sees in the rider on the white horse "a personification of a growing movement or force" of which the beast out of the sea from Revelation 13 will be a part. He is "one of many impostors who constitute this anti-christian force" since he will come at "the beginning of the birth-pains," threatening war but achieving a bloodless victory (the bow is without arrows).[6] Since neither the horse nor the bow can be taken literally (at least since the second- and third-century Parthians, who fought with bows, were no longer posing a threat), a symbolic interpretation is required.

A consistently symbolic interpretation sees the first rider as representing the forces of Satan that were unleashed on the world as a result of Christ's victorious suffering (see the context in Rev. 5:1–14). These forces attempt "to defeat and oppress believers spiritually through deception, persecution, or both."[7] Since this theme of cosmic conflict can be found already in the Old Testament, in Jesus' teaching, in Paul's proclamation, and, most importantly, in many other passages in the Apocalypse, this interpretation is possible.

Some combine a literal (historical) and a symbolic interpretation. The description of the rider reminded readers in the first century of Parthian warriors (who fought on horses with bows). These warriors were not controlled by Rome (hence the crown of the rider) and were even feared by Rome (they defeated a Roman army in 55 B.C. and in A.D. 62). However, John hardly describes a particular Parthian campaign against the Roman Empire. The rider on the white horse with a bow who is given a crown "represents humankind setting themselves up in the place of God," and the entire vision of the first seal describes "the general propensity of sinful humans for conquest."[8] This means that seal 1 (wars of conquest) corresponds to sign 2 in Jesus' prophecy of the end (wars, rumors of war, international unrest). The first seal can then be interpreted as predicting armed conflicts, which have continued to

---

5. See Walvoord, *Revelation of Jesus Christ*, 126–27.
6. Thomas, *Revelation*, 422–23.
7. Gregory K. Beale, *The Book of Revelation: A Commentary on the Greek Text*, NIGTC (Grand Rapids: Eerdmans, 1999), 377 (also see 371, 375–78).
8. Osborne, *Revelation*, 277.

characterize human history after the first century when John wrote. At the same time, linguistic and thematic connections with Revelation 12:12–17 and 13:7 indicate that the first seal introduces the great cosmic war between Satan and the people of God.[9] On account of the allusions to first-century realities and the presence of the theme of cosmic conflict in the biblical tradition and in other parts of John's Apocalypse, this interpretation is plausible.

The First Trumpet Judgment

The first trumpet judgment speaks of "hail and fire, mixed with blood" that are hurled to the earth, with the result that "a third of the earth was burned up, and a third of the trees were burned up, and all green grass was burned up" (Rev. 8:7). Interpreters who insist on a literal interpretation expect that in the last phase of human history an "unfathomable deluge" of hail and fire mixed with blood will be hurled by God onto the earth, with the result that one-third of the vegetation is destroyed.[10] While such an event is possible (e.g., in connection with nuclear war), it would be impossible to say that it is the precise (and only) fulfillment of this text. If one such event can occur, subsequent events of a similar nature could take place as well. In other words, a literal interpretation does not allow us to specify the point at which we have arrived in God's timetable.

A symbolic interpretation takes the first trumpet as depicting God's punishment of unbelievers: "The trumpets portray judgment on unbelievers because of their hardened attitude, thus demonstrating God's incomparable sovereignty and glory. These judgments are not intended to evoke repentance but to punish because of the permanently hardened, unrepentant stance of the unbelievers toward God and his people."[11]

An interpretation that combines symbolic meanings with literal events in history sees both the theme of divine judgment that brings about the fulfill-ment of the judgment prophesied in Joel 2:30–31 (where blood and fire are mentioned together) and the reality of picturing one-third of all the great forests of the world burned down.[12]

---

9. Osborne sees "a description of the extent to which war is the ultimate depravity of hu-manity" (ibid.).
10. Robert L. Thomas, *Revelation: An Exegetical Commentary* [Chicago: Moody, 1995], 15–17. The literal interpretation of the assertion that "all green grass was burned up" creates a problem with the content of the fifth trumpet, where grass still exists (Rev. 9:4). Thomas solves this by assuming a time lapse between the first and fifth trumpets, and by pointing out that in most regions grass is not green year round. He accuses scholars who accept symbolic interpretations as getting into "a hopeless quagmire of contradictions" (ibid., 16–17) but does not see that his interpretation leads to contradictions as well, which need to be solved.
11. Beale, *Book of Revelation*, 472.
12. Osborne, *Revelation*, 350–51.

The First Bowl Judgment

The first bowl judgment announces that "a foul and painful sore came on those who had the mark of the beast and who worshiped its image" (Rev. 16:2). A literal interpretation reckons with an outbreak of agonizing ulcers that refuse to go away which will afflict the unbelievers.[13] A symbolic interpretation understands the effect of the bowl that produces a bad and evil sore in a figurative sense: the people who accept the idolatrous mark of the beast will be punished by being given "a penal mark" that presumably entails spiritual and psychological torment (as in Rev. 9:4–6, 10).[14] Interpreters who combine symbolic and literal interpretations understand the first bowl as emphasizing that the people who have accepted the mark of the beast deserve judgment from God, while pointing out that "the thought of such a plague in a literal sense is fearsome indeed. Medical supplies would be exhausted in a few days with such a universal disaster."[15]

Numerical Symbolism

The presence of symbolism in John's series of seven judgments needs to be taken seriously, even if it undermines the efforts of end-time "specialists." Such "specialists" often use the progression from one to seven in the three series of seven judgments (or other numbers in the Apocalypse) to more precisely calculate the nearness of the end.

The most important numbers in the Apocalypse are three, four, seven, and twelve (or multiples of these numbers).[16] Most acknowledge the presence of symbolism in at least some of the passages in the Apocalypse. It is well known that there were more churches in the province of Asia at the end of the first century than the seven churches that John singles out (Rev. 1:4, 11; 2:1–3:22). For example, there were churches in Troas, Hierapolis, Colossae, Miletus, and Tralles. Whatever the particular reason for the selection of the churches of Ephesus, Smyrna, Pergamum, Thyatira, Sardis, Philadelphia, and Laodicea may have been, they are intended to describe "typical assemblies with regard to their histories and spiritual states."[17]

Seven

Seven is the number of completeness. This means that a list of seven is

---

13. Thomas, *Revelation*, 248–49. He adds, "Happenings on such a catastrophic scale stretch the capacity of human comprehension. No precedent in human history can measure up to the future supernatural intervention of God, but man's inability to grasp the magnitude of it is no reason to deny its literal meaning" (ibid., 249).
14. Beale, *Book of Revelation*, 814.
15. Osborne, *Revelation*, 580.
16. See Richard J. Bauckham, *The Climax of Prophecy: Studies on the Book of Revelation* (Edinburgh: T&T Clark, 1993), 29–37.
17. Thomas, *Revelation*, 63–64; see Osborne, *Revelation*, 60.

representative of all: the seven churches of the province of Asia stand for all the churches; the seven bowl judgments stand for all divine judgments and for the seven trumpet judgments as well. It is probably not accidental that several titles of God occur seven times in the book: the full title "the Lord God Almighty" (Rev. 1:8; 4:8; 11:17; 15:3; 16:7; 19:6; 21:22), "the one who sits on the throne" (4:2, 9, 10; 5:1, 7, 13; 6:16; 7:15; 19:4; 20:11; 21:5). There are also seven "beatitudes" sprinkled throughout the book of Revelation (1:3; 14:13; 16:15; 19:9; 20:6; 22:7, 14). The Greek term *makarios* translated "blessed" is also used in the beatitudes in the Sermon on the Mount (see Matt. 5:3–12).

Four

Four is the number of the world. The earth has four corners (Rev. 7:1; 20:8) and four winds (7:1). The created order of the world can be described in terms of four divisions. Every creature "in heaven and on earth and under the earth and in the sea" offers to God and the Lamb a fourfold doxology of "praise and honor and glory and power" (5:13 NIV).[18] The created order consists of earth, sea, (rivers and) springs, and heaven (8:7–12; 14:7; 16:2–9)— four parts of creation that are the targets of the first four trumpet judgments and the first four bowl judgments. This pattern explains why all three series of seven judgments have a 4 + 3 pattern: in each case the first four judgments are judgments on the earth or the world. This pattern also explains why there were originally four series of judgments, if the seven thunders are included (10:3–7). John was granted visions in which he saw the complete judgment (series of seven) on the entire world (four series). It is perhaps not accidental that the list of cargoes that Babylon imports from "the merchants of the earth" (18:11–13) consists of 28, that is, 4 x 7 items.[19] It is probably also not accidental that the title for Jesus Christ "the Lamb" occurs 28 (i.e., 4 x 7) times, indicating the worldwide scope of his victory. The fourfold phrase that describes the nations of the world—"peoples and tribes and languages and nations"—occurs seven times (5:9; 7:9; 10:11; 11:9; 13:7; 14:6; 17:15; the phrase varies each time it occurs; instead of "tribes" sometimes "kings" [10:11] or "multitudes" [17:15] is used). It may also not be accidental that the title of the sovereign God who created the world—"the one who lives forever and ever"—occurs four times in the book (4:9, 10; 10:6; 15:7). There are four references to "the seven spirits" (1:4; 3:1; 4:5; 5:6), as they represent the fullness of God's power "sent out into all the earth" (5:6). The four references to the seven churches (1:4, 11, 20) suggest that they represent all the churches of the world.

---

18. The other doxologies are either sevenfold (Rev. 5:12; 7:12) or threefold (Rev. 4:9, 11; 19:1b).
19. Note that the items in the list of cargoes are not numbered, nor does John give the figure 28.

Three

Three does not have a consistent meaning. The number three occurs in the book of Revelation in connection with the designations of God: the title with its three elements—the one "who is and who was and who is to come"—occurs three times (Rev. 1:4, 8; 4:8); God is worshiped with the acclamation "holy, holy, holy" (4:8), linked with the threefold doxology of "glory and honor and thanks" (4:9, 11; see 19:1; the third element is "power" in 4:11, and the elements in 19:1 are "salvation and glory and power").

Twelve

Twelve is the number of the people of God. This symbolic significance derives from the twelve tribes of the people of Israel in Old Testament times. The number twelve is squared for completeness (144) and multiplied by a thousand (the 144,000 of Rev. 7:4–8; 14:1; see question 9). The description of the New Jerusalem in Revelation 21:9–22:5 contains twelve references to the number twelve.

Specific Symbolic Numbers

This numerical symbolism suggests that unless there is a clear indication to a literal interpretation, the numbers in John's Apocalypse should be understood to have a symbolic meaning. This clearly also applies to the number 666, which John insists can be understood if readers apply wisdom and insight to the number and if they can do calculations (Rev. 13:18; for details see question 21). Some of John's numbers can be interpreted in the context of Pythagorean mathematics, which conceived of numbers as corresponding to geometrical figures.[20] John uses square numbers for the people of God (144, the twelfth square number, i.e., the square of 12): the figure of God's people is 12 times 1,000 from each of the twelve tribes, that is, 144,000, a figure that can be represented as the square of twelve (12 x 12 = 144; note that 144 is in fact the twelfth square number), multiplied by a thousand. John states that the New Jerusalem is square (Rev. 21:16), and he uses the number twelve exactly twelve times in the description of the New Jerusalem: there are twelve gates,

---

20. Two-dimensional figures represent plane numbers: figures with equal sides and figures with unequal sides. The most important figures with equal sides were triangular and square numbers; the most important figures with unequal sides were rectangular numbers, which can all be depicted as pebbles arranged in patterns. For example: six is a triangular number (the sum of consecutive numbers that add up to six, that is, 1 + 2 + 3 = 6) and can be depicted as a triangle of 1 + 2 + 3 pebbles; sixteen is a square number (the sum of the successive odd numbers, that is, 1 + 3 + 5 + 7 = 16) and can be depicted as a square of 4 + 4 + 4 + 4 pebbles; twelve is a rectangular number (the sum of successive even numbers, that is, 2 + 4 + 6 = 12) and can be depicted as a rectangle of 4 + 4 + 4 pebbles. For this discussion, including the following comments in the text, see Bauckham, *Climax of Prophecy*, 390–407.

twelve angels, the names of the twelve tribes of Israel, twelve foundations, the twelve names of the twelve apostles, the length and the width is twelve thousand stadia, the twelve gates are twelve pearls, and there are twelve kinds of fruit (Rev. 21:9–22:5).

John also uses rectangular numbers: the apocalyptic period of the end times lasts 42 months or 1,260 days (Rev. 11:2, 3; 12:6; 13:5). The number 42 is the sixth rectangular number (6 x 7), and 1,260 is the thirty-fifth rectangular number (35 x 36). The fact that 42 months is three and a half years indicates that this period is borrowed from Daniel, who uses the phrase "a time, times, and half a time" (Dan. 7:25; 12:7), a phrase that John explicitly uses in Revelation 12:14. What is at first sight surprising is the fact that John ignores Daniel's specifications of this phrase, given as 1,290 days and as 1,335 days, respectively (Dan. 12:11, 12). John's figures of 42 months or 1,260 days require the artificial assumption of 12 months of only 30 days each. It seems that John deliberately chose rectangular numbers to describe the period during which the beast reigns (triangular number) persecuting the people of God (square number), using rectangular numbers "to designate this ambiguous period in which the beast and the saints oppose each other."[21]

In sum, the symbolism of these numbers suggest that all, if not most, numbers in John's Apocalypse should be interpreted symbolically, not literally.

Summary

The details of the first four judgments of the seal series indicate that John is not describing new developments: wars of conquest (seal 1) took place in the late first, second, and third centuries, and ever since. The same holds true for international unrest (seal 2), famine and hunger (seal 3), and the effects of warfare (sword), famine, and plagues, all of which kill people (seal 4).

Literal events that resemble the judgments depicted in the seal, trumpet, and bowl judgments are not impossible to imagine—not only because of God's sovereign power, but also because of humankind's seemingly endless capacity for devising, producing, and deploying technologies and weapons that affect or have the potential to affect large parts of the globe.

At the same time, John's concern is not to provide his readers in the first century with a detailed timetable of future events that allows them to establish how close the end is. Even taken literally, many of the judgments described in the three series have been a reality since the first century (and before—for example, during Israel's exodus from Egypt), in varying degrees and in different regions of the earth. The symbolism of most if not all of the numbers in the Apocalypse suggest that John's focus is not on historical events for their own sake but on the meaning of God's judgment both for the world (as a call to

---

21. Bauckham, *Climax of Prophecy*, 401.

repentance) and for the church (as a call to faithful perseverance and coura-
geous witness).

REFLECTION QUESTIONS

1. What are the dangers of a purely literal interpretation? What difference do
   literal interpretations make regarding the time of Jesus' return?

2. Can literal events have symbolic meanings?

3. How can symbolic meanings be established?

4. What are the dangers of a purely symbolic interpretation?

5. What is the meaning of the numbers four and twelve in John's visions?

When Will the Seal, Trumpet, and Bowl Judgments Take Place?

The crucial question concerning John's three series of seven judgments is timing. When will the three series of judgments take place? When do they begin? Do they provide information about strictly future developments? Three important insights help us to answer this question.

A Comparison of the Seven Seal, Trumpet, and Bowl Judgments

A comparison of the three series of judgments shows that each series recapitulates the same period of history and takes the reader to the end. The three series of seven judgments are explicitly numbered. And the three series have a comparable structure of 4 + 3 judgments: the first four bring judgment on the earth, the last three on the people. The judgments of seals 1–4 are introduced with a closely similar wording, and they are connected in each case with a horse and its rider. The judgments of trumpets 1–4 form an obvious group, but John places a stronger emphasis on trumpets 5–7 as a group, each of which is linked with the vision of an eagle proclaiming a threefold "woe" on the inhabitants of the earth. The judgments of trumpets 1–4 and of bowls 1–4 affect the earth, the seas, the inland waters, and the heavens, paralleling the Egyptian plagues.

The three numbered series do not predict a chronology of events, as is sometimes assumed. At least the two following considerations render this assessment unavoidable. First, when stars fall from the sky and when the sky is rolled up (seal 6), there is nothing left of the earth to destroy in order for the trumpet and bowl judgments to take place. Second, the first four plagues of the trumpet judgments would all but end civilization: if one-third of the world's vegetation is destroyed, if one-third of the world's rivers and springs are poisoned and thus eliminating one-third of the world's drinking water (which is already scarce today in many regions of the world), and if one-third of daylight is eliminated, civilization as we know it would come to an end. Governments would not be able to cope with the catastrophes and their aftermath. The disasters of the early bowl judgments also would end civilization: if all sea creatures are killed (bowl 2) and if all rivers turn to blood, rendering drinking water virtually impossible to find (bowl 3), human life quickly would become impossible. The three series of judgments do not prophesy a progression of events: they represent a unity that recapitulates the time until the end with different symbols, "like that of a musical theme with variations, each variation adding something new to the significance of the whole composition."[1]

The disasters of each series evidently happen simultaneously. This is particularly obvious in the seal judgments. Wars and international unrest (seal 1 and 2) are inevitably accompanied by famine and hunger (seal 3) and by plagues and death (seal 4). Each series describes God's judgments in history until the end comes, which itself constitutes judgment (symbolized with the references to lightning, thunder, hail, and the earthquake).

Each subsequent series represents an intensification of judgment. The seal judgments destroy a quarter of the earth (Rev. 6:8), the trumpet judgments affect a third of the earth (8:7, 9, 10, 11, 12; 9:15), and the bowl judgments affect the whole earth: earth, sea, inland waters, and the air (16:1–21). The seal and trumpet judgments affect human beings indirectly, whereas the bowl judgments are poured out directly upon the earth dwellers.

Each series is tied to the other in the seventh judgment by the repetition of a formula, "peals of thunder, rumblings, flashes of lightning, an earthquake" (Rev. 8:5; 11:15, 19; 16:17–18; order of these elements varies), the first three elements of which connect all three series to the vision of the throne of God in Revelation 4 (see 4:5).[2] The deliberate use of this formula indicates that each of the three series reaches the final judgment in the seventh element. The first series (seal judgments) has a close resemblance with the lists of the signs of the end prophesied by Jesus (see question 3). The second series (trumpet judgments) replicates the plagues in Egypt that initiated Israel's exodus and redemption from slavery, bringing Israel to Mount Sinai where God revealed himself. The third series (bowl judgments) is connected with the second series by reference to the angels (Rev. 8:2, 3, 5, etc.; 15:1, 6, 8) and by the first four judgments that also replicate the Egyptian plagues. These connections indicate that in each of the three series of judgments, John takes his readers all the way to the end.

The content of the sixth and seventh element in each of the three series also confirms that John takes his readers three times to the end. In the sixth seal (Rev. 6:12–14), the sun turns black: universal darkness quickly would

---

1. G. B. Caird, *A Commentary on the Revelation of St. John the Divine*, HNTC (New York: Harper & Row, 1966), 106; quoted by many commentators, e.g., Grant R. Osborne, *Revelation*, BECNT (Grand Rapids: Baker Academic, 2002), 270.
2. On the earthquake, see question 29.

end life on earth. The stars falling to earth also would immediately end life on earth (the impact of only several large meteorites, let alone one star or planet, on earth would end life on earth), the dust cloud would block out incoming solar radiation for months, and temperatures would drop throughout the world, creating global winterlike conditions leading to mass extinctions. The graphic description of the sky rolled up like a scroll indicates the disappearance of the sky and thus the end of the world.

The seventh trumpet (Rev. 11:15–19) announces that the Lord God and his Messiah have taken over the kingdom of the world, that God's eternal reign has begun, and that the time for the judgment of the dead and for rewarding God's servants has come. These announcements relate to events connected with the end of human history, a fallen creation that has rebelled against God. The final announcement of the seventh trumpet is the opening of God's temple in heaven, an event that also announces the end of the history of the fallen world—God is about to leave his heavenly temple and become present among his people.

The seventh bowl (Rev. 16:17) begins with the proclamation "It is done!" which announces that God's judgment has taken place and that the end of human history in fallen creation has arrived. The latter is indicated with the announcement that the cities of the nations collapse, that Babylon is finally judged, and that the islands and the mountains vanish (vv. 19–20). The proclamation "It is done!" is repeated in Revelation 21:6 in the vision of the new heaven and the new earth. At this time, the New Jerusalem will come down out of heaven from God, God will make his home among the mortals, death will be abolished, and everything will be made new (21:2–5). The reference to the eschatological earthquake in each series also indicates that the end has come (see question 5). John's three series of seven judgments take his readers from the present (in the first century) to the end and the new beginning of God's new world (in a century whose number is unknown).

The Seal Judgments (John) and the Signs of the End (Jesus)

A comparison of the signs of the end in Jesus' prophecy with the judgments of the seven seals reveals a very close connection. This is especially obvious if we compare Mark's version of Jesus' discourse about the end times in Mark 13 with the seal judgments in Revelation 6:1–8:5 (the additional material in Matt. 24 is indicated in the table in parenthesis). Through John's vision in Revelation 6, the risen Jesus (Rev. 1:1) describes the same time period about which he had prophesied on the Mount of Olives (Mark 13) during his earthly ministry. The obvious conclusion is that if Jesus prophesied events between his first and second coming in Mark 13 (and Matt. 24–25; Luke 21), John's vision describes the same reality, albeit in different terms. The following table summarizes the two prophecies.

THE SIGNS OF THE END AND THE SEAL JUDGMENTS	
JESUS' SIGNS OF THE END **MARK 13:5–20 (MATT. 24)**	**JOHN'S SEAL JUDGMENTS** **REVELATION 6:1–8:5**
1. seduction, messianic pretenders	see Revelation 13
2. wars, rumors of war; international unrest	1. wars of conquest
3. earthquakes	2. international unrest; people kill each other
4. famine	3. famine, hunger
5. persecution	4. sword, famine, plague, wild animals; one-fourth of humankind killed
(6. false prophets)	5. persecution
(7. injustice, lack of love)	
(8. universal proclamation of the gospel)	
9. the destruction of Jerusalem	
10. messianic pretenders, false prophets	see Revelation 13

11. the return of Jesus
  (a) sun becomes dark
  (b) moon becomes dark
  (c) stars fall from the sky
  (d) powers of sky shaken
  (e) sign of the Son in heaven, Son comes on the cloud
  (f) sending of angels; trumpet sound (Matthew); gathering of the elect
	6. earthquake
	  (a) sun darkened
	  (b) moon turns blood red
	  (c) stars fall from the sky
	  (d) sky recedes like scroll

	7. silence
	  (a) thunder
	  (b) voices/rumblings
	  (c) lightning
	  (d) earthquake

Two predictions of Jesus in Mark 13 are missing in Revelation 6: (1) Jesus' warning of seduction by messianic pretenders (sign 1). John may have decided to omit the introductory reference to messianic pretenders because he would later include an entire chapter about the Devil and his earthly allies who seduce the people on earth (Revelation 13).[3] (2) Jesus' prediction of the siege and destruction of Jerusalem (sign 9). The reason for this omission is probably to be seen in the fact that John wrote the Apocalypse around A.D. 95, twenty-five years or so after the destruction of Jerusalem had taken place.

Apart from these two omissions, the correspondence is obvious.[4] The first and second seal judgments (wars of conquest and international unrest) correspond to sign 2. The third and fourth seal judgments (hunger, plagues, death) correspond to sign 4 (famine results in hunger, diseases, wild animals, and death). The fifth seal judgment (persecution) corresponds to sign 5. The sixth seal judgment (earthquake, sun becomes dark, moon turns blood red, stars fall from the sky, the sky recedes like a scroll) corresponds almost exactly to Jesus' description of his return, which included the same cosmic phenomena. The seventh seal (silence, thunder, voices/rumblings, lightning, and earthquake) corresponds to Jesus' description of his return (sign 11) with one important difference: the description of the coming of the Son of Man on the clouds is replaced by silence. John delays prophesying Jesus' return until Revelation 19, creating dramatic suspense for his readers who are waiting since the opening chapter for a description of God "who is to come" (Rev. 1:4) and of Jesus who is "coming with the clouds" (v. 7). The earthquakes of sign 3 in Jesus' prophecy have been moved to the end of the series, linked with the sixth seal judgment. This shift can be explained by the fact that John views the earthquake as a major image of the end.

Jesus' discourse about the end times in Matthew 24–25 / Mark 13 / Luke 21 relates the signs of his return and of the end of the age to the entire period from his first coming to his second coming. Do John's visions of three series of seven judgments take place during the same time period, between Jesus' first coming and his return? Or do they describe a special period of judgment within that period? Some believe that the first series of judgments, the seven seals of Revelation 6, describe events in the future that mark "the beginning of the great day of God's wrath."[5]

---

3. Matthew has multiple references to messianic pretenders and false prophets (signs 1, 6, and 10).
4. This is acknowledged by essentially all commentators, including those who relate the other two judgment series to a later historical period (identified as "the Great Tribulation"). See Robert L. Thomas, *Revelation: An Exegetical Commentary* (Chicago: Moody, 1992), 416.
5. John F. Walvoord, *The Revelation of Jesus Christ* (Chicago: Moody Press, 1966), 122. The quotation is Walvoord's heading for Revelation 6.

The comparison of the seal judgments in Revelation 6 with the signs of the end prophesied by Jesus shows that the prophecy of the earthly Jesus and the visions granted by the exalted Jesus describe the same period of history.

The Three Series of Judgments, the Lamb, and Jesus' Warning

John provides clues at the beginning and end of the three series of judgments that indicate he is writing about the entire time between Jesus' first and second coming. John connects the judgments in Revelation 6–16 with Jesus' victory in his death, resurrection, and exaltation. Jesus is the Lamb that was slain, that stands before God's throne receiving sovereign authority. He alone is worthy to open the seven seals of the heavenly scroll (Rev. 5:1–14). The doubly inscribed scroll—there is writing on the inside and on the back of the scroll (v. 1)—has a twofold background. It represents a contract deed, sealed with seven seals, with a description of the contents written on the back (which means that the contents of the scroll are not entirely secret). Being a heavenly sealed scroll, it represents the heavenly book that contains God's plan of redemption for the fallen world.[6]

As the Lamb opens one seal after the other, events unfold that eventually lead to the end and to the new beginning of the new heaven and the new earth. Note that the first series of the seal judgments is connected with the second series of the trumpet judgments: when seal 7 is opened, the seven angels who stand before God are given the seven trumpets (Rev. 8:2) and they announce the judgments described in the subsequent visions. The contents of the scroll reveal God's redemptive plan behind the visions of Revelation 6–22, visions which describe the events that will end this world and introduce eternity. It is thus not convincing to posit a long historical period between Jesus' death, resurrection, and ascension—celebrated in Revelation 5—and the onset of the reality described in the first and subsequent series of judgments. The seals have been opened at Jesus' death, resurrection, and ascension.

We should not forget that John writes a prophecy (Rev. 1:3) which he was asked not to seal (22:10), nor the fact that he sends his prophecy as a letter (see 1:4–6) to Christians in the first century who are exhorted seven times at the beginning of the book to have ears to listen to what the Spirit is saying to the churches (2:7, 11, 17, 29; 3:6, 13, 22). The fact that John repeats the exhortation ("Let anyone who has an ear listen") in the middle of the vision of the beast from the sea (13:9)[7] confirms that the entire content of John's book is immediately relevant for first-century Christians. There is no doubt that as the Apocalypse was read aloud, the listeners would have applied this exhortation to themselves.

---

6. See *1 Enoch* 47:3; 81:1–3; 106:19; 107:1.
7. This exhortation comes between the trumpet judgments and the bowl judgments.

As John reaches the end of the third series of seven judgments, he briefly interrupts his description of bowl 6 to include the following warning and promise: "See, I am coming like a thief! Blessed is the one who stays awake and is clothed, not going about naked and exposed to shame" (Rev. 16:15). The warning that he will come "like a thief" reminds Christians of the identical statement that Jesus, Paul, and Peter had made (Matt. 24:43; 1 Thess. 5:2–4; 2 Peter 3:10). The image of the coming of a thief underlines the unexpectedness and the suddenness of Jesus' return. Neither John nor his readers have a clue concerning the time or date of Jesus' coming. The blessing is at the same time an exhortation for John's readers and listeners (this is the third of seven beatitudes or blessings). He uses language taken from the messages to Sardis and Laodicea, the two churches that were most in danger of apostasy. The picture is that of "the man who stays awake, fully clothed, contrasted with the man who sleeps and will therefore be caught naked when surprised in the night."[8] John exhorts all Christians to "stay awake" and to "be clothed," that is, to be ready for Christ's return, which will happen unexpectedly and suddenly.

Repeatedly, some end-time "specialists" have used the number, content, and sequence of the seal, trumpet, and bowl judgments to somehow narrow down the time frame of Jesus' return. This is misguided as a matter of principle. The fact that John's readers are warned not to be surprised by Jesus' unexpected and sudden coming as late as the sixth bowl judgment, which is immediately followed by the proclamation of God's and Christ's victory in bowl 7, means that the earlier judgments related in previous visions did not contain any clues about the nearness of Jesus' coming. Later Christian readers of John's book do well to hear his warning: when end-time "specialists" attempt to "locate" the time at which they write in some timetable of end-time events, they automatically assume that Jesus cannot come back "now" because there are other events that need to take place first. John and his readers, if they heeded his exhortation, had a different position: they were ready, at any time, for Jesus' return. This position allowed them to focus on spiritual matters and liberated them from getting caught up in end-time speculations.

Summary

A completely futurist interpretation of the three series of judgments[9] renders the content of John's visions in Revelation 6–16 irrelevant for his readers in the first century. A completely symbolic interpretation runs the risk of ignoring God's intervention in the affairs of history throughout the

---

8. Richard J. Bauckham, *The Climax of Prophecy: Studies on the Book of Revelation* (Edinburgh: T&T Clark, 1993), 109–10; see Gregory K. Beale, *The Book of Revelation: A Commentary on the Greek Text*, NIGTC (Grand Rapids: Eerdmans, 1999), 837; Osborne, *Revelation*, 593.
9. As advocated, e.g., by Walvoord, *Revelation of Jesus Christ*, 125; Thomas, *Revelation*, 413–39.

ages. Events in past, present, and future history may resemble or even seem identical with the judgments depicted in the seal, trumpet, and bowl series— without providing clues to predict the nearness of Jesus' return and of the end. The seal, trumpet, and bowl judgments describe God's judgment of rebellious humanity with increasing intensity. The events described in the three series of judgments are indicators of the last period of human history on this earth in the sense that the last period of history is the period between Jesus' first and second coming. It is Jesus' death, resurrection, and exaltation that has inaugurated the last period of history, during which the forces of evil seek to destroy the people of God. God's people, however, are under God's protection as they continue to witness for the truth of the gospel despite persecution, suffering, and martyrdom.

REFLECTION QUESTIONS

1. How are the seal, trumpet, and bowl judgments connected with each other?

2. How are the three series of judgments connected with Jesus' signs of the end in Matthew 24–25?

3. How are the three series of judgments connected with the death, resurrection, and ascension of Jesus mentioned in Revelation 5?

4. In what way is the image of Jesus coming like a thief in the night important for understanding the number, the sequence, and the progression of the 3 x 7 judgments?

5. How does the exhortation to be prepared for the unexpected second coming of Jesus relate to attempts to calculate how near the end is?

The Future of the Church

Will Christians Live during the Tribulation?

In view of the discussion in section A, this question could be formulated in two different ways: When do the signs of the end that Jesus prophesied (Matt. 24–25) begin? Or what is the starting point of the three series of judgment of Revelation 6–16? The discussion in the previous pages answered these questions already (see question 7). If indeed the period of "great distress" or "great tribulation" belongs to the period between Jesus' first and second coming, then the answer is yes, Christians do live through the period of great distress or tribulation.

The Tribulation

The Greek term (*thlipsis*) sometimes translated as "tribulation" has two senses: (1) the metaphorical sense of "trouble that inflicts distress," which can be translated in English as "oppression, affliction, tribulation" (e.g., Matt. 13:21; Mark 4:17; Acts 11:19; Rom. 5:3; Rev. 1:9); (2) the sense "inward experience of distress" with the translation "affliction, trouble" (e.g., 2 Cor. 2:4; Phil. 1:17).[1]

Jesus illustrates the power of the reality of "distress" (which I will use in this section as the translation for *thlipsis*) in the parable of the sower and the soils: the seed that falls on shallow, rocky ground that cannot produce plants to yield fruit represents people who hear the word and quickly receive it with joy, but who eventually succumb to "distress" or persecution (Matt. 13:21; Mark 4:17). According to John, Jesus predicted that his followers will face "distress" in the world and then gives them the assurance that Jesus has conquered the world (John 16:33). Luke describes the persecution that arose after Stephen's martyrdom as "distress" (Acts 11:19) that forced the inhabitants of Jerusalem to leave the city and move to other regions.

---

1. See BDAG, 457 (*thlipsis*).

Paul encouraged the believers in the newly established churches in southern Galatia to continue in the faith, saying, "It is through much distress [*thlipseōn*, a plural form of *thlipsis*] that we must enter the kingdom of God" (Acts 14:22, author's translation throughout this paragraph). He asserts that married Christians have "distress" that single people are spared (1 Cor. 7:28). He praises God who consoles us "in all our distress" so we may be able to console others who are in "any distress" (2 Cor. 1:4). When Paul worked as a missionary in the province of Asia, there was a time of "distress" during which he was so utterly, unbearably crushed that he "despaired of life itself" (2 Cor. 1:8). When Paul wrote to the Corinthian believers, he wrote out of "much distress and anguish of heart" (2 Cor. 2:4). It is possible to have joy in the midst of "our distress" (2 Cor. 7:4). Paul commends the believers in the Macedonian churches who, during a "severe ordeal of distress," were generous and helped Paul (2 Cor. 8:2). Paul asserts that as Christian believers we boast in "our distress" (*thlipsesin*, a plural form of *thlipsis*) that we experience because "distress produces endurance, and endurance produces character, and character produces hope, and hope does not disappoint us" (Rom. 5:3). He asserts that neither hardship nor "distress" nor persecution, nor famine, nor nakedness, nor peril, nor sword can separate us from the love that God in Jesus Christ our Lord has granted us (Rom. 8:35, 37–39). He admonishes the believers in the city of Rome to "rejoice in hope, be patient in distress, persevere in prayer" (Rom. 12:12; see 2 Cor. 6:4; Eph. 3:13; 1 Thess. 3:3, 7; 2 Thess. 1:4). In two passages the term "distress" describes what the wicked will receive on the day of judgment (Rom. 2:9; 2 Thess. 1:6).

Other passages can be added that show that "the New Testament writers uniformly expected suffering and hardship to be the common lot of believers throughout their earthly existence."[2] Jesus' warning in Matthew 7:14 that the road that leads to life is "narrow" uses a verb (*thlibō*), which is related to the standard term for "distress" or "tribulation" (*thlipsis*). The road to life is "narrow" because it is characterized by distress, affliction, and tribulation. And Paul declares in 2 Timothy 3:12 that "everyone who wants to live a godly life in Christ Jesus will be persecuted." This stark pronouncement "hammers the final nail into the coffin of any aberrant gospel that preaches an abundant life devoid of persecutions."[3]

The Great Tribulation

Among the signs of the end that Jesus prophesies is "distress" (*thlipsis*, Matt. 24:9; RSV, NASB, and ESV have "tribulation"; NET and NIV have "to be

---

2. Craig L. Blomberg, "The Posttribulationism of the New Testament: Leaving 'Left Behind' Behind," in *A Case for Historic Premillennialism: An Alternative to "Left Behind" Eschatology*, ed. Craig L. Blomberg and Sung Wook Chung (Grand Rapids: Baker Academic, 2009), 77.
3. William D. Mounce, *Pastoral Epistles*, WBC 46 (Nashville: Thomas Nelson, 2000), 560.

persecuted"; NRSV has "to be tortured"). The distress of sign 5 may include being killed, and it certainly includes being hated because of one's faith in Jesus. This "distress" belongs to the labor pains (Matt. 24:8), which include wars and rumors of wars, an assertion that is followed by the comment that "this must take place, but the end is not yet" (Matt. 24:6).

Matthew 24:21

When Jesus predicts the siege and destruction of Jerusalem (Matt. 24:15–22), he asserts, "For then there will be great distress [*thlipsis megalē*], unequaled from the beginning of the world until now" (v. 21 NIV; see question 3). The expression translated "great distress" (NRSV and NET translate "great suffering," NLT "greater anguish") is rendered "great tribulation" in older and a few recent translations (KJV, RSV, NASB, ESV).

The expression "great tribulation" or "great distress" refers to the period of horrific extreme suffering during the siege of Jerusalem. This "great tribulation" was a local event, a fact that made it possible for Jesus' followers to flee. Neither Jesus' listeners nor Matthew's readers would have related this prophecy to a much later period of time unrelated to the Jerusalem temple of the first century.

Revelation 7:14

The expression "great tribulation" or "great distress" (*thlipsis megalē*) occurs a second time in the New Testament. In Revelation 7:14, the multitude of believers "that no one could count, from every nation, from all tribes and peoples and languages" (Rev. 7:9) is described as the people "who have come out of the great distress [*ek tēs thlipseōs tēs megalēs*]; they have washed their robes and made them white in the blood of the Lamb" (author's translation of Rev. 7:14; NRSV has "great ordeal"). The tradition of translating the expression here in Revelation 7:14 as "great tribulation" (KJV, RSV, NASB, NLT, ESV, NIV) is so strong that several translations that use different English terms for the same Greek expression in Matthew 24:21 (NET, NLT, NIV) use "great tribulation" here.

Interpreters who assume that the followers of Jesus will be taken up into heaven in the rapture before the great tribulation connect the latter with the trumpet judgments in Revelation 8–9 (some include the seal judgments in Revelation 6). And they interpret the people "who have come out of the great tribulation" (Rev. 7:14 NIV) as people who came to faith after the rapture and who were thus "stuck" on earth during the tribulation where they had to endure persecution and even martyrdom.[4] This interpretation requires, among other assumptions, that the expression "the great tribulation" is a technical term.

---

4. John F. Walvoord, *The Revelation of Jesus Christ* (Chicago: Moody Press, 1966), 145–46; Robert L. Thomas, *Revelation: An Exegetical Commentary* (Chicago: Moody, 1992), 486–87, 495–97.

There is no evidence that requires us to interpret the expression "the great tribulation" (*hē thlipsis hē megalē*) as a technical title for the final seven-year period or three-and-a-half-year period before the end. The term *thlipsis* is used by John in the sense of the distress, that is, the suffering and persecution that Christians have to endure (Rev. 1:9; 2:9, 10). John alludes in Revelation 7:14 to Daniel 12:1, a passage that prophesies "a time of distress" (Greek, *hē hēmera thlipseōs*, "the day of distress") that would be "such as has not occurred since they were born until that day," giving the assurance that "on that day the whole people will be exalted, whoever is found inscribed in the book" (LXX translation, NETS). [5]

It appears that John also alludes to Daniel 11:35 ("Even some of the wise will stumble, resulting in their refinement, purification, and cleansing until the time of the end, for it is still for the appointed time," NET) and to Daniel 12:10 ("Many will be purified, made clean, and refined" [NET]—he asserts that the people before the throne "have washed their robes and made them white in the blood of the Lamb," Rev. 7:14). This means that "the great tribulation" is the particular event (note the definite article) of the final war between the satanic forces and the saints. With the allusion to Daniel 12:1, John makes the point that "the messianic army is an army of martyrs who triumph through their martyrdom because they are followers of the Lamb who participate in his victory by following his path to death."[6]

The great tribulation, taken from Daniel 12:1, is the time of persecution in which the people of God triumph through martyrdom (not through fighting). The phrase "they who have come out of the great tribulation" (Rev. 7:14 NIV) most plausibly presupposes that they have been in the great tribulation, and then left it (through martyrdom). Some limit the reference to the end of the period of distress that Jesus had prophesied and that John describes in his visions.[7] This is not necessary, however.[8] The protection symbolized by the seals is not a protection from martyrdom but speaks of the spiritual preservation of the faith of those living through the judgments that befall the evil world and who endure the attack of the satanic forces.[9]

---

5 A. Pietersma and B. G. Wright, *A New English Translation of the Septuagint* (Oxford: Oxford University Press, 2007)

6. Richard J. Bauckham, *The Climax of Prophecy: Studies on the Book of Revelation* (Edinburgh: T&T Clark, 1993), 229. Note the interpretation of Daniel 12:1 in the Qumran text 1QM I, 11–12; XV, 1; XVII, 5–8 in terms of the war between the faithful and the Kittim (the Romans) in which Michael will intervene in the final stage of the battle (ibid., 226).

7. Grant R. Osborne, *Revelation*, BECNT (Grand Rapids: Baker Academic, 2002), 324–25; Blomberg, "Posttribulationism of the New Testament," 75–76.

8. Osborne argues that the multitude of Revelation 7:14, which he (correctly) identifies with the 144,000 (see question 9), is sealed (i.e., protected) from the judgments that will fall on the land or the sea or the trees (Rev. 7:1–8) (*Revelation*, 325n13).

9. Bauckham, *Climax of Prophecy*, 257; Gregory K. Beale, *The Book of Revelation: A Commentary on the Greek Text*, NIGTC (Grand Rapids: Eerdmans, 1999), 409.

The spiritual nature of the protection of the people of God is evident from the fact that believers endure the same (seal) judgments as unbelievers. When the Lamb opened the fifth seal, John saw "the souls of those who had been slain because of the word of God and the testimony they had maintained" (Rev. 6:9 NIV). Believers who wonder how long it will take until God will judge the inhabitants of the earth who have killed them are told "to wait a little longer, until the full number of their fellow servants and their brothers and sisters were killed just as they had been" (Rev. 6:11 NIV). Whether "the great tribulation" describes the entire time between Jesus' first and second coming or a specific period during that time, believers have no promise and no guarantee that they will never experience suffering and martyrdom.

The Three-and-a-Half Year Period

John, in his vision of the dragon who persecutes the woman, relates that "the woman was given the two wings of the great eagle, so that she could fly from the serpent into the wilderness, to her place where she is nourished for a time, and times, and half a time" (Rev. 12:14). If the word for "time" is interpreted as "year" and the plural "times" as two years, then John speaks of three-and-a-half years. This is the only passage in the New Testament in which this expression occurs. It is a direct allusion to two passages in Daniel. In Daniel 7:25, the prophet speaks of a person who shall "speak words against the Most High, shall wear out the holy ones of the Most High, and shall attempt to change the sacred seasons and the law; and they shall be given into his power for a time, two times, and half a time." The context in Daniel 7 is the theme of the coming of God's kingdom (described in 7:13 as the kingdom of "one like a son of man" and as the kingdom of the saints ["holy ones"] of the Most High). With the deliberate allusion to Daniel 7 and the expression "three-and-a-half years," John asserts that the final period of which Daniel spoke has arrived—the period that will bring about the prophesied transfer of sovereignty over "all peoples, nations, and languages" from the empires of the world, represented as beasts, to the "one like a son of man" and to the people of the Most High.[10] In Revelation 12, the context is the conflict between the great red dragon (Satan who slaughters the people of God, the Serpent)[11] and the woman with the crown of twelve stars, that is, the people of God who give birth to the Messiah (Rev. 12:5) and who are subsequently persecuted by the dragon (v. 17).[12] Thus, the statement in Revelation 7:14 refers to the period between Jesus' ascension and the end, that is, to the time between Jesus' first

---

10. Note Daniel 7:14: "To him was given dominion and glory and kingship, that all peoples, nations, and languages should serve him. His dominion is an everlasting dominion that shall not pass away, and his kingship one that shall never be destroyed" (NRSV).
11. Revelation 16:6; 17:6; 18:24. For the identification of the dragon and the serpent with the Devil and Satan, see Revelation 12:9; 20:2.
12. For the view that the woman's offspring are the 144,000 of Revelation 7, see question 9.

coming and his second coming. This is a time of suffering for the people of God who are attacked by the forces of evil, but also a time in which they experience God's spiritual protection.

In Daniel 12:7, the prophet receives an answer to the question, "How long shall it be until the end of these wonders?" (Dan. 12:6). He is assured that it will be "for a time, two times, and half a time, and that when the shattering of the power of the holy people comes to an end, all these things would be accomplished" (v. 7). John's vision in Revelation 10 clearly alludes to Daniel 12. John is told by the angel with the scroll in his hand that "there will be no more delay, but in the days when the seventh angel is to blow his trumpet, the mystery of God will be fulfilled, as he announced to his servants the prophets" (Rev. 10:6–7). In other words, the scroll that John receives contains the fuller revelation about the last period at the end of history that was predicted in Daniel, which Daniel himself could not understand (Dan. 12:8) as it was to remain sealed until the time of the end (v. 12:9). The fuller prophecy that John receives and passes on to his readers concerns the way in which the transfer of sovereignty from the nations of the world to the "one like a son of man" and the people of the Most High occurs: the universal kingdom of God comes through the church and her faithful witness to the Messiah, a witness that is accompanied by suffering.

The figure of the three-and-a-half years corresponds to the 1,260 days of Revelation 12:6. There the woman is confronted by the dragon who wants to devour the child that the woman is bringing into the world. After the child was snatched away and taken to God's throne, "the woman fled into the wilderness, where she has a place prepared by God, so that there she can be nourished for one thousand two hundred sixty days" (Rev. 12:6). John emphasizes that the people of God will be kept spiritually safe by God for the entire last period before the end.

The figure of the 1,260 days is also mentioned in Revelation 11:3, a passage in which John describes the ministry of two witnesses who are granted by God the authority "to prophesy for one thousand two hundred sixty days, wearing sackcloth." The figure of 1,260 days corresponds to the 42 months, the period during which the "holy city" is trampled by the (Gentile) nations (Rev. 11:2). The "holy city" is probably a reference to the people of God.[13] Since the church's witness began immediately after Jesus' ascension (Acts 1), with Peter's preaching on the day of Pentecost (Acts 2), and since the beast will be shut up only when it is cast into the lake of fire at the time of Jesus' triumphant return (Rev. 19:20), John describes in Revelation 11:2–3, 5 the period of the church between Jesus' first and second coming. This is a period during which the church has been given the task to "prophesy" (i.e., to proclaim God's revealed

---

13. Osborne, *Revelation*, 413.

truth to the people on earth)—the period before the end when God's people are under attack and experience suffering, even martyrdom.

In the vision of the beast from the sea—the enemy of God and of God's people[14]—John relates that "the beast was given a mouth uttering haughty and blasphemous words, and it was allowed to exercise authority for forty-two months" (Rev. 13:5). This figure, which John uses here again for Daniel's three-and-a-half years, stands for the last period of history before the end during which God's people will be opposed. John emphasizes that the authority of the evil forces that attack and oppose the church possess authority that is given by and limited by God.

If the three-and-a-half years or 42 months, or 1,260 days were to be taken literally, and if the church knew when this literal time period begins, Christians could calculate when the end would come. Therefore, this interpretation cannot be correct. Not only John (Rev. 16:15) but also Jesus, Paul, and Peter compare Jesus' return with the coming of a thief, who always comes unexpectedly and suddenly (Matt. 24:43; 1 Thess. 5:2–4; 2 Peter 3:10). Since the time of Jesus' coming is unknown, and since the early church believed that the last days before the end began with Jesus' ministry (see question 1), the time of suffering and persecution that these figures (three-and-a-half years or 42 months, or 1,260 days) entail is now.

Summary

Jesus, Paul, and other New Testament writers unanimously assume, and assert, that believers experience distress, suffering, persecution, and martyrdom. The vision of Revelation 7 promises the spiritual protection of the faith of Jesus' followers, but not physical protection from suffering. The "great tribulation" that Jesus prophesies in Matthew 24:21 describes the horrific events of the siege and destruction of Jerusalem, a prophecy that was fulfilled in the events of A.D. 66–70. The "great tribulation" of Revelation 7:14 is not a particular period of history in which suffering becomes unbearable, but a description of the end times as a time of trouble during which many of Jesus' followers are tested and purified as martyrs. This does not mean that all believers will suffer extreme distress or that all believers will be persecuted, or that all believers will die as martyrs. It means, however, that suffering and persecution should not come as a surprise, and that it must not be avoided through compromise with the secular and immoral values of the world (as championed by the Nicolaitans in Rev. 2:12–16). God will faithfully preserve the followers of the Lamb—Jesus, Israel's Messiah, who himself suffered and was killed by God's enemies. John calls believers to persevere and endure hardships for Jesus' name and not to grow weary (Rev. 2:3).

---

14. The beast from the sea often identified as the Antichrist. See questions 19 and 20.

REFLECTION QUESTIONS

1. What is "tribulation"? What is "the great tribulation"?

2. Why do Jesus, Paul, and John speak of the suffering of Christians?

3. How have Christians suffered in the past? How do they suffer in the present?

4. What is the role of the eschatological earthquake?

5. How can Christians endure suffering?

Who Are the 144,000 in Revelation 7?

In discussion of matters related to the end times, the 144,000 of Revelation have often played an important role. There has been a long debate about who these people are and what their being sealed means. Since there is no consensus regarding the answer to these questions, the wise interpreter refrains from being dogmatic.[1] This does not mean, however, that we cannot attempt to find the most plausible answers to these questions.

Before we address these questions, the following points need to be emphasized. (1) While John speaks of the 144,000 who have been sealed (Rev. 7:4), it is helpful to notice that the number twelve is more important for John: he speaks of twelve thousand people from each of the twelve tribes of Israel being sealed (i.e., the number twelve is used twelve times). This will be important when we consider the possibility of the symbolic meaning of this number. (2) The figure 144,000 also occurs in Revelation 14:1, 3, a passage that must be part of the interpretation of Revelation 7. (3) The seal of God is a central feature in Revelation 7:1–8, mentioned twice as a noun (7:2, 3) and four times as a verb (7:4a, 4b, 5, 8). (4) The context of Revelation 7:1–8, which is an interlude between the sixth and the seventh seal judgment, must be regarded as significant for the interpretation of the passage.

The Identity of the 144,000

The following two identifications are the main interpretations. We will briefly list the pros and cons of each position.[2]

---

1. Labeling the view of competent scholars who disagree with one's own position on the identity of the 144,000 as "ridiculous" is rather unhelpful, implying a categorical unwillingness to learn from others (so John F. Walvoord, *The Revelation of Jesus Christ* [Chicago: Moody Press, 1966,] 143; Robert L. Thomas, *Revelation: An Exegetical Commentary* [Chicago: Moody, 1992], 476).
2. For more technical surveys, see David E. Aune, *Revelation*, WBC 52B (Dallas: Word, 1998), 2:440–45; Gregory K. Beale, *The Book of Revelation: A Commentary on the Greek Text*,

The 144,000 Are Christians from Ethnic Israel

The interpretation that posits that the 144,000 are Christians from ethnic Israel is based on the statement that the 144,000 were "sealed out of every tribe of the people of Israel" (Rev. 7:4) and on the enumeration of twelve tribes of Israel (vv. 5–8).[3] Some argue that this is a special group of Jewish believers who have been "set aside for the purpose of witnessing to a rebellious world. Nothing is said here about the rest of the saved. It is only noted that these will have special protection from the wrath of God while they witness. After their witness is concluded, martyrdom may well be their fate."[4] It is argued that a nonliteral interpretation of the term "Israel" and of the list of twelve tribes makes no sense. Some also argue that since the author of the book is a Jewish Christian, it is not surprising that he envisioned a special role for Jewish Christians in the last period before the end. Some refer to Romans 11:7 where Paul speaks of Jewish Christians as the "elect" and the "remnant" of Israel who accept Jesus as Israel's Messiah (11:5). Some argue that since the distinction between Jewish and Gentile Christians was an important category in the early church,[5] it is not surprising that John speaks of Jewish Christians. A variant of this interpretation identifies the 144,000 with Jewish Christians who emerged as a remnant from among the Jewish people after the destruction of Jerusalem after A.D. 70.[6]

Many scholars find a "literal" interpretation in terms of the twelve ethnic tribes of Israel unconvincing for the following reasons. The twelve tribes no longer existed literally since hundreds of years before John wrote (the ten northern tribes were taken into exile in 722 B.C.). While Josephus speaks of the existence of the twelve tribes in his day,[7] and while Jewish texts speak of the eschatological restoration of the twelve tribes,[8] it is open to debate whether references to the twelve tribes in these texts are meant literally (in a biological sense) or as a reference to God's chosen people, the descendants

NIGTC (Grand Rapids: Eerdmans, 1999), 416–23. The Jehovah's Witnesses have confused many people with their view that the 144,000 are a select group of Christians who will rule in heaven with Christ, while other true believers will be resurrected to a life on earth after Armageddon. There is no hint in Revelation 7, nor anywhere else in the New Testament, that there is an elite group of Christians distinguished from "ordinary" believers.

3. Walvoord, *Revelation of Jesus Christ*, 141–43.
4. Thomas, *Revelation*, 474–78. He does not seem to notice that nothing is said here about witnessing either. For Thomas's arguments for a literal (biological) understanding of "Israel" and the twelve tribes, see ibid., 476–78.
5. See Acts 10:45; 11:1, 19–20; 13:16–17; 19:10; Romans 1:16; 3:29–30; 9:6–8; 10:12–13; 1 Corinthians 1:24; 12:13; Galatians 2:7–8; 3:28; Ephesians 2:11–19.
6. André Feuillet, "Les 144,000 Israélites marqués d'un sceau," *NovT* 9 (1967): 191–224.
7. Josephus asserts that two of the tribes are in the province of Asia and Europe, subject to the Romans, and ten tribes beyond the Euphrates (*Ant. 11.133*).
8. See Isaiah 49:6; 63:17; Ezekiel 47:13, 21–23; 48:30–35; Zechariah 9:1; Sirach 36:10; *Psalms of Solomon* 17:26–28, 43–44; 1QM II, 2–3; III 12–13, 14–15; 1QS I, 15, 29; *4 Ezra* 13:12–13, 39–49.

of Abraham and Isaac and Jacob.[9] The explanation that the identity of tribal membership "is lost to mankind" but "still known to God"[10] is convincing only if it is believed that God will create new tribal identities (assuming that the sealing will take place in the future, as interpreters who hold this position usually do). Intermarriage between the tribes, for hundreds of years (by the time of John) and for several thousand years (by the twenty-first century), effectively dissolves the tribes, whose identity was based on marriage within the tribe. Interpreters who insist on a literal interpretation should be willing to concede that with the exception of descendants of the tribes of Levi, Judah, and Benjamin, the twelve tribes have long disappeared. A literal interpretation of the twelve tribes would necessarily demand a literal interpretation of the 144,000. This interpretation, however, is difficult since it would limit the number of Jews to be saved to a precise figure. Such an interpretation only works if the figure is limited to 144,000 Jewish Christians who survive the tribulation while others Jewish Christians die as martyrs.[11] While the distinction between Jewish and Gentile believers was indeed a continuing issue in the early church, at least Paul regarded such distinctions as a problem since Jews and Gentiles were reconciled through Jesus Christ who "has made both groups into one and has broken down the dividing wall" (Eph. 2:14). Paul asserts that God through Jesus Christ created "one new humanity in place of the two, thus making peace", reconciling "both groups to God in one body through the cross" (vv. 15–16). All who belong to Jesus Christ are "children of God through faith" with the result that "there is neither Jew nor Gentile" because "if you belong to Christ, then you are Abraham's seed, and heirs according to the promise" (Gal. 3:26, 28, 29 NIV; see Col. 3:11). Since many descriptions of "literal Israel" have been applied to the church,[12] the reference to Israel and its tribes is not necessarily literal. Another problem with this interpretation is the implied consequence that only Jewish Christians receive God's seal, while Gentile Christians have to cope without it.

We should not forget that John writes not only a book about matters related to the end, but also a letter conveying a prophecy that was directly relevant for his first-century readers in the churches of Asia Minor. Apocalyptic information for the distant future (in some Great Tribulation two thousand years later, or three thousand years if Jesus continues to delay his return) would be irrelevant for John's first readers, the majority of whom were Gentile

9. Note that there is a rabbinic tradition that held that the ten tribes would never be restored (see *b. Sanh.* 110b; *Avot of Rabbi Nathan* 31b).

10. Thomas, *Revelation*, 478.

11. Thus, Walvoord still seems to shy away from taking the number 144,000 as a "literal" exact figure (*Revelation of Jesus Christ*, 143).

12. For example, John praises, Jesus who has "made us to be a kingdom and priests to serve his God and Father" (Rev. 1:6 NIV; see 5:10; 20:6), alluding to Exodus 19:6, where these terms describe Israel.

believers. They would be left wondering whether the call to be faithful unto death, the prerequisite for obtaining the crown of life (Rev. 2:10), given to the Jewish and Gentile believers in the church of Smyrna, is qualitatively different from the promise implicit in the sealing of the 144,000, if the latter is a group of Jewish Christians only.

The 144,000 Are the Church

The interpretation that argues that the 144,000 are a symbolic representation of the church is often based on Revelation 9:4, where demonic scorpions of the fifth trumpet judgment are ordered "not to harm the grass of the earth or any plant or tree, but only those people who did not have the seal of God on their foreheads" (NIV).[13] The passage assumes a clear and simple distinction between people who do not belong to God and are called to repentance (see Rev. 9:20–21) and the people who belong to God and are under God's protection. The description in terms of "Israel" and in terms of the twelve tribes of Israel is explained by the background of the early Christian description of the church of Jewish *and* Gentile believers as "the Israel of God" (Gal. 6:16; see Rom. 9:6). Gentile believers are described as "Jews" understood in a spiritual sense (Rom. 2:28–29) and thus by faith as sons of Abraham (Rom. 4:11–17; Gal. 3:7). Believers in general are described as "the twelve tribes scattered among the nations" (James 1:1 NIV) and as "the exiles of the Dispersion" (1 Peter 1:1). They are described as the messianic temple built on Jesus the rejected cornerstone (1 Peter 2:4–8), as "a chosen people, a royal priesthood, a holy nation" (v. 9 NIV).[14] The irregular nature of the list of the twelve tribes is regarded as a subtle clue that the list in Revelation 7:5–8 is not a literal reference to ethnic Israel: Judah comes first rather than Reuben (the oldest son of Jacob), Dan is omitted, and Manasseh is added (who is the son of Joseph, who stays in the list, while Ephraim, Joseph's other son, is not mentioned); the unique sequence of the names, particularly the fact that the sons of the slave girl Zilpah are moved up in the list, may, perhaps, point to the inclusion of the Gentiles.[15]

---

13. G. E. Ladd, *A Commentary on the Revelation of John* (Grand Rapids: Eerdmans, 1972), 114–17; Robert H. Mounce, *The Book of Revelation*, rev. ed. (Grand Rapids: Eerdmans, 1998), 154, 158–59; Grant R. Osborne, *Revelation*, BECNT (Grand Rapids: Baker Academic, 2002), 311–12; Ben Witherington, *Revelation*, New Cambridge Bible Commentary (Cambridge: Cambridge University Press, 2003), 137; Akira Satake, *Die Offenbarung des Johannes*, Kritisch Exegetischer Kommentar 16 (Göttingen: Vandenhoeck & Ruprecht, 2008), 226–27. The fact that this is the majority position does not render it correct, of course, although it should caution interpreters not to call this view "ridiculous" (see above).

14. The concept of the church consisting of Jewish and Gentile believers as the new Israel of the messianic period is probably connected with Jesus' promise that his twelve disciples will "sit on twelve thrones, judging the twelve tribes of Israel" (Matt. 19:28; see Luke 22:30).

15. See Christopher R. Smith, "The Portrayal of the Church as the New Israel in the Names and Order of the Tribes in Revelation 7.5–8," *JSNT* 11 (1990): 111–18. See the critique of Richard J. Bauckham, who assumes a list along matriarchal lines and is critical of an

The identification of the 144,000 with Christian martyrs[16] is a variant of their identification with the church. In the immediate context of the seal judgments (of which Revelation 7 is an interlude), the fifth seal introduces a vision of "the souls of those who had been slaughtered for the word of God and for the testimony they had given" who cried out with a loud voice, "Sovereign Lord, holy and true, how long will it be before you judge and avenge our blood on the inhabitants of the earth?" (Rev. 6:9–10). When the figure of 144,000 is repeated in Revelation 14:4, they are described as people who "follow the Lamb wherever he goes. They were purchased from among mankind and offered as firstfruits to God and the Lamb" (NIV). A recent variation of the identification of the 144,000 with Christian martyrs is the view that the 144,000 represent the "army" of the Messiah that is called to fight a holy war, a war to be fought and won by sacrificial death.[17] The complications for this interpretation are twofold. In Revelation 7:1–8, there is no indication that John only has martyrs in view. And the symbolic value of both the number twelve (the complete people of God) and the number one thousand (a large complete number) emphasizes the idea of completeness, as does the listing of all twelve tribes of Israel, rather than a particular subgroup of people.[18]

In sum, the identification of the 144,000 with the worldwide congregation of the followers of the Lamb is most plausible, perhaps with an emphasis on "the church militant on earth" that conquers through suffering and martyrdom.

The Function of the Seal

The most plausible Old Testament background for the seal that the 144,000 receive is Ezekiel 9, where God commands an angel to put a mark on the faithful, which will protect them from the coming wrath to be inflicted by the Babylonians, instructing other angels to slay unfaithful Israelites. A seal or mark can also refer to a special stamp of ownership or approval. For example, Isaiah prophecies about a time when God will pour his Spirit upon Israel's descendants, giving them his blessing. This will be a time when some will "write on the hand, 'The LORD's' and adopt the name of Israel" (Isa. 44:3, 5). The

---

interpretation that is too allegorical ("The List of the Tribes in Revelation 7 Again," *JSNT* 42 [1991]: 99–115).

16. Martin Kiddle, *The Revelation of St. John*, MNTC (New York: Harper), 133–37; G. B. Caird, *A Commentary on the Revelation of St. John the Divine*, HNTC (New York: Harper & Row, 1966), 94–98, 178–181.

17. Bauckham, *Climax of Prophecy*, 210–37. He interprets the 144,000 who "keep themselves ritually pure of the cultic defilement through sexual intercourse" (see Rev. 14:4) as that which was demanded for God's army in Deuteronomy 23:9–14 (see 1 Sam. 21:5; 2 Sam. 11:9–13; similarly (1QM VII, 3–4, 6) and thus they represent an army fighting the Lord's battle (ibid., 231). Also see Beale, *Revelation*, 422–23.

18. On the symbolism of the number twelve, see question 6.

144,000 who have the name of the Lamb and the name of his Father written on their foreheads (Rev. 14:1) are contrasted with all the other people who received the mark of the beast (Rev. 13:16–17). Having the name of the Lamb written on their foreheads means that they belong to the Lamb, in contrast to the people who belong to the beast. The name written on the forehead of the 144,000 in Revelation 14:1 corresponds to the seal (*sphragis*) that the 144,000 in Revelation 7:3 receive on their foreheads. This prepares for the description of God's perfect, new world in Revelation 22:4 where the people of God "will see his face, and his name will be on their foreheads."

The seal speaks of ownership and protection. Those who belong to the Lamb will be protected by God. In view of John's call to be faithful witnesses even in the face of death (Rev. 2:10; 11:1–10),[19] the promise of protection does not speak of physical security but of the protection of the believers' faith and salvation in the midst of the turmoil and tribulation of the present and final period before the end. This is confirmed by the fact that the 144,000 in Revelation receive God's seal during the interlude between the sixth and seventh seal: God promises that his people will be saved amid the havoc caused by Satan and his demonic forces. This is metaphorical language, speaking of spiritual realities (which means that Christians should not expect physical letters appearing on their foreheads).

The function of the divine seal that promises spiritual protection and provides authentication of God's ownership over all the individual members of his people confirms that the 144,000 who receive God's seal can hardly be a select group of people (e.g., ethnic Jews, Christian martyrs) but describes the entire community of the redeemed. This means that the group sealed in Revelation 7:1–8 is identical with the "great multitude that no one could count, from every nation, from all tribes and peoples and languages, standing before the throne and before the Lamb" (Rev. 7:9). This conclusion is confirmed by the fact that the two visions in Revelation 7 have parallels with the vision in Revelation 5. John *hears* that the Lion of the tribe of Judah who is the root of David has won a victory, and he *sees* the Lamb that was slain (Rev. 5:5–6). John *hears* the number of those who were sealed, and he *sees* the great multitude that no one could count (Rev. 7:4, 9). This suggests that John may want his readers to recognize that the relationship between the 144,000 and the great multitude is the same as the relationship between the Lion and the Lamb. For example, the Lion from the tribe of Judah (Rev. 5:5) corresponds to the list of those who were sealed from all the tribes of Israel (with *Judah* listed at the beginning of the list, Rev. 7:5). Furthermore, the slain Lamb that has ransomed for God people from every tribe, language, people, and nation (Rev. 5:6, 9) corresponds

---

19. See Revelation 12:11: "But they have conquered him by the blood of the Lamb and by the word of their testimony, for they did not cling to life even in the face of death."

to the great multitude from every nation, from all tribes, peoples, and languages who stand before the Lamb (7:9).[20]

Summary

The vision of the 144,000 provides a symbolic description of the people of God in its entirety, consisting of Jewish and Gentile followers of the Lamb, Israel's Messiah and Savior. God puts his seal upon them, which "enables them to respond in faith to the trials through which they pass, so that these trials become the very instruments by which they can even be strengthened in their faith. . . . As the saints are empowered to persevere through adversity, the genuineness of their profession is authenticated and they are shown truly to belong to God."[21] The sustaining power of God's presence "is never more real than in times of suffering and persecution. The message of Revelation 7:1–8 reiterates that important truth. Believers have no reason to fear the terrible events of 6:12–17 or the effects of the judgments in chapter 6–16, for they belong to him and are his people."[22]

REFLECTION QUESTIONS

1. What is the symbolic value of the number twelve?

2. What are the best arguments for a literal understanding of the twelve tribes in Revelation 7:1–8 in terms of ethnic Israelites?

3. What are the best arguments for a symbolic understanding of the twelve tribes?

4. Why is the vision of the 144,000 inserted between the judgments of the sixth and seventh seal?

5. How does John encourage his readers with the vision of the 144,000?

---

20. Bauckham, *Climax of Prophecy*, 216.
21. Beale, *Book of Revelation*, 409, 410–11.
22. Osborne, *Revelation*, 302.

Will the Church Disappear in a Rapture to Heaven?

The word "rapture" is not self-explanatory. Merriam-Webster gives three definitions: (1) an expression or manifestation of ecstasy or passion; (2) a state or experience of being carried away by overwhelming emotion, or a mystical experience in which the spirit is exalted to a knowledge of divine things; and (3) (often capitalized) the final assumption of Christians into heaven during the end time according to Christian theology. The discussion in this chapter concerns the third meaning. The expectation of "the rapture" in which all true Christian believers will disappear from earth before the great tribulation in a miraculous event that will unite them with Jesus in heaven has been popularized by the Left Behind series. This sixteen-volume series provides fictional depictions of events related to the apocalypse in general and the rapture in particular.[1] The success of these books does not guarantee the correctness of the underlying end-time scenario depicted, of course.

The view that in the last days all true believers will be taken up to heaven in a secret rapture, leaving behind a world in chaos, was first articulated by John Nelson Darby in 1830. Darby was an itinerant preacher ordained initially into the Anglican Church of Ireland who traveled extensively in North America.[2] The fact that this teaching was unknown to the church fathers and

---

1. Tim LaHaye and Jerry B. Jenkins, Left Behind, 16 vols. (Wheaton: Tyndale, 1995–2007). For a sociological analysis of the "Left Behind" phenomenon see Amy Johnson Frykholm, *Rapture Culture: Left Behind in Evangelical America* (Oxford: Oxford University Press, 2004).
2. The suggestion that Darby heard this view of the end-time events from Margaret MacDonald, a fifteen-year-old prophetess, remains unproven. See Richard R. Reiter, "A History of the Development of the Rapture Positions," in Gleason L. Archer Jr., Paul D. Feinberg, Douglas J. Moo, and Richard R. Reiter, *Three Views on the Rapture: Pre-, Mid-, or Post-Tribulation* (Grand Rapids: Zondervan, 1996), 11n14.

the Reformers, not to speak of all other theologians until the early nineteenth century, does not render it automatically misguided per se. Christians base their convictions neither on the popularity of beliefs nor on the short history of a doctrine, but on what Scripture actually says. We will therefore focus in this chapter not so much on the pros and cons of the discussion,[3] but on the most relevant passages, particularly the key text 1 Thessalonians 4:17.

1 Thessalonians 4:17

The verse in question is situated in a section of Paul's first letter to the Christian believers in the city of Thessalonica in which he addressed the fate of Christians who had died. Paul had established the church in Thessalonica in the last three months of the year A.D. 49, before being abruptly forced to leave the city for Berea and eventually Athens and Corinth (Acts 17:1–9 relates Paul's missionary work in and escape from Thessalonica). He writes his first letter to the Thessalonian believers during his missionary work in Corinth, which is dated from February or March A.D. 50 to September A.D. 51. In the intervening months, Christians in Thessalonica had passed away. It appears that the Thessalonian Christians had understood their present sufferings as belonging to the tribulation of the last days, indicating the imminent return of Jesus. They evidently did not know what to make of the death of fellow believers before Jesus' return and were distressed about their fate, about which they had not received any teaching. Note Paul's comment in 1 Thessalonians 4:13 that he does not want the Thessalonian believers to be uninformed. The following section in 4:13–18 provides them with information that they did not have before.[4] Paul's concern in this passage is to reassure the Christians in Thessalonica that believers who have died will be raised from the dead to join the living believers when Jesus returns. Paul would not have dreamed that his rather straightforward explanation of the future would give rise to the immense amount of speculation that we find in the writings, fictional and otherwise, of end-time "specialists" today.

In his discourse about believers who have died and about the coming day of the Lord, Paul first clarifies the fate of believers who have died, before reminding them of what they already know about the day of the Lord and how the expectation of Jesus' (second) coming should inform how they live. Paul makes the following assertions:

---

3. For an excellent introduction, see Gleason L. Archer Jr., ed., *Three Views on the Rapture: Pre-, Mid-, or Post-Tribulation* (Grand Rapids: Zondervan, 1996). The fact that the position contributors of the volume (Feinberg, Archer, and Moo) are all former professors at Trinity Evangelical Divinity School demonstrates that the question of the rapture is not important enough to divide serious scholars and Christian believers.
4. In other sections of the letter, Paul reminds the Thessalonians of what they already know (see 1 Thess. 1:5; 2:1, 5, 9, 11; 3:3, 4; 4:2; 5:2).

4:13   The Thessalonians should not be uninformed about the following matters:

(a) Christian believers do not have to grieve like the unbelievers when their loved ones die

(b) Christian believers have hope

4:14   Jesus died and rose from the dead

God will bring with Jesus those who have died as believers

4:15   Believers will be alive when Jesus comes

Believers who are alive when Jesus comes will not precede the deceased believers into heaven

4:16   Jesus the Lord himself will come down from heaven

(a) with a loud command

(b) with the voice of an archangel

(c) with the trumpet call of God

The deceased believers will rise from the dead

4:17   The living believers on earth will be caught up

(a) in the clouds

(b) together with the resurrected believers who had been deceased

(c) to meet the Lord Jesus in the air

All believers will be with the Lord Jesus forever

4:18   This information should be used by the believers to encourage one another

5:1   The Thessalonians had already been informed about the times and dates of the Lord's coming .

5:2   The day of the Lord will come like a thief in the night

5:3   (a) Unbelievers will think that they have peace and live in safety

(b) Destruction (on the unbelievers) will come suddenly

(c) Analogy for the unexpectedness of Jesus' coming: labor pains begin suddenly

(d) Unbelievers will not escape the destruction of God's judgment

5:4   Believers will not be surprised by the day of the Lord

5:5   Believers are "children of light" and therefore "children of the day"

Believers do not belong to the night or to the darkness

5:6–8   Exhortation to be awake and sober, that is, to live as "day people" who exhibit faith, love, and hope

5:9   Believers are destined not for God's wrath but for salvation through Jesus Christ (grounds of the exhortation)

5:10   The purpose of Jesus' death "for us" is the believers' (eternal) life together with Jesus

Believers will enjoy (eternal) life with Jesus, whether they are alive when Jesus returns or whether they have died

5:11   This information should be used by the believers to encourage one another and to build each other up

The key passage for any discussion of the rapture is 1 Thessalonians 4:16–17, and thus these verses deserve a closer look. Paul describes the coming of the Lord Jesus as a descent from heaven: he will "come down [*katabēsetai*] from heaven [*ap' ouranou*]" (4:16 NIV). If the Thessalonian believers were familiar with the tradition about Jesus' ascension into heaven, they would have known that Jesus was "taken up" before the eyes of the Twelve, that he was "taken" from them "into heaven" (*eis ton ouranon*) and that two men in white robes (angels) announced that "this same Jesus, who has been taken from you into heaven, will come [*eleusetai*] back in the same way you have seen him go into heaven [*eis ton ouranon*]" (Acts 1:9, 11 NIV). If they were familiar with Jesus' prophecy about the end times and about his return, they would have known Jesus' announcement that at the time when the stars will fall from the sky and the celestial bodies will be shaken (i.e., at the end of the present time), "people will see the Son of Man coming in clouds with great power and glory" (Mark 13:26 NIV). Without specific information to the contrary, Paul's readers connected his description of Jesus' coming down from heaven as the fulfillment of the prophecy that he will come from heaven in the same way in which he had gone into heaven.

A "Secret" Departure?

Three elements in 1 Thessalonians 4:16 confirm that Paul is not speaking of a secret coming (to gather the believers in a secret rapture) but of a public coming: Jesus descends from heaven to earth (a) with a loud command, (b) with the voice of an archangel, and (c) with the trumpet call of God. The last two elements explain the first element: the loud command is conveyed through the voice of an archangel and through a trumpet call. As regards the archangel (not mentioned in the Old Testament but in early Jewish texts), Paul probably thinks of the archangel named Michael.[5] The trumpet call marks Jesus' coming as a theophany (see God's coming on Mount Sinai, Exod. 19:16–20) and as the fulfillment of the prophecy of Zechariah 9:14, where "the Sovereign LORD will sound the trumpet" as he saves his people "on that day" (v. 16).[6] And the trumpet call connects Paul's explanation with Jesus' prophecy of his (second) coming, described as the coming of the Son of Man "on the clouds of heaven" at the time when he "will send his angels with a loud trumpet call" to gather the elect from the earth (Matt. 24:30–31 NIV).

The Last Trumpet

In his discussion of the bodily resurrection of the dead in 1 Corinthians 15, Paul mentions "the last trumpet" as well: "Listen, I tell you a mystery: We

---

5. See *1 Enoch* 20:5; Daniel 12:1 (LXX); Jude 9; Revelation 12:7.
6. Also see Isaiah 27:13; Joel 2:1; Zephaniah 1:16.

will not all sleep, but we will all be changed—in a flash, in the twinkling of an eye, at the last trumpet. For the trumpet will sound, the dead will be raised imperishable, and we will be changed" (1 Cor. 15:51–52 NIV). The parallels with 1 Thessalonians 4:16 are obvious: when the day comes on which believers in Jesus will bear "the image of the heavenly man" (1 Cor. 15:49 NIV), some believers will be alive on earth ("we will not all sleep") while other believers will have died; a trumpet will sound on that day—the "last trumpet" signaling the last day of the first creation, the day on which the dead will be raised. In 1 Thessalonians 4:16, the trumpet is also connected with the deceased believers being raised from the dead. According to Old Testament, Jewish, and early Christian expectations, there is only one day of resurrection—at the end, when God will raise the righteous for eternal life in his presence and the unrighteous for judgment. The fact that Paul does not speak of the fate of the unbelievers is of no consequence. He does not provide, in this passage, a full discussion of the future of the world and all its inhabitants. Rather, he focuses on the believers, who are grieving because some people in the church had died before Jesus had returned.

The last statement in 1 Thessalonians 4:16 describes what will happen to the deceased believers on the day when Jesus will come down from heaven to earth—they will be raised from the dead. The two statements in 4:17 describe what will happen to the believers who are alive on the day when Jesus comes down from heaven.

"Caught Up"

Paul asserts that the living believers on earth will be "caught up" (1 Thess. 4:17). The phrase "we who are still alive" (NIV) describes Christian believers who are alive when Jesus comes from heaven to earth. The explicit personal pronoun "we" (*hēmeis*) in the Greek sentence suggests that Paul thought it possible that he might be among those who will live long enough to experience Jesus' return. The clarifying phrase "[we] who are left" (*hoi perileipomenoi*) describes the living believers in contrast to deceased believers (whose death triggered the necessity that Paul had to write about these matters). The believers who are alive when Jesus comes are "the remainder" of those who believe.[7] The next phrase in the Greek sentence is "together with them" (or "simultaneous with them"), referring to the deceased believers. This is Paul's point of the entire passage: the deceased believers will have no disadvantage; they will meet Jesus at the same time as the believers who are still alive when Jesus comes.

---

7. Gordon D. Fee, *The First and Second Letters to the Thessalonians*, NICNT (Grand Rapids: Eerdmans, 2009), 179; Charles A. Wanamaker speaks of "those who survive until the coming of the Lord from heaven" (*The Epistles to the Thessalonians: A Commentary on the Greek Text*, NIGTC [Grand Rapids: Eerdmans, 1990], 174).

The verb translated "caught up" (*harpagēsometha* from *harpazō*) often has the sense of a sudden and violent action and can be translated as "snatched" (Latin *raptus*, hence the term "rapture").[8] The connotation of violent action is not always present, however. The meaning of the verb, as used in many passages in Greek literature, can be defined as "to grab or seize suddenly so as to remove or gain control," which can be done with force or simply in such a way that no resistance is offered.[9] The Greek verb is regularly used in funerary inscriptions and in letters of consolation to lament the fact that Fate had snatched (*harpazō*) away the deceased from their loved ones to Hades.[10] Paul consoles the Thessalonian believers not by lamenting the fact that death had snatched away their loved ones, but, in a deliberate twist, by asserting that God will snatch up the living believers at the same time as he will raise the dead back to (eternal) life.

"In the Clouds"

The phrase "in the clouds" corresponds to the following description of meeting the Lord who comes down from heaven "in the air" (1 Thess. 4:17). Paul's language echoes Daniel 7:13, where the "one like a son of man" is "coming with the clouds of heaven" (NIV). The following description in Daniel 7 describes this event as universal: "He was given authority, glory and sovereign power; all nations and peoples of every language worshiped him. His dominion is an everlasting dominion that will not pass away, and his kingdom is one that will never be destroyed" (v. 14 NIV). This passage is important because Jesus establishes a connection between his coming as the Son of Man in glory and Daniel's "son of man" (Mark 13:26). Luke describes Jesus' ascent to heaven with the statement "a cloud hid him from their sight" (Acts 1:9 NIV). As the two men (angels) announce that "this same Jesus, who has been taken from you into heaven, will come back in the same way you have seen him go into heaven" (v. 11 NIV), it was natural for Paul to describe the "ascent" of the living and the dead believers as being snatched up "in the clouds" for their meeting with the Lord "in the air."

---

8. See Matthew 11:12; John 6:15; 10:12; Acts 8:39; 23:10; 2 Corinthians 12:4; Revelation 12:5. Many interpreters assume the connotation of violent action here as well. See, e.g., F. F. Bruce, *1 and 2 Thessalonians*, WBC (Waco: Word, 1982), 102. Also see Wanamaker, who writes, "The ascent is brought about by a force outside the individual" (*Epistles to the Thessalonians*, 175).

9. BDAG, 135 (*harpazō* 2a and 2b); Henry George Liddell, Robert Scott, and Henry Stuart Jones, *A Greek-English Lexicon* (Oxford: Clarendon, 1996), 245 (*harpazō*) I.2 ("seize hastily"), I.3 ("seize, overpower, overmaster"). The verb is later used to describe the "taking away" of a slave who is being released (ibid., III).

10. Abraham J. Malherbe, *The Letters to the Thessalonians*, AB 32B (New York: Doubleday, 2000), 276, with reference to inscriptions such as *Inscriptiones graecae* II 1062a, and authors such as Plutarch, *A Letter of Condolence to Apollonius* 111D, 117BD.

Meeting the Lord

The purpose of the "rapture" of the believers who are alive together with the believers who have died is "to meet the Lord [*eis apantēsin*]" (1 Thess. 4:17). The noun that Paul uses here is often taken as a technical term that describes a dignitary who pays an official visit (*parousia*) to a city, denoting "the action of the leading citizens in going out to meet him and escort him back on the final stage of his journey."[11] This interpretation has been effectively criticized on the grounds that *apantēsis* ("meeting") is not a technical term and that the formal elements of such receptions mentioned in Hellenistic sources are missing from 1 Thessalonians 4:17. For example, there is no reference of a "return" of Jesus to earth with those who meet him in the air.[12] The fact that Paul seems to leave Jesus and the "raptured" and risen believers up "in the air" should not overly concern us. There are only two passages in which Paul locates the final destiny of the believers as "in heaven" (2 Cor. 5:1; Col. 1:5). It seems that Paul has "almost no interest whatever in our final eschatological 'geography'; rather, his interest is altogether personal, having to do with their being 'with the Lord.'"[13]

Meeting Jesus at His Second Coming

The following passage in 1 Thessalonians 5:1–11 confirms that Paul speaks of events related to Jesus' second coming. The reference to the Lord coming like a thief in the night (5:2) alludes to Jesus' identical statement in Matthew 24:36, 42–44, as does the analogy of labor pains, which always begin suddenly (see Matt. 24:8). Paul speaks of the "day of the Lord" (1 Thess. 5:2), God's wrath (5:9), and of the believers enjoying (eternal) life with Jesus (5:10). The following table lists the parallels between Paul's description and Jesus' prophecy about his return.[14]

---

11. Bruce, *1 and 2 Thessalonians*, 102. Also see I. Howard Marshall, who concludes that "then we may take the further step of deducing that the Lord's people go to meet him in order to escort him back to the earth and that this is where they shall always be with the Lord" (I. Howard Marshall, *1 and 2 Thessalonians*, NCBC [Grand Rapids: Eerdmans, 1983], 131).
12. See Michael R. Cosby, "Hellenistic Formal Receptions and Paul's Use of ΑΠΑΝΤΗΣΙΣ in 1 Thessalonians 4.17," *BBR* 4 (1994): 15–33; Gordon D. Fee, *The First and Second Letters to the Thessalonians*, NICNT (Grand Rapids: Eerdmans, 2009), 180; Malherbe, *Letters to the Thessalonians*, 277.
13. Fee, *First and Second Letters to the Thessalonians*, 181.
14. The table is adapted from Ben Witherington, *1 and 2 Thessalonians: A Socio-Rhetorical Commentary* (Grand Rapids: Eerdmans, 2006), 136, who follows Gregory K. Beale, *1–2 Thessalonians, IVPNTC 13 (Downers Grove, IL: InterVarsity Press, 2003), 137. Also see David Wenham, Paul: Follower of Jesus or Founder of Christianity?* (Grand Rapids: Eerdmans, 1995), 303–14.

JESUS' SECOND COMING ACCORDING TO PAUL AND JESUS		
	1 THESSALONIANS	MATTHEW
Christit returns	4:16	24:30
from heaven	4:16	24:30
accompanied by angels	4:16	24:31
with a trumpet of God	4:16	24:31
Believers are gathered to Christ	4:17	24:31, 40–41
in clouds	4:17	24:30
at a time unknown	5:1–2	24:36
Jesus comes like a thief	5:2, 4	24:36
Unbelievers are unaware of the coming judgment	5:3	24:37–39
Judgment is like a mother's birth pains	5:3	24:8
Believers are not to be deceived	5:4–5	24:43
Believers are to be watchful	5:6	24:37–39
Warning against drunkenness	5:7	24:49

Paul's concern in 1 Thessalonians 4–5 "has to do not with threat lest they fail to shape up, but with urging them on in the midst of present difficulties."[15] This concern, clearly expressed in the exhortations of 5:6–8 and in the references to encouragement (4:18; 5:11), renders the view that the believers will be removed from earth to heaven before the tribulation extremely unlikely. If this was Paul's view, there would be no reason for him to be concerned that the young Thessalonian believers are strengthened and encouraged in the trials (*thlipsesin*, the plural term that can also be translated as "distress" or "tribulation") that they are facing, adding that "you know quite well that we are destined for them" (3:3 NIV). Paul regularly informed new believers that trials and tribulations were unavoidable for believers in Jesus (see Acts 14:22: "They returned to Lystra, Iconium and Antioch strengthening the disciples and encouraging them to remain true to the faith. 'We must go through many hardships to enter the kingdom of God,' they said"; NIV; also see 2 Tim. 3:12).

It should be noted that the theory of a pretribulation rapture has to assume three comings of Jesus, three resurrections, and two judgments.[16] In this

---

15. Fee, *First and Second Letters to the Thessalonians*, 199.
16. See J. Daniel Hays, J. Scott Duvall, and C. Marvin Pate, *Dictionary of Biblical Prophecy and End Times* (Grand Rapids: Zondervan, 2007), 349.

view, Jesus' first coming is his coming as Jesus of Nazareth, the second coming is in the secret rapture, and the third coming is in glory after the tribulation. It follows that three resurrections have to be assumed: the resurrection of the righteous dead who are raised at the time of the rapture, the resurrection of the righteous who were converted during the tribulation and who consequently died during the tribulation, and the resurrection of the wicked after the millennium. And there are two judgments: the judgment of the righteous at the time of the rapture for the purpose of rewarding the faithful, and the judgment of the unrighteous after the millennium. As the New Testament speaks only of Jesus' first coming and his coming again from heaven, the theory of a secret rapture before the tribulation is an interpretation of 1 Thessalonians 4:17 that leads to major complications with a whole host of passages.

In sum, the key text 1 Thessalonians 4:17 speaks of an event that coincides with Jesus' return on the day in which the dead will be raised. There is no indication of a "secret rapture" in which the believers will disappear from the earth, leaving unbelievers behind.

Matthew 24:40–41 / Luke 17:34–35

The text about two pairs of people described in Matthew 24:40–41 and Luke 17:34–35 as working together is often used to describe what will happen at the rapture. Jesus says that when the Son of Man comes, "two will be in the field; one will be taken and one will be left. Two women will be grinding meal together; one will be taken and one will be left" (Matt. 24:40–41). It is suggested that one person in the two pairs of people is a believer, who is "taken" (by God, to heaven, in the rapture), while the other person is "left" (behind, on earth). If this statement is interpreted in its context, a different meaning is more likely. In Matthew 24:38–39, Jesus compares the coming of the Son of Man with the people living at the time of Noah's flood, who were "swept away" because they were unprepared. Thus, the people who are "taken" in Matthew 24:40–41 are people who are "taken" for judgment (see Jer. 6:11).[17] There is no reference to a sudden disappearance of people from earth.

Revelation 4:1 and 11:12

Some look for the rapture in the book of Revelation before the events in chapters 6–16.[18] John's vision of an open door in heaven, and his hearing of a

---

17. R. T. France, *The Gospel of Matthew, NICNT* (Grand Rapids: Eerdmans, 2007), 941. Craig L. Blomberg writes, "In this context, Christians will be the ones left behind—on earth to enjoy the glory and grandeur of reigning with Christ during the millennium" ("The Posttribulationism of the New Testament: Leaving 'Left Behind' Behind," in A Case for Historic Premillennialism: An Alternative to "Left Behind" Eschatology, ed. Craig L. Blomberg and Sung Wook Chung [Grand Rapids: Baker Academic, 2009], 78).

18. John F. Walvoord admits that "the rapture as a doctrine is not a part of the prophetic foreview of the book of Revelation" (*The Revelation of Jesus Christ* [Chicago: Moody Press,

voice "speaking to me like a trumpet" and saying, "Come up here, and I will show you what must take place after this" (Rev. 4:1) is not a veiled reference to an "invitation" of the church to leave earth and go into heaven. Rather, it is a summons to receive the revelation of visions that John is to communicate to the churches.[19]

The vision of the two witnesses refers to their death and resurrection, followed by a "loud voice from heaven" that said to them, "Come up here!" followed by the comment "and they went up to heaven in a cloud while their enemies watched them" (Rev. 11:12). If the two witnesses (see question 25) are real people, then this passage obviously does not refer to the rapture of the church. If the two witnesses symbolize the church and her calling to missionary witness amid suffering and martyrdom, a rapture of God's people becomes a possibility. On the other hand, the reference to going up to heaven "in a cloud" links this to passages that describes Jesus' second coming (see above). The view that John speaks about a rapture of the believers into heaven some time before the end does not emerge naturally from the text but has to be assumed.[20]

Summary

The "rapture" of the believers, as described by Paul in 1 Thessalonians 4:17, refers to the meeting of the believers who are alive on earth with Jesus who comes from heaven to earth, an event that unites them with the believers who had died and who will be raised from the dead. There is no evidence in the New Testament for a separation between believers and unbelievers in which the believers are taken to heaven before the day of the Lord while the unbelievers are left behind on earth to face unprecedented tribulations. The event of "the rapture" (if one wants to retain the term, based on 1 Thess. 4:17) takes place on the day when Jesus returns to earth.

REFLECTION QUESTIONS

1. How would the belief in a secret rapture of believers, if true, change the way believers live?

2. Why is the theory of a secret rapture of the church problematic?

1966], 103). Since the apostle John gives us the most detailed review of the end times, this is a revealing admission.

19. See Robert L. Thomas, *Revelation: An Exegetical Commentary* (Chicago: Moody, 1992), 1:337.

20. For passages not discussed due to space limitations, such as John 14:3 and 1 Corinthians 15:51–52, see Douglas J. Moo, "The Case for the Posttribulation Rapture Position," in *Three Views on the Rapture*, 169–212, 178–80.

3. Why is the timing of an assumed secret rapture before the onset of "the great tribulation" problematic?

4. What is Paul's main concern in 1 Thessalonians 4–5?

5. What does Paul say about the future of the believers in 1 Thessalonians 4–5?

Will the Work of the Church Bring about a Period of Faith, Righteousness, Peace, and Prosperity on Earth?

Some Christians believe that the work of the church will bring about paradiselike conditions on earth. Interpretations stand and fall with the plausibility or impossibility of the particular interpretation of the sentences, phrases, words, and arguments of the relevant biblical passages. In some cases the historical origin of theological positions can be illuminating. This is the case with the view briefly described above, a position that is known by the label "postmillennialism" (see the introduction). This position has been held nearly exclusively in North America.[1] Most Protestants and Catholics who settled colonial America did not believe in a future, literal thousand-year reign of Jesus on earth before the eternal state. In tune with the positions of the Roman Catholic, Lutheran, and Reformed traditions, they were "amillennialists." In contrast, most of the Puritans who settled New England believed that Jesus' return would usher in a millennial reign on earth, a view that had become popular in England in the seventeenth century.[2] They believed that

---

1. The following historical survey follows Timothy P. Weber, "Dispensational and Historic Premillennialism as Popular Millennialist Movements," in *A Case for Historic Premillennialism: An Alternative to "Left Behind" Eschatology*, ed. Craig L. Blomberg and Sung Wook Chung (Grand Rapids: Baker Academic, 2009), 1–22, esp. 5; see Timothy P. Weber, "Millennialism," in *The Oxford Handbook of Eschatology*, ed. Jerry L. Walls (Oxford: Oxford University Press, 2008), 365–83, esp. 376.
2. Note that it is often difficult and anachronistic to identify people as pre-, post-, or amillennial prior to the nineteenth century, the time when biblical scholars began to use these labels consistently. Some Puritans were premillennialist, some were amillennialist, some

they lived in the last days, that the Antichrist was already at work, and that the signs of the approaching end were becoming increasingly obvious. Then the Great Awakening happened in the 1740s, when thousands of people converted and hundreds of churches were established. Jonathan Edwards (1703–1758), the leading evangelical theologian of the time, concluded that God's dramatic intervention was leading to the Christianization of the world, which would usher in the golden millennial age before Christ's return.[3] These ideas were revived and consolidated during the Second Great Awakening in the early nineteenth century, which brought even more impressive transformations.[4] "Evangelists such as Charles Finney told their converts to apply Christian principles to social and political causes and predicted that if they did so, the millennium was just around the corner."[5]

We will explore the scriptural basis for the claim that "increasing gospel success will gradually produce a time in history prior to Christ's return in which faith, righteousness, peace, and prosperity will prevail in the affairs of people and of nations."[6]

The Expectation That the Vast Majority of People Will Be Saved in the Present Age

The scriptural evidence adduced for the view that the church can expect most people of the world to accept faith in Jesus Christ and be saved includes the following passages and arguments. Since God is powerful, his Word will accomplish his purpose, as Isaiah prophesied: "it shall not return to me empty, but it shall accomplish that which I purpose, and succeed in the thing for which I sent it" (Isa. 55:11). Since God's sovereign power will assure

---

were postmillennialist, but many were difficult to define in these terms. Most of them thought that all Israel would convert to Christianity before the final judgment, but it is often hard to tell whether they thought that Christ would return before or after this conversion. I owe this point to Douglas A. Sweeney.

3. Edwards was influenced by Daniel Whitby (1638–1725), rector of St. Edmund's Church in Salisbury, who held that the population of the world would be converted to Christ, that the Jews would return to the Holy Land, that the pope and the Turks would be vanquished, and that subsequently the world would enjoy a period of a thousand years of peace and happiness, and then Jesus would return.

4. The Bible commentaries of Matthew Henry, Thomas Scott, and Adam Clarke, which were written at that time, gave expression to this "postmillennial" interpretation of biblical prophecy.

5. Weber, "Dispensational and Historic Premillennialism," 5.

6. Kenneth L. Gentry, "Postmillennialism," in *Three Views on the Millennium and Beyond*, ed. Darrell L. Bock (Grand Rapids: Zondervan, 1999), 11–57, esp. 13–14. The discussion that follows above is a critical analysis of Gentry, ibid., 22–57. For a fuller exposition of his position, see Kenneth L. Gentry, *He Shall Have Dominion: A Postmillennial Eschatology* (Tyler, TX: Institute for Christian Economics, 1992). Also see Loraine Boettner, "Postmillennialism," in *The Meaning of the Millennium: Four Views*, ed. Robert G. Clouse (Downers Grove, IL: InterVarsity Press, 1977), 117–41.

that his purposes will be achieved, Jesus' statement that "God did not send the Son into the world to condemn the world, but in order that the world might be saved through him" (John 3:17; see John 1:29; 1 John 4:14) must be taken seriously. The text says that the world, not only a few people, will be saved. Thus Jesus predicted that "I, when I am lifted up from the earth, will draw all people to myself" (John 12:32). When Jesus is described as "the atoning sacrifice . . . for the sins of the world" (1 John 2:2) and as "reconciling the world to himself" (2 Cor. 5:19; see Rom. 11:15), this needs to be seen as accomplished over time: "that is, Christ's labors will eventually effect the redemption of the created system of humanity and things."[7] This interpretation must not be confused with "universalism," which teaches that all human beings will eventually be saved. The parable of the weeds (Matt. 13:24–30) and the parable of the nets (Matt. 13:47–50) warn that the incredible growth of God's kingdom on earth will not lead to absolute perfection, as there will always be a mixture of the righteous and the unrighteous. When Jesus commissions the disciples to make disciples of all nations (Matt. 28:19), he who has been given all authority in heaven and on earth will make sure that this will indeed happen.

Most people prefer to believe an optimistic message, and all Christians would rejoice if indeed all people—all our relatives and friends, and especially our enemies—came to faith in Jesus. The view that Scripture leads us to expect that this will indeed happen, perhaps not in our lifetime but sometime in the future, cannot be maintained, however.[8] Jesus, Peter, Paul, and John believe that the present time, since the coming of Jesus who is Israel's Messiah, is the time of the "last days" or "end time" (see question 1). The concept of the "last days" as a present reality hardly promises a continually progressive development during which most people will come to faith in Jesus. This is particularly true when it is connected, for example, with Paul's conviction that the present time of the Christian life until Jesus' return is a time of suffering and distress (Rom. 8:18; 2 Cor. 1:5–10; Phil. 1:29; 3:10; Acts 14:22; see question 8). The model for the present existence of the church is not Israel's conquest of Canaan (see Deut. 7:22) but Israel's desert experience (Heb. 3:7–19). Christians remain "resident aliens" in the world (Heb. 11:13; 1 Peter 1:1). Jesus is the exalted king at God's right hand now (Acts 2:24–36; Eph. 1:22–23; Heb. 1:3), not in a future period when most of the people in the world will acknowledge him. If the view that Christ's present kingdom leads progressively to the conversion of most of humankind were correct, the missionary work of

---

7. Gentry, "Postmillennialism," 43. For the next point, see ibid., 39, 43.

8. See the responses of Robert B. Strimple and Craig A. Blaising to Gentry in *Three Views on the Millennium and Beyond*, 58–80, for the discussion that follows. For a more sympathetic critique, see Stanley J. Grenz, *The Millennial Maze: Sorting Out Evangelical Options* (Downers Grove, IL: InterVarsity Press, 1992), 83–88.

the Twelve and of Paul must be regarded as not very successful, given the fact that the apostles thought that Jesus might return during their lifetime.

Several passages speak explicitly against the view that there will be a worldwide turning to faith in Jesus. In the context of a discussion about the time when God will finally bring about justice for the elect "who cry out to him day and night" and who wonder whether God will "keep putting them off," Jesus asks, "when the Son of Man comes, will he find faith on the earth?" (Luke 18:7–8 NIV). This question amounts to an exhortation to keep looking forward, with perseverance, to the day when he will return and exercise righteous judgment. It implies the possibility of a lack of faith even among believers.[9] Paul asserts in his letter to Timothy that "everyone who wants to live a godly life in Christ Jesus will be persecuted, while evildoers and impostors will go from bad to worse, deceiving and being deceived" (2 Tim. 3:12–13 NIV). The claim that the prophecies of suffering and anti-Christian distress by Jesus (Matt. 24), Paul (2 Thess. 2), and John (Rev. 6–16) have all been fulfilled in the first century and is thus a thing of the past is convenient, but not convincing.

The Expectation That a Period of Righteousness, Peace, and Prosperity Can Be Achieved

The belief that there will be a period of righteousness, peace, and prosperity for most of humankind is connected by its proponents with God's creation purpose, God's sovereign power, and God's blessed provision. As regards God's creation purpose, it is claimed that since originally all creation was "very good" (Gen. 1:31), since God created the world for his own glory (Rom. 11:36; Col. 1:16), and since Scripture often reaffirms God's love for his creation and his claim of ownership over all creation (e.g., Ps. 24:1; Exod. 9:29; Deut. 10:14; 1 Cor. 10:26, 28), the expectation that there is real hope for the world is rooted in the reality of creation. As God's sovereign power determines "the end from the beginning" (Isa. 46:10 NIV), we can be confident that he "accomplishes all things according to his counsel and will" (Eph. 1:11). This means that our expectations for the future should not be determined by past or present experiences and situations but by confidence in the power of the sovereign God. As regards God's blessed provision, the church has the presence of Christ, who "began a good work among you" and who "will bring it to completion by the day of Jesus Christ" (Phil. 1:6), the indwelling of the Holy Spirit who empowers believers for righteous living, the Word of God that has the power to demolish strongholds (2 Cor. 10:4–5), and the assurance that Satan has been defeated at Jesus' first coming. It is further argued that the redemptive-historical flow from creation and Eden

---

9. To speak of "eschatological pessimism" (Grenz, *Millennial Maze*, 87), is probably too strong.

to the Abrahamic covenant and to the new covenant suggests that the latter will be more glorious than the old or Abrahamic covenant, approximating the conditions in Eden. Proponents argue that Old Testament prophecy expects the incremental progress of redemption among the nations: the water of life flows gradually deeper (Ezek. 47:1–12), and the kingdom of God grows larger (Dan. 2:35) and taller (Ezek. 17:22–24; Matt. 13:31–32).

The exegetical evidence presented for this view is as follows. The messianic psalms of the Old Testament are interpreted as prophetic hymns that predict conditions before the consummation.[10] Thus, it is claimed that Psalm 72:5–7 predicts the messianic victory: "He will endure as long as the sun, as long as the moon, through all generations. . . . In his days the righteous will flourish; prosperity will abound till the moon is no more" (NIV 1984). Isaiah's prophecy for the last days includes the promise that "he shall judge between the nations, and shall arbitrate for many peoples; they shall beat their swords into plowshares, and their spears into pruning hooks; nation shall not lift up sword against nation, neither shall they learn war any more" (Isa. 2:4). Jesus' kingdom parables connect with the expectations of messianic victory in the Old Testament.[11] For example, in the parable of the sower, Jesus predicts a great increase of righteous citizens of the kingdom (Matt. 13:1–17). In John 12:31 Jesus predicted that "now is the judgment of this world; now the ruler of this world will be driven out." In the Great Commission, Jesus directed his disciples to "go therefore and make disciples of all nations" (Matt. 28:19). Since Jesus asserted his sovereign lordship in the Great Commission, it is his intention that this obligation can and will be fulfilled. This prospect constitutes the securing of the nations that Psalm 2:8 speaks of: "Ask of me, and I will make the nations your heritage, and the ends of the earth your possession." Paul prophesies that the end will come when Jesus hands over the kingdom to God the Father, and that this will happen "after he has destroyed every ruler and every authority and power" (1 Cor. 15:24), which will thus happen before the end.

This optimistic view of the future represents a one-sided and selective interpretation of important biblical passages. Psalm 2 speaks not only of the (messianic) king's dominion over the earth, but also of rebellion (Ps. 2:9). The use of Psalm 2 in the New Testament does not allow an interpretation exclusively in terms of a present kingly rule of Jesus: the psalm is applied to Jesus' baptism (Matt. 3:17), to Jesus' resurrection and ascension (Acts 13:33), and to Jesus' second coming (Matt. 25:31–46; 2 Thess. 1:6–12; Rev. 19:15). The

---

10. Gentry thinks that Psalm 2 develops "the redemptive-historical theme of struggle and victory that began with the *proteveangelium* [Gen. 3:15]. It throbs with historical optimism and serves virtually as a postmillennial tract" ("Postmillennialism," 36).

11. Gentry asserts that "the kingdom's gracious and righteous influence will totally penetrate the world system" (ibid., 41).

prophecy in Isaiah 2:2–4 does not speak of a golden age that will gradually develop, only to be replaced by a new earth that will be even more perfect. Rather, the context of Isaiah shows that it refers to the permanently established rule of God following the judgment on the day of the Lord. If the first creation, the fallen world in which we live, could be redeemed to such a substantial degree that it is nearly perfect, there would really be no need for the first heaven and the first earth to pass away to make room for a new heaven and a new earth (Rev. 21:1; see 2 Peter 3:13: "but in keeping with his promise we are looking forward to a new heaven and a new earth, where righteousness dwells"; NIV). The kingdom parables in Matthew 13 do not speak of a gradual development of the kingdom of God toward a golden age on earth. Instead, they contrast the (small) beginning with the end, without specifying what will happen in the intervening period. The parable of the sower (Matt. 13:1–17) speaks more about rejection than about success: while there is certainly a harvest, three of the four soils do not yield fruit. Jesus' Great Commission in Matthew 28:18–20 directs the disciples to "fish for people" among all the nations and assures them of Jesus' powerful presence but does not predict a worldwide turning to faith by a majority of the people living on earth. Christians hope not for the progressive perfection of the world but for Christ's return to establish a new heaven and a new earth. Neither Jesus' prophecy (Matt. 24) nor John's visions about the time until the end encourages readers to anticipate a golden age of righteousness and peace before Jesus' return. The time until the end is like the time since the fall: human society continues to rebel against God and his Messiah, while the gospel is proclaimed by faithful witnesses. God's new world is established only when Jesus comes back.

Summary

The expectation that a steadily increasing number of people will submit to God's kingly rule by coming to faith in Jesus, resulting in a golden age in which all sectors and aspects of society are permeated with righteousness, peace, and prosperity, lacks sufficient support in Scripture. While the reminder that the reign of God is present and real is important, and while the optimism concerning the proclamation of the gospel and the possibilities of the church's involvement in society and in the world is appealing, this view misrepresents the biblical view of the future and minimizes the radical nature of Jesus' second coming and of the creation of a new earth.

REFLECTION QUESTIONS

1. Why is the view that the work of the church will result in a golden age on earth, before Jesus' second coming, attractive?

2. Which Scripture passages are used to establish this claim?

3. What does Scripture say about the success of the missionary work of the church?

4. What does Scripture say about the future of human society?

5. What role should evangelism, missions, and social involvement of Christians have in the church in the light of what Scripture says about the future?

SECTION **C**

The Future of Israel

What Are Israel's Old Testament Promises?

Christians who affirm that national Israel, including the modern state of Israel, has a God-given destiny base their convictions on the Old Testament. The promises of God's covenant with Abraham and the prophecies of the prophets are particularly important for this conviction. We will discuss the promises made by God to Israel in the Old Testament in four parts: God's covenant with Abraham and Moses, God's covenant with Israel, the promises of the Old Testament made through the prophets, and the convictions and hopes of the Jews in the Second Temple period.

The Covenant with Abraham

God made a covenant with Abraham that included the following provisions: (1) Abraham will receive land as an everlasting possession, (2) his descendants will become a great nation in this land, (3) and all the people of the earth will be blessed through Abraham and his descendants. Genesis 12:1–3 states, "Now the LORD said to Abram, 'Go from your country and your kindred and your father's house to the land that I will show you. I will make of you a great nation, and I will bless you, and make your name great, so that you will be a blessing. I will bless those who bless you, and the one who curses you I will curse; and in you all the families of the earth shall be blessed.'"

God repeated these promises for Abraham (Gen. 15:18–21; 17:7–9) and for Abraham's son Isaac and grandson Jacob (Gen. 26:2–4; 28:13–15). In each reiteration, the Promised Land is specifically linked to the covenant. In Genesis 17:9, God reminds Abraham about covenant fidelity: "God said to Abraham, 'As for you, you shall keep my covenant, you and your offspring after you throughout their generations.'" In Leviticus 18:24–30, God warns Israel not to become defiled by the culture of the Canaanites, warning Israel that if they do not keep his statutes and his ordinances, "the land will vomit you out for defiling it, as it vomited out the nation that was before you" (v. 28).

Moses and God's Covenant with Israel

Before Israel entered the Promised Land, Moses warned Israel that if their descendants "become complacent in the land, if you act corruptly by making an idol in the form of anything, thus doing what is evil in the sight of the LORD your God, and provoking him to anger," then Israel "will soon utterly perish from the land that you are crossing the Jordan to occupy; you will not live long on it, but will be utterly destroyed" (Deut. 4:25–26). The stunning severity of these words reminds Israel that "this land is not simply a gift the giver has forgotten. It is a gift that has expectations for covenant holiness and justice. God is watching this land. He has personal expectations for this land. It is a land that should evoke memories of his own holiness."[1]

It is important to note that Israel never "owns" the land in the sense of "private property." God owns the land, which is the reason why plots of land cannot be sold permanently to others: "The land shall not be sold in perpetuity, for the land is mine; with me you are but aliens and tenants" (Lev. 25:23; note the provisions of the jubilee year in Lev. 25). The first crops and first animals of the land belong to God and are offered in sacrifice (Lev. 27:30–33; Deut. 14:22; 26:9–15). The land is holy because it belongs to a holy God.[2]

The Old Testament Prophets, the Covenant, and God's Promises

Because the land ultimately belongs to God, an egoistic and greedy (or what we might call "capitalist") behavior concerning the land is severely criticized by the prophets. Isaiah writes, "Ah, you who join house to house, who add field to field, until there is room for no one but you, and you are left to live alone in the midst of the land! The LORD of hosts has sworn in my hearing: Surely many houses shall be desolate, large and beautiful houses, without inhabitant" (Isa. 5:8–9; similarly Mic. 2:1–3). In Isaiah's famous Song of the Vineyard, Israel is described as God's vineyard, planted with choice vines, which God expected to yield grapes—but it yielded wild grapes. The consequence for the lack of righteousness and the lack of repentance is the loss of the land: "And now I will tell you what I will do to my vineyard. I will remove its hedge, and it shall be devoured; I will break down its wall, and it shall be trampled down" (Isa. 5:5).

The prophets foresee a return of the exiles to the land and the restoration of Israel. Amos writes in the eighth century B.C., relating what God had revealed to him: "I will restore the fortunes of my people Israel, and they

---

1. See Gary M. Burge, *Jesus and the Land: The New Testament Challenge to "Holy Land" Theology* (Grand Rapids: Baker Academic, 2010), 4.
2. See ibid., 4–9.

shall rebuild the ruined cities and inhabit them; they shall plant vineyards and drink their wine, and they shall make gardens and eat their fruit. I will plant them upon their land, and they shall never again be plucked up out of the land that I have given them, says the LORD your God" (Amos 9:14–15). Jeremiah, called as a prophet in 627 B.C., repeatedly prophesies about God's judgment on Israel and the coming exile from the land (see Jer. 25:8–9; 27:6). He writes, "'As the LORD lives who brought the people of Israel up out of the land of the north and out of all the lands where he had driven them.' For I will bring them back to their own land that I gave to their ancestors" (Jer. 16:15; see Hos. 2:14–23; 11:8–11).

Isaiah predicts that "in the latter time" (or "in the future") God "will make glorious the way of the sea, the land beyond the Jordan, Galilee of the nations" (Isa. 9:1–2). This will be a time when "the people who walked in darkness have seen a great light; those who lived in a land of deep darkness—on them light has shined" (v. 2). Isaiah predicts that the rod of their oppressor will be removed and that "all the boots of the tramping warriors and all the garments rolled in blood shall be burned as fuel for the fire" (vv. 4–5). In Isaiah's prophecy, Israel's redemption and restoration is connected with a child that will be born: "For a child has been born for us, a son given to us; authority rests upon his shoulders; and he is named Wonderful Counselor, Mighty God, Everlasting Father, Prince of Peace. His authority shall grow continually, and there shall be endless peace for the throne of David and his kingdom. He will establish and uphold it with justice and with righteousness from this time onward and forevermore. The zeal of the LORD of hosts will do this" (vv. 6–7).

Ezekiel, who writes in Babylon during the time of the exile, reaffirms the connection between the Promised Land as God's gift, Israel's obligations in possessing the land, and God's judgment leading to the loss of the land. Ezekiel conveys God's word to Israel, saying, "My eye will not spare you, I will have no pity. I will punish you for your ways, while your abominations are among you. Then you shall know that I am the LORD" (Ezek. 7:4). God asserts, "The great abominations that the house of Israel are committing" drive him far from his temple (8:6). Israel will be restored only when God returns to the land and to the temple (43:1–4). Interestingly, Ezekiel prophesies that Israel's restoration will be connected with water flowing from the temple (47:1–2) and that, when the tribes of Israel are again allotted land, the aliens who are in Israel shall be treated as "citizens of Israel" and allotted an inheritance in Israel (47:22–23) in a way that was not possible before.

The Jewish Nationalist Hopes during the Period of the Second Temple

The commitment to the Promised Land and to ritual purity was an important characteristic of the Jewish commonwealth because it was reestablished after the exile during the time of Ezra and Nehemiah as well as the subsequent six centuries until the second temple was destroyed in A.D. 70. The author of the *Psalms of Solomon*, who was perhaps of Pharisaic persuasion writing in the first century B.C., acknowledges that when Israel was taken into exile to a foreign country, this happened "when they neglected the Lord, who had redeemed them" (*Pss. Sol.* 9:1). He looks forward to a time when God would raise up "their king, the son of David, to rule over your servant Israel, in the time known to you, O God" (*Pss. Sol.* 17:21). This Messiah will "purge Jerusalem from gentiles who trample her to destruction," "he will gather a holy people whom he will lead in righteousness; and he will judge the tribes of the people that have been made holy by the Lord their God" and "he will distribute them upon the land according to their tribes"(*Pss. Sol.* 17:22, 26, 28). The Qumran community calls its members to purity and covenant faithfulness so that Israel will not lose the land (*Rule of the Community* [1QS] I, 5; VIII, 3).

When Judea came under Roman control in 63 B.C., the political gains of the Maccabean heroes were lost. The Jews had three options: (1) cooperation, the option chosen by King Herod and the leading priestly families of the Sadducees; (2) separation, the option chosen by the Qumran community and to a certain extent the Pharisees; (3) resistance, the option chosen by freedom fighters or zealots. In the years following the death of Herod I in 4 B.C., messianic figures such as Simon and Anthronges fought against foreign pagan rule. A generation later, between A.D. 40 and 50, Theudas and Judas the Galilean sought to reclaim the land and fought the occupying Romans.[3] By A.D. 66, the Zealot movement had become so influential that it started a military revolt against the Roman occupiers. While we do not have an explicit description of their political program, it seems obvious that these freedom fighters derived their yearning for a new era of Jewish sovereignty from Old Testament texts that spoke of God's covenant to Abraham and his descendants and of God's promises of the restoration of Israel. Israel's commitment to the Torah, the temple, and the land could not acquiesce in the occupation by the Romans.

Summary

God's promises given to Abraham speak of descendants (ethnic identity) and land (territorial integrity). Israel's center was the tabernacle and eventually the temple in Jerusalem (religious exclusivity). Sacrifices that allowed the Israelites to remain God's people were possible only in the temple, from which God's holiness flowed and which made the land "the Holy Land" and Israel God's holy people. Life in the Promised Land and worship in the temple were connected with Israel's commitment to the Torah and thus with covenant fidelity. The Abrahamic covenant, repeated by God several times in the time of the patriarchs and reiterated by Moses, emphasized the fundamental

---

3. See Josephus, *Jewish War* 2.55–65; *Jewish Antiquities* 17.271; 20.97–98; see Acts 5:33–39.

importance of continuous fidelity to the covenant. Israel was warned of loss of land if they refused to live in righteousness. The prophets' promise of a future restoration of Israel to land continued to be connected with covenant fidelity.

REFLECTION QUESTIONS

1. What promises did God give to Abraham and his descendants?

2. What is the significance of covenant fidelity?

3. What does the Law say about ownership of the land?

4. What are the two possibilities of Israel's future in the Old Testament prophets?

5. What does Isaiah say about Israel's future restoration?

Does National Israel Have a Special Destiny?

If we answer this question with the help of Old Testament passages only, the answer is yes. If we answer the question on the basis of New Testament passages only, the answer is no. Since Christians, whether Gentile Christians or Jewish Christians, accept the Old Testament as part of Scripture, the answer to the question is thus more complicated than a simple yes or no. Some Christians ignore what the New Testament says, or does not say, about the importance of ethnicity and land in a territorial sense. In view of the foundational significance of the New Testament Scriptures for Christian faith, this is not a defensible position: what Jesus, Paul, Peter, John, and all the authors of the New Testament say about Israel and the church must not be ignored but given a foundational, central place in thinking about this question. On the other hand, some Christians have ignored what the Old Testament says about Israel, missing the consistently "Jewish" roots of the Christian faith and failing to understand the significance of Jesus' messianic dignity and the importance of history for the Christian understanding of salvation and of the church. We will now look at the Old Testament heritage and promises and at the New Testament understanding of the people of God, focusing again on key passages.

Jesus and Israel's Hopes

Some of Jesus' disciples held nationalistic hopes for Israel. Two disciples from Emmaus who had been supportive of Jesus hoped that "he was the one to redeem Israel" (Luke 24:21), thinking that their hopes were dashed when Jesus was crucified. Jesus was certainly aware of such hopes.

In the context of the political climate of his time, Jesus' silence regarding the territorial aspirations and the national politics of his day is surprising. He positively responds to the request of a Roman centurion to heal his slave

(Matt. 8:5–13). He asserts that if someone—in the political context of Judea, a Roman soldier—asks to be accompanied for a mile, one should walk with him two miles (Matt. 5:41). He commands his followers to love their enemies (Matt. 5:44). When he is asked whether it accords with the Law to pay taxes to the Roman emperor, he answers in the affirmative (Mark 12:13–17; see Matt. 17:24–27). The kingdom of God that Jesus proclaimed "could not be co-opted by a nationalistic movement that sought to win back the land by force."[1]

Jesus' Continuity with Israel's National Aspirations

Jesus' ministry displays continuity with Israel's national identity and commitment to the land. He was born in Bethlehem, a town that evokes memories of David (1 Sam. 17). He began his ministry at the Jordan River, evoking memories of Israel's conquest of the land under Joshua. He chose twelve disciples as his inner leadership group, evoking the hopes for the restoration of Israel in the land. He told the Twelve, when he sent them on a preaching tour, not to go to the Gentiles (Matt. 10:5–6).

Jesus anticipates a time when "the renewal [*palingenesia*] of all things" will take place, "when the Son of Man is seated on the throne of his glory," when the Twelve will sit in judgment over the twelve tribes of Israel (Matt. 19:28; see Luke 22:30). This prophecy implies the renewal and restoration of the land in accordance with Old Testament and Jewish expectations.

Jesus' Discontinuity with Israel's Nationalist Hopes

Jesus' ministry also displays discontinuity with Israel's nationalist hopes. When he was born, he was welcomed not by the priests or the pious Pharisees but by Gentile magi from the east (Matt. 2:1–12). He focused his ministry not on Judea and Jerusalem but on Galilee, which is called "Galilee of the Gentiles" (Matt. 4:15). He was followed by people from Syria and the Decapolis (Matt. 4:24–25). He ministered east of the Jordan river (Matt. 8:28–34; Mark 6:30–44).

Jesus declared in his first public sermon that he was the Promised One who declares the year of the Lord's favor (Luke 4:19, 21). But on the same occasion he reminded his Jewish listeners who doubted his credentials that when there were many widows in Israel and when there was a severe famine in the land, "Elijah was sent to none of them except to a widow at Zarephath in Sidon" and that even though there were many lepers in Israel "none of them was cleansed except Naaman the Syrian" (Luke 4:26, 27). The crowd responded by trying to kill Jesus because they could not accept his disregard for

---

1. Gary M. Burge, *Jesus and the Land: The New Testament Challenge to "Holy Land" Theology* (Grand Rapids: Baker Academic, 2010), 29. For the observations that follow in the text above, see ibid., 30–57.

Israel's privileges in the land. Jesus' proclamation of the arrival of the kingdom of God contains no references to geography or to territorial claims.

When Jesus pronounced a blessing concerning the people who will inherit the earth, he spoke of the meek (Matt. 5:5), not of politically active people who seek to push a nationalist agenda. In the parable of the fig tree, he formulated a prophetic critique of Israel due to its lack of fruit, which could lead to its removal from the land (Luke 13:6–9).

In the parable of the vineyard, which takes up and (re)interprets Isaiah's parable of the vineyard (Isa. 5:1–7; see question 12), Jesus announced that the owner of the vineyard will come and destroy the tenants "and give the vineyard to others" (Luke 20:16; see Matt. 21:43; Mark 12:12; Luke 20:19).

In the Cana miracle (John 2:1–10), he took the water that, stored in stone jars, served exclusively the purpose of ritual purification, and transformed it into wine for the wedding celebration. This implies that at least on this occasion, ritual purification through water, replaced by Jesus, was no longer necessary. At one point Jesus asked his audience to pay close attention and understand his announcement that "there is nothing outside a person that by going in can defile, but the things that come out are what defile" (Mark 7:15). This statement comes close to a declaration that the purity laws regulating food are no longer valid.

Jesus teaches Nicodemus, a teacher of Israel, that entrance into the kingdom of God requires a new birth, effected by God who brings about the promised restoration of Israel through the transforming power of his Spirit (John 3:3, 5–8).

When the disciples marvel at the grandeur of the temple, Jesus prophesies the destruction of the temple (Matt. 24:15–22)—without providing a prophecy promising the restoration of Israel and the rebuilding of the temple.

After his death and resurrection, when the disciples ask Jesus whether he will now restore the kingdom to Israel (Acts 1:6), he answers in the affirmative but redefines their still nationalist expectations: Israel's restoration takes places not as a political action but by the proclamation of the gospel, beginning in Jerusalem and Judea, which is made effective through the power of God's Holy Spirit (Acts 1:8).

Stephen and Peter

Stephen, who is accused of speaking against Moses and the temple, affirms in his important speech (Acts 7:1–53) that God's revelation has often taken place outside the Promised Land (not only in the Law of Moses). And he emphasizes that the "holy ground" where God is worshipped can also be found outside the Promised Land (not only in the temple in Jerusalem).

Peter is directed by God through a vision three times repeated to abandon the traditional Jewish commitment not to associate with or visit a Gentile and instead not to call anyone "profane or unclean," Gentiles specifically included

(Acts 10:28). Peter explains God's revelation and his experience in Caesarea, where the Roman centurion Cornelius has been converted to faith in Jesus, to his fellow Jewish believers in Jerusalem: he has been directed by the Spirit "not to make a distinction between them and us" (Acts 11:12). While this new position is not explained beyond the question of table fellowship between Jews and Gentiles, it seems obvious that the change in commitment to the Law would affect the nationalist focus on the temple and the land as well.

Paul and the Promise to Abraham

Paul was proud to call himself a Jew from the tribe of Benjamin (Phil. 3:5). He remained committed to the city of Jerusalem, organizing famine relief in Antioch (Acts 11:27–30) and a collection in the churches of Galatia, Macedonia, and Asia Minor (Rom. 15:25–28; 2 Cor. 8–9). He mentions temple worship in Jerusalem as one of Israel's privileges (Rom. 9:4).[2]

Galatians 3:6–9

Paul argues in Galatians 3:6–9 that the promise God gave to Abraham ("All the Gentiles shall be blessed in you," v. 8) is fulfilled in those who share Abraham's faith, which includes all Gentile believers. In Galatians 3:16–18, he makes the crucial point that God's promise was given to Abraham and "his seed" or "offspring" (singular), not multiple "offsprings" (plural), and that this promise refers to Jesus Christ, who is the one seed or offspring. Jesus is the true heir of God's promise to Abraham, and that means that all who belong to Jesus share in the fulfillment of the Abrahamic promise. This is true both for Jews and Gentiles: the reality of the fulfillment of Abraham's blessing can be experienced *only* in connection with Jesus, Israel's Messiah. Those who belong to Jesus the Messiah form one family.[3]

Romans 4:16–17

In Romans 4, a text in which Paul interprets Genesis 15:6, Paul makes this inclusive point even more decisively. He declares that salvation from the wrath of God depends, for both Gentiles and Jews (Rom. 1:18–3:20), on faith in Jesus Christ "in order that the promise may rest on grace and be guaranteed to all his descendants, *not only* to the adherents of the law *but also* to those who share the faith of Abraham (for he is the father of all of us, as it is written, 'I have made you the father of many nations')" (Rom. 4:16–17, emphasis added). The community of the people of God that deserves the

---

2. See Peter W. L. Walker, *Jesus and the Holy City: New Testament Perspectives on Jerusalem* (Grand Rapids: Eerdmans, 1996), 114. For the observations that follow in the text above, see ibid., 116–60; Burge, *Jesus and the Land*, 73–94.
3. See N. T. Wright, *The Climax of the Covenant: Christ and the Law in Pauline Theology* (Philadelphia: Fortress, 1992), 157–74.

description "the descendants of Abraham" is no longer defined along ethnic lines. There is no longer apartheid between Abraham's biological descendants (Israel, the Jewish people) and Gentiles. God's promise to Abraham is not for Israel only, nor for Israel's restoration in the Promised Land with the temple at its center, but for the world. It is all the people who acknowledge and worship God through faith in Jesus Christ through whose death they have been granted forgiveness of sin and the presence of the promised Holy Spirit.

Paul and Israel

Romans 9:4–5

In Romans 9:4–5, Paul lists Israel's privileges: "They are Israelites, and to them belong the adoption, the glory, the covenants, the giving of the law, the worship, and the promises; to them belong the patriarchs, and from them, according to the flesh, comes the Messiah, who is over all."

It is important to note that Paul, in his letter to the Roman believers whom he addresses as Gentile Christians, links these privileges with believers in Jesus Christ, regardless if they are ethnic Jews or converted Gentiles. (a) Not all Israelites truly belong to Israel. Rather, it is the children of the promise (i.e., those who believe as Abraham believed; Rom. 4) who count as true descendants of Abraham (Rom. 9:6–8). (b) Believers in Jesus have received God's Spirit, who grants them "adoption" into God's family as God's children (Rom. 8:14–15, 23; see Gal. 4:5–7; Eph. 1:5). (c) When people come to faith in Jesus Christ, the glory of God, which humankind has lost, is restored to them because they are believers in Israel's Messiah (Rom. 3:23–24; 5:1–2; 8:17–21). (d) Believers in Jesus experience the benefits of the new covenant (Rom. 8:3–4; see 2 Cor. 3:6; Eph. 2:12). (e) In regards to worship, believers in Jesus have access to God on account of the saving work of Jesus Christ, worshipping God in everyday life (Rom. 5:1–2; 12:1–2). (f) The promises given to Abraham are fulfilled in anyone who believes as Abraham believed (Rom. 4:16; 15:8–9). (g) Gentile believers are counted among Abraham's descendants (Rom. 4:16). (h) Believers in Jesus acknowledge him as Messiah, whether they are Jews or Gentiles, while unbelieving Jews do not know him.

This does not mean that Israel's privileges have been transferred to "the church" (conceived of as consisting of Gentile believers). But these privileges that Jews claimed for themselves, in conscious distinction from the Gentiles, no longer guarantee the salvation of the Jewish people. Paul wants them to be saved, but this means that they have to come to faith in Jesus Christ (see Rom. 10:2–4). Paul rejects the suggestion that God has rejected Israel (Rom. 11:1), but then points to himself and other Jews who have come to faith in Jesus as proof that Israel is still God's people, albeit only a remnant (Rom. 11:1–6). Gentile believers, who once were not God's people but who are now called children of the living God (Rom. 9:25–26, quoting the prophet Hosea), are now added to this remnant.

Romans 11:26

One passage in the New Testament speaks explicitly about a future for Israel. Paul declares in Romans 11:25–26 that "a hardening has come upon part of Israel, until the full number of the Gentiles has come in. And so all Israel will be saved." The interpretation of the seven words "and so all Israel will be saved" (Rom. 11:26) is disputed.

If "Israel" refers to the Jewish people in an ethnic sense, Paul's statement cannot possibly mean that all Jews (or Israelites) of all ages are saved. God's covenant was always dependent on covenant fidelity, and Paul is convinced that salvation is possible only through faith in Jesus, for Jews and for Gentiles (Rom. 1:18–3:20). Since Paul, who worked as a missionary among both Jews and Gentiles, had a burning desire to see the Jewish people saved (Rom. 9:1–3; 10:1), it is unwarranted to assume that there is a separate path to salvation for Jews and for Gentiles. Israel is saved when they no longer stumble over Jesus the Messiah (Rom. 9:32–33). Many suggest that the sentence "all Israel will be saved" prophesies a large-scale conversion of Jews who will accept Jesus as Messiah in the period before the end (with the word "all" referring to Israel as a whole, not to each individual Jew).[4]

Some have argued that the expression "all Israel" refers to the messianic people of God consisting of believing Jews *and* believing Gentiles, saved through the process that Paul described earlier in the chapter. As God's salvation reaches the Gentiles, the Jewish people become jealous as they see what happens when Jews (the remnant) and Gentiles come to faith in the Messiah Jesus (Rom. 11:13–14). They form messianic communities of believers who are transformed by the power of the Holy Spirit, Jewish believers and Gentile believers living together as the new covenant people of God. Paul had already made the point that both Gentile and Jewish believers are true Jews who are truly (inwardly) circumcised (2:28–29; see Phil. 3:3).

There is no consensus on how to interpret the sentence in Romans 11:26. Paul either emphasizes the timing of Israel's conversion (in the future, after the last Gentile has been converted), or he emphasizes the manner of the conversion of Jews (Jews are converted via the conversion of the Gentiles). What is clear, however, is the fact that Paul does not speak of a future of Israel in nationalist or territorial terms.

---

4. See Douglas J. Moo, *The Epistle to the Romans*, NICNT (Grand Rapids: Eerdmans, 1996), 720–23. Arnold G. Fruchtenbaum believes that "all Jews living at that time" are meant (*Israelology: The Missing Link in Systematic Theology* [Tustin, CA: Ariel Ministries, 1989], 785).

Summary

The New Testament does not speak of a special destiny of ethnic Israel. Jesus emphasized the fundamental importance of continuous fidelity to the covenant, warning Israel of loss of land if they refuse to live in righteousness—in full agreement with the Abrahamic covenant, with Moses' exhortation, and with the prophets of the Old Testament. Jesus proclaimed that covenant fidelity and righteousness now depend on accepting and obeying his message about the arrival of the kingdom of God. Paul emphasized that membership in the covenant and righteousness depend on coming to faith in Jesus, whose death and resurrection effects salvation for all who believe, whether Jews or Gentiles. There is no interest in territorial questions, neither for the church nor for Israel. The Promised Land has not become irrelevant, and the Jewish people have not been totally rejected, as a people, by God. But Israel's land cannot claim a lasting theological significance. It is no longer "holy land" in an exclusive sense. Since God revealed himself in Jesus, Israel's crucified and risen Messiah, the locus of divine presence is where Jesus is: at the right hand of God and in the community of Jewish and Gentile believers, which is the temple of the Holy Spirit and the body of Christ.

REFLECTION QUESTIONS

1. What does Jesus say about Israel and the kingdom of God?

2. Why did Jesus choose twelve disciples?

3. What does Jesus' parable of the vineyard mean for national Israel?

4. What does Paul say about the Jewish people of his day?

5. What does Paul say about Israel's future?

Does the Modern State of Israel Represent Fulfillment of Prophecy?

Many Christians are convinced that the emergence of the state of Israel after the Second World War in 1948 is the fulfillment of prophecy. Can this position be maintained? Do the passages that are quoted in support of this position indeed predict the events of 1948?

The State of Israel and Biblical Prophecy

The belief that the foundation of the state of Israel in 1948[1] is the fulfillment of prophecy is usually linked with Jesus' statements in Luke 21:24 and Matthew 24:32–34. An often quoted statement formulates this conviction as follows: "I believe the modern-day state of Israel is a miracle of God and a fulfillment of Bible prophecy. Jesus clearly said that 'Jerusalem would be trodden down of the Gentiles until the time of the nations is fulfilled' (Luke 21:24). It has been 50 years since the founding of that state, but only 30 years since Jerusalem came under the control of Jews for the first time since Jesus made that prediction. Could it be that 'this generation shall not pass until all these things are fulfilled?'"[2]

The last comment connects Luke 21:24 with Matthew 24:34, a connection that has prompted some to give a date for Jesus' return: assuming the length of a generation as forty years, the end (for Christians, in the rapture) could come

---

1. David Ben-Gurion (1886–1973) read the Declaration of Independence of the state of Israel on May 14, 1948, at the Tel Aviv Museum. He became the first prime minister and defense minister of the state of Israel.
2. David Brickner, "Don't Pass Over Israel's Jubilee," Jews for Jesus newsletter, April 1998, http://jewsforjesus.org/publications/newsletter/1998_04/jubilee, quoted by Stephen Sizer, *Zion's Christian Soldiers: The Bible, Israel, and the Church* (Nottingham: Inter-Varsity Press, 2007), 75; Gary M. Burge, *Jesus and the Land: The New Testament Challenge to "Holy Land" Theology* (Grand Rapids: Baker Academic, 2010), 112.

within forty years, that is, by 1988 at the latest.[3] This date was over twenty years ago, which is nearly an entire generation, if a generation is defined as the average time between a mother's first child and her oldest daughter's first child, or the average age of first-time mothers. In 2005, this figure was twenty-five years in the United States.[4] In the Roman Empire, girls were allowed to marry from the age of twelve, but most women of lower social rank were between nineteen and twenty years old at the time of their first marriage.[5] Assuming that a majority of women would have their first child within a year of marriage, a "generation" would have been about 20 years, according to the modern definition. A more general, less technical definition in terms of "contemporaries" extends a "generation" to perhaps forty years. A closer look at these two passages will help us determine whether an interpretation in terms of the events of 1948 (or 1967, when Jerusalem was reunified as a result of Israel's victory in the Six-Day War) is warranted.

Jesus' Prophecy Concerning Jerusalem and Israel

The view that the emergence of the modern state of Israel represents fulfilled prophecy is primarily based on two passages, Matthew 24:32–34 and Luke 21:24. Since the claim that the events of 1948 were predicted by Jesus has far-reaching consequences for understanding Jesus' prophecy of the end times, these passages need to be carefully examined.

Matthew 24:32–34

After Jesus predicted his return in Matthew 24:29–31, he said, "Now learn this lesson from the fig tree: As soon as its twigs get tender and its leaves come out, you know that summer is near. Even so, when you see all these things, you know that it is near, right at the door. Truly I tell you, this generation will certainly not pass away until all these things have happened" (Matt. 24:32–34 NIV).[6] Jesus uses the fig tree as a lesson because the appearance of new shoots in spring is a clear indication that summer is just around the corner when the fruit of the tree can be harvested.

---

3. Hal Lindsey, *The Late Great Planet Earth* (Grand Rapids: Zondervan, 1970), 53–54.
4. "Mean age at first birth: 25." Births and Natality (U.S.), National Center for Health Statistics, http://www.cdc.gov/nchs/fastats/births.htm.
5. See Susan Treggiari, "Marriage," in Hubert Cancik, Helmuth Schneider, and Manfred Landfester, eds., *Brill's New Pauly: Encyclopedia of the Ancient World* (Leiden: Brill, 2006), 8:389; J. Wiesehöfer points out that the median age of marriage derived from census declarations in Egypt was 17.5 years for women. We do not have similar demographic numbers for ancient Israel and Judea, but it can be plausibly assumed that the situation was comparable with other regions in the Mediterranean world ("Marriage, Age at," in ibid., 8:394).
6. The parallel passages in Mark 13:28–30 and Luke 21:29–32 have slightly different wording but essentially agree with Matthew's version; in all three reports Jesus connects "all these things" (Luke only has the word "all" in the Greek) and speaks of "this generation."

There are two key questions. (1) What does the expression "this generation" (Greek, *hē genea hautē*) mean? (2) What does the expression "these things" (Greek, *panta tauta*; v. 33) refer to? The answers to these questions are linked with each other. The following interpretations have been suggested.

The first interpretation suggests that the expression "these things" refers to "the end" mentioned in verses 6, 14. This is assumed in translations such as NRSV and NJB that translate "he is near" in v. 33. If correct, the first part of Jesus' statement, "this generation will certainly not pass away until all these things have happened" (v. 34 NIV), becomes a problem. We either have to assume (1) that Jesus' prophecy was not fulfilled,[7] (2) that the word "generation" has a different meaning, or (3) that the expression "these things" has a different referent than "the end" and Jesus' return.[8] Most Christians want to avoid the conclusion that the first option entails.

The second interpretation posits that the word "this generation" has a different meaning, referring to the "race" of the Jewish people.[9] Jesus says that the Jewish race will not die out before Jesus' second coming and the end. This explanation of the Greek term *genea*, which is usually translated as "generation," is not convincing. The parallel in Matthew 23:35–36[10] leaves no doubt that Jesus uses the term "generation" (Greek, *genean*) with its normal meaning, which is present elsewhere in the Gospel of Matthew, referring to Jesus' contemporaries.[11]

The third interpretation suggests that the expression "these things" does not refer to Jesus' return but specifically to the destruction of Jerusalem.[12] The destruction of Jerusalem and the temple took place in A.D. 70, forty years after

---

7. Cf. Robert H. Gundry who speaks of the "problem of non-fulfilment," which he explains with the statement that "biblical prophecy often undergoes change, often by way of delayed fulfilment" (Robert H. Gundry, *Mark: A Commentary on His Apology for the Cross* [Grand Rapids: Eerdmans, 1993], 790).

8. Since R. T. France interprets the phrase "the end" in Matthew 24:6, 14 and the entire section Matthew 24:4–35 as referring to the destruction of Jerusalem, he can see all of the events predicted by Jesus up to this point as being fulfilled within the generation of Jesus' contemporaries (*The Gospel of Matthew*, NICNT [Grand Rapids: Eerdmans, 2007], 929).

9. See Andrew J. Mattill, *Luke and the Last Things: A Perspective for the Understanding of Lukan Thought* (Dillsboro: Western North Carolina Presss, 1979), 97.

10. Jesus refers to God's judgment on "this generation" before predicting for the first time the destruction of the temple in Matthew 23:38.

11. Matthew 11:16; 12:39, 41–42, 45; 16:4; 17:17; 23:36. BDAG, 191 (*genea* I) connects the definition "those exhibiting common characteristics or interests, race, kind" with Luke 16:8, where the meaning of *genea* is contested, however.

12. See Ben Witherington, *Jesus, Paul, and the End of the World: A Comparative Study in New Testament Eschatology* (Downers Grove, IL: InterVarsity Press, 1992), 43–44; N. T. Wright, *Jesus and the Victory of God, Christian Origins and the Question of God*, vol. 2 (Minneapolis: Fortress, 1996), 365; Craig S. Keener, *A Commentary on the Gospel of Matthew* (Grand Rapids: Eerdmans, 1999), 589.

the beginning of Jesus' ministry in A.D. 30 and thirty-seven years after Jesus gave the prophecy, which is about one generation.

The fourth interpretation argues that the expression "these things" refers to the coming of the end announced as the topic of the discourse in Matthew 24:6, 14, including the destruction of Jerusalem as the last of the signs mentioned before the depiction of Jesus' return in verses 29–31. In other words, "this generation" is the time in which all the prerequisites of Jesus' return mentioned in verses 5–28 were fulfilled, including the destruction of the temple (described in vv. 15–22).[13]

The fourth explanation does justice to the meaning of "this generation" and to the reference of "these things" to Jesus' prophecy regarding the "signs" of the time up until his return. The statement about the fig tree in Matthew 24:32 and the green shoots is not a reference to Israel (either ancient or modern) but a metaphor that uses an image from agriculture to convey a spiritual truth. The word about the fig tree underlines the need to be watchful once "these things" that he has predicted have taken place. Such events include the worldwide proclamation of the gospel (24:14) and the destruction of Jerusalem (24:15–22) as the two new developments in the history of the Jewish people and of the world.

The nations at the "ends of the earth" (Acts 1:8; cf. Matt. 28:19) were reached with the gospel within a generation. The "ends of the earth" in the south (Ethiopia) was reached as an Ethiopian official was converted on the road to Gaza and then returned to his home country (Acts 8:26–39). The western end, Spain, was presumably reached by Paul upon release from his first Roman imprisonment (see his plans in Rom. 15:24, 28). The northern end, Scythia, is mentioned by Paul and thus in his purview (Col. 3:11). And the "end of the world" in the east, India, was probably reached by the apostle Thomas.[14] Once the gospel is proclaimed in the world and once Jerusalem has been destroyed, Jesus could return with unexpected suddenness, as the parables in Matthew 24:36–25:46 illustrate.

Luke 21:24

In Luke's version of Jesus' prediction of the destruction of Jerusalem, we read: "they will fall by the edge of the sword and be taken away as captives among all nations; and Jerusalem will be trampled on by the Gentiles, until the times of the Gentiles are fulfilled" (Luke 21:24). Some end-times "specialists" who regard the state of Israel as fulfillment of prophecy connect Luke

---

13. D. A. Carson, *Matthew*, EBC 8 (Grand Rapids: Zondervan, 1984), 507; Craig L. Blomberg, *Matthew*, NAC 22 (Nashville: Broadman, 1992), 357; Jeffrey A. Gibbs, *Jerusalem and Parousia: Jesus' Eschatological Discourse in Matthew's Gospel* (St. Louis: Concordia Academic Press, 2000), 205–7.
14. See Eckhard J. Schnabel, *Early Christian Mission* (Downers Grove, IL: InterVarsity Press, 2004), 1:448–98, 880–910.

21:24 with the capture of East Jerusalem in the Six-Day War of June 1967 as marking "the end of the time of the Gentiles."[15] A year later, the same end-times "specialist" was more explicit: "We are literally witnessing the last hours of the times of the Gentiles. God's focus is shifting back to his people Israel."[16] Another author was even more convinced when he asserted, "The time of the Gentiles is now past and there has been a changing of the guard. Men may argue and pontificate, but something irrevocable has happened: Jerusalem is no longer trodden down by non-Jews."[17]

The context of Luke 21:24 is Jesus' prophecy about the future, which includes the destruction of Jerusalem. Jesus regarded the destruction of the temple, which stood in first-century Jerusalem, as divine judgment for the people's unfaithfulness. Jesus asserts that the "times of the Gentiles" (the Greek text has the plural *kairoi*, "times") during which the Gentiles will control Jerusalem will be "fulfilled" (Greek, *plērōthōsin*). It is unclear what Jesus means by this statement. Many interpreters suggest that the phrase refers to the period during which the Romans would occupy the city.[18] Jesus' disciples (and the readers of Luke's Gospel) would naturally connect the destruction of Jerusalem with the Roman army—the only power in the first century that could destroy a city such as Jerusalem. If this interpretation is correct, Jesus assures his disciples that the painful period of the siege and destruction of Jerusalem would last only as long as God allows. This interpretation can be confirmed with the parallel passages in Matthew 24:22 and Mark 13:20 where Jesus asserts that "those days" will be cut short for the sake of the elect (i.e., his followers).

Some suggest that the "times of the Gentiles" are a temporary period after which Israel will regain control of Jerusalem. If this interpretation is correct, there is no reason why this event should be connected with the events of either 1948 or 1967. Since Jesus does not further consider Israel's place in God's plan during the end times after the destruction of Jerusalem and the temple— he proceeds to speak about the coming of the Son of Man in a cloud with power and glory (Luke 24:25–27)—it is equally possible, and in this context more plausible, to connect the "times of the Gentiles" being "fullfilled" with the second coming of Jesus.[19]

---

15. Hal Lindsey, *Planet Earth 2000 A.D.: Will Mankind Survive?* (Palos Verdes, CA: Western Front, 1994), 164, cited in Sizer, *Zion's Christian Soldiers,* 107. For the observations made that follow in the text above, see ibid., 107–10.

16. Hal Lindsey, *The Final Battle* (Palos Verdes, CA: Western Front, 1995), 95.

17. Mike Evans, *Jerusalem Betrayed: Ancient Prophecy and Modern Conspiracy Collide in the Holy City* (Dallas: Word, 1997), 193.

18. Bo Reicke, "Synoptic Prophecies and the Destruction of Jerusalem," in *Studies in New Testament and Early Christian Literature,* ed. David E. Aune, NTSup 33 (Leiden: Brill, 1972), 121–34, 127; Joseph A. Fitzmyer, *The Gospel According to Luke,* AB 28A (Garden City: Doubleday, 1981–85), 1347.

19. Peter W. L. Walker, *Jesus and the Holy City: New Testament Perspectives on Jerusalem* (Grand Rapids: Eerdmans, 1996), 100–101.

There is nothing in the text to suggest that the "times of the Gentiles" is followed by the "times of the Jews."[20] Jesus speaks to his disciples who certainly are all Jews, but who are, more importantly, commissioned to proclaim the gospel in Jerusalem and in Judea and among the nations. Also, assuming that Luke's readers are mostly Gentile Christians, Jesus' statement may contain "a thinly-disguised warning that there will be a future judgment for the Gentiles. Any temptation to gloat over the judgment upon Jewish Jerusalem must be dismissed, since there will come a time when this apparent Gentile ascendancy will also come to an end."[21]

Are the Events of 1948 and 1967 Fulfillment of Prophecy?

Even though there is nothing to suggest that Jesus predicted the events of 1948, it is possible to hold the view that the establishment of the state of Israel was God's initiative. Not every initiative of God is the fulfillment of prophecy. There are other historical developments that Christians explain with reference to God's sovereign intervention in world affairs. However, if finite human beings want to be certain about a particular explanation of historical events representing divine action, prophetic revelation is needed: the biblical books of Joshua, Judges, 1 and 2 Samuel and 1 and 2 Kings are called "the former prophets" precisely because it takes prophetic insight to determine which historical events derive from God's blessing or judgment. If the return of the Jews from Babylonian exile and the rebuilding of Jerusalem after 539 B.C. represent fulfillment of biblical prophecy, and if the events of 1948 and 1967 represent fulfillment of biblical prophecy as well, there is no reason why Israel may not again lose Jerusalem, requiring another fulfillment of the same prophecies.

Without the word of a prophet, there is no way of knowing whether the foundation of the state of Israel is the prefiguring of a later fulfillment of specific prophecies or the final fulfillment of these prophecies. The "prophecies" of the end-time "specialists" have been wrong so often that their predictions cannot possibly be taken as prophetic word.

Also, if the prophecy of Luke 21:24 (given in A.D. 33) is a prophecy of events in 1948 or 1967, the apostles could not have believed that they might be alive when Jesus returns—which they clearly did. Either they misunderstood Jesus, or modern end-time "specialists" do.

There may be plausible historical reasons for Christians, particularly for Christians from Germany and Austria, to support the state of Israel. Such a position does not require, however, regarding the events of 1948 or 1967 as the fulfillment of biblical prophecy.

---

20. Darrell L. Bock sees a reference to "a kingdom hope that included Israel's reincorporation in what eventually came to be expressed as millennial hope" (*Luke*, 1681).
21. Walker, *Jesus and the Holy City*, 101.

Whatever our convictions are, there should be no doubt that whether or not the modern state of Israel is the result of God's intervention, the actions of the state of Israel cannot be automatically accepted as divinely sanctioned. For followers of Jesus, all actions must be evaluated in the light of the values and norms of the Law, which demands justice and righteousness. Actions must also be evaluated in the light of the values and norms of Jesus who demands a righteousness that exceeds that of the pious Pharisees who were committed to the Law (Matt. 5:20) and who demands extraordinary love: "love your enemies and pray for those who persecute you" (v. 44).

Summary

While there is some basis for believing that the New Testament envisions future events in which the Jewish people will play a role (particularly Rom. 11:26; see the discussion in question 13), there is no clear scriptural basis for connecting biblical prophecy with the events of 1948 or 1967. The establishment of the modern state of Israel may or may not be the result of God's intervention in history. This does not affect the fact that Christians are called to love the Jewish people, as they are indeed called to love all people, which they demonstrate by bringing the good news of Jesus, Israel's Messiah and the Savior of the world, to all nations.

REFLECTION QUESTIONS

1. What are reasons for believing that the modern state of Israel is God's creation?

2. What does "this generation" in Matthew 24:34 mean?

3. What are the various interpretations for the phrase "times of the Gentiles" in Luke 21:24?

4. How can Luke 21:24 be related to the events during and immediately after A.D. 70?

5. What is the connection between Matthew 24:33 and Luke 21:24 and Jesus' second coming?

What Is Christian Zionism?

Christians who are convinced that the emergence of the modern state of Israel in 1948 is the fulfillment of prophecy sometimes argue that Christians are duty-bound to support the state of Israel. Some go a step further and assert that since the Holy Land belongs to Israel according to God's promises, the state of Israel has a right, even an obligation, to evict the Palestinian people from the territory that God has irrevocably given to Israel. As Joshua removed the Canaanites, so Israel should, and will, remove the Palestinians. Such positions are often labeled "Christian Zionism."

Zionism is defined as "an international movement originally for the establishment of a Jewish national or religious community in Palestine and later for the support of modern Israel." Christians who have sympathies for Israel, who believe that the Jews deserve a state on account of the hundreds of years of suffering inflicted by European governments, or who believe that sometime in the future Jewish believers will play an important role in God's plan, are not Zionists in the strict sense of the word. Christian Zionists have been described as people who are committed "to promote or preserve Jewish control over the geographic area now containing Israel and the occupied Palestinian territories."[1]

What Do Christian Zionists Say?

John Hagee, an influential charismatic preacher, asserted in 2007 in an address before the Policy Conference of the American Israeli Public Affairs Committee (AIPAC): "There are millions of evangelical Christians across America who consider the Jewish people the apple of God's eye, who see

---

1. Robert O. Smith, "Christian Zionism: It Challenges Our Lutheran Commitments," in *The Lutheran 1964* (2009): 1, quoted by Gary M. Burge, *Jesus and the Land: The New Testament Challenge to "Holy Land" Theology* (Grand Rapids: Baker Academic, 2010), 115.

you as the chosen people, a cherished people and a covenant people with an eternal covenant that will stand forever. Ladies and gentlemen of AIPAC, it's a new day in America. The sleeping giant of Christian Zionism has awakened; there are 50 million Christians standing up and applauding the State of Israel."[2] He went on to say, "If a line has to be drawn, draw the line around both Christians and Jews; we are united; we are indivisible; we are bound together by the Torah—the roots of Christianity are Jewish. We are spiritual brothers and what we have in common is far greater than the things we've allowed to separate us over the years." More important than Jesus, it seems, is political support for Israel. The same preacher warns, "[I]t is 1938; Iran is Germany and Ahmadinejad is the new Hitler. Ladies and gentlemen, we must stop Iran's nuclear threat and stop it now and stand boldly with Israel, the only democracy in the Middle East." The political agenda becomes even more explicit in the following paragraph of his speech: "Let the word go forth from Washington, DC tonight. There is a new beginning in America between Christians and Jews. We pledge to God and to the Jewish people to fulfill the words of the Prophet Isaiah; for Zion's sake we will not hold our peace and for Jerusalem's sake we will not rest. You who make mention of the Lord do not keep silent and give the Lord no rest until he makes Jerusalem the praise of all the earth." Hagee's defense of Israel has become so ardent that he claims that is it a myth that the Jews killed Jesus, that the Jews never rejected Jesus as the Messiah, that Jesus did not come to be the Messiah, that Jesus had to live to be the Messiah, and that the old covenant is not dead.[3]

Hagee's position is certainly extreme and not representative of dispensationalists and others who love the Jewish people. However, it serves as a warning where support of a particular political position can lead if it is not qualified by a superior commitment to biblical revelation.

---

2. John Hagee, "A Night to Honor Israel" (keynote address, AIPAC Policy Conference 2007, Washington, DC, March 11, 2007). Part of the speech is quoted by Stephen Sizer, *Zion's Christian Soldiers: The Bible, Israel, and the Church* (Nottingham: Inter-Varsity Press, 2007), 11.

3. John Hagee, *In Defense of Israel: The Bible's Mandate for Supporting the Jewish State* (Lake Mary, FL: FrontLine, 2007), 125, 132, 135, 136, 158. Hagee's book is full not only of theological errors but also of glaring historical mistakes. He claims that Jesus, as a child, studied the Mishnah (p. 96), which was compiled around A.D. 200. He writes that Caiaphas was appointed by Herod (p. 127), when in fact he was appointed high priest by the Roman governor Valerius Gratus in A.D. 15 long after Herod had died. He claims that Acts 11:26 happened forty years after the crucifixion (p. 93), that is, in A.D. 70 or 73 (Jesus was crucified in A.D. 30, perhaps in A.D. 33), when in fact it happened during the reign of Claudius (Acts 11:28), that is, in the early 40s. More examples of a rather careless handling of historical matters can be found, a fact that does not inspire confidence in Hagee's interpretation of historical texts.

Israel and Territorial Claims

The "maps" that the Old Testament gives for Israel's conquest of Canaan (Num. 34:1–12; Deut. 11:24; Josh. 1:1–9) are often taken as "prophecy" that predict the territory that the state of Israel can claim for itself. What is sometimes called "the land covenant" (Deut. 29–30) is interpreted as being based on "the unconditional promises contained within the Abrahamic Covenant," illustrating "the principle that eternal ownership of the land is unconditional but temporal possession of land is conditioned upon obedience to God through the law. The Land Covenant affirms Israel's right to the land solely on the basis of the Abrahamic Covenant, regardless of the nation's unfaithfulness to God and to the Mosaic Covenant."[4] The territorial dimensions of Joshua 1:1–9 are regarded as "a divinely bestowed title to the entirety of the Promised Land" that awaits future fulfillment.[5]

Bizarre Interpretations

The desire to support Israel sometimes leads to bizarre interpretations. For example, some find the United States of America in biblical prophecy. One author interprets Revelation 12:14–17 (John sees that "the woman was given the two wings of the great eagle, so that she could fly from the serpent into the wilderness, to her place where she is nourished for a time, and times, and half a time") as referring to "some massive airlift" transporting Jews who escape: "Since the eagle is the national symbol of the United States, it's possible that the airlift will be made available by aircraft from the US Sixth Fleet in the Mediterranean."[6] John's readers would have had no way of knowing any of this.

Problems of Christian Zionism

The problems with this type of Christian Zionism are immense. First, texts that announce the extent of Israel's settlement in the Promised Land at the time of Joshua are interpreted as prophecies for later times. This is unwarranted. The relevant Old Testament texts are not formulated as prophecies. When we interpret biblical texts, their text-type (or genre) must inform the interpretation: proverbs formulate general truths and not predictions of the future; parables convey theological and ethical truths and are not meant as precise historical reporting on conditions in the first century.[7] Just as not every biblical text is a law, so not every biblical text is a prophetic promise.

4. Tim LaHaye and Ed Hindson, eds., *The Popular Bible Prophecy Commentary* (Eugene, OR: Harvest, 2006), 56–57.

5. Ibid., 65.

6. Hal Lindsey, *There's a New World Coming: A Prophetic Odyssey* (Santa Ana, CA: Vision House, 1973), 185, quoted by Sizer, *Zion's Christian Soldiers*, 35.

7. Note, for example, the ten thousand talents in the parable of the unforgiving servant in Matthew 18:24: this huge amount of money, corresponding to 170,000 years of wages of a day laborer, far surpassed the amount of debt that an individual could incur.

Second, passages that attach conditions to Israel's possession of the Promised Land are either ignored or downplayed. The promise of Genesis 17:8 ("I will give to you, and to your offspring after you, the land where you are now an alien, all the land of Canaan, for a perpetual holding") must be read in its context. For example, Genesis 17:9 ("God said to Abraham, 'As for you, you shall keep my covenant, you and your offspring after you throughout their generations'") and Genesis 17:14 ("any uncircumcised male who is not circumcised in the flesh of his foreskin shall be cut off from his people; he has broken my covenant") clarify that the promise of land is connected with covenant faithfulness. Residence in the land is linked with conditions in Deuteronomy 19:8–9: "If the LORD your God enlarges your territory, as he swore to your ancestors—and he will give you all the land that he promised your ancestors to give you, provided you diligently observe this entire commandment that I command you today, by loving the LORD your God and walking always in his ways." In Deuteronomy 28, blessings are pronounced upon Israel for the people's obedience (28:1–3, 7, 10) and curses for disobedience (28:15–16, 25, 63–64). Similar conditions can be found in the book of Joshua (1:2–5, 7–8; 7:11–12; 23:16). We noted similar conditions in the Old Testament prophets in the discussion of question 13.

Third, selective exegesis focused on Israel fails to do justice to several Old Testament texts. For example, in Deuteronomy 2:1–5, 9, 19 God tells Israel not to provoke the descendants of Esau who live in Seir nor the Moabites nor the Ammonites, "for I will not give you even so much as a foot's length of their land, since I have given Mount Seir to Esau as a possession. . . . I will not give you any of [Moab's] land as a possession, since I have given Ar as a possession to the descendants of Lot. . . . I will not give the land of the Ammonites to you as a possession, because I have given it to the descendants of Lot." The "prophetic significance" of these passages is not discussed in terms of Israel's claims to these territories. Also, the instructions of how the Jews who returned from the Babylonian exile should treat the "foreigners" living in the land are conveniently ignored by Christian Zionists who accept Israel's treatment of the Palestinians or argue for the latter's eviction, yet the text says: "You shall allot it as an inheritance for yourselves and for the aliens who reside among you and have begotten children among you. They shall be to you as citizens of Israel; with you they shall be allotted an inheritance among the tribes of Israel. In whatever tribe aliens reside, there you shall assign them their inheritance, says the Lord GOD" (Ezek. 47:22–23).

Fourth, "exegesis by current events"[8] is highly problematic and requires constant updating. In the nineteenth century, the London Jews' Society believed that the Jewish people would accept Jesus as Messiah, then be restored to

---

8. Charles Haddon Spurgeon, *Lectures to My Students* (London: Passmore & Alabaster, 1893), 100, quoted by Sizer, *Zion's Christian Soldiers*, 85 (for the comments that follow in the text above, see 84–85).

the Promised Land, and then Jesus would return. Cyrus I. Scofield's *Reference Bible* (1909) claimed in a note that biblical prophecy predicts a third restoration of Israel to the land that would coincide with Jesus' second coming. After mostly secular Jews settled in Israel at the beginning of the twentieth century, this interpretation was changed. In the 1967 revision of the *Scofield Reference Bible*, a note was added to Deuteronomy 30:5 that contained the sentence, "In the twentieth century the exiled people began to be restored to their homeland." In the 1984 revision, this sentence was changed to read, "In the twentieth century the exiled people were restored to their homeland." This reversal of the order of events—Israel's repentance, revival, and restoration—to the sequence: Israel's restoration to the land, then repentance and revival, is the standard assumption among many prophecy writers today.[9] The Old Testament prophets expected repentance before restoration (as do many orthodox Jews in Israel today, who do not acknowledge the state of Israel precisely because of its secular nature; David Ben-Gurion, Golda Meir, and other political leaders never made a secret of their secular, agnostic views, despite the fact that they often quoted the Bible).[10]

Fifth, most if not all of the interpretations suggested by Christian Zionists are not explained by careful exegesis (interpretation) but are stated as obvious. Most if not all of the interpretations "by current events" are impossible from the start. John, the author of the book of Revelation, was directed by an angel who said, "Do not seal up the words of the prophecy of this book, for the time is near" (Rev. 22:10), which means that he was to write up the visions about the end times and about the end in such a manner that his readers would be able to understand. If first-century readers would not have been able to understand the meaning of a prophecy because new developments reveal the "real" meaning of a prophecy (as is claimed), then we can never know what a prophecy means, because there could be new developments in a hundred or a thousand years that would reveal the "real" meaning in an even clearer sense.

Sixth, Christian Zionists do not seem to be concerned with the living conditions and the fate of Palestinian Christians. Whatever our political convictions and commitment may be, it should be a matter of course that followers of Jesus love and support fellow believers first and foremost. That this is often not the case gives serious pause about the integrity of the Christian commitment of the proponents of Christian Zionism.

Summary

The support of so-called Christian Zionists for Israel is well-intentioned. However, their political views that support the territorial aims of a "Greater

---

9. See, for example, Hal Lindsey, *The Road to Holocaust* (New York: Bantam, 1989), 180.
10. See Shlomo Avineri, *The Making of Modern Zionism: Intellectual Origins of the Jewish State* (New York: Basic Books, 1981).

Israel" cannot be regarded as necessary interpretation of biblical prophecy. Political support for Israel, which can be justified on historical and moral grounds, must not be allowed to disregard the historical and moral rights of the Palestinian people. This is particularly true in light of the Old Testament stipulations concerning non-Israelites living in Israel. And political support for Israel must never be allowed to disregard the loyalty that Christians owe other Christians, including the Palestinian Christians who are under pressure both from the Israeli government (as Palestinians) and from Palestinian Muslims (as Christians). At the same time we need to remind ourselves that misuse does not preclude proper use. A healthy support for the state of Israel, whether for historical reasons or based on a particular position regarding biblical prophecy, is possible, and indeed desirable.

REFLECTION QUESTIONS

1. What do Christian Zionists believe?

2. Where do they go wrong? What is selective exegesis?

3. What does the Old Testament say about Israel's possession of land?

4. What does the Old Testament say about Israel and non-Israelites living together?

5. What are the criteria by which Christians should evaluate the behavior of governments and their representatives?

Will a Third Temple Be Built in Jerusalem?

Some end-times writers assert that a third temple will be built in Jerusalem before Jesus returns. If this were merely their private opinion, we would not have to discuss this view in a book on what the Scriptures say about the end times. However, since they claim that the construction of a third temple is necessary, fulfilling biblical prophecy, it becomes imperative that we investigate the biblical foundation of this view.

Orthodox Jews and the Building of a Third Temple

Since the foundation of a Jewish state in 1948 and particularly since the unification of Jerusalem in the Six-Day War of June 1967, some orthodox Jews have been planning the building of a third temple.[1] This is not a new idea, however. Rashi (Rabbi Shlomo Yitzchaki, A.D. 1040–1105) believed that the third temple is already completed in heaven, waiting for God's permission to be brought down to earth. Maimonides (A.D. 1135–1204) believed that the third temple will be built by the Messiah, based on the measurements and dimensions that he describes for the future temple. Most orthodox authorities believe that the building of the third temple will occur in the time of the Messiah, at the hand of the Almighty. Rabbi Sofer (Rabbi Moses Schreiber, 1762–1839) argued, for example, that when Jews mourn the destruction of the (second) temple during the time between Tammuz and Av, they are preparing the city of Jerusalem and the temple (which are already being built in heaven) for its descent to earth. When the suffering and the mourning of the

---

1. The first temple, built by Solomon, was destroyed by the Babylonians in 587 B.C. The second temple, built by Zerubbabel and Ezra and rebuilt by Herod I, was destroyed by the Romans in A.D. 70.

Jewish people is complete, the heavenly temple will then be complete and allowed by God to be sent down.[2]

Maimonides's view is the minority position today among orthodox Jews. Several Jewish organizations, however, have the stated goal of working for the rebuilding of the (third) temple, among them the Temple Mount and Eretz Yisrael Faithful Movement[3] and the Temple Institute. The latter writes on their website, "The Temple Institute is dedicated to every aspect of the Holy Temple of Jerusalem, and the central role it fulfilled, and will once again fulfill, in the spiritual wellbeing of both Israel and all the nations of the world. The Institute's work touches upon the history of the Holy Temple's past, an understanding of the present day, and the Divine promise of Israel's future. The Institute's activities include education, research, and development. The Temple Institute's ultimate goal is to see Israel rebuild the Holy Temple on Mount Moriah in Jerusalem, in accord with the Biblical commandments."[4]

Christian End-Time "Specialists" and the Third Temple

Some Christian writers hold that prophecies associated with the temple in Matthew 24:15–22 and in 2 Thessalonians 2:1–12 were not completely fulfilled when the Romans destroyed the temple in A.D. 70. They believe that the events of A.D. 70 prefigured an end-time destruction of the temple. This view necessitates that a third temple will be built (so that there can be the "abomination of desolation").

Hal Lindsey claimed that the rebuilding of the temple at its old site is the event that will "completely set the stage for Israel's part in the last great act of her historical drama."[5] The fact that the Dome of the Rock, Islam's third holiest site, occupies the place where Israel's temple stood is an obstacle, which according to Lindsey is irrelevant, however, since "it is certain that the temple will be rebuilt. Prophecy demands it." The passages that are given as "proof" that prophecy "demands" the erection of a third temple are: (1) Jesus' prophecy in Matthew 24 (alluding to Daniel 9:27, which indicates that the desecration of the temple in the last period before Jesus' return will happen "at the midway point of God's last seven years of dealing with the Jewish people"); (2) Daniel's predictions of a coming prince (the Antichrist) from among the people who destroyed the second temple, making possible the reinstitution of

---

2. See Reb Chaim HaQoton, "Building the Third Holy Temple," *Reb Chaim HaQoton* (blog) http://rchaimqoton.blogspot.com/2007/07/building-third-holy-temple.html, posted July 17, 2007 (accessed June 2010).
3. See the website http://www.templemountfaithful.org/ (accessed June 2010).
4. See the website http://www.templeinstitute.org/main.htm (accessed June 2010).
5. Hal Lindsey, *The Late Great Planet Earth* (Grand Rapids: Zondervan, 1970), 55. For the quotations that follow in the text above, see ibid., 56, 57, 58. His prediction that the third temple would soon be built (ibid., 57) was evidently triggered by the capture of East Jerusalem in June 1967.

the sacrifices; and (3) Paul's prophecy in 2 Thessalonians 2:4. Lindsey regards the rebuilding of the temple "the most important sign of Jesus Christ's soon coming" and "the key piece of the jigsaw puzzle," asserting that "for all those who trust in Jesus Christ, it is a time of electrifying excitement." Since Lindsey believed that these things are in the process of happening, he predicted that "there will soon begin the construction of this Temple." This prediction was published in 1970. Forty years later—an entire generation—the construction of a third temple has still not been initiated.

Some suggest that a third temple will be built in the millennium.[6] The interpretation is based on passages such as Ezekiel 40–46 and not on passages linked with the appearance of the Antichrist. Others interpret Ezekiel as describing "not physical geography but spiritual realities."[7] Since a "millennial temple" plays no role in the end times, it is not discussed by authors who reckon with the building of a third temple before Jesus' second coming.

Jesus and the Temple

On one occasion Jesus declared, "I tell you, something greater than the temple is here. But if you had known what this means, 'I desire mercy and not sacrifice,' you would not have condemned the guiltless. For the Son of Man is lord of the sabbath" (Matt. 12:6–8). According to John 2:19, Jesus asserted on one occasion, "Destroy this temple, and in three days I will raise it up." John clarifies that Jesus was not speaking of the physical temple in Jerusalem, but "of the temple of his body" (v. 21), which was understood by the disciples only after Jesus' resurrection. Jesus' claim to be the (messianic) temple appears to obviate the continuing significance of the Jerusalem temple.

Jesus' view of the temple that stood in Jerusalem during his time is reflected most clearly by his demonstration in the temple (Matt. 21:12–13; Mark 11:15–18; Luke 19:45–47). He drove out the people who were buying and selling in the colonnaded halls surrounding the temple and then made a twofold proclamation. First, Jesus declared that the Jewish leadership had turned the temple into a "den of robbers," quoting Jeremiah 7:11 where the prophet, in the context, announces the destruction of the temple. Second, Jesus declared that the entire temple mount was to be "a house of prayer for all the nations" (Mark 11:17), including the areas (which were outside the Inner Enclosure) where the commercial activities had been located. He alluded to Isaiah 56:7 where the prophet emphasizes the universal significance of the presence of Yahweh in Israel. Jesus announces the destruction of the temple

---

6. Arnold G. Fruchtenbaum, *Israelology: The Missing Link in Systematic Theology* (Tustin, CA: Ariel Ministries, 1989), 810–13; Richard S. Hess, "The Future Written in the Past: The Old Testament and the Millennium," in *A Case for Historic Premillennialism*, ed. Craig L. Blomberg and Sung Wook Chung (Grand Rapids: Baker Academic, 2009), 31–34.
7. Daniel I. Block, *The Book of Ezekiel*, NICOT (Grand Rapids: Eerdmans, 1998), 2:505.

and declares "that the particularism of Jewish worship had come to an end and that the temple would soon to be replaced by an eschatological 'house of prayer.'"[8]

In Matthew 24:15–22, Jesus explicitly announces the destruction of the temple (see question 3) without predicting that the temple would be rebuilt in the future. The claim mentioned above, that the destruction of the temple in A.D. 70 did not completely fulfill Jesus' prediction of the temple's destruction, seems to be born out of a need to prove that a third temple needs to be built. Jesus' prophecy in Matthew 24:15–22 can indeed be seen as fulfilled in the events of A.D. 70. If this is interpreted as only a partial fulfillment, with the destruction of a (future) third temple still to come, it may be possible that the destruction of that third temple might also be a merely partial fulfillment.

Given Jesus' statements about the temple, it is not surprising that the Jewish leaders who wanted to eliminate Jesus believed that they could charge him with plotting the destruction of the temple (Matt. 26:61). This charge was serious. Anybody who announced that the major temple of a city or nation would be destroyed could be accused of a capital crime and be executed. It was only because the testimony of the witnesses who reported on Jesus' statements concerning the temple was inconsistent that this charge was dropped in Jesus' trial before the Sanhedrin.

Stephen and the Temple

Similar to the initial charges against Jesus, Stephen was accused of speaking blasphemous words against "Moses and God"—against "this holy place and the law"—when he explained what Jesus of Nazareth had said when he declared that he will "destroy this place and will change the customs that Moses handed on to us" (Acts 6:11, 13, 14).

In his speech, Stephen declared that God does not live in a temple made by human hands (Acts 7:48–49). He emphasizes that it is not he who speaks against God but the Jewish leaders who offend God by failing to understand God's transcendence of which the temple is only a sign. And they also fail to grasp the full extent of what God demands from them—which now includes, most critically, the acknowledgment of and faith in Jesus as the one who rules on David's throne at God's right hand, fulfilling God's promises for the last days (Acts 7:51–53).

Paul and the Temple

Paul does not dispute that the Jerusalem temple has some significance. When James, the leader of the church in Jerusalem, suggests that he should go

---

8. Andreas J. Köstenberger and P. T. O'Brien, *Salvation to the Ends of the Earth: A Biblical Theology of Mission*, NSBT 11 (Downers Grove, IL: InterVarsity Press, 2001), 78–79.

to the temple and purify himself by immersion in water, Paul complies (Acts 21:18–26).

Paul holds that the congregation of the followers of Jesus is a spiritual temple, built on the foundation that is the life, death, and resurrection of Jesus, Israel's Messiah (1 Cor. 3:16). He emphasizes that the Spirit of God dwells in this temple, which means that God himself is present. This explains why he calls this temple "God's temple" which is "holy" (1 Cor. 3:17). Paul calls the church "the temple of the living God" (2 Cor. 6:16) and connects Ezekiel's version of the covenant promise of the presence of God in the midst of Israel (Ezek. 37:27) to the church (2 Cor. 6:16–7:1). He explains to the Gentile Christians in the province of Asia that they are no longer "strangers and aliens" but "citizens with the saints and also members of the household of God, built upon the foundation of the apostles and prophets, with Christ Jesus himself as the cornerstone. In him the whole structure is joined together and grows into a holy temple in the Lord; in whom you also are built together spiritually into a dwelling place for God" (Eph. 2:19–22). When Paul argues for sexual purity, he declares that the individual believer's body is a "temple of the Holy Spirit" (1 Cor. 6:19). Important to note is the teaching that the church is messianic Israel (Rom. 9–11; Gal. 6:16).

2 Thessalonians 2:1–12

In 2 Thessalonians 2:3–4, Paul writes that Jesus' return cannot happen quite yet. He argues as follows: "Let no one deceive you in any way; for that day will not come unless the rebellion comes first and the lawless one is revealed, the one destined for destruction. He opposes and exalts himself above every so-called god or object of worship, so that he takes his seat in the temple of God, declaring himself to be God."

Paul announces that the Lawless One is obviously a pagan ruler who declares himself to be a god (note the allusion to Dan. 11:36; Ezek. 28:2). The self-deification of the Roman emperors was well known to the Thessalonian believers, who had seen coins in circulation that portrayed the emperor on one side accompanied by the word *theos* ("God"). Interpreted against the background of Daniel 9:26–27,[9] Paul is convinced that this Lawless One is empowered by Satan (2 Thess. 2:9). And he believes that "the mystery of lawlessness is already at work" (2:7), in the period before the appearance of the Lawless One.

Ten years before Paul wrote his letters to the Thessalonian Christians, the emperor Gaius Caligula ordered to have his statue set up in the temple in Jerusalem, an event that caused great alarm among the Jews and nearly

---

9. The "prince who is to come" will "make sacrifice and offering cease; and in their place shall be an abomination that desolates, until the decreed end is poured out upon the desolator" (Dan. 9:26–27).

led to a revolt in A.D. 39–40 in Judea.[10] Emperor Claudius was honored on coins minted in Philippi, close to Thessalonica, which displayed the image of Claudius and Augustus on one side, with the inscription DIVUS AUG ("divine Augustus"). In A.D. 44, the Jewish king Herod Agrippa accepted divine honors at games in Caesarea.[11] When Claudius died in A.D. 54, his successor Nero minted coins that announced the divine status of Claudius. It is thus likely that had Paul lived long enough, he would have seen the destruction of the Jerusalem temple by the Roman general (and later emperor) Titus in A.D. 70 "as a fulfillment of much of what he says" in 2 Thessalonians 2:1–12.[12] Some scholars who do not find this convincing suggest that the reference to the "temple" is used metaphorically and typologically: "Taking up a motif derived from Ezekiel and Daniel and given concrete illustration in previous desecrations of the Jewish temple, both actual and attempted, he has used this language to portray the character of the culminating manifestation of evil as an anti-theistic power which usurps the place of God in the world. No specific temple is in mind, but the motif of sitting in the temple and claiming to be God is used to express the opposition of evil to God."[13]

Paul links the appearance of Jesus with the destruction of the Lawless One (2 Thess. 2:8). The expression "and then" in the sentence "And then the lawless one will be revealed, whom the Lord Jesus will destroy with the breath of his mouth" is an emphatic way of saying "and not before."[14] It is only after the events of 2 Thessalonians 2:3–4 that the Lawless One will be revealed, which means that contrary to the Thessalonians' belief, the day of the Lord had not already arrived (2:2).[15] Perhaps Paul has brought two distinct events together: the judgment on Jerusalem that Jesus' had prophesied as an event that will take place before the end and the event of Jesus' return. The purpose of this

---

10. Cf. Philo, *Legatio ad Gaium*, 203–346.

11. Acts 12:21–23; Josephus, *Jewish Antiquities* 19.343–47.

12. Ben Witherington, *1 and 2 Thessalonians: A Socio-Rhetorical Commentary* (Grand Rapids: Eerdmans, 2006), 212; for the imperial cult mentioned above, see ibid., 218–19. Cf. F. F. Bruce, *1 and 2 Thessalonians*, WBC (Waco: Word, 1982), 168–69, 177. On the Antichrist, see questions 17–21.

13. I. Howard Marshall, *1 and 2 Thessalonians*, NCBC (Grand Rapids: Eerdmans, 1983), 191–92.

14. Gordon D. Fee, *The First and Second Letters to the Thessalonians*, NICNT (Grand Rapids: Eerdmans, 2009), 290. N. T. Wright suggests that "the day of the Lord" in 2 Thessalonians 2:2 does not refer to Jesus' return (*parousia*, a term not used here) but to God's awaited judgment on Jerusalem. Paul's statement in 2 Thessalonians 2:1 links the "coming of our Lord Jesus Christ" with "our being gathered to him" (NIV), which suggests that Paul does speak of Jesus' return ("Jerusalem in the New Testament," in *Jerusalem Past and Present in the Purposes of God*, rev. ed., ed. Peter W. L. Walker [Grand Rapids: Baker Academic, 1994], 53–78).

15. The person of the Lawless One will be discussed in question 18.

juxtaposition of distinct events was the argument "that the latter cannot take place until the former has occurred."[16]

Paul and his readers could not have thought of a (third) temple that would be built sometime in the future after the present (second) temple had been destroyed sometime in the future. End-time "specialists" who assume the building of a third temple have to assume the following sequence: destruction of the (second) temple ➞ building of a third temple ➞ appearance of the Lawless One ➞ self-deification of the Lawless One in the (third) temple. Paul, in 2 Thessalonians 2:1–12, does not mention the first two events, which means that the fourth event cannot plausibly have been thought to take place in a third temple. Paul and his readers could only have thought of the present (second) temple standing in Jerusalem. Paul's prophecy in 2 Thessalonians 2:1–12 does not speak of a third temple, nor does it make the assumption of the building of a third temple a necessity.

Finally, we should note that Paul's argument had two main goals. First, he wanted to convince the believers in Thessalonica that Jesus' return, while possibly imminent ("the mystery of lawlessness is already at work"), cannot happen yet, since the Lawless One, who would declare himself to be a god in the temple of God, had not yet appeared. Second, rather than wanting to provide a detailed timetable of the end times, he wanted to reassure the persecuted believers that God had not forgotten either them or their persecutors.[17]

Summary

Will a third temple be built? This is a possibility, although at present it is impossible to imagine how this could happen, given the political and religious situation in Jerusalem in particular and in the world at large. Orthodox Jews who want to build a third temple would be able to do so only if they could get the Israeli government to occupy the temple mount and either tear down the Dome of the Rock and build the third temple at the spot some believe was the location of Solomon's temple, or build the temple between the Dome of the Rock and the Al-Aqsa Mosque (as others suggest for the location of Solomon's temple). This scenario is not feasible politically, as the violent reaction of the Muslim world can only be imagined,[18] and as none of the (mostly secular) Israeli governments have any motivation to build a Jewish temple and renew the sacrificial cult.

---

16. Peter W. L. Walker, *Jesus and the Holy City: New Testament Perspectives on Jerusalem* (Grand Rapids: Eerdmans, 1996), 135n80.
17. Fee, *First and Second Letters to the Thessalonians*, 292.
18. Lindsey thinks that an earthquake could do the trick. While an earthquake could theoretically destroy the Dome of the Rock, it would not make the building of a Jewish temple automatically possible, since the Muslim world would rush to finance the rebuilding of the Dome (*Late Great Planet Earth*, 57).

Given the significance of Jesus as described in the New Testament, both for Jewish and Gentile believers, the building of a third temple would have no theological, salvific, or spiritual significance.[19] Believers in Jesus accept his word that "salvation is from the Jews" (John 4:22). And they are convinced that the hour has come when the true worshippers "worship the Father neither on this mountain [Garizim] nor in Jerusalem" but everywhere "in spirit and truth" (vv. 21, 23).

Will there be a new temple in the millennium? This is possible, given Ezekiel's prophecy of a temple, which has not been built. On the other hand, this is not certain given Jesus' assertion that he is God's temple, given Paul's assertion that the Jewish and Gentile church is God's holy temple, and given the teaching that the church is the messianic people of God.[20]

REFLECTION QUESTIONS

1. What is the basis for the belief that a third temple will be built?

2. What does Ezekiel say about a third temple?

3. What does Matthew 24:15–22 say about a third temple?

4. What does 2 Thessalonians 2:1–12 say about a third temple?

5. What is possible? What is certain?

---

19. On a biblical theology of the temple, see Gregory K. Beale, *The Temple and the Church's Mission: A Biblical Theology of the Dwelling Place of God*, NSBT 17 (Leicester: Apollos; Downers Grove, IL: InterVarsity Press, 2004).

20. Hess acknowledges that he "cannot easily harmonize the two streams of teaching in the New Testament. . . . If we cannot completely flatten out all the bumps in this picture, I will not worry. The future is a long time, and there is plenty of opportunity for God to demonstrate his presence in a purified and magnificent temple on this earth as well as in the expected glorious presence of the Father and the Son in the life of the world to come" ("Future Written in the Past," 35).

PART 2

The Return of Jesus Christ

Events before the Return of Jesus

What Is the "Abomination of Desolation" in Jesus' Prophecy?

The concept of a figure that opposes God's Anointed One is rooted in Old Testament and Jewish traditions that speak of two distinct figures.[1] One tradition describes a false prophet who opposes the "prophet like [Moses]" within the community of God's people who misleads the righteous with signs and wonders (see Deut. 18:18–22; ; Jer. 23:9–40; Ezek. 13:1–23). The other tradition describes a tyrannical ruler from outside the community who oppresses the righteous (Dan. 8:23–25; 11:2–45). The Jewish text *Testament of Moses* (first century A.D.) combines features of King Antiochus IV with traits of King Herod I (the Great), portraying a figure who would appear in the last days opposing God and his people, only to be destroyed by God. These traditions are connected with the expression "abomination of desolation" in Jesus' prophecy, which derives from Daniel's prophecy.

Daniel's Prophecy of the "Little Horn"

Daniel's vision in Daniel 11 prophesies events that scholars identify with developments beginning with the end of the reign of King Cyrus (530 B.C.), involving Alexander the Great (336–323 B.C.) and the military conflicts between "the southern king" (the Ptolemaic rulers in Egypt) and the "northern king" (the Seleucid rulers in Damascus and later in Antioch), focusing on the career of Antiochus IV (the "little horn"). Daniel's prophesy in Daniel 7:20–25; 8:8–12; 9:26–27 and especially in 11:21–45 is often linked with Antiochus IV, "his achievements, his intrigues, his campaigns, his unconscious fulfillment of Scripture, his dealings with a covenant people and their sanctuary, his god-like and god-defying assertiveness, his plunder, and his fall."[2]

---

1. The Greek term *antichristos* ("antichrist") means "adversary of the Messiah."
2. John E. Goldingay, *Daniel*, WBC 30 (Dallas: Word, 1987), 288.

Daniel 11:29–32 describes a person who comes to Jerusalem and plunders the temple, setting up "the abomination of desolation" (also Dan. 12:11 NASB). The expression "the abomination of desolation" (Matt. 24:15; cf. Mark 13:14 ESV; Greek, *to bdelygma tēs erēmōseōs*) renders the Hebrew expression *shiqquts shomem*, which means "an/the abomination that makes desolate." It is a derogatory pun from the Hebrew expression *ba'al shamayim*, a term that describes the Syrian god who was the counterpart of Zeus Olympius, in whose honor Antiochus had renamed the Jerusalem temple (2 Macc. 6:2). The term "abomination" (Hebrew, *shiqquts*) is used in the Old Testament in connection with pagan worship or idolatry, which defiles and pollutes the land.[3] The expression "came to symbolize an unspeakable affront to the sanctity of God's house and to God himself."[4]

Prototypes in Jewish History during the Second Temple Period

The understanding of the prophecies of Israel's and Judea's prophets was shaped by subsequent historical experiences. Of particular importance was the rule of the Seleucid (Syrian) king Antiochus IV Epiphanes (175–164 B.C.). His title "King Antiochus God Manifest" (Greek, *Theos Epiphanes*) expresses his claim to divine status. According to 1 Maccabees 1:54, the "abomination of desolation" (KJV) was set up on the altar in the Jerusalem temple on 15 Chislev of the year 145 (of the Seleucid Era, corresponding to December 167 B.C.). According to Josephus, the abomination was a pagan altar on which pigs were offered (*Ant.* 12.253). The description in Daniel 9:27 and 11:29–32 most likely also refers to the setting up of a pagan altar. Ten days later the first pagan sacrifices were offered on this altar: a pig was slaughtered, which was meant to deliberately offend the Jews. The temple was dedicated to Zeus Olympius. A cult statue of the god was placed in the temple, alongside statues of King Antiochus, whose birthday was to be celebrated by regular, monthly sacrifices.

The outrage of the Jewish people prompted Antiochus to follow a policy of extermination against the Jews in 168 B.C. Pagan altars were erected in other towns and villages in Judea, and the Jews were forced to sacrifice pigs to the pagan gods. Antiochus issued a decree in which he prohibited the celebration of the sabbath, Jewish festivals, and circumcision of newborn babies. In addition, the Holy Scriptures were to be confiscated. Faithful Jews—a minority—who refused were arrested, tortured, and killed, and women and children were sold into slavery.[5] The sons of Mattathias, a priest from Modein

---

3. E.g., see Deuteronomy 29:16[17]; 1 Kings 11:5, 7 (2x); 2 Kings 23:13 (2x), 24; Isaiah 66:3; Jeremiah 4:1; 7:30; Ezekiel 5:11.
4. Craig A. Evans, *Mark 8:27–16:20*, WBC 34B (Nashville: Thomas Nelson, 2001), 318.
5. Otto Mørkholm, "Antiochus IV," in *The Hellenistic Age*, ed. W. D. Davies and Louis Finkelstein, *The Cambridge History of Judaism*, vol. 2 (Cambridge: Cambridge University Press, 1989), 286–87.

near Jerusalem, organized an armed rebellion against the Syrians that eventually led to military victory and the rededication of the temple. In Daniel 12:11, the prophet states that "from the time that the regular burnt offering is taken away and the abomination that desolates is set up, there shall be one thousand two hundred ninety days."[6] This figure represents three-and-a-half lunar years, and "can be related to several sets of events between 168 and 164 B.C., terminating perhaps with the victories of Judas Maccabaeus and the rededication of the temple in Jerusalem."[7]

Jesus' Prophecy of False Prophets and False Messiahs

Jesus predicts the coming of false prophets (*pseudoprophētai*) and false messiahs (*pseudochristoi*) in his speech about the time until the end (Matt. 24:5, 24; Mark 13:5–6, 22; Luke 21:8). These imposters will performs signs and wonders and lead many people astray, if possible even the elect. They are mentioned in connection with the appearance of the "desolating sacrilege standing in the holy place" (Matt. 24:15; cf. Mark 13:14).[8]

The expression "the desolating sacrilege"—often translated as "abomination of desolation" (*to bdelygma tēs erēmōseōs*)—derives from the Greek text of Daniel 12:11 (the exact words are used there, see above) and Daniel 11:31 (also see Dan. 9:27). Jesus says that this abomination will be "standing where he must not" (Mark 13:14, author's translation). The masculine gender of the participle (*hestēkota*) translated "standing," which follows the neuter noun (*bdelygma*, "abomination") can suggest that the abomination is a statue, a pagan deity, or a deified man.[9] In Daniel 9:26–27, the masculine participles in the Greek text refer to Antiochus IV, who set up an abomination in the temple. Antiochus IV, the "little horn" of Daniel 8:8–12, became the "prototype" for the supreme opponent of God on earth. It should be noted, however, that these false prophets and false messiahs whom Jesus predicts do not demand worship, nor do they cause the suffering of the last days, in contrast to the "beast" of Revelation 13.

Some suggest that Jesus' prophecy was fulfilled in the attempt of emperor Gaius Caligula to place his image in the form of a statue in the Jerusalem temple.[10] The horror with which the Jews received the news of the emperor's

---

6. See the account in 1 Maccabees 1:54: "Now on the fifteenth day of Chislev, in the one hundred forty-fifth year [i.e., 167 B.C.] they erected a desolating sacrilege [Greek, *bdelygma erēmōseōs*] on the altar of burnt offering."

7. Goldingay, *Daniel*, 310.

8. Luke 21:20 speaks here of Jerusalem being surrounded by armies as a signal that the city's desolation is near.

9. The assertion by commentators that the masculine participle refers to a person is not necessary: a statue (for example, *ho kolossos)* or a male pagan deity can be referred to with a masculine term as well.

10. See Josephus, *Jewish Antiquities* 18.261, 271.

plans suggests that they would have regarded this action as an "abomination of desolation." Caligula, however, was assassinated in Rome before the Syrian governor Petronius was able to comply with his command.

Some suggest that Jesus' prophecy was fulfilled by the events in the summer of A.D. 70 when the Roman commander (and later emperor) Titus entered the temple after the occupation of the temple mount by Roman troops, before its destruction. Josephus relates that Titus and his generals walked into the temple and viewed "the holy place of the sanctuary and all that it contained," and that subsequently Roman troops "carried their standards into the temple court and, setting them up opposite the eastern gate, there sacrificed to them, and with rousing acclamations hailed Titus as imperator" (*J. W.* 6.260, 316). The main problem with this interpretation is the fact that Jesus advises his disciples to flee once they see the "abomination of desolation" standing in the temple. When Titus entered the temple and when the Roman standards were set up in the temple court, it was too late to flee. By that time the city was already destroyed, after having been surrounded by Roman troops for months.

A better suggestion is the desecration of the temple by Zealot militants, which preceded the destruction of Jerusalem. At the beginning of the war, in the winter of A.D. 67/68, Zealots occupied the temple mount and usurped the high priesthood.[11] Josephus, who was initially involved in the war as a general in the Jewish army, describes the Zealots' actions as a desecration of the holy courts of the temple, calling them "abominations."[12] The "abomination of desolation" refers to the revolutionary leaders such as Eleazar son of Simon, who occupied the temple mount and stained it with blood, or Phanias, the high priest whom the Zealots appointed despite the fact that he was not of high priestly descent.[13] The time of these events would have allowed the Christians to flee Jerusalem.

Summary

Jesus prophesied that before the end and his return, false prophets and false messianic pretenders would come, and that "the abomination of desolation" would be standing in the temple before its destruction. Some point out that Jesus' prophecy of the "abomination of desolation" standing in the temple was nearly fulfilled in the attempt of emperor Gaius Caligula, who insisted on receiving divine honors, to set up his image in the temple. Some argue that Jesus' prophecy was fulfilled in the occupation of the temple mount by the leaders of the Zealot movement who usurped the high priesthood. Some suggest that Jesus' prophecy was fulfilled when the Roman commander (and later emperor) Titus entered the temple, set up the Roman standards in the temple court complete with attendant sacrifices, and subsequently destroyed

---

11. Josephus, *Jewish War* 4.151–157; 5.5.
12. Ibid., 4.163; also see 4.182–183, 201, 388; 6.95.
13. Joel Marcus, *Mark*, AB 27B (New York: Doubleday/Yale University Press, 2009), 891.

the temple. Whatever the specific event, connecting "the abomination of desolation" with the events in A.D. 70 (and the destruction of Jerusalem and the temple) is the most plausible interpretation.

Some argue that the prophecy has not (yet) been fulfilled. If correct, this would mean one of three things: (1) Jesus' prophecy was never fulfilled, although some events could qualify as partial fulfillments. (2) Jesus' prophecy will be fulfilled in the future, in a third temple that will be built (note, however, that New Testament prophecy nowhere suggests that a third temple will be built; see question 16). (3) Jesus' prophecy will be fulfilled in the future when someone will appear who claims divine authority—not in a literal "temple" in which the "abomination of desolation" stands, but metaphorically in terms of his demand for absolute obedience.

Since Jesus himself does not know the time of his second coming (see question 4), Satan does not know the time either. This means one of two things for the concept of the Antichrist (also see questions 18 and 19). If the Antichrist is a figure of history, we would have to conclude that Satan has an evil person "ready" in every generation who would deceive and persecute, and that the devastating effects of his actions could manifest themselves very quickly. Jesus' repeated emphasis that he will come unexpectedly and suddenly suggests, however, that Christians will not be certain whether this man is indeed "the" Antichrist. Or, if the antichrist is a symbolic figure for the evil forces that set themselves up against God, disputing God's authority, ridiculing Christ, and persecuting Christians, then Jesus' second coming is not tied to the appearance of a particular evil person. After the destruction of Jerusalem in the first century, an event that fulfilled Jesus' one specific prediction, Jesus' return could take place in any generation, unexpectedly and suddenly.

REFLECTION QUESTIONS

1. What is a "false messiah"? What is a false prophet?

2. What is the Old Testament background of the expression "abomination of desolation"?

3. Why is Antiochus IV Epiphanes important?

4. How can "the abomination of desolation" be connected with events in the first century?

5. What could be a future "abomination of desolation"?

Who Is the "Lawless One" in Paul's Prophecy?

The person of the Antichrist has been connected with "the abomination of desolation" in Jesus' prophecy about the time until the end as well as with Paul's statements about a Lawless One who must appear before Jesus' return.

The Lawless One

Paul predicts that before Jesus' return "the Lawless One" (Greek, *ho anthrōpos tēs anomias,* "the man of lawlessness") will appear (2 Thess. 2:3). He will lead a rebellion (Greek, *apostasia*), which can refer either to a political rebellion, religious defection, or both, the last option being the most plausible in light of the context of Paul's statements in 2 Thessalonians 2:1–12.

He is called "the Lawless One" because he opposes God's law, which explains why he is described as "the one destined for destruction" (2:3). Since his appearance is described with the same term as Jesus appearance in 1:7 (noun *apokalypsis*; in 2:3 the verb *apokalyptō* is used), same term*is* (he can be viewed as in some sense a rival Messiah, the *antichristos* (a term that Paul does not use).[1] He is further described as "the one who opposes" (Greek, *ho antikeimenos*; 2:4), which has been explained as rendering the Hebrew term *shatan* ("adversary," also the title of Satan).[2]

The Lawless One "exalts himself above every so-called god or object of worship" (2 Thess. 2:4). He thinks that his importance is superior to the true and living God and every other so-called (pagan) god and that he deserves more worship than any other existing object of worship. This echoes the description in Daniel 11:36–37: "The king shall act as he pleases. He shall exalt

---

1. F. F. Bruce, *1 and 2 Thessalonians,* WBC (Waco: Word, 1982), 167.
2. See Zechariah 3:1, where the Greek translation (LXX) uses the verb *antikeisthai* for the Hebrew verb *shatan* ("to oppose").

himself and consider himself greater than any god, and shall speak horrendous things against the God of gods. He shall prosper until the period of wrath is completed, for what is determined shall be done. He shall pay no respect to the gods of his ancestors, or to the one beloved by women; he shall pay no respect to any other god, for he shall consider himself greater than all."

Paul adds that "he takes his seat in the temple of God, declaring himself to be God" (2 Thess. 2:4). The first part of the statement is most plausibly connected with the temple in Jerusalem (the definite article before "temple" suggests a particular temple), which was still standing when Paul wrote to the Thessalonian Christians. This interpretation links Paul's statement with Jesus' prophecy about the "abomination of desolation" standing in the temple. Paul's readers were familiar with emperor worship in which Roman emperors were accorded divine honors.

Paul's description of the Lawless One combines the two types of antimessiah figures of Second Temple Judaism: the figure of the false prophet, and the figure of the tyrant who opposes God. Paul appears to be thinking of a future pagan ruler who will recapitulate the blasphemy of Antiochus IV Epiphanes (see question 17) and who will be the supreme embodiment of evil which will appear at the end.

The Restrainer

Paul asserts that the Thessalonian believers know that something is currently restraining the Lawless One (2 Thess. 2:6). Since a restraining power is not mentioned anywhere else in the New Testament, this seems to be Paul's contribution to Christian thought regarding the end times. The problem for modern readers is that they do not know what the Thessalonian believers knew, and Paul's remarks are too cryptic to allow certainty. In 2 Thessalonians 2:6, he refers with a neuter expression to "what restrains" (*to katechōn*) while in 2:7 he uses the masculine expression "he who restrains" (*ho katechōn*). There are a variety of interpretations:

First, some suggest that the restraining power is the mission of the church, which needs to be completed before the end, and specifically the mission of Paul to the Gentiles.[3] There is no evidence, however, that Paul believed himself to be holding back the Lawless One.

Second, some suggest the presence of the church and the present influence of the Holy Spirit are the "restraining one." This is not convincing since Paul would surely have spoken of the church and of the Holy Spirit in more direct, clear terms. It is also difficult to see how the Holy Spirit would be removed before Jesus' return.

---

3. For this and the following suggestions, see Leon Morris, "Man of Lawlessness and Restraining Power," in *Dictionary of Paul and His Letters*, ed. Gerald F. Hawthorne, Ralph P. Martin, and Daniel G. Reid (Downers Grove, IL: InterVarsity Press, 1993), 592–94.

Third, some connect the Lawless One sitting in the temple with Jesus' prophecy about "the abomination of desolation" in the temple and the fall of Jerusalem. In this case, the restraining power is the Jewish state, while the restrainer is perhaps James, the leader of the Jerusalem church.[4] The appearance of the Lawless One is held back until the Jerusalem temple is destroyed, then the Roman emperors will persecute the church. It is difficult to see, however, how James could be restraining the evil forces of the Roman Empire.

Finally, many interpreters have concluded that Paul refers to the Roman Empire (*to katechōn*) personified in the emperor (*ho katechōn*). Thus, it has been suggested that "Paul viewed established government as imposing a salutary restraint on evil (Rom. 13:3, 4) . . . He knew that Roman rule would not last forever, and that its benevolent neutrality could not be counted on indefinitely, but in the present situation a welcome curb was placed on the forces of lawlessness."[5] This interpretation can be generalized in terms of the principle of order (in Paul's time the Roman state, in later times other governmental systems) and its personification in a particular ruler (in Paul's time the Roman emperor).[6]

The Fulfillment of Paul's Prophecy

When the temple was destroyed in A.D. 70, Titus did not take a seat in the Jerusalem temple declaring himself to be God. It is quite possible, however, that Paul, had he lived long enough, would have seen the occupation of the temple mount by the (later) pagan emperor claiming divine honors, his entrance into the temple, the offering of sacrifices to the Roman standards, and the subsequent destruction of the temple as a fulfillment of his prophecy.[7]

It is important to note that Paul believed that "the mystery of lawlessness is already at work" (2 Thess. 2:7). This suggests that he was not thinking of events in the distant future but of events already unfolding in the year A.D. 50 when he wrote to the believers in Thessalonica. Paul could have been thinking of emperor Gaius Caligula's attempt to set up a statue of himself in the Jerusalem temple only ten years earlier, an "abomination" that was avoided at the last moment but an event which demonstrated what could happen in the context of emperor worship in a Roman province.

If this interpretation is regarded as unconvincing, it does not follow that Paul's prophecy implies the building of a third temple (so that the Lawless

---

4. B. B. Warfield, "The Prophecies of St. Paul" [1886], in *Biblical and Theological Studies*, ed. Samuel G. Craig (Philadelphia: P&R, 1952), 463–502, 471–74.

5. Bruce, *1 and 2 Thessalonians*, 172. He adds that "one merit of the imperial interpretation . . . is that it accounts at one and the same time for the diplomatic allusiveness of the language and for the alternation between the neuter and masculine genders" (ibid., 188).

6. Morris, "Man of Lawlessness and Restraining Power," 593.

7. Ben Witherington, *1 and 2 Thessalonians: A Socio-Rhetorical Commentary* (Grand Rapids: Eerdmans, 2006), 212.

One has a temple to sit in; see question 16). It is possible to assume that while Paul speaks specifically of the Jerusalem temple, he means the reference metaphorically: a Lawless One will come and usurp the authority of God, demanding obedience and worship that is due to God alone.[8]

Summary

Paul reminds the believers in Thessalonica of matters related to the end times that he does not fully explain again in his letter. This makes certainty about what he means difficult. He describes a person who rebels against God's law, who thinks that he is superior to the true and living God, and who believes that he deserves to be worshipped. The appearance of this figure is delayed by a restraining power, which is why Jesus cannot return just yet. Paul may have predicted events that were fulfilled in connection with the destruction of the temple in Jerusalem in A.D. 70, but this is not certain. At the same time he does not seem to speak of a distant future but of a time that the Thessalonian believers may yet live through.

REFLECTION QUESTIONS

1. What does Paul say about the Lawless One?

2. How can the Lawless One in Paul's prophecy be connected with the "abomination of desolation" in Jesus' prophecy?

3. How has "the restraining power" been explained?

4. How can Paul's prophecy be linked with the events of A.D. 70?

5. How can Paul's prophecy be linked with a more distant future?

---

8. Bruce, *1 and 2 Thessalonians*, 169.

Who Is the Beast in John's Prophecy?

In several visions, John describes a Beast from the sea that is usually identified with the ultimate adversary of God, of Jesus Christ, and of God's people, and thus identified with the Antichrist (see question 20). The various descriptions have a rich Old Testament background, particularly in Daniel's prophecy of the four beasts. John's statements about the Beast can be summarized as follows in the table below:

THE BEAST FROM THE SEA		
REV.	DESCRIPTION	OT PARALLEL
	ORIGIN	
11:7	the Beast comes from the bottomless pit	Dan. 7:3 – fourth beast
13:1	Beast comes out of the sea	Job 40:25 – sea dragon Dan. 7:3–4 – four beasts come out of sea
	DESCRIPTION	
13:1	ten horns and seven heads	Dan. 7:7 – fourth beast has ten horns
	ten diadems on horns	Dan. 7:24 – fourth beast's ten horns: ten kings
	blasphemous names on heads	Dan. 7:8, 11 – horn with a mouth that boasts
13:2	like a leopard	Dan. 7:6 – third beast like a leopard
	feet like a bear's	Dan. 7:5 – second beast like a bear
	mouth like a lion's	Dan. 7:4 – first beast was like a lion
16:10	the Beast has a throne and a kingdom	

THE BEAST FROM THE SEA		
REV.	DESCRIPTION	OT PARALLEL
17:3	the Beast is scarlet	
	the Beast is full of blasphemous names	
	a woman sits on the Beast	
	the Beast has seven heads and ten horns	see Rev. 13:1 (description)
17:8	the Beast was, is not, and will come up from the bottomless pit	Dan. 7:3–4 – four beasts come up out of the sea
	the Beast is destined for destruction	Dan. 7:11, 18, 26 – the beast is judged, destroyed
	IDENTITY	
17:9	the seven heads are seven mountains	
17:9–10	the seven heads are seven kings of whom five have fallen, one is living, and the other is yet to come	Dan. 7:4–7, 17, 23 – the seven heads of the four beasts are seven kingdoms
	the seventh remains only a little while	
17:11	the Beast that was and is not is an eighth king who belongs to the seven	
17:12	the ten horns are ten kings	Dan. 7:7–8, 20, 24 – ten horns are ten kings
	they have not yet received a kingdom	
	EVENT	
13:2	the Beast receives from the dragon power, throne, authority	Dan. 7:6 – third beast receives authority to rule over the earth and persecute
13:3	one of its heads seemed to have received a death-blow	Gen. 3:15 – head of the serpent is struck
	its mortal wound was healed	
	the whole earth followed the Beast	
	they worshipped the Beast	Dan 7:8 – the horn's war against saints
14:10	the people who worship the Beast and its image and who receive the Beast's mark are judged by God	
16:2	the people who have the mark of the Beast are judged with foul and painful sores	Exod. 9:9–11 – the Exodus plague of sores

THE BEAST FROM THE SEA		
REV.	DESCRIPTION	OT PARALLEL
16:10	the kingdom of the Beast is plunged into darkness	Exod. 10:22 – the Exodus plague of darkness
17:8	the inhabitants of the earth are amazed when they see the Beast: because it was and is not and is to come	
17:12	the ten kings will receive authority for one hour together with the Beast	Dan. 4:16 – period during which God caused Nebuchadnezzar to become like a beast
17:13	they yield their power and authority to the Beast	
17:14	they will make war on the Lamb	
	the Lamb who is Lord of lords and King of kings will conquer them	Dan. 7:21 – the horn overpowers the saints
17:16	the ten horns and the Beast will hate the harlot	Ezek. 16:37–41 – God judges Israel who is a harlot
	the ten horns and the Beast will destroy the harlot	Ezek. 23:25–34, 47 – God judges Jerusalem (the harlot)
17:17	the ten horns will give their kingdom to the Beast until the words of God are fulfilled	
19:19–20	the Beast is captured together with the false prophet	Dan. 7:11 – the beast was slain
	the Beast is thrown into the lake of fire that burns with sulfur	Dan. 7:11 – the beast was thrown into fire
20:10	is tormented day and night forever and ever	
ACTION		
11:7	the Beast will make war against the two witnesses	Dan. 7:21 – wages war against the holy people
	conquers and kills the two witnesses	Dan. 7:21 – defeats the holy people
13:5	utters haughty and blasphemous words	Dan. 7:6–8 LXX – mouth speaking great things
	exercises authority for forty-two months	Dan. 7:25: persecution – a time, times, half a time

THE BEAST FROM THE SEA		
REV.	**DESCRIPTION**	**OT PARALLEL**
13:6	utters blasphemies against God's name	Dan. 7:8, 11, 20, 25 – the little horn of the fourth beast; see Dan. 11:32, 36
	utters blasphemies against those who dwell in heaven	Dan. 7:25 – fourth beast speaks against God, oppresses his holy people Dan. 8:10-13 – tyrant overthrew God's sanctuary
13:7	makes war on the saints	Dan. 8:10, 25; 11:36
	conquers the saints	Dan. 7:21 – the little horn defeated the holy people
	has authority over every tribe, people, language, and nation	Dan. 7:14 – authority was given to him
13:8	worshipped by all the inhabitants of the earth whose name is not written in the book of life	Dan. 7:14 – the nations of the earth served him Dan. 7:10 – in God's court books were opened
13:12	the Beast is worshipped because of the activity of the second beast (the false prophet)	
13:13	the second beast (false prophet) performs signs on behalf of the Beast	Exod. 4:17, 30; 10:12; 11:10 – ironic echo of the acts of Moses
13:14	the inhabitants of the earth make an image of the Beast that had been wounded by the sword yet lived	Isa. 27:1 – God brings the sword on the dragon
13:15	makes the image of the Beast speak	
	all who do not worship the image of the Beast are killed	Daniel 3 – Nebuchadnezzar kills all who do not worship the image
13:16	the mark of the Beast is put on the right hand or the forehead by the false prophet (14:9)	
13:17	no one will be allowed to buy or sell who does not have the mark of the Beast	
13:18	the number of the Beast is 666, which is the number of a person (15:2)	
16:13	spits out a foul spirit like a frog, a demonic spirit that deceives people regarding idol worship	Exod. 8:2–11 – the Exodus plague of frogs

THE BEAST FROM THE SEA		
REV.	**DESCRIPTION**	**OT PARALLEL**
16:14	assembles the kings of the whole world under the influence of demonic forces for battle	Zech. 13:2 LXX – false prophets and the unclean spirit active when the nations gather (see Zech. 12:3)
	prepares for battle on the great day of God Almighty	Joel 2:11; Zeph. 1:14 – great day of God, day on which God decisively judges the unrighteous
16:16	assembles the kings of the earth at Armageddon	Zech. 12:3–4; 14:2, 13–14 – God will gather the nations in Israel for the final war of history
19:19	gathers with the kings of the earth and their armies to make war against the rider on the white horse and his army	Ezekiel 39 – God's battle against Gog and Magog Ps. 2:2: the kings of the earth stood up and gathered against the Lord and his Anointed

Revelation 13 and Daniel 7

The description of the Beast coming up from the sea (Rev. 13:1) is based on Daniel 7:2–3, and the reference to ten horns is based in Daniel 7:7, 20 and 24. The seven heads of the Beast refer to Leviathan[1] and/or to the combined heads of the four beasts in Daniel 7 (the first three beast have one head each, while the fourth beast has four heads; Dan. 7:6). The blasphemous names of the Beast that John describes are connected with the "little horn" that comes up among the ten horns of Daniel's fourth beast and speaks blasphemy (Dan. 7:8).

John uses the prophecy of Daniel 7 in his description of the ultimate adversary of God and of his people. This is confirmed by a recurring threefold pattern in Daniel 7 and in Revelation 13: an agent arises; the agent is given power; the effect of the agent's acquisition of power is described.[2] In Daniel 7, four beasts rise from the sea (7:4–6); the beasts receive authorization (7:4, 6); the effect of the fourth beast's authorization is described (7:7–8). In Revelation 13, the beast steps forward (vv. 1–2); the beast receives authority from the dragon (v. 2, 4) and from God (v. 5, 7); the effect of the Beast's authorization is described (vv. 3–4, 6, 8). Many have observed that the so-called trinity of the dragon, the Beast from the sea, and the beast from the land is a parody of the trinity of the Father, the Son, and the Holy Spirit.

---

1. In ancient Near Eastern legends, the sea monster has seven heads.
2. See Gregory K. Beale, *The Book of Revelation: A Commentary on the Greek Text*, NIGTC (Grand Rapids: Eerdmans, 1999), 728.

John's reference to forty-two months during which the Beast was granted authority on earth (Rev. 13:5) is based on Daniel 7:25 (and Dan. 12:7). While Antiochus IV Epiphanes may have been the first fulfillment of Daniel's prophecy (see question 18), John saw Daniel's prophecy of the fourth beast and his little horn as fulfilled in the Beast, which he would have linked with Rome and its successors.

The reason John drew on Daniel's description can be explained by his concern to critique "the status quo of apostasy, compromise, and syncretism. The world system in which the Christians of Asia Minor lived was a Satanic parody of God's ordering of the world. The corrupt system is characterized by the blasphemy of rulers who claim deity and by the apostasy of so-called Christians acquiescing to the compromising demands of emperor worship and of the institutions of pagan society."[3]

The Beast as Sea Monster

In the Old Testament, the sea monster is an image for evil kingdoms whose rulers persecute God's people. For example, the pharaoh at the time of the Exodus is described as a sea dragon, as well as pharaohs of later historical periods.[4] The Dragon that John describes in Revelation 12:3-4 is the ultimate force behind the Beast from the sea in Revelation 13:1-10 and behind his sidekick, the beast from the earth (Rev. 13:11-17). The Sea Dragon is behind the earthly kingdoms that the Beast represents and controls. In Revelation 16:14 the Dragon, the Beast from the sea, and the beast from the earth (the false prophet) are described as demonic spirits who cause the "kings of the whole world" to assemble for battle against God.

The concept of two satanic beasts opposing God (in Revelation 13, the Beast from the sea and a beast from the earth) takes up Job 40-41 where we find a land beast (Behemoth), which will be killed by God with a sword, and a Sea Dragon (Leviathan), which conducts a war waged by his mouth. Job describes the defeat of the Dragon, the incarnation of evil, by God in the primordial past,[5] while implying a future battle in which the continued defiance of the defeated Dragon will be finally vanquished.

The Seven Heads of the Beast

The Beast from the sea described in Revelation 13:1 has ten horns and seven heads. This corresponds to the description of the beast in 17:3, which also has seven heads and ten horns. In 12:3 it is the Dragon (Satan, the Devil)

---

3. Ibid., 729.
4. Psalm 74:13-14; 89:10; Isaiah 30:7; 51:9; Ezekiel 29:3; 32:2-3; Daniel 7; Habakkuk 3:8-15.
5. According to ancient Jewish tradition, on the fifth day of creation God created Leviathan (a sea creature) and Behemoth (a land creature). After their rebellion against God, these two beasts become symbolic of the powers of evil who would be destroyed at the final judgment.

who has seven heads and ten horns. Note that in 17:3 the Beast possesses heads, while in 17:9 it is described as being heads. Correspondingly, in 17:3 the woman sits on the beast, while in 17:9 she sits on the heads = mountains = kings. The identification of the Beast with its heads suggests that John speaks of the (evil) authority that the Beast claims for himself.

The seven mountains are often identified with the seven hills of Rome:[6] John speaks of the blasphemous claims and the corrupting influence of the Roman Empire and the persecution that it inflicts upon the church. It is quite plausible that John's description reminded his readers of the topography of the city of Rome and, by extension, of the reality of the Roman Empire. At the same time, "mountains" often symbolize kingdoms in the Old Testament.[7]

Again, John's readers might be tempted to think of seven individual kingdoms in history or of seven kings. In view of the frequent figurative use of the number seven (in the Old Testament and particularly in John), symbolizing fullness or completeness, it is more plausible to interpret this description of the Beast having seven heads as representing "the oppressive power of world government throughout the ages, which arrogates to itself divine prerogatives and persecutes God's people when they do not submit to the evil state's false claims."[8] Just as the Dragon with seven heads and ten horns is active throughout the history of the world, so the Beast with seven heads and ten horns is active in the political, cultural, and religious systems of history that refuse to submit to the one true and living God and his Savior. This interpretation is confirmed by the fact that John regards the "antichrist," the adversary of God and his Messiah, not as a future figure but as a reality that is manifested in the false teachers of the church (1 John 2:18, 22; 4:4; 2 John 7; see question 20).

The Seven Kings

In Revelation 17:9, John identifies the seven heads of the Beast as seven kings. Horns are often images of power. In 17:10–11 he writes that of these seven kings "five have fallen, one is living, and the other has not yet come; and when he comes, he must remain only a little while. As for the beast that was and is not, it is an eighth but it belongs to the seven, and it goes to destruction." The identification of the seven kings with literal political rulers has been often attempted but is fraught with difficulties. Most suggestions identify the seven kings with Roman emperors.

If we begin with the first emperor, Julius Caesar, then Nero (A.D. 54–68) is the sixth emperor—who would have been living when John wrote. Dating the

---

6. The seven hills of Rome are the Aventine, Caelian, Capitoline, Equiline, Palatine, Quirinal, and Viminal.

7. See Isaiah 2:2; Jeremiah 51:25; Ezekiel 35:3; Daniel 2:35, 45.

8. Beale, *Book of Revelation*, 869.

composition of the book of Revelation during Nero is not impossible but unlikely. Most scholars date Revelation to around A.D. 95. Moreover, the fate of the seventh emperor and his successor is problematic: in the year after Nero's suicide, three emperors (Galba, Otho, and Vitellius) all ruled for very short periods. Some suggest that these three "interim" emperors should be omitted, which would take us to Vespasian as the seventh and Titus as the eighth emperor—both generals who led the war against the Jewish rebellion, with Titus destroying Jerusalem in A.D. 70. A major problem of the identification of Nero as the sixth king is the portrayal of the sixth king in Revelation 17:10–11 as less oppressive, which does not fit Nero. According to both Christians and pagan historians, Nero was infamously known as the greatest persecutor of the followers of Jesus in the first century.

If we begin with Augustus, the first emperor who claimed divine status (for Julius Caesar, his deceased predecessor), successors six through eight are the ill-fated Galba, Otho, and Vitellius, who are insignificant. Omitting these three takes us to Vespasian (A.D. 69–79) as the sixth king and to Titus and Domitian who followed him.

If we begin with Caligula, who has more antichrist characteristics than Caesar or Augustus, and if we omit Galba, Otho, and Vitellius, we have Domitian (A.D. 81–96) as the sixth king "who is." This identification coincides with the near-consensus view that John wrote the book of Revelation during the reign of Domitian. However, the question arises in what sense Nerva (A.D. 96–98) and Trajan (A.D. 98–117) as kings number seven and eight are in view in John's prophecy.

A general problem with this kind of identification is the description of the eighth king: if the seven kings represent seven political rulers, how can the eighth be one of the seven? Some see this as a reference to the *Nero Redivivus* legend (see question 20): Nero was emperor, than vanished, only to return.[9] While not impossible, this is unlikely.

The reference to an "eighth" after a "seventh" in Revelation 17:11 seems to introduce a figurative element. In early Jewish and early Christian texts, the eighth day is the day after the seven days of creation, the day in which the regular operation of the created world began. Also, in "graded numerical sayings" that we find in the Old Testament, two consecutive numbers are mentioned to indicate a reality that illustrates and represents, rather than makes a literal statement about a certain sequence.[10] The eighth head has the same evil nature as the seven that came before him, but "he is different from them in that he is

---

9. This view is already found in church father Victorinus's commentary on Revelation, written in the third century.
10. Proverbs 6:16: "There are six things that the LORD hates, seven that are an abomination to him." Micah 5:5: "If the Assyrians come into our land and tread upon our soil we will raise against them seven shepherds and eight installed as rulers." See Richard J. Bauckham, *The Climax of Prophecy: Studies on the Book of Revelation* (Edinburgh: T&T Clark, 1993), 405.

an even fuller embodiment of Satanic power and in that his reign concludes history."[11] John's point is that even this climax of evil political power is destined for destruction (Rev. 17:11).

Clearly there is symbolism present. John speaks not of seven kings pure and simple, but of seven heads. Since he had described the Dragon as having seven heads, and since he identified the Dragon with "the Devil and Satan, the deceiver of the whole world" (Rev. 12:9), it is plausible to see a symbolic meaning of the number seven in the reference to the seven heads of the Beast as well. The frequent use of the number seven in Revelation as a reference to "the divine arrangement and design of history and the cosmos"[12] confirms a symbolic interpretation. The seven heads, identified as seven kings, stand for the empires of the world, the systems of political rule and religious loyalties of human history that stand against God. We must not forget that John described the Lamb as having "seven horns" (Rev. 5:6), which is clearly figurative, speaking of the completeness of Jesus' power as a result of his death and resurrection.

John and his readers may have thought of Domitian as the (seventh) reigning emperor. The symbol of the number seven and the statement that when the seventh king comes, "he must remain only a little while" (Rev. 17:10) indicate John's belief that "the Roman tyranny was a temporary phenomenon about to be completed (in the seventh short-lived ruler) and would lead to the eschaton."[13]

The Ten Kings

In Revelation 17:12, John identifies the ten horns of the Beast as ten kings. This identification is taken from Daniel 7:24, which interprets the ten horns of the fourth beast (Dan. 7:7) as ten kings. These ten kings, "who have not yet received a kingdom, but they are to receive authority as kings for one hour, together with the beast" (Rev. 17:12), are sometimes identified with ten literal rulers of the ten Roman provinces. Others identify the ten kings with Roman client kings (such as existed, at various periods, in Adiabene, Armenia, Bosporus, Cappadocia, Commagene, Emesa, Judea, Galatia, Mauretania, Nabatea, Osrhoene, Paphlagonia, Pontus, and Thrace), some of which became Roman provinces in the first century.[14]

End-time "specialists" have suggested that the European Union is the fulfillment of John's statement.[15] The six founding nations in 1950 are Belgium, France, Germany, Italy, Luxembourg and the Netherlands. When Denmark,

---

11. Beale, *Book of Revelation*, 876.

12. David E. Aune, *Revelation,* WBC 52C (Dallas: Word, 1998), 3:948.

13. Grant R. Osborne, *Revelation*, BECNT (Grand Rapids: Baker Academic, 2002), 620.

14. See Fergus Millar, *The Roman Empire and Its Neighbours*, 2nd ed. (1981; repr., London: Duckworth, 1996).

15. Hal Lindsey, *The Late Great Planet Earth* (Grand Rapids: Zondervan, 1970), 88–97. He predicted that by around 1980 "Rome" (the "great harlot" of Revelation 17), will be revived in a ten-nation United States of Europe.

Ireland and the United Kingdom joined the European Union on January 1, 1973, raising the number of member states to nine, some believed that the last period of history was about to begin. The excitement increased when Greece became the tenth member in 1981—only to be deflated when Spain and Portugal joined in 1986, when Austria, Finland, and Sweden joined in 1995, when ten new countries (Cyprus, Czech Republic, Estonia, Hungary, Latvia, Lithuania, Malta, Poland, Slovakia and Slovenia) joined in 2004, and when Bulgaria and Romania joined in 2007. As of 2010, the European Union has twenty-seven member countries, a far cry from the "ten kings" of revelation.[16]

John's description of the ten kings suggests that he does not speak of ten literal rulers. John says that these ten kings have yet to appear: they receive their authority from a higher authority "together with the beast" (Rev. 17:12). This suggests that they receive their authority from the Dragon, that is, from Satan. The ten kings "are united in yielding their power and authority to the beast; they will make war on the Lamb, and the Lamb will conquer them, for he is Lord of lords and King of kings, and those with him are called and chosen and faithful" (17:13–14). These ten kings seem to be identical with "the kings of the earth" (17:18).[17]

The figure ten symbolizes perhaps the great power of these evil forces and "the multiplicity of sovereignties" that enhance the power of the Beast.[18] Their rule will only last "one hour" (17:12)—clearly a figurative expression for "a very brief period" after which they will be defeated by the Lamb. John contrasts these ten "kings" with the Lamb, Jesus, who is "Lord of lords and King of kings" and with "those with him" who are "called and chosen and faithful" (17:14). The "ten kings" are earthly agents of Satan, the evil forces through whom he hopes to defeat God and his Messiah and the people who belong to him. They are working toward this end throughout history and in the last period before the end.

Jesus' Victory

John's interpretation of the vision of the Beast with the seven heads and the ten horns in Revelation 17:8 is crucial. He describes the Beast as "it once was, now is not, and yet will come up" (NIV), which parodies the threefold description of God as "who is, and who was, and who is to come" (1:8; cf. 4:8;

---

16. See the EU official website http://europa.eu/index_en.htm (accessed June 2010).
17. Also see Revelation 16:14, 16; 17:2; 18:3, 9; 19:19. As "kings from the east" (16:12), they would have been seen as Parthians rulers coming from the east in a contemporary (first-century) literal reading.
18. Beale, *Book of Revelation*, 878. He refers to the introduction to the second Targum (Aramaic translation) of Esther, in which it is asserted that all of world history is ruled by only ten kings.

11:17; 16:5). The elements "is not" and "come up" parodies Jesus' death and resurrection.

The assertion that the Beast "is not" refers to the effects of Jesus' death and resurrection on the forces of evil. Jesus' death on the cross and his resurrection on the third day constituted the decisive victory over God's enemy. When he died on the cross, he ransomed for God "saints from every tribe and language and people and nation" and "made them to be a kingdom and priests serving our God, and they will reign on earth" (Rev. 5:9–10).

The assertion that the Beast "will come up" (NIV; or "is about to ascend") means that the evil forces seem to have recovered from their defeat. The Roman Empire, and all past and future empires, seem to be unaffected by Jesus' victory on the cross. They continue to prosper, their cultures and religions continue to defy God, and they continue to persecute the followers of Jesus.

The assertion that the Beast will "go to destruction" (17:8), the last element in the description of the "career" of the Beast, describes that one day on which Jesus will demonstrate the reality of his victory on the cross by destroying Satan's forces finally and completely when the end comes. When John says that the last king, the last manifestation of the forces of evil, remains "only a little while" (17:10) and that the ten kings have authority for only "one hour" (17:12), he underlines his conviction that the end is not far off. The end was imminent, it could come quickly. At the same time John recognizes that there is an undetermined time between the present and the future when the end comes (see 6:11; 12:12; 22:6–7, 12).[19]

Summary

John's description of the Beast depicts a figure inspired by Satan, the Dragon who also comes from the Abyss. The Beast mimics Jesus, the Lamb, whose death and resurrection signaled his defeat, seeking to maintain his influence over the earth dwellers. The Beast demands worship and loyalty from the inhabitants of the earth, using the kingdoms and rulers of the earth to exercise control. The seven kings and the ten kings that John associates with the seven heads and ten horns of the Beast could have been understood in the first century as depicting specific Roman emperors and their allies, or as depicting the political system and cultural and religious practices of the Roman Empire more generally. John's interpretive comments suggests that he understands the Beast as the political, cultural, religious, and economic systems that Satan uses in order to thwart God's purposes—to no avail, as God will destroy the forces of evil when the end comes. The connections that John establishes with Old Testament traditions and with his own statements about God the Almighty and about Jesus the Lamb confirm that he wants to

---

19. See Beale, *Book of Revelation*, 866, 871.

assure his readers that Jesus' victory at the cross and resurrection was decisive. Despite the continuing activity of Satan and his minions, God's victory at the end will come swiftly, ending the ability of Satan to influence history.

REFLECTION QUESTIONS

1. How does John describe the characteristics of the Beast?

2. What actions of the Beast does John describe?

3. What is the connection between John's description of the Beast from the sea and Daniel's prophecy of the appearance of four beasts?

4. What is the connection between the claims of the Beast and Jesus' death and resurrection?

5. What is John's purpose in writing about the Beast?

Who Is the Antichrist?

A recent dictionary on biblical prophecy begins the entry on "antichrist" with the statement, "surprisingly, the term *antichrist* (Greek, *antichristos*) is only used four times in the Bible."[1] The fact that the term *antichristos* or *antichrist* is found only four times in the New Testament (1 John 2:18, 22; 4:3; 2 John 7) is surprising only in a certain Christian culture where authors and "prophecy speakers" talk about the Antichrist in such a fashion that the unsuspecting Christian may get the impression that this totally evil man is mentioned on just about every page of the Bible. While the term *antichrist* is rare, the concept of a figure opposing God and God's people is more frequent in the Bible. Jesus' prophecy about the "abomination of desolation" (Mark 13:14 ESV) and Paul's prophecy of the Lawless One who takes a seat in the temple of God (2 Thess. 2:1–12) are examples that we have discussed in questions 17 and 18. Here we want to investigate what John (the only New Testament author to use this term) means when he uses the term *antichrist*.

John's Statements about Antichrists in His Letters

In 1 John 2:18, the apostle reminds his readers that they have "heard that antichrist [Greek, *antichristos*] is coming." This prophecy about which they had been instructed has been fulfilled: "now many antichrists [*antichristoi polloi*] have come." And this proves that "it is the last hour." The antichrists are people who deny that Jesus the man was the divine Messiah who has come in the flesh: "Who is the liar but the one who denies that Jesus is the Christ [the Messiah]? This is the antichrist, the one who denies the Father and the Son" (2:22). Similarly, he asserts in 2 John 7, "many deceivers have gone out into the world, those who do not confess that Jesus Christ has come in the flesh; any such person is the deceiver and the antichrist!"

---

1. J. Daniel Hays, J. Scott Duvall, and C. Marvin Pate, *Dictionary of Biblical Prophecy and End Times* (Grand Rapids: Zondervan, 2007), 31.

For John, the prediction of a coming Antichrist is fulfilled in the activity of false teachers in the church. In 1 John 4:3, the apostles declares that "every spirit that does not confess Jesus is not from God. And this is the spirit of the antichrist, of which you have heard that it is coming; and now it is already in the world." Some conclude from the expression "the spirit of the antichrist" that John regards the false teachers of his time as precursors of the final Antichrist who will be active at the time of Jesus' return.[2] While possible, this is not what John actually says but an interpretation made in light of the book of Revelation. Like Paul, John does not speak of events in the distant future but of events that are unfolding before his eyes.

The Antichrist in Revelation 13

The Beast from the sea in Revelation 13 (see question 19) is sometimes identified with an individual Antichrist, a specific human being who will appear during the last stage of world history. This interpretation can be found in the earliest church fathers.[3] The view that the Antichrist will be an individual is supported by the consideration that since he is a counterpart to Jesus Christ, who is a person, he must be a person also.

Others identify the antichrist with a (religious and political) system inspired by evil forces that spread false teaching and oppose God, the Messiah, and God's people. This interpretation can be found in the New Testament (1 John 2:18, 22; 4:3; 2 John 7) and in the earliest church fathers as well.[4]

These two interpretations are not incompatible: the adversary of the Messiah (in Greek, *antichristos*) can be both a religious and political *system* that spreads false teaching and persecutes God's people and a religious and/or political *leader* who, as the incarnation of the forces of evil, opposes God and his people.

John combines the characteristics of all four beasts in Daniel 7 in order to underline the fierceness of the Beast described in Revelation 13. The Dragon and the Beast represent the empires of the world of the past, the present, and the future. This also emerges from the fact that the Old Testament uses the image of the sea monster for successive evil kingdoms spanning hundreds of years (see question 19). As satanic evil manifested itself in the kingdoms of Egypt, Assyria, Babylon, Persia, and Greece, John's readers in the first century would have identified the Beast with Rome and with the emperor as Rome's incarnation. Later Jewish writings regularly identify the fourth beast of Daniel 7 with Rome, which was also described as "Edom" and "Babylon."[5] Indeed,

2. Grant R. Osborne, *Revelation*, BECNT (Grand Rapids: Baker Academic, 2002), 493.
3. *Didache* 16; Justin, *Dialogue with Trypho* 32; Irenaeus, *Against Heresies* 5.25–30.
4. Polycarp, *To the Philippians* 7; Tertullian, *Against Marcion* 5.16.
5. See, e.g., *Midrash Rabbah* Genesis 44.17; 76.6; *b. Avodah Zarah* 2b. For Edom and Babylon, see *Sibylline Oracles* 5.137–161.

"this system of evil will continue so to manifest itself in yet future kingdoms of the world, and has ability to manifest itself as well in economic, social, and religious structures on earth."[6]

The emergence of the Beast from the "sea," which is the "abyss," describes his origins in the dark realm of evil. The seven heads and the ten horns underline the completeness of the oppressive power of the Antichrist and the completeness of the effect of this power upon the world. The crowns speak of the Beast's claims to royal, universal sovereignty, in opposition to Jesus, who is the true "King of kings and Lord of lords" wearing many crowns (Rev. 19:12, 16). The blasphemies that are written on the Beast's head speak of his claims to earthly kingship, in opposition to Jesus' kingship, and of his claims to divine status, in opposition to Jesus' divine sonship. The power that drives the Beast's rule is satanically inspired: the Antichrist denies the authority of the true God and the salvation of Jesus the true King.

The Beast receives a wound, leading to the Beast's death (Rev. 13:3).[7] The wound of the Beast was fatal. However, as a result of the power of the Dragon (Devil) who continues to be active through the beast from the earth (the false prophet), the death wound of the Beast was healed (vv. 3, 14). Satan parodies Jesus' passion, death, and resurrection, in order to cover up the fact that he has been vanquished and that his authority has been removed.

The Beast and the Emperor Nero

Many commentators identify the Beast of Revelation with the emperor Nero (A.D. 54–68), for two main reasons. First, Nero was the incarnation of a system whose rulers claimed divine status, made public on coins and in the emperor cult that was celebrated in the provinces. Also, he instigated a long series of political murders that culminated in the shocking murder of his mother, Agrippina. As a result of these murders, and his tendency to absolutism and his self-indulgent personality, Nero was sometimes called a beast, for example, by Marcus Aurelius.[8] Apollonius of Tyana relates how Philostratus, a first-century philosopher, who visited Rome during the reign of Nero, described the emperor as a beast:

---

6. Gregory K. Beale, *The Book of Revelation: A Commentary on the Greek Text*, NIGTC (Grand Rapids: Eerdmans, 1999), 686.

7. Most English translations of Revelation 13:3 (emphasis added) are misleading, rendering the expression *hōs esphagmenēn* as "*seemed* to have received a death-blow" (NRSV), "*seemed* to have had a fatal wound" (NIV; similarly RSV, ESV), "*as if* it had been slain" (NASB), "*appeared* to have been killed" (NET). The comparative particle *hōs* does not express a condition. The genitive expression *hē plēgē tou thanatou* in the second part of 13:3, often translated as "mortal wound," is epexegetical (or descriptive): the "wound" involved "death," which means that the Beast died as the result of a wound inflicted by a sword (13:14).

8. Miriam T. Griffin, *Nero: The End of a Dynasty* (1984; repr., New York: Routledge, 2000), 210. Also see Richard J. Bauckham, *The Climax of Prophecy: Studies on the Book of Revelation* (Edinburgh: T&T Clark, 1993), 407–23.

In my travels, which have been wider than ever man yet accomplished, I
have seen many, many wild beasts of Arabia and India; but this beast, which
is commonly called a Tyrant, I know not how many heads it has, nor if it
be crooked of claw, and armed with horrible fangs. However they say it is
a civil beast and inhabits the midst of cities; but to this extent it is more
savage than the beasts of mountain and of forest, that whereas lions and
panthers can sometimes by flattery be tarried and change their disposition, stroking and petting this beast does but instigate it to surpass itself in
ferocity and devour at large. And of wild beasts you cannot say that they
were ever known to eat their own mothers, but Nero has gorged himself on
this diet.[9]

Since the Jewish war against Roman rule broke out during Nero's reign
in A.D. 66, he could be held responsible for the destruction of the temple and
Jerusalem. He was the first emperor to persecute the church, killing Peter and
Paul.

Second, the fate and legend of Nero have some similarities with John's description of the Beast's fatal wound that was subsequently healed. After being
deposed by the Senate, Nero killed himself by plunging a sword into his throat
on June 9, A.D. 68. Confusion surrounding his death, fueled in part by the fact
that it was unclear who had actually seen his corpse, led to rumors that he
was still alive (this is called the *Nero Redux* or *Nero Redivivus* legend). At least
three impostors appeared in Greece and in Asia who looked and spoke like
Nero and claimed to be Nero (in A.D. 69, 80, and 88).[10] Furthermore, in the
fifth Sibylline oracle (which dates from the reign of emperor Hadrian, A.D.
117–138), Nero is portrayed returning to power. Moreover, he is described as
opposing the Jews during the time after his return, causing a war of destruction. Having conquered the entire empire, he will attack Jerusalem. But the
oracle predicts that he will be defeated by God, who will send the messianic
king against him. His defeat is followed by the final judgment.[11] After Nero's
death, a year of civil war with three emperors (Galba, Otho, and Vitellius)
followed. Vespasian, who became emperor in A.D. 69, was able to consolidate
the power of the Roman Empire, which could be interpreted in terms of the
recovery of the Roman dragon.

It is thus possible that John saw Nero as an Antichrist.[12] Like other emperors, he claimed divine status; he persecuted the Christians; he was killed by
sword; he was rumored to be still alive. This does not mean that John would

---

9. Philostratus, *Vita Apollonii* 4.38.
10. See Tacitus, *Historiae* 1.2.1; 2.8–9; Dio Casssius 63.9.3; 66.19.3; Suetonius, *Nero* 57.2. On
    the false Neros see Griffin, *Nero*, 214–15; Bauckham, *Climax of Prophecy*, 407–31.
11. *Sibylline Oracles* 5.106–110, 150–151, 365. See Bauckham, *Climax of Prophecy*, 416–18.
12. Note the discussion of the figure 666 in question 21 with regard to Nero.

have identified Nero as *the* final Antichrist (which he clearly was not: the end did not come in the first century). John might have seen Nero as one antichrist in a series of *antichristoi*, a series that includes the false teachers mentioned in his letters. He could hardly have seen Nero as the final Antichrist, since Nero committed suicide in A.D. 68, while John wrote the book of Revelation probably between A.D. 80 and 90.

The Beast and Satanic Evil

The parallels between the description of the Beast in Revelation 13 and the description of Jesus the Messiah in the book of Revelation make it plausible to assume that the Beast is meant to be seen as the God's grand adversary.[13] The fatal wound that the Beast receives on the head can be taken to reflect the promise of Genesis 3:15 ("I will put enmity between you and the woman, and between your offspring and hers; he will strike your head, and you will strike his heel"). The passive voice of the verb in Revelation 13:3 ("one of its heads *had received* a death blow") can be interpreted as a divine passive: it was God who administered a fatal wound. John can be read to mean that the Beast has been mortally wounded as the result of Jesus' death and resurrection, as fulfillment of Genesis 3:15 and as the initial fulfillment of Isaiah 27:1 (see the allusions to this passage in Rev. 12:3, 9, 17).

Jesus has won the decisive victory over the Devil at the cross. The fact that the Devil and the Beast continue to exist does not mean that their defeat has been reversed: even though Satan and his forces of evil continue to have influence in the world, they have irreversibly lost the authority to accuse Jesus' followers and condemn them to eternal damnation (Rev. 12:7–12).

The Actions of Antichrist

The Beast's evil actions, after his defeat and his pseudo-resurrection, are described in Revelation 13:4–8. The Beast manages to win the allegiance and praise of the inhabitants of the earth. He attempts to mimic God's incomparability, claiming to have unsurpassed dignity and power. His authority is exercised mostly through speech, which is blasphemous: he exalts himself above God by claiming to be God. He persecutes God's people, Jesus' followers, so much so that he can "overcome" them, which means that Christians are

---

13. Beale lists the following parallels: both Jesus and the Beast have a sword, have followers who have their names written on their foreheads (13:16–14:1), have horns (5:6; 13:1, 11), are slain (5:6; 13:3, 8), rise to new life and are given new authority, have authority over "every tribe and language and people and nation" (5:9; cf. 7:9; 13:7; 17:12, 15), and receive worldwide worship (5:8–14; 13:4, 8). Beale concludes that "these parallels between Christ and the beast are closer than any extrabiblical parallels to the beast. They show that the beast is set up as the supreme enemy of Christ and his people. The only figure who fits the description of the beast is the devil himself, as he repeatedly works through his chosen agents throughout history" (*Book of Revelation*, 691).

dying as martyrs. His influence reaches every class or group of people ("every tribe") through the entire earth ("every people and language and nation"). The only exception to his influence is the people "whose name has not been written from the foundation of the world in the book of life of the Lamb that was slaughtered"—the followers of Jesus whose names have been recorded in God's census record are assured of salvation. The followers of the Beast reject the true "Lamb who was slain" and worship the Beast "who was slain"(RSV, NIV). This is the reason why their names are not written in the book of life of the Lamb. The Beast, together with the false prophet, seeks to validate his authority through signs and wonders, which may include pseudo-magical tricks and demonic activity.

Refusal to participate in the worship of the Beast will bring suffering upon the followers of the Lamb. Many of them are killed because they refuse to publicly express their loyalty to the Beast (Rev. 13:15; on the "mark" of the beast, see question 23). All Christians suffer, as the state imposes economic measures against them (vv. 16–17). The refusal to participate in the imperial cult or to sacrifice to the deities worshipped by one of the local or provincial guilds and associations could very quickly lead to ostracism, discrimination, and economic hardship (the guilds controlled who could trade).

The Goals and End of Antichrist

This description indicates that the Beast has primarily religious goals. This is confirmed by the fact that he is closely associated with the beast from the earth, the false prophet (Rev. 13:11–17; 16:13; 19:20; 20:10). The Beast from the sea speaks blasphemous words against God, while the beast from the earth makes the first Beast's claims sound plausible, convincing the people to worship the Beast, who is inspired by the Dragon, that is, Satan.

The context of idolatry is also evident in the fact that John alludes to the Old Testament story of Shadrach, Meshach, and Abednego's refusal to bow down to the statute that was the image of king Nebuchadnezzar (Rev. 13:15; see Daniel 3). John encourages his Christian readers to remain faithful even in the face of arrest and certain death. The reference to the "image of the beast" that people are required to worship may allude to "the establishment of the provincial cult of Domitian at Ephesus, with its colossal cult statue."[14]

---

14. Simon R. F. Price, *Rituals and Power: The Roman Imperial Cult in Asia Minor* (Oxford: Oxford University Press, 1984), 712. Emperor Domitian granted Ephesus the right to establish the third provincial cult in the province of Asia in A.D. 89/90. In the "cult of the Sebastoi," the emperors Vespasian, Titus, and Domitian were venerated. Thirteen inscriptions were discovered that are connected with the establishment of this cult. See Steven Friesen, *Twice Neokoros: Ephesus, Asia, and the Cult of the Flavian Imperial Family* (Leiden: Brill, 1993), 29–49; also Steven J. Friesen, *Imperial Cults and the Apocalypse of John: Reading Revelation in the Ruins* (Oxford: Oxford University Press, 2001). Friesen clarifies that the

Increasingly, Christians came under pressure to participate in festivals connected with the imperial cult.

The rule of the Beast comes to an end when Jesus returns to earth and wins the last battle against the forces of evil (Rev. 19:11–21). He will be captured together with the false prophet and thrown into the lake of fire (19:19–20; 20:10).

The Antichrist and Rome, and Other Identifications

If we interpret the Beast as a corporate entity—the evil forces of the world system that oppose God and his Messiah—the main goal of the Beast's actions is total integration of the people into the idolatrous institutions of the state. As far as the church is concerned this means that the Antichrist, empowered by the false prophet, seeks to bring Christians to compromise with the institutions of state and culture. The latter was indeed the teaching of the Nicolaitans, false apostles teaching advice as that of Balaam and "Jezebel"—people who were active in the churches in Ephesus, Smyrna, Pergamum, and Thyatira (Rev. 2:2, 6, 10, 14–15, 20–23). These evil actions of the Beast are not limited to a time of tribulation in the distant future (from John's vantage point). They describe the entire period in history from Jesus' death and resurrection to his second coming at the end. Jesus' death and resurrection brought about the Devil's defeat, and his second coming will mean the final and complete elimination of the Devil.[15] Gregory the Great (bishop of Rome in A.D. 590–604) held that while Antichrist is a future enemy of the church, he is present in the hypocrisy and pride of Christians. John Wycliffe (1324–1384) believed that the papacy was the Antichrist, as did the Reformers, including Luther and Calvin.[16]

If we interpret the Beast as an individual, John's readers would have thought of Nero and/or other emperors who demanded that the citizens worship the deceased emperors as divine and who persecuted Christians because they refused to do so. In later periods, Christians identified the Antichrist with a host of figures, both historical and contemporary. Joachim of Fiore (A.D. 1135–1202) saw individuals such as Herod, Nero, Constantius, Muhammad, and Saladin as antichrists. He believed that the final, greatest Antichrist was already born and present in the world. Around A.D. 1210, the Amalricians in Paris believed that the pope was the Antichrist, the prelates his members, and that Rome was Babylon. Pope Gregory IX claimed in a letter (June 21, 1239) that the German emperor Friedrich II was the Beast arising

---

colossal statue, parts of which have been discovered in Ephesus, was not that of Domitian (A.D. 81–96) but of his immediate predecessor, Titus (A.D. 79–81).

15. This is confirmed by the reference to the forty-two months, which is based on Daniel 7:25, in Revelation 12:6, 14.

16. Bernhard McGinn, *Antichrist: Two Thousand Years of the Human Fascination with Evil* (San Francisco: HarperCollins, 1994), 80–83, 182, 202–3, 212–13.

from the sea, while Friedrich's publicists declared that Pope Innocent IV was the Antichrist. Jean de Roquetaillade (1310–1365) believed that the German emperor Ludwig of Bavaria was the Antichrist. Oswald J. Smith regarded Benito Mussolini in 1927 as a candidate for the Antichrist. Finally, since the increase in the writings of end-time "specialists" in the 1970s, a whole host of contemporary figures have been identified as the Antichrist.[17]

Few would doubt that a political or religious system can have anti-Christian goals and policies. The identifications of specific figures of history with the Antichrist, understood as an individual, have not yet been successful—history has continued beyond the lifetime of the people so identified. The diversity of these identifications and the regular need to abandon such identifications does not give much hope that if John indeed described a future historical figure, Christians would agree about a "candidate" whose identity would then be confirmed by the second coming of Jesus. More important than such speculations is John's concern to encourage the followers of Jesus to remain faithful in their commitment to Jesus as Israel's crucified and risen Messiah in the face of discrimination, suffering, arrest, and even death. This concern should be ours as well.

Summary

In Revelation 13, John describes the incarnation of evil, a figure inspired by Satan who opposes Jesus Christ and who seeks to usurp his place among the inhabitants of the earth as an object of worship and loyalty. He parodies Jesus' death and resurrection in order to hide the fact that he has lost the battle against God. He deceives people with false teaching and seeks to validate his claims to divine authority with signs and wonders. He persecutes Christians who refuse to acknowledge him through economic discrimination and death. He will be defeated when Jesus returns.

There are reasons to regard John's description of the Beast from the sea as prophecy of a future historical figure, patterned on "prototypes" in Jewish history and in contemporary history. And there are reasons to understand John's description of the Beast from the sea as a symbolic portrayal of the world system—past, present, and future, from Jesus' first coming to Jesus' second coming—that idolizes human authority and refuses to acknowledge the authority of the one true and living God and his Messiah. It is important to note that while John describes the evil activities of the Beast, he also emphasizes with the phrase "it was given" or "it was allowed" that the Beast can do what he does only because God allows it. God always remains firmly in control.

---

17. Oswald J. Smith, *Is the Antichrist at Hand?* (Toronto: Tabernacle, 1926). See McGinn, *Antichrist,* 135–42, 153–54, 175, 256, 260.

REFLECTION QUESTIONS

1. Whom does John identify as the Antichrist in his letters?

2. What does the Beast do to the inhabitants of the earth?

3. What does the Beast do to the followers of Jesus?

4. In what sense is the Beast the Antichrist?

5. What lesson can be learned by the identification of the Beast with numerous historical figures as the Antichrist?

What Is the Meaning of the Number 666?

John ends his description of the Beast from the sea in Revelation 13 with the statement, "this calls for wisdom: let anyone with understanding calculate the number of the beast, for it is the number of a person. Its number is six hundred sixty-six" (Rev. 13:18). The number 666 that John gives in the last comment has been interpreted in essentially two ways: the number indicates the name of a person who is the Beast (Antichrist), or the number indicates in a symbolic manner the character of the Beast.

Identification of the Number with a Name

The identification of the name of a person with a number was possible in antiquity because numbers were represented by letters of the Hebrew, Greek, or Latin alphabet. The representation of a personal name as a number is generally called *gematria* (a Hebrew loan word from Greek, *geōmetria*). The relevant Greek term is *isopsēphos* ("equal in numerical value").

This practice was very common. Worshipers of pagan gods sometimes referred to the god by using the numerical value of his or her name. For example, Jupiter was known as 717. In difficult and dangerous political settings, people wrote their opinions about an emperor "encoded" in numbers on walls, afraid to speak their mind openly. Suetonius relates several such graffiti in Greek and in Latin. One reads as follows: "A calculation new. Nero his mother slew."[1] The first word in this sentence, translated as "a calculation new" (Greek, *neopsēphon*), based on the verb *psēphizō* ("count"; with pebbles, *psēphos*) signals to the reader to detect the fact that the numerical

---

1. Suetonius, *Nero* 39; see Suetonius, *Lives of the Caesars*, trans. J. C. Rolfe, Loeb Classical Library (1913; repr., Cambridge: Harvard University Press, 1998), 3:152 with n. (a).

value of the name Nero (Greek, *Nerōn*), which is 1005,[2] is the same number as the numerical value of the following sentence. In other words, this graffito affirmed that the rumor was correct that Nero indeed killed his mother, Agrippina. In Pompeii, the city that was destroyed in A.D. 79 as the result of the eruption of Mount Vesuvius, the following graffito was discovered on a wall: "I love her whose number is 545 [Greek, ΦΜΕ]."[3] The man responsible for this graffito evidently had an affair with a married woman, for which, had it become public, he would have been punished. But he still wanted to publicly confess his affection and assumed that his lover would understand that it was her name written on the wall. Since the numerical riddle could "encode" the first name, the family name, the nickname, or a combination of these, all resulting in different numbers, the woman would have to know that 545 was "her" number. No one in the city would be able to identify from the number 545 the person whose number was written on the wall. Many names yielded the numerical value of 545. Even names that did not have a value of 545 could be written in such a manner that the number 545 would emerge since the orthography of names was not fixed.

In Jewish exegesis, *gematria* was known as an exegetical tool, formulated as the twenty-ninth of the thirty-two hermeneutical rules. One rabbinic tradition regarding the name of the Messiah asserted that his name would be Menahem ("the Comforter," see Lam. 1:16). In the argument for this assertion, the rabbis pointed out that the name Menahem (written with the four Hebrew letters mem, nun, khet, mem) has the same numerical value, which is 138, as the word "branch" (the three Hebrew letters tsade, mem, khet), which is given in Zechariah 3:8 and 6:12 as the title of the Davidic Messiah. In another example from the Jewish and Christian *Sibylline Oracles*, the authors included a prophecy about world leaders from Alexander the Great to Hadrian, including eleven emperors from Julius Caesar to Vespasian for which no names but only the numerical value of the first letter of their name is given (*Sib. Or.* 5:12–51).

A majority of interpreters understand John's statement in Revelation 13:18 as a numerical riddle that can be solved with *gematria*. This means that one needs to find a name or a word that consists of letters whose numerical value is 666. Such attempts will yield different results depending on which alphabet one uses. Since John and many of the Christians in the province of Asia were Jewish Christians who spoke Aramaic and read the Hebrew Scriptures, the basis for the *gematria* could be the Hebrew alphabet.

---

2. Nu: 50, epsilon: 5, rho: 100, omega: 800, nu: 50.
3. Phi: 500, mu: 40, epsilon: 5. See Adolf Deissmann, *Light from the Ancient East Illustrated by Recently Discovered Texts of the Graeco-Roman World* (1927; repr., Grand Rapids: Eerdmans, 1980), 276.

Since John writes in Greek and since all the Christians in Asia Minor spoke Greek, the number riddle could likewise be based on the Greek alphabet. The following table lists the suggested identifications of the number 666 derived from the numerical value of the letters of the Greek alphabet.

INTERPRETATIONS OF THE NUMBER 666		
GREEK NAME	TRANSLITERATED GREEK	REFERENT
ευανθας	Euanthas[4]	"the one who blossoms beautifully," the god Dionysos (Irenaeus, *Haer.* 50.30.3)
λατεινος	Lateinos[5]	"the Latins," Roman Empire (Irenaeus)
τειταν	teitan[6]	"titans" who rebelled against the gods (Irenaeus)
	teitan	emperor Titus (A.D. 79–81) who destroyed Jerusalem
	teitan	the Flavian emperors (Vespasian and his sons Titus and Domitian)
	teitan	a third Titus, identified with Domitian (A.D. 81–96)
Γαιος Καισαρ	Gaios Kaisar[7]	emperor Gaius Caligula (A.D. 37–41)
Α ΚΑΙ ΔΟΜΕΤ ΣΕΒ ΓΕ	A Kai Domet Seb Ge[8]	Autocrator Caesar Domitian Sebastus (Augustus) Germanicus
ΔΚΛΧVI, DKLXVI[9]		emperor Domitian, in the sixteenth year of his reign

---

4. Epsilon: 5, upsilon: 400, alpha: 1, nu: 50, theta: 9, alpha: 1, sigma: 200.
5. Lambda: 30, alpha: 1, tau: 300, epsilon: 5, iota: 10, nu: 50, omicron: 70, sigma: 200.
6. Tau: 300, epsilon: 5, iota: 10, tau: 300, alpha: 1, nu: 50.
7. Gamma: 3, alpha: 1, iota: 10, omicron: 70, sigma: 200, kappa: 20, alpha: 1, iota: 10, sigma: 200, alpha: 1, rho: 100 = 616 (this is the number that Codex Ephraemi gives in the text instead of the number 666).
8. Abbreviated title: A(utokratōr) Kai(sar) Domet(ianos) Seb(astos) Ge(rmanikos).
9. Delta Kappa Lamba, for D(omitianus) C(aesar) L(ykabantos) (the last term refers to the "year"), and the Roman numeral XVI—"in the 16th year of his reign." The phrase "Domitianus Caesar" is not attested as a title of Domitian.
10. Kappa: 20, alpha: 1, iota: 10, sigma: 200, alpha: 1, rho: 100, theta: 9, epsilon: 5, omicron: 70, sigma: 200 (yields 616, which some regard as the original reading of the Greek text).

INTERPRETATIONS OF THE NUMBER 666		
GREEK NAME	TRANSLITERATED GREEK	REFERENT
Μ. Νεπουα	M. Nepoua	emperor Nerva (A.D. 96–98)
ουλπιος	Oulpios	emperor Trajan (A.D. 98–117)
Μαρκυς Αυρελιυς	Markus Aurelius	emperor Marcus Aurelius (A.D. 270–275)
αντενος	Antenos	"opponent" (Victorinus, third century)
γενσερικος	Genserikos (Genserich)	king of the Goths who conquered Rome in A.D. 455
λαμπετις	Lampetis	daughter of the sun god (Andrew of Caesarea, sixth century)
παλαιβασκανος	Palaibaskanos	"old sorcerer" (Andrew of Caesarea, sixth century)
βενεδικτος	Benediktos	blue bastard (Andrew of Caesarea, sixth century)
κακος όδηγος	Kakos hodēgos	"evil leader" (Andrew of Caesarea, sixth century)
αληθης βλαβερος	Alēthēs blaberos	"truly evil" (Andrew of Caesarea, sixth century)
αμνος αδικος	Amnos adikos	"unjust lamb" (Andrew of Caesarea, sixth century)
αρνουνη	Arnounē	"the one who denies" or "apostate" (Primasius, sixth century)
δαμνατυς	Damnatus	"the condemned" (Beatus, eighth century)
αντιχριστυς	Antichristus	"antichrist" (Beatus, eighth century)
ιταλικα εκκλησια	Italika ekklēsia	"the Italian church" (the Roman Catholic church)
ή λετανα βασιλεια	Hē letana basileia	"the Latin kingdom" (Rome; Clemens second/third century)
παπεισκος	Papeiskos	"the pope"
καισαρ θεος	Kaisar Theos[10]	title "Caesar is god"
Μαομετις	Maometis	Mohammed

INTERPRETATIONS OF THE NUMBER 666		
GREEK NAME	TRANSLITERATED GREEK	REFERENT
Λουθερανα	*Loutherana*	Luther
σαξονειος	*Saxoneios*	the Saxon (Luther was from Saxony)
Ναβοναπαρτι	*Nabonaplarti*	Napoleon Bonaparte (Tolstoy)

Since John lived and wrote during the Roman Empire, the Latin alphabet could be used (although not all letters of the Latin alphabet had numerical equivalents).

Diocles Augustus	emperor Diocletian (A.D. 284–305)
Julian Apostata	emperor Julian (A.D. 361–363), who attempted to restore paganism
Vicarius filii De	title of the pope (Adventists)
Ellen Gould	Adventist prophetess

The introductory statement in Revelation 13:18 ("Let anyone with understanding calculate the number of the beast"), and the way in which the *gematria* of personal names works suggest that the number and the name that it represents was not a secret riddle for John's readers. He appeals to the wisdom and understanding of his readers, which suggests that at least some of them did know who the number represented. This in turn may suggest that John did not calculate the number 666 himself but found it in Jewish or Jewish-Christian tradition. This would point to the use of the Hebrew alphabet as the basis for the calculation. Thus most commentators assume that the Hebrew alphabet has to be used in order to see which personal name John identified with the number 666.

נרון קסר	*NRWN QSR* or *Neron Caesar*[11]	"Nero Caesar," emperor Nero (A.D. 54–68)
תריון	*TRYWN* or *Terion*[12]	"the beast"
קסר רומית	*QSR RWMYT* or *Caesar Romith*	"Caesar [emperor] of Rome"

---

11. Nun: 50, resh: 200, vav: 6, nun: 50, qof: 100, samek: 60, resh: 200.
12. The Greek term *thērion* written in Hebrew; tav: 400, resh: 200, yod: 10, vav 6, nun: 50.

There are several reasons why the identification of the number 666 with Nero is plausible. First, in an Aramaic document discovered at Wadi Murabba'at (near Qumran), the name and title of Nero is transliterated as *QSR NRWN* ("Neron Caesar"), derived from the Greek form of the name, with the combined numerical value of 666.[13]

Second, Nero was the first emperor to take action against Christians, killing many of them in the most horrible manner, among them Peter and Paul. It would have been natural for John to regard Nero as a manifestation of the Beast that he described in Revelation 13 (as one of a series of antichrists, among them the false teachers that he mentions in his letters).[14]

Third, Nero was designated as a "beast" (Greek, *thērion*) by several Greek authors.[15] It is probably not a coincidence that the numerical value of *Neron Caesar* is the same as the numerical value of *Beast*, which can be achieved if the Greek term meaning "beast" (*thērion*) is transcribed into Hebrew.[16] John states in Revelation 13:18 that the number of the beast (666) is *also* the number of a person (666), challenging his readers to "calculate [*psēphisatō*] the number of the beast," using a verb that suggests using the method of isopsephism.[17] Using the method of isopsephism, John indicates that the numerical value of Nero's name has a meaning. The *gematria* emphasizes not only that Nero is the Beast: it *demonstrates* that he is the Beast. The numerical value of Nero's name identifies him as the one who is the fulfillment (or one of the fulfillments) of the Beast in Daniel's prophecy.

An interpretation of a different sort was suggested by Johann Albrecht Bengel (1687–1752), a pietistic scholar renowned for his biblical commentaries. He argued that 666 refers not to a name but to years. By combining Revelation 13:18 with 13:5, he concluded that 666 years are the equivalent of 42 months, which means that a "prophetic month" equaled 15 6/7 years (666 divided by 42). He believed that the period of the time, times, and half a time (a total of 777 7/9 years) had begun in the year A.D. 1058 when the pope won independence from the Roman emperor. By adding 777 7/9 to 1058, he

---

13. Pierre Benoit, Jozef T. Milik, and Roland de Vaux, *Les grottes de Murabba'ât*, Discoveries in the Judean Desert 2 (Oxford: Clarendon Press, 1961), 100–104; see David E. Aune, *Revelation*, WBC 52B (Dallas: Word, 1998), 2:770.
14. This conclusion is accepted by many interpreters. For a critique, see Gregory K. Beale, *The Book of Revelation: A Commentary on the Greek Text*, NIGTC (Grand Rapids: Eerdmans, 1999), 719–20.
15. Philostratus, *Vita Apollonii* 4.38; *Sibylline Oracles* 5.343; 8.157.
16. The procedure of transcribing a Greek word into Hebrew is found in *3 Baruch* 4:3–7 and 4:10; *3 Baruch* is a Jewish apocalyptic text that was written at the same time or slightly later than the book of Revelation.
17. Isopsephism is the method by which a connection between two different words is established by means of demonstrating that the numerical value of the words is the same (the words are then *isopsēpha*).

arrived at the figure of June 18, 1836, as the date for Jesus' second coming and the beginning of the millennium.[18]

Symbolic Explanations

The interpretation of the number 666 as an identification of Nero with Daniel's fourth beast, and thus as an antichrist who fights against God and his Messiah and against the people of the Messiah, can be combined with a symbolic explanation. Some have suggested that the significance of the number 666 is to be seen in the fact that 666, the number of the Beast, does not reach 777, the figure of divine perfection. The number 666—six repeated three times—is intended as a contrast with the divine sevens used in other passages in the book of Revelation and thus "indicates the completeness of sinful incompleteness found in the beast. The beast epitomizes imperfection, while appearing to achieve divine perfection."[19] Some see a contrast with 888, the numerical value of the name "Jesus" (*Iēsous*) in Greek.[20] The difference between 666 and 888 reveals the difference between Satan's agent and God's Messiah: "the Antichrist of Satan falls as far short of being the true deliverer of mankind as the Christ of God exceeds all the hopes of man for a redeemer."[21]

Summary

The number 666 is mentioned in Revelation 13:18 as the "number of a person," which is also "the number of the beast." If the method of *gematria* is employed, the number 666 is interpreted as the numerical equivalent of the

---

18. See William Baird, *History of New Testament Research*, vol. 1: *From Deism to Tübingen* (Minneapolis: Fortress, 1992), 79. Note that Bernhard McGinn misunderstands Bengel's scheme, assuming that Bengel expected the arrival of the Antichrist for 1836 (*Antichrist: Two Thousand Years of the Human Fascination with Evil* [San Francisco: HarperCollins, 1994], 236).
19. Beale, *Book of Revelation*, 722. Thus already Irenaeus, *Against Heresies* 5.29–30.
20. Iota: 10, eta: 8, sigma: 200, omicron: 70, upsilon: 400, sigma: 200. The figure 888 is mentioned in *Sibylline Oracles* 1:324.
21. G. R. Beasley-Murray, *The Book of Revelation*, NCBC (1974; repr., Grand Rapids: Eerdmans, 1981), 221. Another reason why John may have used the number 666 is the significance of this number in Pythagorean mathematics, which conceived of numbers as corresponding to geometrical figures (see Richard J. Bauckham, *The Climax of Prophecy: Studies on the Book of Revelation* [Edinburgh: T&T Clark, 1993], 390–407). The number 666 is the double triangle of 8: it is triangle of the number 36 (i.e., $1 + 2 + 3 \ldots + 36 = 666$), and the number 36 is both the triangle of 8 ($1 + 2 + 3 \ldots + 8 = 36$) and the square of 6 (i.e., $6 \times 6 = 36$). In Revelation 17:11, the Beast is specifically designated as "the eighth" (a triangular number has the symbolic value of the last integer used to calculate it). Numbers that are the triangle of a number that is both triangular and square are extremely rare: the next such number after 666 is 750,925 (the triangle of 1225). John thus uses triangular numbers for the beast (666) and for those who worship the beast. These are the people who are marked with the number of the beast's name on the right hand or on the forehead (Rev. 13:16–17). In contrast, John uses square numbers for the saints (144,000).

name of a person. The results of efforts to find such a name vary depending on the choice of the Greek, Hebrew, or Latin alphabet as the basis for the calculation. Since many names yield the numerical value of 666, since names and titles can be combined (and abbreviated) in many different ways, and since there was no fixed orthography of personal names in antiquity, it has to be assumed that John's readers knew the individual to whom he was referring. John refers, perhaps, to a tradition known to some of his readers regarding the person associated with the number 666. The emperor Nero is the best candidate for such an identification, not least because the numerical value for the Greek term for "beast" is also 666. Since John describes the false Christian prophets who put congregations at risk as "antichrist," it is possible that he regarded "Nero the Beast" as a fulfillment of Daniel's prophecy regarding evil forces who oppose God, claiming to have divine authority and persecuting God's people.

It is also possible to interpret the number 666 symbolically, pointing to the Antichrist's failure to achieve divine perfection: the number 666 signifies "complete incompleteness" in comparison with 777, the number of the "complete completeness" of divine perfection.

Due to the endless possibilities of calculating the numerical value of personal names, it is impossible to identify a particular person on the basis of the number 666. This is confirmed by the numerous interpretations of the number 666.

REFLECTION QUESTIONS

1. What is *gematria*?

2. What names have been suggested with the numerical value of 666?

3. Why is the identification of 666 with the emperor Nero more plausible than other suggestions?

4. Does the symbolic interpretation of the number 666 make sense?

5. Why is it impossible to use the number 666 to determine the identity of the Antichrist?

Who Is the False Prophet?

John describes a false prophet who is inspired by Satan and who forces the inhabitants of the earth to worship the Antichrist. Described as the beast from the earth in Revelation 13, he forms an unholy trinity together with the Dragon and the Beast from the sea. As is the case with the beast from the earth, this figure can be interpreted in terms of first-century realities, as a symbolic depiction of a universal reality, and as a prophecy of future events.

The False Prophet

The false prophet, the second beast in Revelation 13, is consistently linked with the first beast. John describes him as follows (Rev. 16:13–14; 13:11–17; 19:20; 20:10), summarized in the table below.

THE FALSE PROPHET		
ORIGIN	13:11	is a beast that comes out of the earth
DESCRIPTION	13:11	two horns like a lamb; speaks like a dragon
ACTION	13:12	exercises all the authority of the first Beast on its behalf makes the earth and its inhabitants worship the first Beast
	13:13	performs great signs, including fire coming down from heaven
	13:14	deceives the inhabitants of the earth through the signs it performs on behalf of the Beast (cf. 19:20) tells the inhabitants of the earth to make an image for the Beast that had been killed but came back to life

ACTION	14:15	gives breath to the image of the Beast so that the image could speak causes all people who refuse to worship the image of the Beast to be killed
	14:16	causes all people to be marked on the right hand or the forehead with the mark of the Beast
	14:17	prevents all people who do not have the mark of the Beast from buying or selling anything
	16:14	spits out a foul spirit like a frog, a demonic spirit that deceives people about idol worship helps to assemble the kings of the earth for the final battle
EVENT	19:20	is captured together with the Beast is thrown into the like of fire that burns with sulfur
	20:20	will be tormented day and night forever and ever

The Description of the False Prophet

John describes the false prophet as "rising out of the earth" (Rev. 13:11).[1] While the first beast that arose from the sea echoed the four beasts of Daniel 7, the second beast that ascended from the earth echoes the four kingdoms of Daniel 7:17. Since Daniel 7:17 interpreted the four beasts as four kingdoms, John's two beasts are intimately connected. It is a "beast" (Greek, *thērion*) like the Devil (Dragon) and the Antichrist (the Beast). This evil trinity parodies the true God: "As Christ received authority from the Father (Matt. 11:27), so Antichrist receives authority from the Dragon (Rev. 13:4), and as the Holy Spirit glorifies Christ (John 16:14), so the false prophet glorifies the Antichrist (Rev. 13:12)."[2]

The second beast, like the first Beast, parodies Jesus, the Lamb with seven horns (Rev. 5:6): it has "two horns like a lamb" (13:11). While the seven horns of the messianic Lamb symbolized the fullness of his strength as conquering Messiah, the two horns of the counterfeit lamb mimic the two witnesses who are the two lampstands and the two olive trees (Rev. 11:3–4) and the two horns of the evil ruler mentioned in Daniel 7:7 and 8:3 (where the Medo-Persian Empire is described in its opposition to God). The second beast "spoke like a dragon" (Rev. 13:11): like the first beast, it is the agent of the Devil, speaking with his full authority.

Actions of the False Prophet

The activities of the beast from the earth are firmly linked with the authority of the Beast from the sea. The authority that the first Beast had received

---

1. The identification between the second beast of Revelation with the false prophet is made in 16:13; 19:20; 20:10.
2. Robert H. Mounce, *The Book of Revelation*, rev. ed. (Grand Rapids: Eerdmans, 1998), 255.

from the Dragon (13:2) is given by the first Beast to the second beast (v. 12). The authority of the false prophet is satanic and anti-Christian authority. The primary task of the second beast is to cause the inhabitants of the earth to worship the first Beast (vv. 12, 15). This worship is expressed in a mark that people accept on the right hand or the forehead (v. 16). This "mark of the beast" allows the false prophet to prohibit anybody who has not accepted the mark and who is not worshipping the Beast to buy or sell anything.

The fact that the false prophet is successful in bringing the inhabitants of the earth to worship the Beast and his image is described as deception (Rev. 13:14). The repetition of the description of the false prophet as deceiver (16:14; 19:20; 20:10) underlines that deception is the main work of this evil reality. This deception is achieved by great signs that the false prophet performs (13:13).

The False Prophet and the Imperial Cult

John's readers would have identified the description of the second beast with the reality of their own day. We must remember that John does not write about distant events. Rather, he writes a letter to Christian believers in which he conveys a prophecy whose content he was not to "seal up" or hide with cryptic, unintelligible descriptions (Rev. 22:10). John's readers understood what John wrote. Since Jesus did not come back in the first century, and since John describes the entire period between Jesus' first and second coming, his prophecy applies to past centuries as well as to the present and future.

John's readers would have connected the description of the beast from the sea with the false prophets and false messiahs. Jesus had prophesied that "false messiahs and false prophets will appear and produce great signs and omens, to lead astray, if possible, even the elect" (Matt. 24:24; see Matt. 24:5, 11). And Jesus had warned about false prophets who are ravenous wolves in sheep's clothing (Matt. 7:15). John had spoken of antichrists who promulgate false teaching (1 John 2:18, 22; 4:3; 2 John 7), and he had warned the churches about false prophets (Rev. 2:2, 14–15, 20–24).[3]

John's readers would have linked the Beast from the sea with the Roman imperial system. In particular, they would have connected the sea-Beast with the imperial priests who were active in the emperor cult ensuring the "integrity" and the expansion of the worship of the deceased emperors. If John wrote the book of Revelation around A.D. 95, his readers would have been confronted with the claims of Domitian (A.D. 81–96) who called

---

3. The authority of the second beast is modeled on the authority of the apostles: the ministry and authority of the second beast succeeds his master (Rev. 13:12; cf. Acts 1:1–11); the beast's attempt to persuade people to worship his master is linked with his master's resurrection (Rev. 13:12, 14; cf. Acts 2:22–47); the second beast performs miraculous signs as manifestation and validation of his authority (Rev. 13:13; cf. Acts 2:43; 6:12; 15:12). See Gregory K. Beale, *The Book of Revelation: A Commentary on the Greek Text*, NIGTC (Grand Rapids: Eerdmans, 1999), 709.

himself *dominus et deus* ("Lord and God"). The false teachers of the church (the Nicolaitans of Rev. 2 whose activity is compared with that of Jezebel and Balaam) taught and encouraged compromise with the institutions of the Roman Empire, particularly those requiring participation in the emperor cult.

These prophets pose as spokesmen for truth, but instead they promulgate lies. They bring down fire from heaven (Rev. 13:13), a description that implies claims to divine authorization.[4] But they do so on behalf of the Beast (not the Lamb) and with the purpose that people worship the Beast (not the Lamb), as Revelation 13:12–14 shows. The true Christian prophets are portrayed in Revelation 11:5 as speaking as "fire pours from their mouth and consumes their foes." The fire in 11:5 is clearly symbolic (John does not speak of literal fire breathers!): the missionaries and teachers of the church speak God's true word that convicts and judges sinners. In contrast, the false prophets appear to speak the truth but in reality promote the values and falsehoods of the Devil. They advocate continued integration and participation in the institutions of pagan society, arguing that compromise with pagan religious practices is harmless and without consequences for the salvation of believers in Jesus.

The command of the second beast to perform idolatry alludes to the pressure on the people living in the province of Asia to give homage to the image of the emperor in the imperial temples. At the end of the first century, these temples existed in all the large cities of the province. Gaius Caligula promoted the erection of temples dedicated to his own divine genius. In A.D. 89/90, Ephesus was granted the right to establish the third provincial cult in the province of Asia, in a temple dedicated to the worship of Vespasian and his sons Titus (A.D. 79–81) and Domitian (A.D. 81–96).[5] Titus had destroyed Jerusalem and Domitian claimed to be a god. The colossal statue that was erected, parts of which have been discovered in Ephesus, was an image of Titus (not Domitian, as has been previously assumed). John portrays the veneration of the emperor as satanic deception, diverting the worship that is due only to the true and living God to human beings who are not divine, good, or eternal.

The local enthusiasm for the imperial cult put the Christians under increasing pressure. John emphasizes that when the willingness to worship the emperor becomes a matter of life and death (Rev. 13:15), Christians have to be faithful and refuse to worship the image of a human being, even if it means

---

4. Note Elijah's miracle of fire in 1 Kings 18:38. The motif of fire falling from heaven, often understood as lightning, refers to divine judgment in Revelation 20:9 (also in Luke 9:54), as often in the Old Testament (Gen. 19:24; 2 Kings 1:10, 12, 14; Job 1:16; Ps. 11:6; Lam. 1:13; Ezek. 38:22; 39:6).

5. Steven Friesen, *Twice Neokoros: Ephesus, Asia, and the Cult of the Flavian Imperial Family* (Leiden: Brill, 1993), 29–49. Also see Steven J. Friesen, *Imperial Cults and the Apocalypse of John: Reading Revelation in the Ruins* (Oxford: Oxford University Press, 2001).

certain death. They have to persevere as Daniel's friends persevered even in the face of being thrown into the fiery furnace (Rev. 13:14–15 echoes Daniel 3). Particularly those Christians who held government positions, who served in the military, or who had to prove their loyalty to the emperor, were in danger.[6] In Pergamon, Antipas had been executed because he remained steadfast and faithful (Rev. 2:13), and other Christians also died for their faith (Rev. 6:9, 11; 12:11; 20:4).

The false prophet not only fosters false worship, he also enforces economic sanctions against those who refuse to participate (Rev. 13:16–17). While the role of the false prophet is described as primarily religious, his enforcement of political and economic loyalty makes him an agent of the secular state (on the "mark of the beast" see question 23).

The False Prophet and False Prophets

Many have connected John's description of the false prophet with false prophets in the church. There have been countless false teachers in the church, as even a quick perusal of any book on church history will demonstrate. There are thousands of movements that call themselves "Christian" but that in effect draw people away from exclusive loyalty to the one true and living God and from Jesus, the Savior of the world. If we do not see it already, we need to realize that secularism and consumerism demand just as much "worship" in terms of loyalty and obedience to the rules and values of "the game" as the Roman emperors demanded in the first century.

Summary

Whether there will be a final false prophet during the last period of history is unclear. If the "final" Antichrist is regarded as a specific figure at the end of history who opposes God, Jesus, and Christians, then it is plausible to assume that he will be accompanied by a person who ensures that the peoples of the world are loyal to him through supernatural means, economic pressure, and outright persecution of dissenters.[7] Since it is most unlikely that Christians could ever agree about the identity of the Antichrist if understood as a figure during the last period of history, it is equally unlikely that they could agree on the identity of the false prophet.

More important than speculations about whether there will be a final false prophet is a renewed emphasis on the truth of the gospel. There will always be teachers, Christian and otherwise, who declare that truth is relative,

---

6. See the description of Pliny, the governor of Pontus and Bithynia in the early second century (Pliny, *Ep.* 10.96).
7. Hal Lindsey states, without any hesitation, that this person "is going to be a Jew," adding that "many believe he will be from the tribe of Dan" (*The Late Great Planet Earth* [Grand Rapids: Zondervan, 1970], 112). There is no evidence whatsoever either for the first or the second statement.

that absolute truth does not exist, and that adaptation to the values of the contemporary political and economic system is not only wise but also necessary. John's description of the beast from the sea and its activities calls Christians of all historical periods to renew their commitment to the one true God, to faithfully and courageously express their confession of faith in Jesus and be willing to risk discrimination, persecution, and martyrdom.

REFLECTION QUESTIONS

1. What is the difference between the Beast from the sea and the beast from the earth? What are the similarities?

2. What do Jesus and Paul say about false prophets?

3. What are the main characteristics of the false prophet according to Revelation 13? What is his main goal?

4. How did John's readers in the first century understand the vision of the beast from the earth?

5. What are the main lessons of John's vision in Revelation 13 for us today?

What Is the Mark of the Beast?

John speaks of the "mark of the beast" in connection with the efforts of the false prophet (the beast from the earth) to force the inhabitants of the earth to worship the Beast (the beast from the sea) on the basis of economic sanctions. He writes in Revelation 13:16–17: "Also it causes all, both small and great, both rich and poor, both free and slave, to be marked on the right hand or the forehead, so that no one can buy or sell who does not have the mark, that is, the name of the beast or the number of its name." Since John assumes that his readers understand what he is writing, the meaning of the "mark of the beast" needs to be analyzed within its first-century context and theological "world."

What Is the Mark of the Beast?

The term translated "mark" (Greek, *charagma*) designates "a mark that is engraved, etched, branded, cut, imprinted" on something.[1] The term occurs seven times in the book of Revelation.[2] It always refers to the brand or stamp that indicates loyalty to the Beast. Three times John says that this brand is located on either the forehead or on the right hand of the people who accept the satanically inspired claims of the Beast.[3] There are four main suggestions for understanding the "mark" as a contemporary historical practice.

First, the model for the mark of the Beast was the wearing of *tefillin*. Jewish *tefillin* or phylacteries were two small black leather boxes that contained Scripture passages and that were commonly worn on the upper left arm and forehead, following a literal understanding of Exodus 13:9, 16 (also Deut. 6:8; 11:18).[4] The wearing of phylacteries was originally part of the

---

1. BDAG, 1077 (*charagma* 1).
2. Revelation 13:16, 17; 14:9, 11; 16:2, 19:20; 20:4.
3. Revelation 13:16; 14:9; 20:4. For the following suggestions mentioned, see David E. Aune, *Revelation*, WBC 52B (Dallas: Word, 1998), 2:767–68.
4. See Matthew 23:5; early Jewish texts: *Letter of Aristeas* 159; Josephus, *Jewish Antiquities* 4.213; *m. Shevi'it* 3:8, 11.

remembrance of the exodus from Egypt. One difficulty with this interpretation is that phylacteries were worn on the left arm, while the mark of the Beast was applied to the right arm. Thus, this Jewish practice could have served only as a model and assumes that the false prophet who demands that all people have the mark of the Beast is understood as a Jewish prophet. If, however, the Beast is (initially) understood as a reference to the Roman Empire, using a Jewish background to interpret the false prophet and the mark of the Beast is unhelpful.

Second, the mark of the Beast refers to Roman coins on which the images and names of Roman emperors were engraved. The inability to buy and sell commodities would be the result of refusing to use Roman coins. The Jewish Zealot movement, which eventually caused the Jewish rebellion against Rome resulting in the destruction of Jerusalem in A.D. 70, believed that the prohibition of images in the first of the Ten Commandments applied to the image of the emperor on Roman coins.[5] This suggestion, however, is not plausible: the mark of the Beast is connected with the right hand and the forehead of the people, which would be an odd way of referring to coins.

Third, the mark of the Beast may refer to imperial seals. Stamps called *charagma* were printed on deeds of sale with the name and year of the reigning emperor.[6] There is no evidence, however, that people were stamped on their hands or foreheads. This suggestion makes sense only if the "mark" is understood figuratively as a reference to measures of the state keeping check on whether people were submitting to the emperor via participation in the imperial cult: "Possibly, as in the later persecutions under Diocletian and Decius, certificates were issued to those loyal to the emperor and participating in the required ritual of the imperial religion."[7]

Fourth, the mark of the Beast may refer to the tattooing or branding of slaves, soldiers, and the devotees of certain gods. Runaway slaves were branded on the forehead, as a sign of ownership meant to prevent future attempts of escape. Devotees of Cybele and Attis were "sealed" by a tattoo, as a sign of dedication. Barbarian peoples used tattooing as a status mark. Under Augustus, the imperial government issued tiles (Latin, *tesserae*), possibly inscribed, which served as proof of entitlement to the grain dole.[8] When a person was marked off on the roll listing the names of the people who were entitled to receive grain, they probably received one of these tiles to hand in at the granary. Edwin Judge suggests that we may imagine "those who entered the market of Ephesus having first to make their sacrifice, and then receiving

---

5. See Martin Hengel, *The Zealots* (Edinburgh: T&T Clark, 1989), 190–95.
6. Adolf Deissmann, *Light from the Ancient East Illustrated by Recently Discovered Texts of the Graeco-Roman World* (1927; repr., Grand Rapids: Eerdmans, 1980), 341, fig. 51.
7. Gregory K. Beale, *The Book of Revelation: A Commentary on the Greek Text*, NIGTC (Grand Rapids: Eerdmans, 1999), 715.
8. Suetonius, *Divus Augustus* 40.2; 42.3.

their mark in ink on wrist or forehead, just as in Ezekiel 9:2–6. There is no evidence that such a test was actually applied at this time. But there is just enough miscellaneous information on comparable practices for us to say that this is what might have sprung to mind for those listening to Revelation, when they heard that to enter the market you had first to receive the mark of the beast."[9]

Historical Background

The Roman state generally did not impose economic sanctions against religious cults that it regarded with suspicion. Augustus prohibited the cult of Isis in Rome with two decrees (28 and 21 B.C.), measures that are interpreted as "control measures in social policy."[10] Tiberius banished Jews and Isis worshippers from Rome, an action that "publicly demonstrated the political power of the *princeps* [chief or leader] and symbolized the restoration of order."[11]

In the cities of each province, the various guilds provided a means of social control. The guilds were private, voluntary associations with a social nature. Membership in the guilds meant participation in cultic ritual, which could involve eating meat sacrificed to the pagan gods (to which John was opposed, see Rev. 2:14, 20), and paying homage to the emperor. Some have suggested that John anticipates a trade boycott that the Koinon of Asia would recommend to the cities in the province of Asia, "that the disloyal should be discountenanced by the loyal, and that all loyal subjects should try to restrict their custom to those who were of proved loyalty."[12] Once participation in the imperial cult was expected of the citizens of a city as a sign of loyalty, the Christians' refusal could lead them very quickly to commercial ruin.

While exact historical parallels do not exist, it can be readily imagined how commercial boycotts could be imposed on the followers of Jesus who refused participation in the cultural and religious life of the city. The public proof of loyalty to the city and the state was the performance of the cultic ritual; there were other acts of homage to the emperor, such as personal involvement as cult official. Perhaps John describes these public acts of loyalty symbolically as the mark on the right hand or on the forehead: people who confess loyalty to the emperor have the "mark" on the hand, and people who officiate as cult officials in the imperial cult have the "mark" on their forehead. We do not know whether this is what John had in mind. But the problems for Christians who refused to participate in the cultural and religious life of the

---

9. Edwin A. Judge, "The Mark of the Beast, Revelation 13.16," *TynBul* 42 (1991): 160.

10. S. Takacs, "Isis II. Greece and Rome," in *Brill's New Pauly: Encyclopedia of the Ancient World; Antiquity*, ed. Hubert Cancik and Helmuth Schneider; Christine F. Salazar and David E. Orton (Leiden: Brill, 2002–2012), 6:970.

11. Ibid.

12. William M. Ramsay, *The Letters to the Seven Churches*, rev. ed. (Peabody, MA: Hendrickson, 1994), 75.

city were real enough. Once city magistrates or provincial officials decided that someone was refusing to express their loyalty to the emperor, they were ostracized.

The Mark of the Beast and the Seal of God

The mark of the Beast is a parody of the "seal of God" that the followers of the Lamb have received, marking them as belonging to God's people (Rev. 7:2, 4, 5, 8; 9:4). The followers of the Lamb, many of whom are killed "for their testimony to Jesus and for the word of God," are described as people who "had not worshiped the beast or its image and had not received its mark on their foreheads or their hands" (Rev. 20:4). In contrast, Christians who are "marked . . . with a seal" (*sphragizōmen*) or have the "seal" (*sphragis*) of God on their foreheads (Rev. 7:4; 9:4).[13] In Revelation 14:1, John states that the followers of the Lamb had "his name and his Father's name written on their foreheads."

The expression "seal of God" is based on Ezekiel 9:1–11 where a "mark" is mentioned as a sign of the physical protection of the righteous remnant in Israel. Here the prophet sees a man with a writing case who is asked to scour the city for people who share the prophet's broken heart over the abominations perpetrated in Israel and his grief over the impending doom. Those who exhibit such response are to be marked with a *taw* (a letter that had the shape of an X in the archaic cursive script) on the forehead. This mark on the most visible part of the body served "as a distinguishing mark to separate the righteous from the wicked" and, as a mark of ownership, as "Yahweh's signature, his claim on those who were citizens of the true kingdom of God."[14]

The mark on the foreheads of the believers in Revelation—the "seal of God," which is the name of Jesus the Lamb and the name of God the Father—is a symbolic portrayal of the fact that they belong to the true and living God and that they can be assured of the authenticity of their faith and of the spiritual protection of their salvation. Furthermore, the seal and name of God encourage and empower true believers to remain loyal to Jesus Christ even in the midst of immense political and social pressure.Some end-time "specialists" suggest that the "mark of the Beast" is 666 and that in the last period of history the world's population will be branded with this number (perhaps invisibly or in connection with credit cards), which would allow the state to control all economic transactions. Some suggest that the kind of technology that makes this possible is available only today, which (allegedly) "proves" that we live in the end times. This belief misses the point that social control was possible, and practiced quite successfully, even in antiquity. New technology only changes the ways in which social control is encouraged or enforced. John

---

13. The occurrence of this expression in Revelation 9:4 demonstrates that the 144,000 sealed in Revelation 7 are Christians in general, not a select (Jewish) group within the church.
14. Daniel I. Block, *The Book of Ezekiel*, NICOT (Grand Rapids: Eerdmans, 1998), 1:307.

speaks about realities that were already threatening his readers in the first century.

Summary

The expression "mark of the Beast" is a symbolic way of describing the state's measures that are designed to ensure that people submit to compulsory idol worship. The background may be the branding of slaves (as a sign of being property) or the branding of soldiers and devotees of particular pagan cults (as a sign of being faithful followers). Christians have the "seal of God" on their foreheads, which means that they live under God's sovereign authority who assures them of spiritual protection in the midst of persecution.

REFLECTION QUESTIONS

1. When was branding practiced in antiquity? Who was branded and why?

2. What does the presence of a brand (or tattoo) communicate?

3. Why would a state want to control the economic activity of its citizens?

4. Are there historical examples of social and economic control by the state?

5. What can Christians be sure of?

Who Is the Great Harlot of Babylon?

In a long vision that comprises two chapters toward the end of the book of Revelation, John describes a "great Harlot" who is called "Babylon the great, mother of whores and of earth's abomination" (Rev. 17:5). Who is the "great Harlot," and what is "Babylon the Great" with whom the prostitute of John's vision is connected?

The "great Harlot" of Revelation 17 has been identified with various entities throughout church history.[1] Bonaventure (1221–1274), the influential medieval theologian, describes the error of Aristetolian philosophy as "the Great Harlot Reason" of Revelation 17. Dante Alighieri (1265–1321), the supreme poet of the Middle Ages, treats the "whore of Babylon" in the *Divine Comedy* as a symbol of the corrupt (Roman Catholic) church (Inferno XIX). In the prophetic literature of the fourteenth century, the Avignon papacy was identified with "Babylon" of Revelation 17, giving rise to the concept of the "Babylonian captivity" of the church. Martin Luther (1483–1546) entitled the text in which he attacked the Roman Catholic view of the sacraments *The Babylonian Captivity of the Church* (October 1520). He included the declaration, "The papacy is indeed nothing but the kingdom of Babylon and of the true Antichrist." In Elizabethan England, the papal church was regularly described as the "rose-colored harlot with whom the kings of the earth have committed fornication." More recently, John Walvoord suggested that the "great harlot" will be a "super-church" consisting of Catholic, Protestant, and

---

1. For the following, see Bernhard McGinn, *Antichrist: Two Thousand Years of the Human Fascination with Evil* (San Francisco: HarperCollins, 1994), 236, 171–72, 174, 203, 219, 326n48. The quotations are from Luther (ibid., 203) and from Edwin Sandys (ibid., 219).

Orthodox Christians.[2] Dave Hunt has sought to revive this interpretation in a long book.[3]

A careful reading of Revelation 17 in its context helps us to separate fact from fiction and John's meaning from interpretations that are either anachronistic or mere polemical propaganda. John's statements about the Harlot can be summarized as follows in the table below.

THE GREAT HARLOT		
DESCRIPTION	17:1	great Harlot is seated on many waters
	17:3	the woman sits on a scarlet beast the beast has seven heads and ten horns and is full of blasphemous names
	17:4	clothed in purple and scarlet adorned with gold and jewels and pearls
	17:5	the woman's name, written on her forehead, is "Babylon the great, mother of whores and of earth's abominations"
	17:9	the woman sits on the beast's seven heads = seven mountains = seven kings
	17:15	the woman sits on waters = peoples and multitudes and nations and languages
	17:18	the woman = the great city that rules over the kings of the earth
EVENT	17:2	the kings of the earth have committed fornication with the harlot
	17:2	the inhabitants of the earth have become drunk with the wine of her fornication
	17:16	the Harlot will be hated by the ten horns (ten kings) and the Beast the Harlot will be made desolate and naked the Harlot's flesh will be devoured, and she will be burnt up with fire
	19:2	the great Harlot has been judged by God

2. John F. Walvoord, *Armageddon, Oil, and the Middle East Crisis: What the Bible Says about the Future of the Middle East and the End of Western Civilization* (Grand Rapids: Zondervan, 1974), 108–9.

3. Dave Hunt, *A Woman Rides the Beast: The Roman Catholic Church and the Last Days* (Eugene, OR: Harvest, 1994), 456.

ACTION	17:6	the woman was drunk with the blood of the saints and the blood of the witnesses to Jesus
	17:4	holds in her hand a golden cup full of abominations and the impurities of her fornication
	19:2	the great Harlot corrupted the earth with her fornication the great harlot is responsible for the blood of God's servants

The Great Harlot's Symbolism

It is generally recognized, even by "literalists," that the "great Harlot" in Revelation 17 is not a description of a particular female prostitute that will have a corrupting influence on the world's population in the last days. The image of a harlot (or whore, or prostitute) was immediately intelligible in antiquity. Prostitution was not only legal in the Roman Empire, it was widely practiced. It was even regarded as both unavoidable and socially expedient by the conservative politician Cicero who wrote, "If there is anyone who holds the opinion that young men should be interdicted from intrigues with the women of the town, he is indeed austere! That, ethically, he is in the right, I cannot deny: but nevertheless, he is at loggerheads not only with the license of the present age, but even with the habits of our ancestors and what they permitted themselves. For when was this not done? When was it rebuked? When found fault with?"[4] It is not a coincidence that Latin had about fifty synonyms for the term "prostitute."[5]

In the Old Testament, the image of the harlot depicts both immorality and idolatry: as a harlot leads men astray from being faithful to their wives, so Israel has been corrupted to such a degree as to abandon the covenant faithfulness that bound her to the one true and living God, preferring instead to worship and serve foreign gods.[6] Since harlots provide sexual services for payment, an economic connotation is often present as well. Thus, Israel "whores" after other gods because of her leaders' belief that other nations can provide economic and political security. While most of the harlot metaphors in the Old Testament refer to Israel, sometimes reference is made to Tyre (see Isa. 23:15–17) and to Nineveh (see Nah. 3:4).

Therefore, the image of the Harlot refers to abandoning God and his covenant (spiritual unfaithfulness), worshipping and serving other gods

---

4. Cicero, *Pro Caelio*, 20.
5. James N. Adams, "Words for Prostitute in Latin," *Rheinisches Museum für Philologie* 126 (1983): 321–58.
6. See Exodus 34:15–16; Leviticus 17:7; 20:5; Deuteronomy 31:16; Jeremiah 3:1–13; Ezekiel 16:1–63; 23:1–49; Hosea 2:1–23; 4:10–18; 5:3–4; 6:10; 9:1. In Ezekiel 16, the prophet describes "Jerusalem's unrestrained nymphomaniacal adventures with her lovers" (Daniel I. Block, *The Book of Ezekiel*, NICOT [Grand Rapids: Eerdmans, 1998], 1:465), in sometimes very graphic terms (Ezek. 16:25–26, 36–37).

(idolatry), and looking for security through alliances (economic and political priorities).

The Great Harlot's Description

We begin with the name of the great Harlot written on her forehead: "Babylon the great, mother of whores and of earth's abominations" (Rev. 17:5). A name written on the forehead is a symbol for the true character of someone that defines one's relationship to either the true and living God (7:3; 14:1; 22:4) or Satan (13:16; 14:9; 20:4). The reference to "Babylon" takes the reader back to Revelation 14:8, where the second angel had announced God's judgment upon Babylon, with the words, "Fallen, fallen is Babylon the great! She has made all nations drink of the wine of the wrath of her fornication." This proclamation is derived from Isaiah 21:9: "Fallen, fallen is Babylon; and all the images of her gods lie shattered on the ground." This connection shows that "Babylon" is a symbol for the idolatrous commitment of the world. The title "Babylon the great" is derived from Daniel 4:27[30], where king Nebuchadnezzar declares, "Is not this the great Babylon I have built as the royal residence, by my mighty power and for the glory of my majesty?" (NIV; the expression "the great Babylon" occurs nowhere else in the Old Testament). The reference to "Babylon the great" is part of the king's self-glorification, for which he is about to be judged. Babylon was the pagan world power that had destroyed Jerusalem and forced Israel to live in exile. The prophets Daniel and Ezekiel show that the Jewish people living in Babylonia were tempted to compromise with the social, political, and economic system of Babylon. After the victories of King Cyrus, Babylon became a province in the Persian Empire and was eventually taken over by Alexander the Great, who wanted to make Babylon the center of his world empire. Gradual decline led eventually to the abandonment of the site. Today, only ruins remain about 80 kilometers (50 miles) south of Baghdad in the vicinity of modern Hillah.[7]

The reference to "mother of whores" reveals the harlot's seductive character. The reference to the "earth's abominations" reveals her idolatrous disposition. The description of the Harlot as "sitting" connotes sovereignty: she is able to control the people and the Beast through her powerful influence. That the Harlot sits "on many waters" (Rev. 17:1) associates her with evil. That the Harlot is seen by John in "a desert" or "a wilderness" (17:3) is not a contradiction but indicates that John's point is not literal but symbolic geography: "desert" is often a symbol for the place of fierce animals (serpents) and

---

7. Tim LaHaye and Thomas Ice (*Charting the End Times* [Eugene, OR: Harvest, 2001], 105), and other end-time "specialists" who are committed to a literalist reading of biblical prophecy construct a (new) prophecy when they claim that the city of Babylon will be rebuilt (so that the harlot has a place to sit, although the "harlot" is not interpreted literally but symbolically as "the false religious system"; ibid., 62).

evil spirits. The combination of "waters" and "desert" is an allusion to Isaiah 21:1 which also, uniquely in the Old Testament, combines the images of the desert and of the sea, associating both with Babylon. This description implies a note of judgment: Babylon the great city becomes both "many waters" and a "desert" where only satanic spirits dwell (thus explicitly in Rev. 18:2).

The Beast is "scarlet" (or "red"), as is the Harlot, whose color is also described as being "purple" (Rev. 17:3, 4). The Dragon (Satan) has the same color (12:3). Both colors associate the beast and the harlot with royal attire and hence with the claim to political authority and sovereignty. At the same time, the color refers to the blood of the Christians who have been killed in persecutions (see 12:3; 17:3). The attire of the woman—she was clothed in purple and scarlet, and adorned with gold and jewels and pearls (repeated in 18:16)—indicates that this represents not only (spiritual) idolatry but also economic interests: gold, silver, jewels, pearls, as well as purple and scarlet and more are listed (18:12). She is a symbol of human culture that glories in commerce and prosperity. At the same time, the attractiveness of her attire symbolizes the seductive nature of the Harlot.[8]

The Great Harlot's Actions

The woman has a golden cup, but all that she has to offer in this cup are "abominations and the impurities of her fornication" (17:4). This corresponds to the description given: "with the wine of her fornication the inhabitants of the earth have become drunk" (17:2). The figure of the cup with intoxicating drink "symbolizes Babylon's promise of prosperous earthly welfare for its willing subjects, which intoxicates them. The intoxicating influence blinds them to Babylon's evil nature and her ultimate insecurity and deceives them about God as her future judge and as the only true foundation for true prosperity."[9] The reference to "abominations" and "fornication" speaks of idolatry in which the Beast and the people belonging to its realm are involved.[10] In the cities of the Roman Empire, economy and idolatry were closely related. Many temples, such as the great temple of Artemis in Ephesus, served as banking centers of the city and the province. The members of trade guilds worshipped patron gods of the guild, which put enormous pressure on Christians who refused to participate in such worship.

---

8. In Jeremiah 4:30, Israel the harlot is described as follows: "And you, O desolate one, what do you mean that you dress in crimson, that you deck yourself with ornaments of gold, that you enlarge your eyes with paint?"
9. Gregory K. Beale, *The Book of Revelation: A Commentary on the Greek Text*, NIGTC (Grand Rapids: Eerdmans, 1999), 855. He refers to Jeremiah 51:7–8 as a parallel for the way in which the symbol of the cup is used here.
10. Note the figurative meaning of the noun *porneia* and verb *porneuō* as a reference to idolatry in Revelation 2:14, 20–21; also 9:21.

The woman persecutes Christians, who are described as "witnesses to Jesus" (17:6). They are ostracized, marginalized, and even killed because they refuse to submit to the economic and political system that requires participation in (literal) idolatry.

The Great Harlot's Fate

The whole point of John's description of the great Harlot in Revelation 17 is the message that God will bring judgment. The angel who introduces the vision of the Harlot to John says, "Come, I will show you the judgment of the great prostitute" (17:1 NIV). The judgment of the great Harlot (Babylon) is described in two ways. First, the woman is destroyed because the kings of the earth become disenchanted with her (v. 16). The political system of the state (the Beast) and its allies turn against the economic-religious order, attempting to destroy the Harlot before they destroy the Lamb.[11] The destruction of the Harlot is total: "they will make her desolate and naked; they will devour her flesh and burn her up with fire" (v. 16).[12] Second, the woman is judged by God. This is made clear in Revelation 19:2: "Hallelujah! Salvation and glory and power to our God, for his judgments are true and just; he has judged the great whore who corrupted the earth with her fornication, and he has avenged on her the blood of his servants."

The Great Harlot's Interpretation

"Babylon" is a symbol of the ungodly political, economic, and religious system under which the Jewish people lived in the sixth century B.C. (literally) and which the Christians faced in the Roman Empire (figuratively). The reference to the "seven mountains" (Rev. 17:9) and the description of the woman as "the great city that rules over the kings of the earth" (v. 18) is taken most naturally in a first-century context as a reference to the city of Rome and the political and economic power emanating from there.[13] Jewish texts used the term "Babylon" to describe Rome, which destroyed Jerusalem and the temple in A.D. 70 and exiled Israel again in the second century after the Bar Kokhba revolt.[14]

Some link the great harlot with the cult of the goddess Roma, the personification of Rome, because she is depicted as sitting on seven mountains understood as referring to the city of Rome. Bronze coins depict the emperor

---

11. On this point, Grant R. Osborne thinks of the eschatological civil war in which vassal kings destroy Babylon/Rome (*Revelation*, BECNT [Grand Rapids: Baker Academic, 2002], 625).
12. The parallel in Ezekiel 16:37–41 and 23:31–34 suggests that John describes the Harlot being punished and destroyed by her own sin.
13. We should note that the seven mountains are identified with seven kings (Rev. 17:9). For details on the "seven kings," see question 19.
14. See *Midrash Rabbah*, on Numbers 7:10; *Midrash Psalm* 137:1, 8; *Targum Lamentations* 1:19. David Aune lists further passages. Note the use of "Babylon" in 1 Peter 5:13 for Rome. David E. Aune, *Revelation*, WBC 52B (Dallas: Word, 1998), 2:829–30.

Vespasian on one side and the goddess Roma, sitting on the seven hills of Rome on the other. While the cult of Roma may be part of the background of John's vision, it does not exhaust his description of "Babylon" and of the loyalties it demands.

The portrayal of the great harlot ("Babylon the great") as sitting on the Beast (17:3; also 13:1) indicates that she represents the ungodly economic and religious system that controls the political and social system (the Beast), which was for John and his readers the Roman Empire.[15] Any attitude or institution that is characterized by self-glorifying pride, economic overabundance, idolatry, and persecution of Christians is "Babylon."

The contrast between the woman-harlot (Rev. 17) and the woman-mother (Rev. 12) is instructive and demonstrates the necessity to interpret the great Harlot not in terms of merely past events in the first century or in terms of merely future events in the last days immediately before the end. The woman-mother of Revelation is a portrayal of the followers of the Lamb (i.e., of Jesus, the Messiah). Both women are pictured as being in the desert: for the Harlot, the desert is the dwelling place of demons; for the mother, the desert is a place of protection. The scarlet woman is a harlot; the woman-mother is a bride (Rev. 19:7–8). Both women are portrayed as cities: the Harlot is Babylon, while the mother represents the heavenly Jerusalem (21:2, 10). As the woman-mother who is the bride represents the followers of Jesus throughout history, so the Harlot represents the satanically inspired economic and religious system of the various kingdoms, republics, and empires (and democracies) in the various periods of history.

John's comment that he was amazed when he saw the gloriously dressed Harlot (Rev. 17:6) expresses the allure of the economic system of the Roman Empire and the immensity of the pressure to conform and participate in the social and religious institutions of the city and the empire. John is protected from succumbing to the seductive influence of the woman because the angel reveals to him the "mystery of the woman, and of the beast" (v. 7). The mystery is the unexpected way in which Babylon will be defeated—it will self-destruct from the inside even before Jesus' returns (vv. 8–18). The kingdom of evil will destroy itself, as the political elements will turn against the religious and economic elements.

Summary

The image of the great harlot who is "Babylon the Great" symbolizes the prevailing economic and religious institutions that are in alliance with

---

15. Beale comments, "That she rides the beast connotes her alliance with the state. The woman must represent that part of the ungodly world that works together with the state, such as the social, cultural, economic, and religious aspects of the world" (*Book of Revelation*, 853). For the point made that follows in the text above, see ibid., 856.

the political and social systems throughout history. John is concerned that an unfaithful segment of the church may participate in the economic, social, and religious institutions of contemporary society (Rev. 2:14–15, 20–24; 3:2–4; 17–18). And he knows that Jews may participate in the persecution of Christians (Rev. 2:9–10; 3:9). Thus, "Babylon the Great" includes hostile Jews and apostate Christians. But the main concern is to warn the churches not to participate in the idolatry of the economic and religious institutions of the empire. Thus, interpretations of the harlot in terms of the Roman Catholic Church alone miss John's point. The influence of the Roman Catholic Church today is neither economic nor wielded through political institutions worldwide. Sectors of Protestant churches have become apostate both economically and morally. For example, many who claim to be Christians justify unfettered capitalism and consumerism, champion a so-called health and wealth gospel, divorce as easily as unbelievers, or advocate the practice of homosexuality. Indeed, "the repulsive immorality, idolatry, luxury, and misuse of power that characterized Rome has been reproduced many times throughout history; and we must all recognize the same depravity in our way of life today."[16]

REFLECTION QUESTIONS

1. What does the image of the great Harlot communicate?

2. Why does the Old Testament, on occasion, describe the people of Israel as a "harlot"?

3. What is the relationship between the great Harlot and the Beast?

4. What is John's main concern when he describes the economic and religious realities of society as the great Harlot?

5. What should our response be to John's vision of the great Harlot?

---

16. Osborne, *Revelation*, 628.

Who Are the Two Witnesses of Revelation 11?

John describes two witnesses who appear in the city in which the temple of God stands (Jerusalem). They are given by God the "authority to prophesy for one thousand two hundred sixty days, wearing sackcloth" and the authority to perform miracles that resemble those of Moses and Elijah. They are killed by the Beast, but God brings them back to life and takes them up to heaven (Rev. 11:1–13). Some suggest a literal interpretation, while others argue for a symbolic interpretation. Still others seek to combine the two approaches. A discussion concerning the interpretation of this passage, as important as it is, must not obscure the message that John wanted to convey to his readers.

Literalism versus Symbolism

A literal interpretation assumes that the prophecy speaks of the city of Jerusalem in which a temple stands (which would have to be a third temple, yet to be built). It is assumed that there will be two specific individuals who will preach the gospel in Jerusalem during the last three-and-a-half years of history.[1]

A symbolic interpretation takes the temple to be the church, the city as secular civilization that rebels against God, and the two witnesses as referring to the missionary mandate of the church and/or to the martyrs of the church throughout history.[2]

---

1. See, e.g., John F. Walvoord, *The Revelation of Jesus Christ* (Chicago: Moody Press, 1966), 175–83; Robert L. Thomas, *Revelation: An Exegetical Commentary* (Chicago: Moody, 1995), 78–100.
2. See, e.g., Robert H. Mounce, *The Book of Revelation*, rev. ed. (Grand Rapids: Eerdmans, 1998), 215–24; Gregory K. Beale, *The Book of Revelation: A Commentary on the Greek Text*, NIGTC (Grand Rapids: Eerdmans, 1999), 556–608.

Some combine the two interpretations: the two witnesses represent the corporate witness of the church and symbolize the ministry of the church, while they are also two individuals who will appear during the final period of history reproducing the ministries of Elijah and Moses.[3]

The Symbols of John's Vision in Revelation 11

It is quite obvious that John's description of his vision in Revelation 11 includes symbols. While literalists, if pressed, probably would say that the two witnesses are literally wearing sackcloth (Rev. 11:3) and affirm that the two witnesses are protected by literal fire (v. 5),[4] they do not seem to be willing to say that the two witnesses kill their opponents by fire that comes literally out of their mouths. The gospel never prompts missionaries and evangelists to slay their opponents by fire. On the contrary, Jesus' witnesses are willing to suffer and die as martyrs.[5]

The Two Lampstands and the Two Olive Trees

Revelation 11:4 clarifies that the two witnesses are not two individuals but symbols for larger realities: "These are the two olive trees and the two lampstands that stand before the Lord of the earth." In his introductory vision, John sees seven golden lampstands (Rev. 1:12) in the midst of which was one like the Son of Man (v. 13), and he hears Jesus explaining to him that "the seven lampstands are the seven churches" (v. 20). It is not likely that the lampstands in Revelation 11 are different from the lampstands in Revelation 1. This is supported by the fact that the lampstands in Revelation 1 are identified as "a kingdom and priests" (1:6 NIV), which is a phrase that describes the entire church (5:10). Similarly, the two lampstands in Revelation 11 have kingly and priestly functions. The light from the lampstands in the tabernacle and the temple represented God's presence (priestly function). Lampstands and olive trees are mentioned together in Zechariah 4:14. This passage assures God's people that God will provide his Spirit (oil) and cause it to be conveyed by the priest (Joshua) and the king (Zerubbabel), symbolized by the olive trees, which will guarantee that the opposition will be overcome and the rebuilding of the temple will be completed.[6]

The Two Witnesses

If the two witnesses symbolize the church since they are identified as two lampstands, why are there seven lampstands in Revelation 1 and only two

---

3. See Grant R. Osborne, *Revelation*, BECNT (Grand Rapids: Baker Academic, 2002), 408–36.
4. Thomas, *Revelation*, 90.
5. Beale points to Luke 9:54–62 and 10:1–16 where an allusion to Elijah's judging by (literal) fire is followed by Jesus' teaching on the difficulty of discipleship and then applied (figuratively) to the preaching of judgment by the seventy disciples (*Book of Revelation*, 584).
6. Ibid., 577; Osborne, *Revelation*, 420–21.

lampstands in Revelation 11? The change from the number seven to the number two is easily explained. Seven, symbolizing completeness, describes the entire church as the recipient of Jesus' revelation conveyed through John. Two is the number of witnesses that the Old Testament Law required for the validation of testimony before a court of law.[7] The Greek term for "witness" (*martyria*) is often used for testimony in court. The two witnesses stand for the entire church whose calling is to testify to the world about the one true and living God and to his Messiah and Savior, to testify to the truth that is the light of the world (note the symbol of the lampstands!).

The description of the witnesses' opposition confirms that John intends a symbolic (corporate) understanding of his vision. The two witnesses are opposed not by "literal" people in Jerusalem. Rather, "the beast that comes up from the Abyss will attack them, and overpower and kill them" (Rev. 11:7 NIV). The allusion of this description to Daniel 7:21 and the description of the Beast in Revelation 13 and 17 clarifies that it is the followers of Jesus—which are appropriately called "saints" in 13:7—who are attacked by the satanically inspired forces of evil.

The description of the world's reaction to the killing of the two witnesses also suggests a symbolic interpretation. Many people "from every people, tribe, language and nation will gaze on their bodies and refuse them burial" (Rev. 11:9 NIV). This description suggests a global confrontation between the witnessing church and the unbelievers.[8]

The Temple of God

John is given a measuring rod and told, "go and measure the temple of God and the altar, with its worshipers" (Rev. 11:1 NIV). This directive, and the resulting action, alludes to Ezekiel 40–48. There an angel measures various features in a temple that exists in heaven, portraying the certain establishment and the divine protection of the future temple as the place of his presence. The measuring secures the temple against contamination by abominations that profane the sanctuary. This background (and the fact that throughout the book of Revelation John speaks of a heavenly temple) makes it very plausible to see here a reference to the heavenly, true temple,

---

7. Numbers 35:30; Deuteronomy 17:6; 19:15. In the New Testament, see Matthew 18:16; John 8:17; 2 Corinthians 13:1; 1 Timothy 5:19; Hebrews 10:28. This is the reason why God sends, on occasion, two angels (see Luke 24:3–9; Acts 1:10–11).

8. Literalists suggest that "the only way the people of earth could all see the two witnesses is by satellite television, which could easily be fulfilled literally" (Tim LaHaye and Ed Hindson, eds., *The Popular Bible Prophecy Commentary* [Eugene, OR: Harvest, 2007], 522; also Hal Lindsey, *There's a Coming: A Prophetic Odyssey* [Santa Ana, CA: Vision House, 1973], 151). Since John wrote for readers in the first century, and since John was directed not to seal the words of his prophecy (Rev. 22:10), interpretations that require modern technology are illegitimate.

which is the church.[9] The beginning of John's vision assures the church of spiritual protection and of God's continued presence. The "measuring" of the worshippers signifies that they belong to the spiritual temple and that they are under God's protection.

The Holy City

Literalists interpret the reference to the "holy city" (Rev. 11:2) as a reference to the city of Jerusalem in the Holy Land. When John wrote the book of Revelation, the city of Jerusalem had been destroyed by the Roman troops under the command of Titus and lay in ruins for over twenty years.[10] While the expression "holy city" often refers to Jerusalem,[11] the term "city" (Greek, *polis*) always refers in the book of Revelation to the future heavenly city of God (e.g., Rev. 3:12; 21:2, 10).[12] Note Revelation 3:12 where both "temple" and "city" are used symbolically as a reference to the place of God's presence: "The one who is victorious I will make a pillar in the temple of my God. Never again will they leave it. I will write on them the name of my God and the name of the city of my God, the new Jerusalem" (NIV). Thus, the "holy city" in Revelation 11:2 refers to the heavenly city of God, specifically to that part of the heavenly city that is comprised of the followers of Jesus living on earth. This interpretation is confirmed by the fact that the holy city is "trampled," that is, attacked by opposing forces "for forty-two months" (11:2). This is the same time period given for the persecution of the woman by the Dragon and the Beast (11:3; 12:6, 14; 13:5).

Forty-Two Months

Interpreters who insist on literal interpretations wherever possible take this time reference as predicting a period of forty-two months (or three and a half years), described as the second (sometimes as the first) part of the last seven years of history before Jesus' return.[13] While generally accepted among "prophecy writers," this understanding is very unlikely, since it would allow

---

9. The reference to the outer court that "has been given to the Gentiles" can be understood as a reference to the fact that the entire temple, the Court of the Gentiles included, has become a house of prayer as a result of Jesus' work (see Matt. 21:12–13).

10. Thomas argues that the vision refers not to the Jerusalem of the first century but to the rebuilt Jerusalem of the future and of its fate during the period of the great tribulation. This interpretation implies the rebuilding of Jerusalem and of a third temple, thus effectively constructing a new prophecy that John's readers in the first century could not have understood (*Revelation 8–22*, 84).

11. See Matthew 4:5; 27:53; in the Old Testament see Nehemiah 11:1, 18; Isaiah 48:2; 52:1; Daniel 9:24.

12. See the reference to the heavenly city in Hebrews 11:10; 12:22; 13:14.

13. Thomas asserts that "sane biblical interpretation requires that words be taken in their natural meaning unless contextual factors require something other than a literal interpretation." Note the "context" that the following comments establish (*Revelation 8–22*, 84–85)!

believers to predict the year of Jesus' return—assuming that they agree on the beginning of the seven-year period (the explanation that the rapture will remove believers to heaven before beginning of the seven-year period is not convincing; the book of Revelation and other New Testament texts clearly assume that there will be believers on earth when Jesus comes back).

The number of the forty-two months (Rev. 11:2), which corresponds to 1,260 days (Rev. 11:3), is a symbolic figure for the period of tribulation before the end (on the tribulation see question 8).[14] In Revelation 13:5 (and 12:14), the forty-two months or "a time, times, and half a time" (usually interpreted as three and a half years) are clearly based on Daniel 7:25. There, the phrase "a time, times, and half a time" is not a convoluted way of saying "three years and half a year" (which can be expressed in a very straightforward manner). Rather, the expression "suggests a time that threatens to extend itself longer: one period, then a double period, then a quadruple period . . . but the anticipated sequence suddenly breaks off, so that the seven periods (in effect an eternity) that were threatened are unexpectedly halved."[15] John relates this number to the period between Jesus' first and second coming, or more precisely between Jesus' death and resurrection and Jesus' second coming. Jesus' ministry lasted three and a half years, as did Elijah's ministry (Luke 4:25; James 5:17) with whom the two witnesses are connected in John's vision (Rev. 11:5–6). The time of the ministry of the witnessing church is a time of tribulation.

The Ministry of the Witnesses

The witnesses, representing the church, give testimony about Jesus and proclaim the word of God: they are his witnesses and they prophesy (Rev. 11:3). They carry out their ministry of witness in the time of tribulation between Jesus' death and resurrection and his return (vv. 2–3; the reference to the forty-two months or 1,260 days). Their message includes the proclamation of God's judgment, a tragic reality that calls for mourning (11:3; the sackcloth). As they convey the light of God's truth, they are empowered by God's presence (v. 4; the lampstands that stand before the Lord). They are opposed by people who want to harm them, but they stand under God's protection (v. 5). The people who want to harm the witnesses will be judged by God, whose judgment over the world and the unrighteous they proclaim (v. 5; the fire that comes out of their mouth).[16] The ministry of the witnesses is like that of Moses and Elijah (vv. 5–6): as the church proclaims God's truth, including the message of the final judgment, it "unleashes torment toward those who

---

14. Later Jewish interpreters read Daniel's three and a half years as a general time of tribulation for the righteous (*Midr. Ps.* 10:1), or as the time of Israel's Babylonian captivity (*b. Sanh.* 97b).

15. John E. Goldingay, *Daniel*, WBC 30 (Dallas: Word, 1987), 181; also David E. Aune, *Revelation*, WBC 52B (Dallas: Word, 1998), 2:609.

16. Note Revelation 1:16; 19:15, 21 where John describes Jesus as judging his enemies by means of a sword that proceeds from his mouth.

remain ultimately unrepentant. The torments anticipate the final judgment and harden the reprobate in their sinful stance, making them ever more ripe for the punishment of the great day. These torments primarily affect the spiritual realm of a person, especially plaguing his or her conscience."[17] When the time of the witness of the church is complete, the forces of evil will intensify the persecution and attempt to exterminate the church (vv. 7–10). John appears to envision a period of intense suffering before Jesus' second coming, leading to the resurrection and final vindication of the witnesses, who are the followers of the Lamb (vv. 11–12).[18]

Summary

The two witnesses symbolize the witnessing church. Two witnesses testify to and validate truth. God expects the followers of Jesus to proclaim the truth of the gospel even in times of suffering and persecution. The church, portrayed as the temple of God and the holy city, is assured of God's continued presence and protection—which is a spiritual protection since many believers will suffer and some will die as martyrs. Since God's victory over the forces of evil is certain, the followers of the Lamb can be sure that they will be ultimately vindicated when God raises them from the dead and takes them into his presence.

REFLECTION QUESTIONS

1. Which words and expressions of John's vision in Revelation 11:1–13 can be understood literally? Which must be understood symbolically?

2. What is the task of witnesses of Jesus?

3. Why do witnesses of the gospel have to suffer?

4. What can witnesses of the gospel be sure of?

5. What is the relationship between missionary work and the judgment of the unbelievers?

---

17. Beale, *Book of Revelation*, 584. He refers to Revelation 11:10 where the two witnesses are described as having "tormented" the inhabitants of the earth (NIV).

18. The description of the earthquake in Revelation 11:13 in which a tenth of the city collapses and seven thousand people are killed (the numbers may describe the totality of the followers of the Beast who are judged at the end) seems to refer to the beginning of the end when God will judge the inhabitants of the earth. The "survivors" who are "terrified and gave glory to the God of heaven" (NIV) probably do not represent last-minute converts but represent the unbelievers who are forced at the end by God to acknowledge his sovereignty after all (note the allusion to Nebuchadnezzar's response to God's judgment in Dan. 4).

Who Are Gog and Magog in Ezekiel?

In the book of Revelation, "Gog and Magog" describes "the nations in the four corners of the earth" (Rev. 20:8), the forces of evil that attack the people and the city of God. It is an attack that ends in total defeat as "fire came down from heaven and devoured them." The expression "Gog and Magog" comes from Ezekiel 38–39 where we read of "Gog, of the land of Magog, the chief prince of Meshech and Tubal" (38:2) and of his allies "Persia, Ethiopia, and Put are with them, all of them with buckler and helmet; Gomer and all its troops; Beth-Togarmah from the remotest parts of the north with all its troops" (38:5–6).

The *Dictionary of Biblical Prophecy and End Times* begins an entry on "Gog and Magog" with the explanation that "Gog is the leader of a future coalition that will attack Israel, an event described in Ezekiel 38."[1] Interpreters throughout the ages have identified Gog and Magog with very different peoples and places: (1) the invading Goths in the fourth and fifth centuries; (2) the invading Huns in the fifth and sixth centuries; (3) Hungarian raiders in the tenth century; (4) the pope and the papacy in the fourteenth century (John Wycliffe), (5) Hitler's Germany and Russia in the twentieth century; or (6) more generally as heretics.[2] The *Scofield Reference Bible* identified Gog with Russia, which was a popular identification among "prophecy writers" in the twentieth century, particularly after Russia became a Communist country.[3]

---

1. J. Daniel Hays, J. Scott Duvall, and C. Marvin Pate, *Dictionary of Biblical Prophecy and End Times* (Grand Rapids: Zondervan, 2007), 188.
2. Bernhard McGinn, *Antichrist: Two Thousand Years of the Human Fascination with Evil* (San Francisco: HarperCollins, 1994), 236, 91, 99, 182, 257, 308, 311.
3. See Hal Lindsey, *The Late Great Planet Earth* (Grand Rapids: Zondervan, 1970), 59–71 (chap. 5 is entitled "Russia Is a Gog"). Walvoord maintains that the nation described in Ezekiel 38–39 is "most likely Russia or another state of the former Soviet Union" (John F. Walvoord, *The Final Drama: Fourteen Keys to Understanding the Prophetic Scriptures* [Grand Rapids: Kregel, 1998], 123). Also see Tim LaHaye and Ed Hindson, eds., *The Popular Bible*

After the fall of the Soviet Union, different interpretations were offered. Some suggest a version of the older identification with Communist Russia: the invading coalition that is thought to invade Israel is identified by some with the Islamic republics of Kazakhstan, Kyrgystan, Uzbekistan, Turkmenistan, Tajikistan, and the Ukraine, all former Soviet satellite states.[4]

These various and very different interpretations have one element in common: they all depend on contemporary political and military threats. These identifications can be justified only temporarily and then must be modified to match the ever-changing regional or global political climate changes. What do we learn about Gog and Magog from Ezekiel's prophecy?

Gog and Magog

The location of Ezekiel's Gog is uncertain. Even the interpretation of the name is difficult. Suggestions for the derivation and meaning of the name "Gog" include the following: (1) a mythological "locust giant" (see Amos 7:1, where the Greek translation reads *Gōg*); (2) a personification of darkness (from the Sumerian word *gug*, "darkness"); (3) from the place Gaga mentioned in the Amarna Letters; (4) from Gaga, a deity mentioned in Ugaritic literature.[5] (5) More plausible is the connection with Gyges, the name of a king of Lydia who ruled from 668 to 644 B.C.[6] Since this king had died by the time Ezekiel wrote down his prophecy, this identification is unlikely. Some have suggested that Gog/Gyges is not a personal name but the name of a royal dynasty, and that Ezekiel refers to Gyges' great-grandson Alyattes who revived Lydia as a dominant power in western Asia Minor (modern Turkey). There is no hint that the kings of Lydia ever posed a threat to Judah. To assume that Ezekiel prophesied events in the twenty-first century creates the problem that the long prophecy in Ezekiel 38–39 would be irrelevant for his audience, which is unlikely. Ezekiel's prophecies concerning Tyre and Babylon all refer to contemporary nations in the sixth and fifth century B.C.

The homeland of Gog is identified as "the land of Magog" (Ezek. 38:1; also 39:6). The location of Magog is uncertain. The suggestion that is the most plausible explains Magog as a contraction of the expression *mat Gugi* ("land of God"), interpreted as a reference to the region of Lydia in western Asia Minor. In Genesis 10:2 (1 Chron. 1:5), Magog is described as the second son

---

   Prophecy Commentary (Eugene, OR: Harvest, 2007), 190–93; Joel C. Rosenberg, *Epicenter* (Carol Stream, IL: Tyndale, 2006), 81–87.

4. Mark Hitchcock, *After the Empire: The Fall of the Soviet Union and Bible Prophecy* (Oklahoma City: Hearthstone, 1992), 13–26.

5. Daniel I. Block, *The Book of Ezekiel*, NICOT (Grand Rapids: Eerdmans, 1998), 2:433n31. For the comments that follow in the text above, see ibid., 433–36, 439–40.

6. Date according to Walter Eder and Johannes Renger, *Chronologies of the Ancient World: Names, Dates and Dynasties, Brill's New Pauly, Supplements 1*, trans. and ed. Wouter F. M. Henkelman (Leiden: Brill, 2007), 90.

of Japheth together with Gomer, Madai, Javan, Tubal, Meshech, and Tiras. In other words, it is identified with persons rather than with geographical territories. This use of Magog as a personal name is taken up by later traditions, such as the passage in Revelation 20:8 where "Gog and Magog" appear as a fixed pair of personal names involved in the final battle of history.[7]

Gog's Allies

Ezekiel 38:2 describes Gog as "chief prince" of Meshech and Tubal. The Hebrew expression (*nesi' ro'sh*) translated as "chief prince" (KJV, RSV, NRSV, NIV, NET, ESV) has also been interpreted as referring to three names, which leads to the translation "the prince of Rosh, Meshech, and Tubal" (NASB, JB). The Hebrew term *ro'sh* is interpreted by the (much later) Masoretic pointing (and by the Septuagint [LXX]) in a way indicating that the term should be taken as a noun expressing ethnicity. Many prophecy writers identify "Rosh" with Russia.[8] This identification is based on faulty etymology: the name "Russia" derives from a northern Viking language and not from a Semitic language. It was first used for the region of what we today call the Ukraine in the ninth century A.D.[9] The similarities between the Hebrew term *ro'sh* and the term "Russia" are accidental (which sometimes happens with words from two unrelated languages). Since Ezekiel's use of the term *ro'sh* and the first use of the term "Rus" for the Ukraine are fifteen hundred years apart, the identification of the Hebrew term *ro'sh* with "Russia" is anachronistic. It cannot be the basis for an interpretation of Ezekiel's prophecy. More plausible is the suggestion to link *ro'sh* with the neo-Assyrian word *rashu* or *reshu*, terms that refer to a region far to the east (not in the north). It is a territory on the border between Babylon and Elam, which are geographically distant from Meshech and Tubal to which *ro'sh* is related in Ezekiel 38:2. It is therefore preferable to treat *ro'sh* as the common Hebrew noun it is and interpret it as providing a closer definition of *nasi'* (thus the translation "chief prince"). Ezekiel emphasizes with his use of *ro'sh* that "Gog is not just one of many Anatolian princely figures, but the leader among princes and over several tribal/national groups."[10]

Meshech is attested in neo-Assyrian sources as *Mushki* ruled by King Mitas of Phrygia in western Asia Minor, probably King Midas of Sardis.[11] Tubal was known to the Assyrians as *Bit Buritash*, a kingdom in the interior of central Asia Minor. Ezekiel describes an alliance of God (Lydia), located farthest west, with Meshech on Lydia's eastern border and Tubal, which is

---

7. Also see *Sibylline Oracles* 3:319–20, 512.
8. For example, LaHaye and Hindson, *Popular Bible Prophecy Commentary*, 190.
9. Edwin Yamauchi, *Foes from the Northern Frontier: Invading Hordes from the Russian Steppes* (Grand Rapids: Baker Academic, 1982), 20–21.
10. Block, *Book of Ezekiel*, 2:435.
11. Herodotus, *Histories* 3.94 describes Meshech as part of the nineteenth satrapy of king Darius.

east of Meshech. Why did Ezekiel refer to these peoples in Asia Minor? These were not peoples with whom Judea had direct contact. The answer may be related to the fact that "the peoples in the distant north were shrouded in mystery. The reports of these mysterious people groups that filtered down spoke of wild peoples, brutal and barbaric. This combination of mystery and brutality made Gog and his confederates perfect symbols of the archetypal enemy, rising against God and his people."[12]

Ezekiel mentions five additional allies of God and his forces (Ezek. 38:5–6): Persia (Paras),[13] Ethiopia (Cush), Put (Libya in northern Africa), Gomer (a wild tribe living north of the Black Sea), and Beth-Togarmah (on the border of Tubal in central Asia Minor, in the region of the later kingdom of Cappadocia, in the modern Turkish province of Sivas). This list indicates that Ezekiel envisions a great conspiracy against Israel over which Yahweh has total control.

Gog's Invasion

Ezekiel describes the timing of the invasion by Gog: "After many days you shall be mustered; in the latter years you shall go against a land restored from war, a land where people were gathered from many nations on the mountains of Israel, which had long lain waste; its people were brought out from the nations and now are living in safety, all of them" (Ezek. 38:8).

Two conditions need to be met before this event happens. First, Israel will have recovered from the destruction of a previous invading army. This destruction is a reference to the invasion of Nebuchadnezzar that devastated Judea and brought Ezekiel and other Judeans into exile in Babylonia in 587 B.C. Second, Israel's population will have gathered from many nations. Ezekiel prophesies that this invasion of hostile forces will occur "in the latter days" (Ezek. 38:16), a reference to the "many days" of Ezekiel 38:8. The Hebrew expression translated "in the latter days" (be'acharit hayyamim) does not refer to the last days before the end of history, but to the distant future, to be reckoned from Ezekiel's time. The prophet's later contemporaries would most naturally have seen this prophecy as predicting Israel's return from exile between 539and 516 B.C.,[14] a time that is indeed "many days" after Ezekiel's

---

12. Block, *Book of Ezekiel*, 2:436.
13. The identification of Paras is disputed. A connection with Persia seems mistaken. Old Testament scholars suggest "a reference to some commercial or military power with strong links to Tyre and Egypt, but which is to date unattested in extrabiblical records, or an alternative, perhaps Egyptian, spelling for Pathros, 'Southland'" (Block, *Book of Ezekiel*, 2:439–40).
14. In 539 B.C. the Persians defeated Babylonia, and King Cyrus gave permission to the Jews to return to Judea. In 520 B.C., a large number of Jewish exiles returned during the reign of Darius I, under the leadership of Zerubbabel and Joshua. In 516 B.C., the rebuilt (second) temple was dedicated.

deportation into exile. After the return from exile, Ezekiel's prophecy would be related to another attack on Jerusalem.

Gog's Defeat

The utter and total defeat of Gog and his allies, whose troops are buried in mass graves (Ezek. 38:14–39:20), suggests that these enemies from the distant regions of the earth will never again threaten God's people. The stage is set for Yahweh's return to Israel and to his temple (Ezek. 43:1–7).

The Fulfillment of the Gog Prophecy

Josephus interpreted Ezekiel's writings as a reference to the Scythians who invaded the Middle East around 630 B.C.[15] Later Jewish texts connect Ezekiel's prophecy with the Messiah who will help Israel vanquish Gog and his allies—interpreted not as nations in Asia Minor and adjacent areas but as the nations generally—"at the end of the days."[16] Some have connected Ezekiel's Gog prophecy with the events during the time of Esther (during the reign of the Persian king Ahasuerus, probably Xerxes I who ruled from 486 to 465 B.C. when Israel's enemies wanted to plunder the Jews, only to be slaughtered).[17] Others see Ezekiel's Gog prophecy fulfilled during the time of Antiochus IV Epiphanes (175–164 B.C.) when the Jews in Judea were persecuted but eventually won an astounding victory under Judas Maccabeus and his brothers. While not entirely impossible, if we do not press the details of Ezekiel's Gog prophecy, these interpretations fail to account for the apparent connection of the victory over Gog with Yahweh's total defeat of the forces that threaten Israel in connection with the building of a new temple (Ezekiel 40–48).

Prophecy writers who demand a literal fulfillment believe that Ezekiel's Gog prophecy has not been fulfilled because none of these historical events had all the details of Ezekiel's prophecy. They expect a yet future fulfillment, debating whether it will occur before, during, or after "the Tribulation" or at the end of the millennium.[18] If a literal interpretation is demanded, it must be admitted that a literal fulfillment has become impossible. In Ezekiel's prophecy, Gog and his allies fight on horses with swords, shields, and helmets (Ezek. 38:4–5, 15, 21; 39:20). In "literalist" interpretations of the Gog prophecy which anticipate a future invasion of Gog and Magog by a northern alliance, horses become horsepower, arrows become guided missiles or atomic

---

15. Josephus, *Jewish Antiquities* 1.123.
16. *Targum Pseudo-Jonathan* on Exodus 40:11; also see *3 Enoch* 45:5 (fifth/sixth century A.D.).
17. Gary DeMar, *End Times Fiction: A Biblical Consideration of the Left Behind Theology* (Nashville: Thomas Nelson, 2001), 12–15.
18. LaHaye and Hindson, *Popular Bible Prophecy Commentary*, 191–92.

weapons.[19] One cannot have it both ways: either the fulfillment of Gog's invasion is "literal" in the literal sense of Ezekiel's description, complete with horses and swords and shields, or it is not intended to be taken literally. In this case, a fulfillment of the prophecy has to be sought in a historical period before the invention of gunpowder. Or, Ezekiel conveys a symbolic vision of God's ultimate victory over the enemies of his people.

It seems plausible, therefore, to interpret the Gog prophecy as Ezekiel's vision of the radicalized conflict between Yahweh and the nations in which Yahweh wins the final victory over the cosmic forces of chaos (represented by Gog and his allies).[20]

Summary

The prophet Ezekiel prophesies that in the more distant future, seen from his "place" in history in the sixth century B.C., the conflict between the God of Israel and the evil in the world will come to a climax in which the nations who seek to harm God's people will be utterly and completely destroyed.

REFLECTION QUESTIONS

1. Which geographical identifications have been suggested for Gog and his allies?

2. Which events have been suggested for the fulfillment of Ezekiel's Gog prophecy?

3. How have these nations been interpreted by end-time writers?

4. Why and when do end-time writers revise their identifications?

5. What is Ezekiel's main concern in the Gog prophecy?

---

19. More recent end-time writers (such as Rosenberg, *Epicenter*) identify Gog and his allies with an alliance of Islamic nations who invade Israel, introducing a religious element that is entirely absent from Ezekiel's prophecy.
20. Thus Block, *Book of Ezekiel*, 2:429.

Who Are Gog and Magog in Revelation?

John describes the invasion of Gog and Magog as follows: "When the thousand years are ended, Satan will be released from his prison and will come out to deceive the nations at the four corners of the earth, Gog and Magog, in order to gather them for battle; they are as numerous as the sands of the sea. They marched up over the breadth of the earth and surrounded the camp of the saints and the beloved city. And fire came down from heaven and consumed them. And the devil who had deceived them was thrown into the lake of fire and sulfur, where the beast and the false prophet were, and they will be tormented day and night forever and ever" (Rev. 20:7–10).

Many have noted the general parallels between Revelation 20:1–22 and Ezekiel 37–48. The first resurrection and the messianic millennial kingdom (Rev. 20:4–6) correspond to the revival of the dry bones and the reunited kingdom under the Davidic messiah (Ezek. 37:1–28). The final battle against Gog and Magog (Rev. 20:7–10) has its counterpart in Ezekiel 38–39. The descent of the heavenly Jerusalem (Revelation 21–22) corresponds to Ezekiel's vision of a new temple and a New Jerusalem (Ezekiel 40–48).

Identification of Gog and Magog

Three major identifications of "the nations at the four corners of the earth, Gog and Magog" have been suggested.[1] First, Gog and Magog stand for a demonic army. This raises the question why John does not speak more

---

1. For the discussion that follows in the text above, see David E. Aune, *Revelation*, WBC 52C (Dallas: Word, 1998), 3:1095; Grant R. Osborne, *Revelation*, BECNT (Grand Rapids: Baker Academic, 2002), 713, who argues for the second option; J. Webb Mealy, *After the Thousand Years: Resurrection and Judgment in Revelation 20*, JSNTSup 70 (Sheffield: JSOT Press, 1992), 126–42, who argues for the third option.

explicitly of demons, which he can easily do (see Rev. 9:20; 16:14; 18:2, where the Greek term *daimonion* is used). In the book of Revelation, the word "nations" refers to humans.

Second, Gog and Magog represent the inhabitants of the earth who were not destroyed in the battle described in Revelation 19:17–21. The problem with this interpretation is the fact that the human participants in the battle of Revelation 19 are not *only* "the beast and the kings of the earth with their armies" (v. 19) but "all, both free and slave, both small and great" (v. 18). In antiquity, only free people fought in armies, not slaves (Hollywood movies notwithstanding). This means that Revelation 19:17–21 does not describe an actual military battle between armies but the confrontation between the followers of the Beast and (the followers of) Jesus Christ.

Third, Gog and Magog represent all the inhabitants of the earth who had followed the Beast, that is, all unbelievers who in their rebellion against God had sided with God's arch-rebel.

The third suggestion seems the most plausible. John identifies the expression "Gog and Magog" (which occurs only here in the New Testament: Ezekiel speaks of "Gog, of the land of Magog") with "the nations at the four corners of the earth." Gog and Magog *are* the "nations"—the followers of the ancient Serpent and of the Beast, the sinners—rather than a select few nations.

The Four Corners of the Earth

Why are the nations described as being "at the four corners of the earth" (Rev. 20:8)? If the phrase "four corners of the earth" is taken literally, it would be a strange description of the location of "the nations" (who are Gog and Magog) who live through the millennium and are then seduced once more by Satan. The expression "four corners of the earth" seems to refer to the Abyss.

In the Old Testament and in Jewish texts, the outer edges of the world are regarded as the entrances to the underworld.[2] The phrase "four corners of the earth" is connected in Revelation 7:1 with four angels who restrained the attack of the evil forces from the Abyss (Rev. 8:7–8; 9:3–4). Note Revelation 9:1: "And the fifth angel blew his trumpet, and I saw a star that had fallen from heaven to earth, and he was given the key to the shaft of the bottomless pit." Some translations render the last word of the Greek sentence, which is *abyssou*, as "Abyss" (NIV, NET). In a revealing parallel in the Jewish apocalyptic text *1 Enoch*, the seer is shown "a place, beyond the great earth, where the heavens come together. And I saw a deep pit with heavenly fire on its pillars . . . . This place is the (ultimate) end of heaven and earth: it is the prison house for the stars and the powers of heaven . . . Here shall stand in many different appearances the spirits of the angels which have united themselves with women. They have defiled the people and will lead them into error so that they will

---

2. See Psalm 61:2: "From the end of the earth I call to you, when my heart is faint."

offer sacrifices to the demons as unto gods, until the great day of judgment in which they shall be judged till they are finished" (*1 En.* 18:10–11, 14; 19:1). In Revelation 9:2, the Abyss is also a place of fire: "he opened the shaft of the bottomless pit, and from the shaft rose smoke like the smoke of a great furnace, and the sun and the air were darkened with the smoke from the shaft."

In Revelation 20:9, Satan (together with Gog and Magog) "comes up" onto the expanse of the earth. The Greek word that is used here (*anabainō*) denotes "to be in motion upward" and should be translated "go up" or "ascend."[3] This verb is used in Revelation for smoke rising up (Rev. 4:1), the two witnesses going up into heaven (11:12), the evil forces (the demonic locusts) coming out of the Abyss (9:2–3), the Beast coming up out of the sea (13:1), the second beast coming up from the earth (13:11), and the Beast coming up out the Abyss (11:7). This word is very unnatural if it is taken to describe a march of "the nations" who live on earth to some place where God's people are gathered.

The phrase "plain of the earth" in Revelation 20:9 (NASB, NET, NLT, ESV) is unusual. It occurs only twice in the Greek translation of the Old Testament. The closest parallel is Daniel 12:2: "And many of those who sleep *in the flat of the earth* will arise, some to everlasting life but others to shame and others to dispersion [and contempt] everlasting" (LXX; Old Greek)[4] This suggests that the place from which Satan and "the nations" identified with Gog and Magog come is the Abyss, the place of the dead and the realm of Satan.

The Unrepentant

Consequently, John seems to identify "Gog and Magog" with the "nations" who have been in the Abyss together with Satan as prisoners (Rev. 20:7). They appear to be identical with "the rest of the dead" (Rev. 20:5), that is, with the unrepentant. This is confirmed by the description of "the nations at the four corners of the earth" as being "in number . . . like the sand on the seashore" (20:8 NIV; Greek, *hōs hē ammos tēs thalassēs*). In Revelation 13:1 (in the Greek text this is 12:18), the Dragon, who is Satan, stood "on the shore of the sea" (NIV; Greek, *epi tēn ammon tēs thalassēs*) to meet the Beast as it came out of the sea, that is, out of the Abyss (11:7; also 20:13).

Satan had been confined to the Abyss as a prisoner, unable to influence the earth for a thousand years since the Beast and the false prophet had already been thrown in the lake of fire for eternal punishment (19:20).[5]

---

3. The NIV is misleading when it translates "they marched across the breadth of the earth."
4. Translation quoted from R. T. McLay, in Albert Pietersma and Benjamin G. Wright, eds., *A New English Translation of the Septuagint* (Oxford: Oxford University Press, 2007), 1022 (emphasis added).
5. Mealy compares Isaiah 24:1–27:1 with Revelation 19:19–20:10 (*After the Thousand Years*, 99–101). He writes that the unrepentant "are trapped in the nether world for 'many days' (Isa. 24:22), together awaiting the divine summons for judgment" (ibid., 101).

After the thousand years, Satan and the unrepentant "come up" from the place of the dead onto the earth. Satan's imprisonment should have taught the unrepentant that the pseudo-god who had deceived them in the past has lost his power: his deception is unmasked as he can no longer deceive the nations through the Beast and the false prophet for a thousand years.

The irony of Revelation 20:8 is that "when the unrepentant are released, they are immediately willing to forget the truth that they have just been compelled to face for a thousand long years . . . all the 'rest of the dead' are still blind enough to believe that Satan can overcome God's people."[6]

The punishment for this continuing rebellion is banishment into "the lake of fire and sulfur, where the beast and the false prophet were, and they will be tormented day and night forever and ever" (Rev. 20:10). If this interpretation is correct, there is no literal final battle between Gog and Magog (interpreted as "those who lived through the millennium and then been immediately seduced once more by Satan"[7]). There is, at the end of the thousand years, the final punishment of Satan as the supreme force of evil together with all the unrepentant.

Summary

The prophet John explains that at the end, before God's new world becomes a reality, God will utterly and completely remove from the face of the earth the instigator of all evil and all who followed him in rebellion. In Revelation 20:8, Gog and Magog are not individual nations from the north consisting of military troops. "Gog and Magog" are all the inhabitants of the earth who follow the Beast rather than the Lamb, that is, all the unbelievers who persist in their rebellion against God. Many interpret Revelation 20:7–10 as the final battle between the nations who have been deceived by Satan after the millennium. Others interpret the event as the final judgment upon Satan and the unrepentant at the time of Jesus Christ's return. The choice between these two possibilities depends on how we interpret the millennium (see question 33). Chronological questions aside, there is agreement that the judgment of "God and Magog" is God's final judgment on unrepentant sinners.

REFLECTION QUESTIONS

1. What links John's reference to Gog and Magog with Ezekiel's Gog prophecy? What is similar? What is different?

---

6. Mealy, *After the Thousand Years*, 130.
7. Osborne, *Revelation*, 713.

2. What are the main interpretations of John's prophecy concerning Gog and Magog?

3. How is the final rebellion of Gog and Magog in Revelation 20:8–9 related to the rebellion in Revelation 19:19?

4. What is the meaning of the "nations" with which Gog and Magog are identified?

5. What is the outcome of Satan's last rebellion?

What Is the Battle of Armageddon?

The place called "Armageddon" is mentioned only once in the Bible. John explains that demonic spirits assembled the kings of the world for battle on the great day of the Lord "to the place that in Hebrew is called Armageddon" (Rev. 16:16 NIV). The outcome of this battle between the forces of evil and the almighty God is described in Revelation 17:14 and 19:11–21 (and, some argue, in 20:7–10). Although not explicitly connected with the name Armageddon, a final battle between the assembled wicked nations and Israel's God is mentioned repeatedly in the Old Testament.

The City of Megiddo

Biblical Megiddo is identified with modern el-Lejjun, about one kilometer (0.6 miles) south of Tel Megiddo. The location of the city "at the point where Nahal ʿIron (Wadi ʿAra) enters the Jezreel Valley gave it strategic control in ancient times over the international Via Maris, which crossed from the Sharon Plain into the Valley of Jezreel by way of the ʿIron Valley. This position, astride the most important of the country's roads, made Megiddo the scene of major battles from earliest times through our own."[1] In the fifteenth century B.C., Megiddo appears in Egyptian sources as the city that led a confederation of Canaanite cities against Egypt, which controlled Canaan and Syria. The decisive battle, in which Egypt was victorious after laying siege to Megiddo for seven months, took place at the Qinnah Brook near Megiddo. In the subsequent period, Megiddo was one of the mightiest cities in the Jezreel Valley.

Megiddo is listed among the cities not conquered by the tribe of Manasseh (Josh. 17:11–13). The city continued to be one of the major Canaanite cities

---

1. Yohanan Aharoni, "Megiddo," in *The New Encyclopedia of Archaeological Excavations in the Holy Land*, ed. Ephraim Stern (Jerusalem: Israel Exploration Society and Carta; New York: Simon & Schuster, 1993), 1003. Aharoni describes in detail the excavations on Tel Megiddo.

during the period of the judges (Judg. 5:19). Megiddo later fell into Israelite hands and is listed among the cities fortified by King Solomon (1 Kings 9:15). Around 925 B.C., Pharaoh Shishak conquered Megiddo in his campaign against Israel. After King Tiglath-pileser conquered the northern part of Israel in 733–732 B.C., he made Megiddo the capital of the new Assyrian province of Magiddu, which included the Jezreel Valley and Galilee. The battle between Judah's King Josiah and Pharaoh Necho in 609 B.C. took place at Megiddo (2 Kings 23:29; 2 Chron. 35:22).

After Josiah's defeat, nothing more is heard of Megiddo. When the Roman governor consolidated control over the region after the revolt of Bar Kokhba (A.D. 132–136), he stationed the Sixth Roman Legion not in Megiddo but in Kefar Othnai, a village guarding the 'Iron Pass,' which became known as Legio (the name of the Arabic village at the site is el-Lejjun).

Armageddon in Hebrew

John wants his readers to notice that the term Armageddon is derived from Hebrew. Armageddon in Hebrew is *har-megiddon*, which means "mount" or "mountain" (*har*) of Megiddo. The problem is that while Megiddo was a famous city, there is no "mountain" connected with Megiddo. There is a tell at Megiddo, rising 40 to 60 meters (130 to 200 feet) near the surrounding plain, but no mountain.[2] Settlements on hills were sometimes referred to with the Hebrew term *har*, but the usual term for a hill is *gib'a* while *har* refers to a mountain. Other explanations of the meaning of Armageddon have been offered. Some suggest a reference to a wider area that includes Mount Carmel; however, this mountain is never connected with Megiddo. Others suggest a derivation from the Hebrew term *'ir megiddon* ("city of Megiddo"), which would make sense as a reference to the city, but is not convincing since it requires the assumption of an unusual transcription of a Hebrew word into Greek.

The difficulty of these geographically based explanations has prompted scholars to look for other interpretations. Some derive "Armageddon" from Hebrew *har mo'ed*, which means "mountain of assembly," and see a reference to Mount Zion or to the throne of God, which Babylon's king tries to ascend (Isa. 14:12–14). The assumed emendation of the text makes this suggestion implausible. Others suggest that the Hebrew element *megiddon* comes from a verb meaning "to attack," which then yields "marauding mountain" as the meaning of Armageddon—which has been interpreted as another name for Babylon. Others suggest a connection with the Hebrew term *maged* ("a place

---

2. A tell is an "artificial mound or hill resulting from the accumulation of occupation debris over a long period of time" when "successive phases of settlement were constructed upon the ruins of their predecessor and then in turn leveled to provide a platform for succeeding structures" (Timothy Darvill, *The Concise Oxford Dictionary of Archaeology* [Oxford: Oxford University Press, 2002], 422).

of gathering troops"), which would mean that Armageddon is a reference to the gathering of the nations for the final battle (as in Joel 3:2, 12). Others suggest a connection with Hebrew *har migdō* ("his fruitful mountain") or with *har hemda* ("beautiful city") as a reference to Jerusalem and its vicinity where Ezekiel 38–39 expects the final battle to take place (also Joel 3:2; Zech. 14:2). None of the suggestions mentioned above are fully convincing.

The Meaning of Armageddon

It is ironic that John's reference to Hebrew in Revelation 16:16 does not clarify the identification of Armageddon but seems to complicate the explanation. This may be deliberate. John probably intends the term "Armageddon" as a *general reference* to Megiddo and the battles and other events that took place in the region: the defeat of the kings of Canaan who oppress God's people "by the waters of Megiddo" (Judg. 5:19–21); the confrontation between Elijah and the (false) prophet of Baal during the reign of Ahab and Jezebel on Mount Carmel and their destruction in the Kishon Valley (1 Kings 18:40); the death of Josiah, Judah's misled king, at Megiddo at the hands of Pharaoh Necho (2 Kings 23:29); and the expectation of a future defeat of "all the nations that come against Jerusalem," which is connected with a reference to "the one they have pierced" and to "the mourning for Hadad-rimmon in the plain of Megiddo" (Zech. 12:9–12).[3] The last reference (which contains the only place in the Old Testament where the Hebrew text spells "Megiddo" as *megiddon* rather than *megiddo*, thus agreeing with John's spelling) evokes also the "Gog, of the land of Magog" tradition of Ezekiel 38–39 that expects the final defeat of God's and Israel's enemies over kings from the north and their armies who invade the mountains of Israel (38:8, 21).

This suggests that "Armageddon" is not a specific place that can be located on a map or reached with the help of GPS equipment. Like "Babylon" and "Euphrates" in the book of Revelation, "Armageddon" is a typological symbol of the final battle between God and his enemies, and between Jesus and God's people. This is confirmed by the fact that the Old Testament prophecies about the final battle of history place it in the vicinity of the city of Jerusalem and Mount Zion and the surrounding mountains—about a two-day march south of Megiddo.

The Battle of Armageddon

The Old Testament prophecies about the final battle of history can be compared with John's references to the final battle, summarized in the table below.

---

3. Gregory K. Beale, *The Book of Revelation: A Commentary on the Greek Text*, NIGTC (Grand Rapids: Eerdmans, 1999), 840; Grant R. Osborne, *Revelation*, BECNT (Grand Rapids: Baker Academic, 2002), 596. On Gog and Magog, see questions 26 and 27.

THE FINAL BATTLE		
	OLD TESTAMENT	**REVELATION**
DATE	• on the "day of the Lᴏʀᴅ" (Joel 2:1) • on "the day of the Lᴏʀᴅ [that] is great" (Joel 2:11; Zeph. 1:14) • "great day of the Lᴏʀᴅ" (Zeph. 1:14) • "the great and terrible day of the Lᴏʀᴅ" (Joel 2:31)	• when the sixth angel pours his bowl on the great river Euphrates (16:12) • on "the great day of God the Almighty" (16:14)
LOCATION	• Mount Zion and Jerusalem (Joel 2:1, 32) • Jerusalem (Zech. 12:2–3; 14:2, 4) • the mountains of Israel (Ezek. 38:8; 39:2, 4)	• Armageddon (16:16)
PHENOMENA	• the sun turns to darkness and the moon to blood before the great day of the Lord (Joel 2:31) • clouds and thick darkness (Joel 2:2; Zeph. 1:15)	• lightning, thunder, earthquake, hailstones (16:18, 21)
ENEMY	• a great and powerful army: "their like has never been from of old, nor will be again after them in ages to come" (Joel 2:2) • "the northern army" (Joel 2:20) • Gog, of the land of Magog and his allies (Ezek. 38:2–6) • nations and kingdoms (Zeph. 3:8) • the nations of the earth (Zech. 12:3; 14:2) • many nations (Mic. 4:11)	• kings from the east (16:12) • the kings of the whole world (16:14) • kings, captains, the mighty (19:18) • the Beast and the kings of the earth (19:19) • "all, both free and slave, both small and great" (19:18)
WEAPONS	• horses and chariots (Joel 2:4–5) • horses (Zech. 12:4) • horses, shields, bucklers, and swords (Ezek. 38:4) • bucklers, shields, bows, arrows, handpikes, spears (Ezek. 39:9)	

GOD'S ARMY	• a vast host that is "numberless" (Joel 2:11) • the holy ones (Zech. 14:5)	• rider on a white horse (Jesus returning) (19:11–13) • the armies of heaven (19:14)
GOD'S ACTION	• "the LORD utters his voice" (Joel 2:11) • the Lord is "a warrior who gives victory" and removes disaster from his people (Zeph. 3:17–18) • God destroys "all the nations that come against Jerusalem" (Zech. 12:9) • God will remove the false prophets (Zech. 13:2–6)	• Jesus: sharp sword come from his mouth with which to strike down the nations (19:15) • Jesus: treads the wine press of the fury of the wrath of God the Almighty (19:15) • Jesus: "King of kings and Lord of lords" (19:15) • God captures the Beast and the false prophet (19:20) • God throws the Beast and the false prophet into the lake of fire (19:20) • Jesus: kills "the rest" (the "all" of 19:18) with the sword from his mouth (19:21)
ENEMY'S DEFEAT	• "in the fire of my passion all the earth shall be consumed" (Zeph. 3:8) • the Lord strikes the nations with a plague: "their flesh shall rot while they are still on their feet; their eyes shall rot in their sockets, and their tongues shall rot in their mouths" (Zech. 14:12–15) • the birds are summoned for the great sacrifice that the Lord prepares, to "eat the flesh of the mighty, and drink the blood of the princes of the earth" (Ezek. 39:18)	• birds are summoned to gather for the great supper of God, to "eat the flesh of kings, the flesh of captains, the flesh of the mighty, the flesh of horses and their riders" (19:17) • the birds are gorged with the flesh of the dead (19:21)

The final battle takes places when Jesus returns at the end of human history. This is clearly confirmed by the content of the sixth and seventh bowl (Rev. 16:12–16 / 17–21). The sixth bowl judgment speaks of the gathering of the "kings from the east" who are assembled by demons sent by the Dragon (Satan). As these demons gather "the kings of the whole world," the "kings from the east" and the "kings of the whole world" are identical. The "kings" represent the political leaders of the world who do not follow the Lamb (Jesus), and their "armies" represent whose whom they control (i.e., the unrighteous). The sixth bowl announces the "battle on the great day of God the Almighty" (i.e., the final battle of human history), which takes place at "Armageddon" (Rev. 16:16). The seventh bowl announces God's victory and the dissolution of the cosmos.

In Revelation 19:11–21, John provides the most detailed description of the defeat and judgment of the ungodly forces at the end of history. John first describes Jesus as a rider on a white horse whose sharp sword strikes down the nations (vv. 11–16). Part of this description is a reference to the heavenly armies who come with Jesus (v. 14). Second, John describes the victory over God's enemies (vv. 17–21). How is this victory achieved? The description of Jesus as "The Word of God" (v. 13) portrays Jesus as executing God's justice by means of God's word. His description as having "a sharp sword with which to strike down the nations" come from his mouth (v. 15) is an allusion to Isaiah 49:2 ("He made my mouth like a sharp sword, in the shadow of his hand he hid me"), where the prophet speaks of God's Servant and his ability of accomplish God's mission of restoring the nation of Israel and saving the nations by means of his word (Isa. 49:6). The victory is accomplished not with military weapons (swords are not wielded with the mouth) but with the word of God (words come from the mouth). This description of Jesus suggests that there is no military battle at a specific location.[4] The so-called battle of Armageddon happens when Jesus returns to judge the unrighteous with the justice of the word of God.

The battle of Armageddon is a symbolic description of the victory of Jesus over the forces of evil at the end, accomplished with the word of God. This symbolic interpretation is confirmed by the description of the heavenly army as "wearing fine linen, white and pure" (Rev. 19:14). This is not battle dress (not in the first century, and certainly not in the twentieth, twenty-first or later centuries). The description of the saints' attire as "linen, white and pure" enforces the idea that "the cause of truth proclaimed by the righteous and maligned by the impious is being declared right" as they take part in the final judgment "in that their testimony is the legal evidence condemning their oppressors" (see 17:14; 19:8).[5]

---

4. Literalists would have to assume a real battle fought on horses with swords and arrows, which is literally inconceivable in the twenty-first century or any later century.
5. Beale, *Book of Revelation*, 960.

No battle is described. The angel "standing in the sun" (Rev. 19:17) announces the destruction of the Beast, the false prophet, and their followers. As the birds are summoned to eat the flesh of the slain, the victory seems to have already happened. The armies are arrayed and ready for battle in Revelation 19:19, but no battle is described. Jesus the Warrior Messiah wins not with military means but with the word of God that comes from his mouth (19:15). Here, the "word of God" is the word of judgment that Jesus speaks when he judges the unrighteous, vindicating the "testimony of Jesus" (19:10) that his followers have kept.

While the reference to kings, captains, the mighty, horses, and their riders in Revelation 19:18 may describe a military army, the subsequent reference to "all" (Greek, *panta*), explained as "both free and slave" (Greek, *eleutheroi kai douloi*) and as "both small and great" (Greek, *mikroi kai megaloi*) renders unlikely an interpretation in terms of an actual military confrontation. The expressions "free and slave" and "small and great" (19:18; also 16:13) are idioms describing the totality of people of all stations in life, of all ages, and from every social class. Note that in Revelation 20:12, all the dead, "great and small" stand before God's throne or judgment. This description clarifies that "Armageddon" is not an actual military battle. In antiquity, slaves did not fight in armies.

No one survives. The Beast and the false prophet are thrown into "the lake of fire that burns with sulfur" (Rev. 19:20). That is, they are consigned to eternal punishment in hell. The "rest," that is, all people—the political leaders (the kings of the earth) and all of humanity irrespective of age and social class—are then judged by Jesus (v. 21).

Summary
The battle of Armageddon brings the final defeat of the evil forces that rebel against God and resist Jesus Christ. It is not an actual military battle in Israel. A literal fulfillment would have been theoretically possible in the first century when armies fought on horses with swords and spears and arrows. However, even then it would have been impossible to picture all the people of the earth assembled at Megiddo in the Jezreel Valley in order to wage war against God's people, not to mention that Old Testament prophecies expected the final battle to take place in Jerusalem and on Mount Zion. The final battle of history is the destruction of the political, cultural, and religious systems of the world (the Beast and the false prophet) that opposed God and the defeat of the ungodly who refuse to follow Jesus (the Lamb). This last battle takes place when Jesus returns for the final judgment. Jesus wins the final victory of human history—not with military might, but with the word of God.

REFLECTION QUESTIONS

1. What is the meaning of the term *Armageddon*? What are the more plausible suggestions?

2. What is the significance of Megiddo in Israel's history?

3. What does the Old Testament say about the final battle of history?

4. What does John say about the final battle?

5. Will there be an actual military battle?

What Is the Great Earthquake?

In the book of Revelation, John mentions an earthquake at the end of the seal, trumpet, and bowl judgments. Is this a prophecy of a real earthquake that signals that the end has come? Do these prophecies predict suffering through earthquakes that believers have to endure?

Earthquakes as Signs of Theophany

In the Old Testament and in later Jewish texts, an earthquake accompanies God's coming into his creation (theophany).[1] Jesus ben Sira, a priest and wisdom teacher in Jerusalem, writes in the second century B.C.: "Lo, heaven and the highest heaven, the abyss and the earth, tremble at his visitation! The very mountains and the foundations of the earth quiver and quake when he looks upon them" (Sir 16:18–19). In the book of Judith we read, "For the mountains shall be shaken to their foundations with the waters; before your glance the rocks shall melt like wax" (Jdt 16:15).

The creation shakes before God's coming as a warrior who defeats his enemies, who will rule over the nations, and who will judge the wicked. In Judges 5:4–5, we read: "LORD, when you went out from Seir, when you marched from the region of Edom, the earth trembled, and the heavens poured, the clouds indeed poured water. The mountains quaked before the LORD, the One of Sinai, before the LORD, the God of Israel."

Joel 2:10–11 says, "The earth quakes before them, the heavens tremble. The sun and the moon are darkened, and the stars withdraw their shining. The LORD utters his voice at the head of his army; how vast is his host! Numberless are those who obey his command. Truly the day of the LORD is great; terrible indeed—who can endure it?" (also see Mic. 1:4; Ps. 78:7–8).

---

1. For the following, see Richard J. Bauckham, *The Climax of Prophecy: Studies on the Book of Revelation* (Edinburgh: T&T Clark, 1993), 199–209.

God's coming to rule over the nations is described in similar terms. Psalm 97:3–5 reads, "Fire goes before him, and consumes his adversaries on every side. His lightnings light up the world; the earth sees and trembles. The mountains melt like wax before the LORD, before the Lord of all the earth" (also see Ps. 99:1).

Earthquake and the Last Judgment

God's coming to judge the wicked is described with the same imagery. Isaiah 24:18–20 prophecies, "Whoever flees at the sound of the terror shall fall into the pit; and whoever climbs out of the pit shall be caught in the snare. For the windows of heaven are opened, and the foundations of the earth tremble. The earth is utterly broken, the earth is torn asunder, the earth is violently shaken. The earth staggers like a drunkard, it sways like a hut; its transgression lies heavy upon it, and it falls, and will not rise again."[2]

The Great Earthquake when God Comes at the End

All these aspects are combined in Jewish texts that describe the great cosmic earthquake that will accompany God's coming at the end. In the apocalyptic text *1 Enoch*, we read in the first paragraph:

> The God of the universe, the Holy Great One, will come forth from his dwelling. And from there he will march upon Mount Sinai and appear in his camp emerging from heaven with a mighty power. And everyone shall be afraid, and Watchers shall quiver. And great fear and trembling shall seize them unto the ends of the earth. Mountains and high places will fall down and be frightened. And high hills shall be made low; and they shall melt like a honeycomb before the flame. And earth shall be rent asunder, and all that is upon the earth shall perish. And there shall be a judgment upon all, including the righteous. And to all the righteous he will grant peace. He will preserve the elect, and kindness shall be upon them. They shall all belong to God and they shall prosper and be blessed; and the light of God shall shine unto them. Behold, he will arrive with ten million of the holy ones in order to execute judgment upon all. He will destroy the wicked ones and censure all flesh on account of everything that they have done, that which the sinners and the wicked ones committed against him. (*1 En.* 1:3–9;[3] also see *1 En.* 102:1–2; *T. Mos.* 10:1–7; *2 Bar.* 32:1).

---

2. Also see Isaiah 13:13; 34:4; Jeremiah 51:29; Ezekiel 38:20; Nahum 1:5; *Sibylline Oracles* 3:675–93.
3. Quotation of *1 Enoch (Ethiopic Apocalypse)*, trans. E. Isaac, in *The Old Testament Pseudepigrapha*, vol. 1: *Apocalyptic Literature and Testaments*, ed. James H. Charlesworth (New York: Doubleday, 1983).

Some texts describe a great earthquake as belonging to a series of natural and man-made disasters leading up to the end. In the apocalyptic text *2 Baruch* 27:1–7, we read: "That time will be divided into twelve parts, and each part has been preserved for that for which it was appointed. In the first part: the beginning of commotions. In the second part: the slaughtering of the great. In the third part: the fall of many into death. In the fourth part: the drawing of the sword. In the fifth part: famine and the withholding of rain. In the sixth part: earthquakes and terrors" (also see *2 Bar.* 70:8; *4 Ezra* 9:3; *Apoc. Ab.* 30:6). This description is reminiscent, in general terms, of Jesus' description of a series of signs of the end that includes an earthquake (Matt. 24:7; Mark 13:8; Luke 21:11).

The Great Earthquake and the Destruction of the Cosmos

The earthquake is mentioned as destroying the cosmos to make way for God's new world. In the Jewish apocalyptic text *4 Ezra* 6:11–16, we read: "I answered and said, 'O sovereign Lord, if I have found favor in your sight, show your servant the end of your signs which you showed me in part on a previous night.' He answered and said to me, 'Rise to your feet and you will hear a full, resounding voice. And if the place where you are standing is greatly shaken while the voice is speaking, do not be terrified; because the word concerns the end, and the foundations of the earth will understand that the speech concerns them. They will tremble and be shaken, for they know that their end must be changed'" (also see *1 En.* 83:3–5).

The Great Earthquake and Sinai

The origin of such descriptions is God's coming on Mount Sinai, which was accompanied by an earthquake: "On the morning of the third day there was thunder, lightning, as well as a thick cloud, and a blast of a trumpet so loud that all the people who were in the camp trembled. . . . Now Mount Sinai was wrapped in smoke, because the Lord had descended upon it in fire; the smoke went up like the smoke of a kiln, while the whole mountain shook violently" (Exod. 19:16, 18).

In later poetic and prophetic descriptions, the imagery of earthquake and thunderstorm accompanying God's theophany on Mount Sinai is frequent. The most dramatic description is perhaps Psalm 114: "When Israel went out from Egypt, the house of Jacob from a people of strange language, Judah became God's sanctuary, Israel his dominion. The sea looked and fled; Jordan turned back. The mountains skipped like rams, the hills like lambs. Why is it, O sea, that you flee? O Jordan, that you turn back? O mountains, that you skip like rams? O hills, like lambs? Tremble, O earth, at the presence of the Lord, at the presence of the God of Jacob, who turns the rock into a pool of water, the flint into a spring of water" (also see Ps. 68:8; 77:17–18; Isa. 64:3; Hab. 3; *4 Ezra* 3:18; *L.A.B.* 11:4–5).

The Old Testament uses this kind of language in other descriptions of God's intervention, both in the past and on the future day of the Lord.[4] Both in the Old Testament and in Jewish texts we find the expectation of a new intervention of God, whose description is patterned on Israel's deliverance in the exodus from Egypt and God's theophany on Mount Sinai.[5]

The Earthquake in the Book of Revelation

John mentions earthquakes not as part of preliminary judgments during the course of history. Rather, in line with their traditional role in the Old Testament, he refers to an earthquake as a sign that heralds God's coming in judgment. Beginning with the vision of God's throne in Revelation 4, John creates series of references to Exodus 19 that is progressive, summarized in the following table.

THE EARTHQUAKE IN REVELATION				
4:5	flashes of lightning	voices/ rumblings	peals of thunder		
8:5	peals of thunder	voices/ rumblings	flashes of lightning	an earthquake	
11:19	flashes of lightning	voices/ rumblings	peals of thunder	an earthquake	a great hailstorm
16:18–21	flashes of lightning	voices/ rumblings	peals of thunder	a violent earthquake, none like has ever occurred since the human race has been on earth	huge hailstones, each weighing about a hundred pounds

The description of the earthquake in Revelation 4:5 uses language from the Sinai theophany (Exod. 19:16, 18) and the throne vision of Ezekiel (Ezek. 1:13). The earthquake in Revelation 6:12 (sixth seal) accompanies the coming

---

4. Judges 5:4–5; 2 Samuel 22:8–16 (= Ps. 18:7–15); see *Liber antiquitatum biblicarum* 11:5; future: Joel 2:1–2, 10; Micah 1:3–4; Nahum 1:3–6.
5. Isaiah 64; Habakkuk 3; *1 Enoch* 1:3–9; *Testament of Moses* 10:1–7. These descriptions seem to read Deuteronomy 33:2–5 as a prophecy of the end.

of God as Judge, and the description of the earthquake in Revelation 8:5 (seventh seal) combines Exodus (19:16, 18) and Ezekiel (10:2). The earthquake in Revelation 11:19 (seventh trumpet) follows the opening of the heavenly temple, signaling the coming of God in power and glory. The description of the earthquake in Revelation 16:18–20 (seventh bowl) is connected with the last plague and the fall of Babylon that happens at the end (more fully described in Rev. 17:1–19:10). The fullest description of the earthquake is given in Revelation 16:18–20, in the last of the seven plagues of the last series of judgments, again patterned on the Sinai theophany.

Summary

For John, the earthquake is an image of the end. The relevance of the Old Testament and Jewish tradition of the eschatological earthquake makes this a powerful symbol of God revealing himself in power and glory, in judgment and vindication. John expects that God, whose voice shook Mount Sinai, will at the end once again shake heaven and the earth. The eschatological earthquake is not a sign of the approaching end: it *is* the end.

Will this earthquake be a literal event? Since the earthquake of Mount Sinai was a physical phenomenon, and since John's readers in Asia Minor were all too familiar with real earthquakes, wreaking havoc on their cities, it is very plausible that the end will begin with a violent earthquake. Since the Old Testament writers also used the earthquake as a symbol of God's revelation, power, and judgment, we cannot be certain, however.

REFLECTION QUESTIONS

1. What role do earthquakes have in the Old Testament?

2. What is the connection between an earthquake and God's coming in Revelation?

3. What is the connection between the great earthquake mentioned in prophetic texts and God's appearance on Mount Sinai?

4. What role do earthquakes play in Jesus' and John's prophecy about the end of history?

5. In what sense does the great earthquake connect John's three series of judgments in the book of Revelation?

The Return of Jesus

Why Will Jesus Return?

The answer to the question, why will Jesus return? reveals something about the level of our commitment to the Christian faith. If we believe that the early Christians' prayer *Marana tha* (Aramaic phrase for "Lord Come!" 1 Cor. 16:22) still has relevance for today, we should be able to explain why Jesus will return.

Jesus Will Return Because the Bible Says So

One reason Jesus will return is because the Bible says so. This answer is formally correct. The Bible indeed says that Jesus will return. When Jesus tells his disciples that one day the nations will see "'the Son of Man coming on the clouds of heaven' with power and great glory" (Matt. 24:30), he speaks about himself, announcing his return. At the end of the Gospel of John, Jesus charges his disciples to follow him "until I return" (John 21:22–23 NIV). When the angels tell the disciples, "this Jesus, who has been taken up from you into heaven, will come in the same way as you saw him go into heaven" (Acts 1:11), they announce Jesus' return. When Paul asserts that "the Lord himself, with a cry of command, with the archangel's call and with the sound of God's trumpet, will descend from heaven" (1 Thess. 4:16), he speaks of Jesus' return to earth. Paul speaks of "the coming of our Lord Jesus Christ" that will happen after the Lawless One has been revealed (2 Thess. 2:1, 3; see question 18). Paul speaks of Jesus' return when he emphasizes that "at his coming those who belong to Christ" will be bodily raised from the dead (1 Cor. 15:23). Peter responds to scoffers who make fun of Christians who believe in "the promise of his coming" (2 Peter 3:4). He argues that the delay of Jesus' coming is not surprising given God's supremacy over time, his patience in granting people time to repent, and the unexpectedness ("like a thief") of the day of the Lord (2 Peter 3:8–10). In the introduction to the book of Revelation, John writes, "Look! He is coming with the clouds; every eye will see him, even those who pierced him; and on his account all the tribes of the earth will wail. So it is to be. Amen" (Rev. 1:7). At the end of the book, Jesus announced repeatedly, "See, I am coming soon" (Rev. 22:7, 11).

The answer "the Bible says so" is correct: Jesus comes back because the Bible says that he will come back. The reason for Jesus' return is much deeper, however. The question at the end of the day is not only whether the Bible is true but whether God will fully and finally achieve his purposes. The assertion that Jesus must return so that God's promises will be fulfilled is an answer that is formally correct but one that does not give us much understanding beyond that. The biblical authors are not content to make formal claims or give formal directions. They explain the connection with God and his purposes in history. We must therefore look for theological answers.

Jesus Will Return Because God Will Restore His Perfect Creation

One of the theological reasons for Jesus' return is connected in a fundamental way with God's creation and the fall. At the end of the sixth day of creation, "God saw everything that he had made, and indeed, it was very good" (Gen. 1:31; the phrase "very good" in Hebrew is *tob me'od*). The next time that the Hebrew term for "very" (*me'od*) is used in the book of Genesis is in the statement "Cain was very angry" (Gen. 4:5), a disposition that quickly led to the first murder in history. The fact that Cain was "very angry" was a vivid demonstration of the fact that God's creation was no longer "very good." The event that changed God's "very good" creation was the decision of Adam and Eve to act in deliberate disregard of the will of God, following the Serpent rather than obeying the One who had created a perfect world (Gen. 3:1–6).

The consequences of the fall were swift, decisive, and numerous (Gen. 3:7–19). First, the relationship of Adam and Eve with God was fractured: they had to hide from God, no longer being naturally comfortable in his presence, a predicament that required their banishment from paradise. Human beings have lived outside of paradise ever since. Second, the relationship between Adam and Eve became selfish: she desired her husband while he established his rule over her. It was competition between their sons Cain and Abel that led to the first murder. Much of the crime and much of the grief throughout history is the result of selfish competitiveness. Third, the place of Adam and Eve in creation was no longer "natural" but intimately connected with pain, sweat, and death. The ground of the earth was cursed by God (Gen. 3:17), which explains the difficulties of earning a living. Because Adam and Eve doubted God's goodness expressed in a perfect creation, God's blessing has become limited—limited to fallen people who die and limited to fallen creation under God's curse.

Thus one of the theological reasons that Jesus will return is this: God will restore his perfect creation in which all things will be new (Rev. 21:5) and which will be inhabited by people who are righteous and holy and who will never die (Rev. 21:4, 27; 22:3). Since Adam's descendants are "naturally" unrighteous and unholy, it is only people who have accepted God's offer of righteousness and holiness who will live in God's new world. God will restore his perfect creation in a new heaven and a new earth in which death, mourning, crying, and pain will be no more (Rev. 21:1–4).

Jesus Will Return Because God Will Vindicate His Goodness

Adam and Eve doubted God's goodness, believing the doubts that the Serpent had cast on God's intentions. The Serpent asked, "Did God really say, 'You must not eat from any tree in the garden'?" (Gen. 3:1 NIV). The introduction of the question ("really") insinuated surprise, indeed skepticism, while the reference to "any tree" (instead of "one particular tree") is a travesty of God's generous permission to eat from all trees of the garden except one. And the reference to "God" instead of "LORD God" (which is the characteristic phrase for God in Genesis 2–3) indicates distance from God, perhaps even rejection of his authority as Lord. The Serpent's apparently innocent curiosity highlights the enemy's denial of God's goodness, suggesting that a greater fullness of enjoyment could be found apart from obeying God.

Eve's answer adopts the Serpent's distancing from God, speaking of "God" rather than of "LORD God." While she corrects the Serpent's mistake regarding God's command, she adds that God might have been a little harsh: "God said, 'You shall not eat of the fruit of the tree that is in the middle of the garden, nor shall you touch it, or you shall die'" (Gen. 3:3). Eve started to doubt God's goodness and followed the Serpent's suggestion with disastrous results.

This is why Jesus will return: God will restore his creation in a new heaven and a new earth (Rev. 21:5), sustaining the people who live there with water from "the spring of the water of life" (v. 6), dwelling with them in their midst as their God who removes all tears and pain and death (vv. 3–4). God's people will inherit these things, and they will enjoy God as the One who indeed cares for his children (v. 7).

Jesus Will Return Because God Will Vindicate His People

People who obey God's will have often been discriminated against, persecuted, and killed. This history of prejudice, ridicule, and opposition began with Cain killing Abel, upon whom the Lord God had looked with favor (Gen. 4:4–5). From that time onwards, many of God's people have experienced reproach and affliction in various ways (see Heb. 11:35–38). This history of opposition continues until today: the execution of Jesus, Steven, James, Peter, Paul, and countless other Christians throughout the ages being only the more explicit examples of prejudice and discrimination.

This is also why Jesus returns: when God restores his perfect creation, he will vindicate all those who have obeyed his will throughout the ages. It is not "the cowardly, the faithless, the polluted, the murderers, the fornicators, the sorcerers, the idolaters, and all liars" who will live in God's new world (Rev.

21:8). It is "those who conquer" (v. 7), that is, the people who followed the revealed will of God in a fallen world, the people who followed God's provision for dealing with sin (sacrifices in the Old Covenant; Jesus and his death and resurrection in the New Covenant), the people who refused to compromise their faith in God and his salvation despite the hardship and the persecution that following God and his Messiah may bring. The cry of the blood of Abel (Gen. 4:10) and the cry of the Christians martyrs (Rev. 6:10) will be answered when Jesus returns. God is indeed just, and he will punish sin because he is the "Sovereign Lord, holy and true" (v. 10). When Jesus returns, God will execute his judgment against the unrighteous and unholy who have refused him, who have refused Jesus, and who have refused God's people.

Summary

Jesus returns not simply because the Bible says that he will and because his return fulfills promises that God will keep. Jesus will return because God has yet to write the last chapter of the history of humankind: the restoration of his perfect creation that was seriously damaged by the fall into sin, which affected every human being as well as nature. Jesus' return brings about the new heavens and the new earth. This is why Christians pray *Marana tha*, "Lord come!" Jesus returns because God then will vindicate his goodness, which was doubted by Adam and Eve and which continues to be doubted not only by atheists and skeptics but by God's people as well. The new creation that follows Jesus' return will demonstrate beyond doubt that God loves the people he created, and that he will and can live in their midst in the perfect new earth. And Jesus returns because then God will vindicate his people, bringing judgment upon the unrighteous who have disobeyed his will and who ridiculed and persecuted those who loved God.

REFLECTION QUESTIONS

1. What is the connection between Jesus' return and Adam and Eve?

2. What is the link between Jesus' return, the first creation, and the new creation?

3. Why is the truth of God's goodness significant?

4. Why is God's judgment of the unrighteous important?

5. How are Jesus' return and God's purposes for humankind connected?

How and Where Will Jesus Return?

Jesus was a historical figure, and he will return as a historical figure. Because historical figures exist in space and time, Jesus' first coming can be localized in time and space: he was born probably in the year 6 B.C. in Bethlehem. After his birth, he was taken by his parents first to Egypt then to Nazareth in Galilee. He lived in Capernaum once he began his public ministry probably in the year A.D. 28. He died on Friday, the 14th of the month of Nisan (7 April) of the year A.D. 30 in Jerusalem, rose from the dead on Sunday, the 16th of the month of Nisan of the year A.D. 30, and ascended to the Father forty days later from the Mount of Olives outside of Jerusalem (Acts 1:9–12). Because historical figures exist in space and time, it is appropriate to ask how and where Jesus will return.

Jesus Will Return as He Left

When Jesus ascended to the Father, "he was lifted up, and a cloud took him out of their sight" (Acts 1:9). The passive voice of the first verb ("he was lifted up") describes divine action: it was God who took Jesus back into heaven, to sit at his right hand (2:33). The cloud is not the "vehicle" that transported Jesus into heaven because God's dwelling place is not "up there." The cloud signals to the apostles that Jesus has just left them permanently— not as he left them during the last forty days, only to appear again for further instruction and fellowship. The reference to the cloud, which was real enough, provides a clear demarcation between earth and heaven. It emphasizes that Jesus is in heaven, the place where God dwells, sovereign and independent of the control of human beings.[1] Jesus' departure for heaven must not be misunderstood in terms of Jesus now being absent from earth. Luke's narrative in the book of Acts demonstrates that the heavenly Jesus Christ continues to be

---

1. See Matthew Sleeman, *Geography and the Ascension Narrative in Acts*, SNTSMS 146 (Cambridge: Cambridge University Press, 2009), 77–78.

present and actively involved in the mission of the church. The ascension is a moment of "spatial realignment" as Jesus relocates from earth to heaven, from his earthly ministry to his heavenly ministry.[2]

The "two men in white robes" (angels) assure the disciples that Jesus' ascension is a guarantee that he will return in the same manner in which he was taken to heaven: "Men of Galilee, why do you stand looking up toward heaven? This Jesus, who has been taken up from you into heaven, will come in the same way as you saw him go into heaven" (Acts 1:11). This had been prophesied by Jesus, when he told his disciples that when the end comes, the people "will see 'the Son of Man coming in a cloud' with power and great glory" (Luke 21:27; also Mark 14:62). The two angels speak about the manner of Jesus' return: he will return "in the same way"[3] in which he ascended into heaven (Acts 1:11). What does this mean?

Does Jesus Return in a Cloud?

Jesus, the angels, and Paul mention clouds in connection with Jesus' return (Luke 21:27; Mark 14:62; Acts 1:11; 1 Thess. 4:17). As Jesus' ascension to the Father was marked by clouds that hid him from the sight of the disciples, so his return could be accompanied by literal clouds as well. However, if the clouds are literal, Jesus' return would be an event in a particular region: if Jesus' return took place in the city of Jerusalem in Israel, accompanied by clouds, his return could be witnessed only in that city, nowhere else.

The explanation that satellite technology makes a worldwide viewing of Jesus' return is technically (pun intended) correct, but it is inadequate as an explanation for what Jesus, the angels, and Paul could have meant and what his readers could have understood.

When Paul writes to the Thessalonian believers that "we who are still alive and are left" will meet Jesus "in the clouds" (1 Thess. 4:17 NIV), he does not seem to understand the "clouds" as a meeting point above a particular geographical location. As an itinerant missionary, he did not know where he would be if Jesus were to return while he was still alive. And he speaks of all believers wherever they live, including the believers in Jerusalem, Damascus, Antioch, southern Galatia, Philippi, and all the other cities where people had come to faith in Jesus. This seems to rule out a geographically restricting, literal interpretation of the clouds at Jesus' return.

In Luke 21:25–27, Jesus links his coming with a situation on earth when the nations will be in anguish and people faint from terror because there are signs in the sun, moon, and stars: "At that time they will see 'the Son of Man coming in a cloud' with power and great glory" (v. 27). The people who will see Jesus coming "in a cloud" appears to be all the inhabitants of the earth.

---

2. See ibid., 80.

3. The Greek expression here, *hon tropon*, means "in the same manner in which."

This statement also seems to rule out a literal, geographically restrictive interpretation of the clouds.

It is important to note that when Jesus speaks of his return in a cloud (Luke 21:25–27; Mark 14:62), he derives this description from Daniel 7, where the prophet sees "one like a son of man, coming with the clouds of heaven" (Dan. 7:13 NIV). This reference is important because Jesus referred to himself as the Son of Man. When Jesus refers to clouds in connection with his affirmation that he will return from heaven, he may be more interested in making the connection with Daniel's prophecy than in making a comment on an atmospheric phenomenon accompanying his return.[4]

Whether or not Jesus will come on literal clouds, there is no doubt what the reference to the clouds communicates. They emphasize that Jesus' return is a theophany: in the Old Testament God appears in clouds. When Jesus returns, he comes with full, visible, divine dignity and power. Also, the clouds emphasize that Jesus' return is a public event: clouds cannot be kept a secret, but they are seen by everyone looking at the sky in wider region.

Neither Jesus, the angels, nor Paul seem to be overly interested in the clouds. Compare the following description in a pre-Christian Jewish apocalyptic text: "And they took me up onto their wings, and carried me up to the first heaven, and placed me on the clouds. And, behold, they were moving. And there I perceived the air higher up, and higher still, I saw the ether. And they placed me on the first heaven" (2 En. 3:1–3). Neither Jesus nor Paul is interested in the "geography" of the clouds. They are not interested in clarifying how the clouds in which Jesus returns can be seen by the worldwide assembly of believers.

Will Jesus Return on the Mount of Olives in Jerusalem?

The angels told the disciples that Jesus will return "in the same way" in which he ascended to heaven (Acts 1:11). Does that mean that he will return on the Mount of Olives, "a Sabbath day's walk from the city" east of Jerusalem (Acts 1:12 NIV), where this event took place? The prophecy in Zechariah 14 seems to confirm this: "On that day his feet will stand on the Mount of Olives, east of Jerusalem . . . . Then the LORD my God will come, and all the holy ones with him" (vv. 4–5 NIV). However, the angels' reference to the "manner" of Jesus' ascension refers to the heavens and to the cloud, not to the location of Jesus' return. The context of the angels' explanation clarifies that the task that the disciples have been given is more important than the details of Jesus' return. Indeed, even more important than waiting for Jesus' return in Jerusalem. The question "why do you stand here looking into the sky?" (Acts

---

4. Note the context Daniel 7:14: "To him was given dominion and glory and kingship, that all peoples, nations, and languages should serve him. His dominion is an everlasting dominion that shall not pass away, and his kingship is one that shall never be destroyed."

1:11 NIV) reminds them that they have been commissioned by Jesus to wait for the bestowal of the Holy Spirit and his power, and then to be his witnesses "in Jerusalem, and in all Judea and Samaria, and to the ends of the earth" (1:8 NIV). Jesus' followers do not worry about the place of Jesus' return because they work and live as Jesus' witnesses in many cities between Jerusalem and the remotest nations on earth.

How and Where Will Jesus Return?

While Jesus, the two men in white robes (angels), and Paul leave no doubt that Jesus' return will be a "literal" (physical) event that will take place in time and space, they do not clarify how that "space" should be understood. In our present experience, only a limited number of people can witness a physical event such as the appearance of a person, satellite television notwithstanding. What people see on the television screen is an image of a physical event, but not the physical event itself (apart from the fact that such an interpretation is anachronistic and thus irrelevant for understanding the biblical text written in the first century).

Jesus' first coming was full of surprises: only shepherds were present, not the powerful chief priests of Jerusalem nor the learned scribes or the pious Pharisees. And when he was crucified even his followers gave up, sad and disillusioned, only to be surprised on Easter morning by Jesus' resurrection. The Old Testament Scriptures had not prophesied these details about the coming of the Savior. We should thus not be surprised if we find it difficult to understand the details of Jesus' second coming.

Summary

The prophecies that link Jesus' return with clouds emphasize that Jesus' second coming is a theophany. When Jesus returns to earth, God returns. And the reference to clouds emphasize that Jesus' return will be a public event. It cannot be missed; it will be seen by all people. While it is possible that the clouds will be a literal, atmospheric phenomenon, this seems unlikely given the assertion that all people will see Jesus returning and that all believers will meet Jesus when he comes in the clouds. This assertion seems to suggest a symbolic meaning of the "clouds" mentioned in these passages, but it also makes a literal understanding of Jesus' return difficult to comprehend. Despite these difficulties in comprehending the details of Jesus' return, there is no doubt, however, that it will be physical (literal), public, and incontrovertible.

REFLECTION QUESTIONS

1. What are the key passages that describe Jesus' return?

2. What is the connection between Jesus' ascension and Jesus' return?

3. What could the reference to the clouds be referring to?

4. What can be said about the geographical location of Jesus' return?

5. What was more important to the disciples than waiting for Jesus' return in Jerusalem?

Will Jesus Return Soon?

Christians throughout the ages believed that Jesus would return soon, within their lifetime. Hilary of Poitiers in France, who lived in the fourth century, believed that the emperor Constantius was the Antichrist and concluded, "Let us look for Christ's coming, for Antichrist is already in power."[1] In the eleventh century, Fulbert, bishop of Chartres in France, believed that the last judgment was imminent.[2] Melchior Hoffman (1495–1543), one of the radical Reformers who was active in the Netherlands and in Strasbourg (which he predicted would be the New Jerusalem), announced that the end would come in 1533. Jan Mathijs and John Beukels, apocalyptic fanatics among the radical Reformers, took over the city of Münster in Germany in February 1534. Matthijs predicted the end of the world for Easter Sunday, April 5, 1534.[3] Charles Taze Russell, the leader of the movement that would become the Jehovah's Witnesses, predicted in 1910 that the end of the world would come in 1914. His successor, Joseph Rutherford, amended the date in 1918 to the year 1925.[4] The evangelical pastor and evangelist Oswald J. Smith announced in 1926 that the battle of Armageddon and thus the end

1. Hilary of Poitiers, *Invective against Constantius*, trans. E. W. Watson and L. Pullan, in *Select Library of Nicene and Post-Nicene Fathers of the Christian Church: Second Series*, ed. Philip Schaff and Henry Wace (1899; repr., Grand Rapids: Eerdmans, 1973), 9:25; see Francis X. Gumerlock, *The Day and the Hour: A Chronicle of Christianity's Perennial Fascination with Predicting the End of the World* (Atlanta: American Vision, 2009), 25.
2. Bernhard McGinn, *Antichrist: Two Thousand Years of the Human Fascination with Evil* (San Francisco: HarperCollins, 1994), 236, 100. For the example that follows in the text above, see ibid., 214–15.
3. Walter Klaassen, *Living at the End of the Ages: Apocalyptic Expectation in the Radical Reformation* (Lanham, MD: University Press of America, 1992), 46–48.
4. Later the Jehovah's Witnesses announced the year 1975 as the date when the battle of Armageddon would take place (Gumerlock, *Day and the Hour*, 285).

would come in 1933.[5] In 1979, televangelist Pat Robertson planned to go to Jerusalem to film and broadcast the second coming.[6] In 1983, Mary Relfe created a "prophecy chart" in which 1997 was given as the date of the second coming.[7]

These dates passed without the second coming happening. While many of these prophetic announcements were made by apocalyptic enthusiasts who did not seem to care much about what the Bible actually says about the end times, a few were made by serious Christians and spiritually minded preachers and teachers. In view of this sad history of misguided interpretations and false predictions, the question arises whether Christians should ever think that Jesus' return is imminent. What did the early Christians believe?

The End Times Have Begun with Jesus' First Coming

As we have seen in the answers to questions 1–7, the early Christians were convinced that Jesus' first coming marked the beginning of the end times. Jesus' life and work, in particular his death and resurrection, inaugurated the messianic age in which God began to fulfill his promise that he would establish his kingdom. The signs of the end that Jesus named describe world history (Matt. 24:4–28), with the one specific prediction of the destruction of Jerusalem and the temple (vv. 15–22), an event that took place in A.D. 70. The judgments of the seals, trumpets, and bowls that John describes (Revelation 6–16) are parallel to the "signs" enumerated by Jesus and also largely describe world history, rather than specific events that have to be fulfilled. Paul's prophecy of the Lawless One (2 Thess. 2:3) anticipated the arrival of a rebel who first has to appear before the end comes. While it is possible, but not certain, that Paul was speaking about events that he expected to be fulfilled in connection with the destruction of the temple and of Jerusalem, he does not to appear to speak of events in the distant future but of a time that both he and the Thessalonian believers might live to see.

Since the final period in history has been inaugurated with Jesus' coming as Israel's Messiah in the first decades of the first century, and since the political situation in Judea was getting worse in the early second half of the first century, the early Christians believed that the end might soon come, uniting them with Jesus Christ and ushering in the last judgment and God's new world.

---

5. Oswald J. Smith, *Is the Antichrist at Hand?* (Toronto: Tabernacle, 1926), 19; see Gumerlock, *Day and the Hour*, 267.

6. Gumerlock, *Day and the Hour*, 287. See the self-critical account in Gerard T. Straub, *Salvation for Sale: An Insider's View of Pat Robertson's Ministry* (Buffalo: Prometheus, 1986), 160–63.

7. See Mary S. Relfe, *Prophetic Fallout of 9-11: The Final Generation* (Prattville, AL: League of Prayer, 2005).

The Early Christians Prayer for Jesus' Second Coming

This conviction of the "presence" of the end times is the reason why the early Christians included in their prayers the petition "Come, Lord Jesus!" (Greek, *erchou kyrie Iēsou*; Rev. 22:20). This prayer translates the Aramaic expression *Maranatha*, which was even used by believers who did not speak Aramaic (see 1 Cor. 16:22).[8] In the Greek text of Revelation 22:20, the formulation of the imperative "Come!" with the present tense is highly unusual, as God is addressed in the Greek translation of the Old Testament (Septuagint [LXX]) and in the New Testament almost always with imperatives in the aorist tense. The present tense expresses a strong emotional emphasis and thus "adds a special urgency to the church's desire for Christ to return."[9] This urgent petition comes in the context of the immediately preceding statement by Jesus, "Yes, I am coming soon" (Rev. 22:20 NIV), the third such announcement in the last paragraph of the book of Revelation after 22:7 and 22:12.[10] The Greek term translated as "soon" (*tachy*) usually refers to "a very brief period of time, with focus on speed of an activity or event" (translated as "quick, swiftly, without delay"), but also describes "a relatively brief time subsequent to another point of time" ("in a short time, soon").[11]

How should we understand this reference to Jesus' imminent return, made in the first century?[12] The explanation that the Greek word *tachy* means not "soon" but "quickly" is not helpful, since it seems to suggest that John assumes Jesus' coming as being either slow or quick and thus prays for a "quick" coming. Some explain John's "preoccupation" with immediacy in terms of that fact that "his message was and is one of life and death."[13] While there is certainly a "life and death" dimension of the gospel that calls for immediate repentance of sins and faith in the Lord Jesus Christ, it is less helpful to explain the apparent "immediacy" of Jesus' second coming. Another explanation suggests, "Christ's coming is a series of comings in blessing and judgment and will be consummated by a climactic coming in final blessing

---

8. The Greek text of 1 Corinthians 16:22 uses the transcribed words *maran atha*, not the Greek translation used in Revelation 22:20. The traditional spelling *Maranatha* stands for the two Aramaic words *maran* ("our Lord") and *tha* ("come!").

9. Grant R. Osborne, *Revelation*, BECNT (Grand Rapids: Baker Academic, 2002), 797; see David E. Aune, *Revelation*, WBC 52C (Dallas: Word, 1998), 3:1234.

10. This declaration by the exalted Jesus Christ is also found in Revelation 2:16; 3:11.

11. BDAG, 993–94 (*tachos* 1–2).

12. Some suggest that Jesus refers to his coming in the Eucharist (i.e., the Lord's Supper; see John P. M. Sweet, *Revelation*, Pelican Commentaries [London: SCM, 1979], 318; Gregory K. Beale, *The Book of Revelation: A Commentary on the Greek Text*, NIGTC [Grand Rapids: Eerdmans, 1999], 1155), or to his coming at the time of the destruction of Jerusalem (in A.D. 70; Kenneth L. Gentry, *Before Jerusalem Fell* [Tyler, TX: Dominion Press, 1989], 142–45). These interpretations are not convincing because the context suggests a reference to, and desire for, Jesus' final coming.

13. Robert L. Thomas, *Revelation: An Exegetical Commentary* (Chicago: Moody, 1995), 498.

and condemnation."[14] This inaugurated sense of "soon" certainly makes sense: when the risen Lord says to the church in Pergamon, "Repent therefore! Otherwise, I will soon [*tachy*] come to you and will fight against them with the sword of my mouth" (Rev. 2:16), he announces a coming in judgment not on the future day of judgment but in the more immediate future when he judges the church if they do not repent. On the other hand, the declaration "I am coming soon" at the end of the book of Revelation, made after John's vision of Jesus' return (19:11–21), the millennium (20:1–6), the last judgment (20:7–15), and the new heaven and the new earth (21:1–22:5), more naturally refers to Jesus' second coming.

Jesus asserts that he is coming soon, and John prays that Jesus may come soon, "but on whose clock?"[15] Jesus' declaration that he is coming "soon" has to be interpreted in the context of the book of Revelation, a prophecy in which the readers' sense of timing is complicated by the repeated series of kaleidoscopic visions. John's visions aim at describing God "who is and who was and who is to come" (Rev. 1:4) and the coming of Jesus with the clouds when "every eye will see him" (v. 7). It is not a coincidence that John interrupts the description of his visions by interludes.[16] It is only in Revelation 19:11–21 that John describes Jesus' return, followed by the vision of the millennium and the final judgment, before finally God's perfect new world is described. Seen in connection with Jesus' statement, "See, I am coming like a thief!" in Revelation 16:15, the announcement that he is coming soon is not likely to indicate that the thief in the night will appear within a certain time period. Jesus' announcement that he is coming soon is a warning that he *could* be coming soon and that the believers should always be prepared for his coming.

The Early Christians Never Predicted Jesus' Second Coming

As Paul called upon the believers in the city of Philippi to rejoice, to let their gentleness be evident to all, and not to be anxious, he added the affirmation, "The Lord is near" (Phil. 4:5 NIV), in order to encourage them. Paul believed that Jesus' second coming was imminent.[17] God's promises have been

---

14. Beale, *Book of Revelation*, 1127; also R. C. H. Lenski, *The Interpretation of St. John's Revelation* (Minneapolis: Augsburg, 1961), 660.
15. Ben Witherington, *Revelation*, New Cambridge Bible Commentary (Cambridge: Cambridge University Press, 2003), 279. For the comments that follow in the text above, see ibid., 280.
16. Revelation 7:1–17 interrupts the seal judgments between the sixth and seventh seal; Revelation 10:1–11:14 interrupts the trumpet judgments between the sixth and seventh trumpet; Revelation 12:1–14:20 interrupts the transition from the trumpet judgments to the bowl judgments.
17. P. T. O'Brien comments, "Clearly Paul believed in an imminent advent, in the sense that it might happen at any time, and his words are akin to Jesus' direction to his disciples to be 'like servants who are waiting for their master' (Lk. 12:46)" (*The Epistle to the Philippians*, NIGTC [Grand Rapids: Eerdmans, 1991], 489). Also see Benjamin L. Merkle, "Could Jesus

mostly fulfilled through Jesus' first coming. His plan of salvation for humanity and for the earth is nearly complete. The next event in God's plan of salvation is Jesus' second coming. Paul is careful not to set a date. He predicts neither here nor in 1 Thessalonians 4:13–5:3 that he will still be alive when Jesus returns. Like the apostle John, he reckons with the possibility that he might live to see Jesus returning to earth but does not "hype" the possibility in terms of a certainty.

The Early Christians Were Prepared for a Delay of Jesus' Second Coming

Paul is not certain exactly when Jesus will return because he knows that Jesus' second coming is being delayed. He writes to the believers in the city of Thessalonica, "As to the coming of our Lord Jesus Christ and our being gathered together to him, we beg you, brothers and sisters, not to be quickly shaken in mind or alarmed, either by spirit or by word or by letter, as though from us, to the effect that the day of the Lord is already here. Let no one deceive you in any way; for that day will not come unless the rebellion comes first and the lawless one is revealed, the one destined for destruction" (2 Thess. 2:1–3). He knows that Jesus cannot come quite yet. Jesus' return is delayed by a restraining power (about which he provides no information) and by the appearance of the Lawless One who has yet to come (2 Thess. 2:6–8; see question 18).

Jesus himself spoke about a delay of his return. After speaking about the signs of the end, he tells the parable of the faithful and unfaithful slave (Matt. 24:45–51). In the parable, there is a master who leaves two of his slaves in charge of his household. One of the slaves, when he recognizes that the master is "delayed,"[18] begins to mistreat his fellow slaves and eats and drinks with drunkards, only to be surprised when his master returns. In the parable of the ten bridesmaids, "the bridegroom was delayed" (Matt. 25:5) until midnight. In the parable of the slaves entrusted with money, the man who owns the slaves goes on a journey and comes back only "after a long time" (Matt. 25:19).[19]

How Soon Will Jesus Return?

Jesus insists that "about that day and hour no one knows, neither the angels of heaven, nor the Son, but only the Father" (Matt. 24:36). A few verses later he repeats, "Keep awake therefore, for you do not know on what day

---

Return at Any Moment? Rethinking the Imminence of the Second Coming," *TrinJ* 26 (2005): 279–92.

18. The Greek verb used in Matthew 24:48 means "to extend a state or an activity beyond an expected time, take time, linger, fail to come or stay away for a long time" (BDAG, 1092, *chronizō* 2).

19. The Greek phrase here, *meta de polyn chronon*, can also be translated as "after a long period of time."

your Lord is coming" (v. 42). He uses the sudden and unexpected intrusion of thieves in the middle of the night to underline the urgency of his affirmation that "you also must be ready, for the Son of Man is coming at an unexpected hour" (v. 44). In the parable of the faithful and unfaithful slave, the wicked slave will realize that his master "will come on a day when he does not expect him and at an hour that he does not know" (v. 50). At the end of the parable of the ten bridesmaids, Jesus warns, "Keep awake therefore, for you know neither the day nor the hour" (25:13).

Jesus will come like a "thief in the night" (1 Thess. 5:2, 4; also Matt. 24:43; Luke 12:39; 2 Peter 3:10; Rev. 3:3; 16:15)—suddenly and unexpectedly. Thieves do not announce themselves to the occupants of the houses they wish to rob. Jesus announced his return, but not the time of his return. We do not know when Jesus will return. But we know that we should live in such a way that he could come any day. The fact that we could die at any time—through a heart attack, a stroke, a car accident—highlights the importance of this imperative. Committed Christians are like the obedient slaves and the wise bridesmaids—ready at any time for meeting the master and the bridegroom, whether through departing from this life or seeing him when he returns to earth.

What Shall We Then Do?

What should Christians do in view of the possibility of Jesus' imminent return and the uncertainty of knowing how soon this will be? There are two answers. First, Christians should not succumb to the pressure to calculate the time of Jesus' second coming. The examples given above demonstrate the foolishness and futility of such calculations. If Jesus did not know the chronological timing of his return, we will never know it either. Second, Christians should engage in the work that Jesus has entrusted to them. They are like the faithful slaves in Jesus' parable of the faithful and unfaithful slave (Matt. 24:45–51) and in the parable of the good and trustworthy slaves and wicked and lazy slave entrusted with money (25:14–30): they do the work that the master gives them to do.

When Jesus returned to the Father and the disciples were "staring into the sky while he was going" (Acts 1:10 NET), the two men in white clothing (angels) assured them that "this Jesus, who has been taken up from you into heaven, will come in the same way as you saw him go into heaven" (v. 11). Right before this announcement, the angels ask an important question: "Men of Galilee, why do you stand looking up toward heaven?" (v. 11). The question implies a reproach. Jesus' earlier announcement that he would return "'in a cloud' with power and great glory" (Luke 21:27) had implied his departure. And Jesus commission to be his "witnesses in Jerusalem, in all Judea and Samaria, and to the ends of the earth" (Acts 1:8) also implied his absence. The angels tell the disciples not to stand around, wishing for Jesus to remain with them, or waiting for his return on the Mount of Olives. The disciples already know what they should be doing in Jesus' absence: go back into Jerusalem, wait for the promised Holy Spirit, and then preach the gospel and do the same in Judea, Samaria, and in other cities until they reach the end of the world. Christians wait for Jesus' second coming, but they wait while they faithfully live as followers of Jesus, bringing the truth of the gospel to other people near and far.

Summary

The early Christians prayed that Jesus might come back soon. They believed that Jesus' return was imminent, allowing for the possibility that this might happen during their lifetime. Yet they never mention a time frame within which Jesus would return. They never calculate how close the end might be. They never set a date. They waited, but they did not speculate. They did not make false predictions: Jesus could indeed have returned in the first century, after Jerusalem and the temple had been destroyed. At the same time, the early Christians knew that Jesus' return might be delayed. Jesus repeatedly spoke about a delay and about the fact that his return would be sudden and unexpected. This must be our attitude as well if we heed Jesus' exhortation and the apostles' anticipation: we eagerly wait for Jesus' return, we do not speculate about dates, and we do the work of the Lord in the meantime, until he comes back.

REFLECTION QUESTIONS

1. Why is it justified to expect Jesus' imminent return?

2. Why is it justified to expect a delay of Jesus' return?

3. Why is this attitude not schizophrenic?

4. What is Jesus' advice concerning the time of his second coming?

5. Why must we avoid speculations about the date of Jesus' second coming?

PART 3

The Millennium and the Last Judgment

The Millennium and the New Jerusalem

What Is the Millennium?

The word *millennium* does not actually occur in the Bible. It is taken from the Latin translation of Revelation 20:2 where Satan is described as being bound "for a thousand years," which in Latin reads *per annos mille* (*mille*, "thousand," and *annus*, "year"). Since the word for "thousand" in Greek is *chilioi*, early theologians who held that there would be a thousand year reign of Christ on earth were called "chiliasts." Interpreters who understand John's description in Revelation 20:1–6 as referring to a literal historical period take a "millennial" position. For the debate about when the millennium will take place, see question 34. Indeed, "few issues have divided the church for as long a time as this,"[1] and there is no consensus on the interpretation of Revelation 20:1–6 in sight.

Jewish Expectations of a Messianic Kingdom on Earth

According to *1 Enoch* 91:12–17, righteousness will flourish during the eighth and tenth "weeks" before a new heaven appears in the tenth week. The length of the "week" is not indicated. The author of *Jubilees* 23:27–30 mentions the number "one thousand," clearly understood figuratively for the eternal era of blessing for God's people. In *4 Ezra* 7:28–31, we find the expectation of the messianic period that will last for four hundred years. Later rabbinic reflections on the six days of creation in the light of Psalm 90:4 ("For a thousand years in your sight are like yesterday when it is past") sometimes assumed to be a messianic era that lasts two thousand years (*b. Sanh.* 97). The range of the proposed length of the messianic reign ranges from 40 to 365,000 years.

---

1. Grant R. Osborne, *Revelation*, BECNT (Grand Rapids: Baker Academic, 2002), 696. For a presentation of the history of the discussion, see Craig A. Blaising, "Premillennialism," in *Three Views on the Millennium and Beyond*, ed. Darrell L. Bock (Grand Rapids: Zondervan, 1999), 157–92.

Old Testament Expectations of an Earthly Kingdom

More important than Jewish expectations are Old Testament passages that describe the coming kingdom of God as an earthly reign (Isa. 2:1–4; 4:1–6; 11:6–9; Jer. 23:5–8; Zech. 14:5–17; Ezek. 37:24–28; 40–48). A text directly linked with Revelation 20:1–6 is Daniel 7:13–14: "I saw one like a human being coming with the clouds of heaven. And he came to the Ancient One and was presented before him. To him was given dominion and glory and kingship, that all peoples, nations, and languages should serve him. His dominion is an everlasting dominion that shall not pass away, and his kingship is one that shall never be destroyed."

None of these texts refers to the duration of a thousand years of the earthly kingdom. This allows interpreters to link these texts (or at least elements within these passages) with one of two options: (1) These texts describe the kingdom of God that became a reality with the ministry, death, and resurrection of Jesus, Israel's Messiah, which is visible in the life of the followers of Jesus. (2) These texts describe the new heavens and the new earth as God's new creation.

The Binding of Satan

John begins the description of his vision in which he "sees" the thousand-year reign of the saints and of Jesus Christ with a description of the binding of Satan. The reference to the angel's "key to the bottomless pit" (Rev. 20:1) is a symbol of God's sovereign control over all demonic powers. The seizure and binding of Satan (20:2) represents a judgment scene: Jesus' second coming (19:11–21) marks his victory over all evil forces, which here results in the judgment of Satan. He is guilty because he is "that ancient serpent" who deceived Adam and Eve and introduced rebellion and sin into God's perfect creation (Gen. 3). He is the Dragon, the sea monster Leviathan who introduced chaos and sin. He is the Devil and Satan, the great adversary who accuses God's people day and night (Rev. 12:10). The banishment of Satan to the Abyss, the prison house of the demonic spirits, which is locked and sealed after him, ensures that he can no longer deceive the nations (Rev. 20:3). The main activity of the forces of evil has been deception (12:9; 13:14; 18:23). This banishment will last for a thousand years.

The Thousand Years

Are the "thousand years" literal years or symbolic years? Some argue for a literal interpretation.[2] Since similar numbers in Jewish texts have a figurative meaning and, more importantly, since many numbers in the book of Revelation are symbolic (see question 6), it seems probable that the number "one thousand" years is symbolic as well. Thus, it refers to a long epoch—a

---

2. Robert L. Thomas, *Revelation: An Exegetical Commentary* (Chicago: Moody, 1995), 407–9.

period that is markedly longer than the forty-two months during which the Beast "reigns."

Those Seated on the Thrones

Who are the people seated on thrones, "given authority to judge" (Rev. 20:4a)? If the answer to this question is connected with the following statement in 20:4b, then the martyred saints are in view, "those who had been beheaded for their testimony to Jesus and for the word of God." This is not the most plausible interpretation, however.

The first tendency of John's audience who heard about people sitting on thrones would have been to think of the twenty-four elders in Revelation 4:9–10 with crowns on their heads, indicating that they have executive and judicial authority. In Revelation 5:8–9, these elders have a priestly role: they reign and serve, while in Revelation 11:16–17 the elders on their thrones praise God in response to the announcement of Jesus' second coming. In view of the defeat of the Beast and the earthly kings and all their subjects (19:11–21), the readers who have reached Revelation 20:4 would expect the twenty-four elders to help decide matters related to the judgment of the dead and the reward of the faithful. This is confirmed by the following statement in 20:4c which speaks of "those who [*hoitines*] had not worshiped the beast or his image, and had not received the mark on their forehead and on their hand" (NASB).[3] Further evidence is found in the parallel in Daniel 7:9–10, which speaks of God holding court with heavenly helpers. John hints at a wider group than the martyrs who are the Lamb's followers who come through the tribulation and who are not killed for their faith.

We should also note that John does not use the word "elders" for the people seated on the thrones in Revelation 20:4. In light of John's description of the "armies of heaven" in 19:14, the readers would have seen themselves as coming back to judge with Jesus Christ.[4] Since Christians are involved in both judging and reigning (2:26–27; 3:11, 21), and since it had been promised that they would reign on earth in 5:10, the readers would have seen themselves as reigning with Jesus Christ. This corresponds to the last statement in 20:4d: "they came to life and reigned with Christ a thousand years." In 20:9 the "camp of the saints" is mentioned, supporting the view that all believers are present in the millennium.[5]

---

3. The Greek expression that introduces the phrase, *hoitines*, can be rendered "whoever" or "every person who."

4. J. Webb Mealy, *After the Thousand Years: Resurrection and Judgment in Revelation 20*, JSNTSup 70 (Sheffield: JSOT Press, 1992), 108–10.

5. There is no room in John's description of the millennium in Revelation 20:1–6 for the view that ethnic Israel will play a major role during this period. This theory is based on the assumption that unfulfilled Old Testament passages that made predictions for Israel will be fulfilled in the millennial kingdom (e.g., John F. Walvoord, *The Revelation of Jesus Christ*

Thus, it seems that those seated on thrones in 20:4 are not only the twenty-four elders but all those who have overcome, who refused to follow the Beast. The judgment in which the resurrected saints participate must be the judgment of the followers of the Beast who were last mentioned in the preceding context, the "rest" that the returning Jesus Christ dealt with following the defeat and destruction of the Beast and the false prophet (19:21).

The Blessings of the Millennium

The description of the one-thousand-year period is sparse. The immediate context of the description in Revelation 20:4–6 is decisive for a correct understanding. The millennium follows Jesus' return for judgment in which the earth's destroyers are destroyed, together with "the rest" of all the inhabitants of the earth who had been followers of the Beast (19:11–21). It follows the preliminary judgment of Satan who is locked up in the Abyss (20:1–3). This means that the one-thousand-year reign is pictured as a period of paradise-like enjoyment of God's earth. It is a period without deception and temptation, a period of life in the presence of Jesus Christ.

The life of the millennium is resurrection life. The martyrs and all who had not followed the Beast "came to life and reigned with Christ" (Rev. 20:4d). After the reference to the Beast and his followers who were all thrown into "the lake of fire" in Revelation 19:20 and after the reference to thrones in 20:4, the statement "they came to life" (which in Greek is only one word, *ezēsan*) most obviously refers to bodily resurrection.[6] This is confirmed by the statement in 20:5b, "this is the first resurrection." The critical question as to how the resurrected believers (with new, glorified bodies) can be living together during the millennium with unbelievers who have survived the great tribulation will be addressed in question 34.

The only explicit statement about the blessings of life in the millennium comes in Revelation 20:6: "Blessed and holy are those who share in the first resurrection. Over these the second death has no power, but they will be priests of God and of Christ, and they will reign with him a thousand years." The reference to the people who live in the millennium as "blessed and holy" also appears to fulfill the promise of 7:13–15, where the saints "robed in white" (indicating holiness) are described as those "who have come out of the

---

[Chicago: Moody Press, 1966], 284, 301–2). John constantly alludes to Old Testament passages: he does not allude to promises for ethnic Israel or for the Jewish people here. The reference to the "beloved city" in Revelation 20:9 (see question 35) cannot be taken as a basis for this position.

6. Scholars who take an amillennial interpretation interpret this expression either in terms of new spiritual life following conversion (see Col. 3:1; Eph. 2:6) or as a reference to the reign of the deceased saints after death in the intermediate state before the day of resurrection (Gregory K. Beale, *The Book of Revelation: A Commentary on the Greek Text*, NIGTC [Grand Rapids: Eerdmans, 1999], 1000–1016).

great ordeal [tribulation]; they have washed their robes and made them white in the blood of the Lamb" and who are therefore now "before the throne of God, and worship him day and night within his temple, and the one who is seated on the throne will shelter them."

Over What Do the Saints Reign?

Since Revelation 21:21 describes that all the people who had followed the Beast had been removed, the resurrected saints obviously reign over the earth itself. This is the fulfillment of the promise of 5:10: "you have made them to be a kingdom and priests serving our God, and they will reign on earth." This also fulfills the promise of 2:7: "to everyone who conquers, I will give permission to eat from the tree of life that is in the paradise of God." In 7:16–17, the followers of the Lamb who have come out of the tribulation are assured that "they will hunger no more, and thirst no more; the sun will not strike them, nor any scorching heat; for the Lamb at the center of the throne will be their shepherd, and he will guide them to springs of the water of life, and God will wipe away every tear from their eyes."[7]

The resurrected saints join God and his Messiah in the management of his creation, finally fulfilling the purpose for which they were originally created: "Let us make humankind in our image, according to our likeness; and let them have dominion over the fish of the sea, and over the birds of the air, and over the cattle, and over all the wild animals of the earth, and over every creeping thing that creeps upon the earth" (Gen. 1:26).

Summary

The millennium is the one-thousand-year period in which the resurrected saints participate in Jesus' reign over the earth. The people who enjoy the blessings of the millennium are not only the martyrs but all the followers of the Lamb, who share in the first resurrection. They are the believers who have conquered the forces of evil through their allegiance to the Lamb. They participate in Jesus' judgment on the ungodly. They are blessed because they live on the earth on which God bestows his blessings, unhindered by evil. They are holy because they are like priests living in the presence of God. They are resurrected to life; they cannot be touched by the second death, because they are together with Jesus Christ.

REFLECTION QUESTIONS

1. What does the Old Testament say about a future earthly kingdom of God?

---

7. See Mealy, *After the Thousand Years*, 115–16.

2. What is the significance of the binding of Satan?

3. Is the number of one thousand years literal or symbolic?

4. Who are those pictured sitting on thrones and reigning with Jesus Christ?

5. What are the blessings of the millennium?

When Will the Millennium Take Place?

The "date" of the millennium in the end-time scenario has divided Christians from earliest times. The main questions concern the relationship between the millennium and Jesus' second coming and the relationship between the millennium and the church.

Three Main Answers

Some link the millennium with the past and present (the age of the church), some with the present and future (a golden age before Jesus' return), and some with the future (a messianic kingdom on earth after Jesus' second coming).

Interpreters who think that this historical period is a reality in the past and in the present, identical with the age of the church resulting from Jesus Christ's victory on the cross and in the resurrection, take an amillennial position (they do not believe that there will be a millennium in the future). Historically this has been the position held by most Catholics (since Augustine), mainline Protestants (including the Reformers), and conservative Reformed denominations.

Those who think that the millennium is a golden age that will take place in the present age before Jesus returns take a postmillennial position. This is a minority position today, although it was popular in eighteenth- and nineteenth-century America, held by Jonathan Edwards and Charles Grandison Finney (see the discussion in question 11).

Interpreters who hold that the millennium is a historical period in the future after Jesus' second coming take a premillennial position; the prefix *pre-* (from Latin *prae*, "before") signifies that Jesus will return before the thousand-year reign. Historically, this has been the view of some of the early teachers of the church (such as Irenaeus of Lyon) and of a majority of evangelicals.

The Sequence of Events

Some argue that the recurring phrase "Then I saw" or "And I saw" in Revelation 19:11, 17, 19; 20:1, 4, 12; 21:1 "strongly implies a sequence of visions that carries through from the appearance of the Rider on the white horse (19:11) to the establishment of the new heaven and the new earth (21:1ff.)."[1] This is not a decisive argument, however. A sequence of visions is not the same as a sequence events: the same event can be the subject of several visions, which by their very nature as self-contained visions have to be narrated in sequence. The use of the expressions "Then I saw" or "And I saw" throughout the book of Revelation indicates that the phrase as such cannot be taken as a chronological marker.[2]

It can hardly be doubted that there is a chronological sequence of *some* of the events narrated in Revelation 19–21. No one doubts the chronological sequence of Jesus' second coming (19:11–21) ➝ final judgment (20:11–15) ➝ a new heaven and a new earth (21:1–22:5). The question is where 20:1–6 / 7–10 belongs.

There are chronological markers in Revelation 20:1–10. First, the reference to the one-thousand-year period during which Satan is bound in verse 1 is followed by the statement that Satan is locked up in the Abyss "until the thousand years were ended" (v. 3), followed by the statement "after that, he must be set free for a short time" (v. 3 NIV). This indicates the chronological sequence in the fate of Satan: there is a period in which he deceives, followed by a period of one thousand years in which he is prevented from deceiving, followed by a short period in which he deceives again.

Second, the statement "the rest of the dead did not come to life until the thousand years were ended" (20:5a) implies a chronological sequence between the resurrection of the saints who reign with Christ during the one-thousand-year period, a resurrection that must have taken place in conjunction with Jesus' second coming described in 19:11–21, and the (later) resurrection of all the unbelievers who were removed from earth (v. 21; see 20:5, 13–15).

Third, the statement "this is the first resurrection" (20:5b) indicates a chronological sequence between a first and a second resurrection, separated by the one-thousand-year period. The first resurrection describes the one-thousand-year reign of the saints with Jesus Christ. The "second" resurrection must refer to the event when the unbelievers face God's judgment before the great white throne (20:11–15).

---

1. Robert H. Mounce, *The Book of Revelation*, rev. ed. (Grand Rapids: Eerdmans, 1998), 361.
2. Grant R. Osborne, *Revelation*, BECNT (Grand Rapids: Baker Academic, 2002), 699.

Fourth, the parallels between Isaiah 24:1–27:1 and Revelation 19:19–20:10 demonstrate a common pattern of end-time events.[3] The sequence of events in Revelation with their parallels in Isaiah order themselves as follows:

1. On the day of the Lord, heavenly and human powers are punished and imprisoned (Isa. 24:1–22). On the day of Jesus' second coming, the forces of evil and rebellious human beings are punished and imprisoned (Rev. 19:19–20:3).

2. God establishes his reign, and the messianic banquet follows (Isa. 24:23; 25:6–9). God establishes his reign on earth, together with Jesus Christ and the resurrected saints (Rev. 20:4–6), an event described as the "wedding supper of the Lamb" (Rev. 19:9 NIV).

3. Resurrection of those who are in distress, but not of the wicked (Isa. 26:14–19). Resurrection of the saints persecuted by the Beast, but not of "the rest of the dead" (Rev. 20:4–6).

4. Punishment of the inhabitants of the earth, predicted as fire sent from the Lord (Isa. 26:11, 20–21). Destruction of "Gog and Magog" by fire from heaven (Rev. 20:9).

5. The enemies are destroyed because they attack Israel or Jerusalem (Isa. 27:2–4; 26:1, 11–12). The enemy "Gog and Magog" are destroyed by fire because they attack "the camp of the saints and the beloved city" (Rev. 20:7–9).

6. Punishment of "Leviathan the fleeing serpent" (Isa. 27:1). Satan who has been called "that ancient serpent" (Rev. 20:2; he was pictured as Leviathan in Revelation 12) is destroyed in the lake of fire (Rev. 20:10).

Thus, we must assume the following sequence of events. Jesus' second coming marks God's judgment on the forces of evil and on the ungodly. This is "the first death" of the unbelievers who were alive at the time of Jesus' second coming. His second coming also marks the resurrection of the saints. Jesus' return is followed by the millennium, his one-thousand-year reign together with the resurrected saints. The millennial reign is followed by a final attack, which is thwarted by God's final judgment when the unbelievers will be consigned to "the second death" (20:6). This period of one thousand years follows Jesus' return and the resurrection of the saints, and it ends with the final attack and the final judgment.

---

3. J. Webb Mealy, *After the Thousand Years: Resurrection and Judgment in Revelation 20*, JSNTSup 70 (Sheffield: JSOT Press, 1992), 100.

Who Are the Nations That Satan Deceives after the Thousand Years?

The answer to this question is important for understanding the sequence of events in Revelation 19:11–22:5. John sees in his vision that "when the thousand years are ended, Satan will be released from his prison and will come out to deceive the nations" (20:7–8). These "nations" are located "at the four corners of the earth" and identified with "Gog and Magog" (v. 8). In the answer to question 27, we identified them with the unrepentant of human history before Jesus' second coming, who had been consigned to the Abyss. The Abyss is the place of the dead and the realm of Satan, the realm to which Satan had been restricted at the beginning of the millennium (20:1–3). The "kings of the earth" and their armies, and indeed "all, both free and slave, both small and great" (19:18–19), all the followers of the Beast who refused to follow the Lamb, were slain (v. 21). By implication they are imprisoned in Hades, the Abyss that is the realm of the dead, together with rebellious humanity that had gone before them. All these unrepentant sinners are evidently "the rest of the dead" who "did not come to life until the thousand years were ended" (20:5; see Isa. 24:23).[4]

Satan is released from the Abyss after the one-thousand-year period (Rev. 20:2–3), and the "nations" that Satan deceives come upon the earth after the one-thousand-year period (vv. 7–9). John expects his readers to link Satan's release from the Abyss, which results in his final punishment in the lake of fire (v. 10), with the "second resurrection" of the unrepentant sinners who had been consigned to Hades and who will be punished together with Satan in the lake of fire (vv. 11–15).

What Is the Meaning of the Final Deception?

The "nations" are the multitudes of sinners consigned to Hades that had been in Satan's company there for a thousand years. During this time Satan was also imprisoned in the Abyss, unable to leave and deceive the saints on earth. Satan's followers saw that following the ancient Serpent, and his claim to godhood, only leads to death. They were able to see his lies: wanting to be like God by knowing good and evil (Gen. 3:5) indeed leads to death, just as God had told Adam and Eve. The Serpent's deception is unmasked: he has nothing to offer but death.

John does not provide an explicit answer to the question as to why it is part of God's plan (note the term "must" in Rev. 20:3) that the "nations" be deceived a final time. The answer is to be found in the following thought: the fact that the sinners who had been deceived by Satan before are now deceived by him again, after being in his company in the Abyss for a thousand years,

---

4. See ibid., 124. For the comments that follow in the text above, see ibid., 124–38.

proves their total depravity "and demonstrates once and for all the necessity of eternal punishment."[5]

The Millennium and the New Earth

When we follow John's description of his vision of the millennium in Revelation 20:1–6, we are led to believe that we should not make a hard and fast distinction between life during the millennium and life on the new earth. Several considerations support this conclusion.

The statement "the earth and the heavens fled from his presence, and there was no place for them" (20:11) comes after the description of the millennium (20:1–6) and of the last rebellion that ends in destruction and judgment in the lake of fire (20:7–10). When we link this statement with the very similar statements in 6:14, 16 and 16:20,[6] we see that this dissolution of the existing heaven and earth, which describes the theophany of God's appearance, is tied to Jesus' second coming described in 19:11–21 when all evil forces were vanquished.

If the people who live during the millennium are people who have come to life (20:4), who have experienced the first resurrection (v. 5), over whom the second (eternal) death has no power (v. 6), and who live as priests of God and his Messiah and reign as kings (v. 6), then the thousand years are connected with God's new world.

Texts such as Isaiah 11:6–9 are often taken to describe conditions during the millennium. Here the prophet states not only that "the earth will be filled with the knowledge of the Lord" but also that the wolf will lie with the lamb, the leopard with the goat, the calf with the lion, and the "infant will play near the cobra's den"; the young child will put its hand into the viper's nest" (NIV). If this and similar texts indeed describe conditions during the millennium,

---

5. Osborne relates the final deception to the people living on earth during the millennium who supported the Beast but were not part of his army and thus were not destroyed with the rest (*Revelation*, 702–3). At the same time he emphasizes, correctly in my view, that those who came to life to reign with Christ for a thousand years (Rev. 20:4) and who are part of the first resurrection (v. 5) are "all the saints" who have been raised from the dead (ibid., 708). This raises, however, the difficult question of how the resurrected believers who have new, glorified, and incorruptible bodies can live side by side during the millennium with unregenerate unbelievers who still have mortal bodies.

6. Revelation 6:14, 16 (sixth seal): "The sky vanished like a scroll rolling itself up, and every mountain and island was removed from its place. . . . 'Fall on us and hide us from the face of the one seated on the throne and from the wrath of the Lamb.'" Revelation 16:20 (seventh bowl): "And every island fled away, and no mountains were to be found." The Old Testament background for this imagery is found in Isaiah 34:4 ("All the host of heaven shall rot away, and the skies roll up like a scroll. All their host shall wither like a leaf withering on a vine, or fruit withering on a fig tree"); also see Jeremiah 4:23–26; Psalm 97:1–5; Daniel 2:35.

then a fundamental change of the DNA of the world seems to be required, which suggests the conditions of the new heavens and the new earth.

This connection between the millennium and the new earth is confirmed in Revelation 20:9: the "beloved city," which is mentioned in connection with the former, is identical with the New Jerusalem (21:1–27), which is linked with the latter. The identity of the New Jerusalem will be explored in question 35.

Summary

The millennium begins with Jesus' second coming, and it ends with the last judgment when Satan and all unrepentant sinners are consigned to the lake of fire for eternal punishment. The confinement of Satan to Hades at the beginning of the millennium, lasting for the entire thousand-year period, marks the initial judgment on Satan. At the same time it unmasks his deception of the inhabitants of the earth: the promise of the ancient Serpent to be able to take better care of humankind than God the Creator is exposed as a lie. The people who followed Satan's deception find themselves for a thousand years in the company of Satan, who has been rendered absolutely helpless. When Satan is allowed to leave the Abyss, the people who fell for his deception the first time fall for it a second time, confirming that they indeed deserve eternal punishment. This takes place while the resurrected saints enjoy the presence of God and of Jesus Christ, serving as priests and reigning as kings.

REFLECTION QUESTIONS

1. Which clues does John give that help us to determine the beginning of the millennium?

2. What is the sequence of the events that begin with Jesus' second coming?

3. How are the people whom Satan deceives after the millennium described?

4. Is there a connection between the millennium and the new earth?

5. Why are the chronological questions connected with the millennium difficult?

What Is the New Jerusalem?

The New Jerusalem is mentioned in Revelation 20:9 and described in Revelation 21:1–27. John's vision of the city of God is a vision of the dwelling place of God and of God's people, indeed of the new heaven and the new earth.

The Descent of the New Jerusalem from Heaven

When John sees "the holy city, the New Jerusalem, coming down out of heaven from God" (Rev. 21:2; repeated nearly verbatim in 21:10), he sees God coming down to earth. This will happen when "the first heaven and the first earth" pass away and are replaced by "a new heaven and a new earth" (21:1). The picture of the New Jerusalem coming down to the new earth means that the hope and promise of Isaiah 25:6–9 will be fulfilled. What connects these statement in Revelation 21:1 and 21:2 is the statement "and the sea was no more" (21:1).

What is the "sea" that will be abolished? The term "sea" (Greek, *thalassa*) seems to encompass here all the five meanings found in the book of Revelation:[1] (1) the "sea" as the origin of evil in the cosmos (4:6; 12:18; 13:1; 15:2); (2) the "sea" as the place of the dead (20:13); (3) the "sea" as the rebellious nations who cause suffering for the people of God (12:18; 13:1); (4) the "sea" as the central place of the idolatrous commerce of the world (18:10–19); and (5) the "sea" as the literal ocean representing the old creation (5:13; 7:1–3; 8:8–9; 10:2, 5–6, 8; 14:7). If an allusion to Isaiah 65 is involved, the emphasis could be on the removal of tribulation and suffering that was caused by the "sea" for God's people: God will "wipe every tear from their eyes. Death will be no more; mourning and crying and pain will be no more, for the first

---

1. Gregory K. Beale, *The Book of Revelation: A Commentary on the Greek Text*, NIGTC (Grand Rapids: Eerdmans, 1999), 1042; J. Webb Mealy, *After the Thousand Years: Resurrection and Judgment in Revelation 20*, JSNTSup 70 (Sheffield: JSOT Press, 1992), 193–212.

things have passed away" (Rev. 21:4). If there is a connection with the "sea of glass, like crystal" described in Revelation 4:6 (with an allusion to Ezekiel 1:22 and Exodus 24:10), then the "sea" that is abolished is the expanse on which God's throne was pictured, fulfilling the yearning of Isaiah 64:1, "O that you would tear open the heavens and come down."[2]

The barrier that separated God from his creation since the fall in Genesis 3 will finally be removed. Thus, John writes, "See, the home of God is among mortals. He will dwell with them as their God; they will be his peoples, and God himself will be with them" (Rev. 21:3). Heaven and earth will no longer be separate but will become one. The "new heaven" and the "new earth" will be a single reality, characterized by the full, immediate presence of God among his people.

The Identity of the New Jerusalem

The New Jerusalem coming down out of heaven from God (Rev. 21:10) is "the bride, the wife of the Lamb" (21:9). The "holy city Jerusalem" is God's true people, the followers of Jesus who had remained faithful to the Lamb (rather than joining the Great Harlot of Babylon; see question 24),[3] described in 20:9 as "the camp of the saints and the beloved city." The New Jerusalem is the community of the redeemed, the faithful who have refused to commit immorality through idolatry, the believers in Jesus who have persevered even in the midst of suffering and martyrdom. The people are themselves the city and also the temple in which God's presence resides (21:2–3, 12–14).

This is why the New Jerusalem is described as having "the glory of God" (21:11), which is the presence of God himself. The glory of God is reflected in the "radiance like a very rare jewel, like jasper, clear as crystal" (21:11; note the allusion to Ezek. 43:2, 4–5). This means that the New Jerusalem is God's throne: in Revelation 4:3 God's throne is described as being "like jasper." This new reality is the fulfillment of Jeremiah 3:17: "At that time Jerusalem shall be called the throne of the Lord, and all nations shall gather to it, to the presence of the Lord in Jerusalem, and they shall no longer stubbornly follow their own evil will."

The Appearance of the New Jerusalem

John uses Ezekiel's language to describe the New Jerusalem as the reality of the new earth, where the people of God are themselves both the city and the temple in which God's presence resides (Rev. 21:2–3, 12–14). The idea of twelve gates arranged around the one city-temple is taken from Ezekiel

---

2. See Mealy, *After the Thousand Years*, 194.
3. The contrast between the Harlot, which is Babylon, and the Bride, which is the holy Jerusalem, renders impossible the interpretation that asserts that only Jewish believers will reside in the New Jerusalem.

48:30–35. The twelve gates with the names of the twelve tribes of Israel and the twelve foundation stones with the names of the twelve apostles symbolizes the unity of the two covenant peoples who have been united into one messianic people of God. Since the names of the twelve tribes and the names of the twelve apostles yields the sum of twenty-four names, John's description possibly also symbolizes the service of God's people in God's presence.[4]

The measuring of the New Jerusalem (Rev. 21:15–17; note the allusion to Ezek. 40:3–5) symbolizes the security of God's presence in the city and the guarantee that the community of the redeemed is forever free from danger and persecution. The cube shape matches the shape of the Holy of Holies (1 Kings 6:20; 2 Chron. 3:8–9): the entire city is the place of God's presence.[5]

The precious material of which the city is built (Rev. 21:18–21) symbolizes the perfection of God's new world and the presence of God's glory among the community of the redeemed.

The vision of the city's garden, river, and inhabitants (22:1–5) describes the glorious presence of God among his people, ensuring that there will never be any curse again. The followers of the Lamb, who are the servants of God, "will see his face, and his name will be on their foreheads. And there will be no more night; they need no light of lamp or sun, for the Lord God will be their light, and they will reign forever and ever" (vv. 4–5).

The New Jerusalem as Promise and Challenge

The vision of the New Jerusalem is connected with a promise and a challenge. The promise is the assurance that in God's new world, "all things" are new (Rev. 21:5), that the One who is the Alpha and the Omega, the beginning and the end, has fulfilled all promises and grants "the water of life" as a gift (v. 6).

The challenge is to recognize that God grants the gift of the water of life only to those who are "thirsty" (v. 6), that is, to all those who acknowledge that they are in need of the most basic essentials that only God can give (unlike believers in Laodicea who believe that they are rich and that they need nothing; 3:17). The challenge is to see the irreconcilable difference, contrast, and contradiction between the reign of God (20:1–6) with the heavenly Jerusalem (21:1–27) and the empire of Babylon (17:1–19:5). The challenge is to conquer the temptation and deception of the ancient Serpent and the Beast who demands integration into the empire of Babylon. The challenge is to persevere as God's children following the Lamb, refusing to be among "the

---

4. Note that David had organized the cult of temple servants into twenty-four orders of priests (1 Chron. 24:3–19).
5. The immense measurements (the length and width of the city is 1,500 miles) can be compared with the geographical extension of the Greco-Roman world, with a perimeter of about 5,454 miles (numbers from Beale, *Book of Revelation*, 1074).

cowardly, the faithless, the polluted, the murderers, the fornicators, the sorcerers, the idolaters, and all liars" whose place will be "in the lake that burns with fire and sulfur" (21:7–8).

Summary

The New Jerusalem is the community of the redeemed, the place where all Christians will be who have followed Jesus and persevered in adverse circumstances and persecution, refusing to conform to the secular values of God's enemy. They are themselves the city in which heaven and earth have become one, the city that is a temple because it is the place where God dwells.

REFLECTION QUESTIONS

1. Why is God's new world called "New Jerusalem"?

2. What is the connection between the New Jerusalem and Old Testament prophecy?

3. How is the New Jerusalem described?

4. How are the inhabitants of the New Jerusalem described?

5. Who will live in the New Jerusalem?

The Day of Judgment

When Will the Day of Judgment Take Place?

The Bible repeatedly speaks of God judging the earth. God brings judgment on sinners during their lifetime. Abraham acknowledges God's right to judge the inhabitants of the cities of Sodom and Gomorrah when he pleads to spare those who are just: "Shall not the Judge of all the earth do what is just?" (Gen. 18:25). God judges human beings in the present through the judicial system that he has ordained (Deut. 16:18–18:13; cf. Rom 13:1–7). Sometimes God exercises judgment in the context of war (2 Chron. 35:20–24). Israel was convinced that there would be a future judgment. This conviction is often expressed in the context of Israel's apostasy and in the context of evils experienced from hostile nations. This final judgment is often referred to as "the day of the LORD" or "that day" (Isa. 2:11–12; Zeph. 1:7; Ezek. 7:7). Sometimes God's judgment is linked with God's coming down to earth: "He is coming to judge the earth. He will judge the world with righteousness, and the peoples with his truth" (Ps. 96:13).

Before the prophet Isaiah describes God's future new creation (Isa. 65:17–25), he announced God's final judgment: "See, it is written before me: I will not keep silent, but I will repay; I will indeed repay into their laps their iniquities and their ancestors' iniquities together, says the LORD" (65:6–7). Among Israel's sins (listed in Isa. 65:7, 11–12), the most serious is the charge that "when I called, you did not answer, when I spoke, you did not listen, but you did what was evil in my sight, and chose what I did not delight in" (v. 12). The result of the final judgment is the division of the people into two groups who receive God's blessing and God's judgment, respectively (vv. 13–15). References to a future judgment of all human beings are rare, but they are unambiguous: "for by fire will the LORD execute judgment, and by his sword, on all flesh" (Isa. 66:16; also Jer. 25:31; Zech. 14:1–12; Mal. 4:1–6).

Jesus spoke of the coming day of judgment. When he sent his disciples on a preaching tour through Galilee, he said to them: "If anyone will not welcome you or listen to your words, shake off the dust from your feet as you leave that house or town. Truly I tell you, it will be more tolerable for the land of Sodom and Gomorrah on the day of judgment than for that town" (Matt. 10:14–15). Paul spoke about the coming day of judgment in no uncertain terms: "But by your hard and impenitent heart you are storing up wrath for yourself on the day of wrath, when God's righteous judgment will be revealed. For he will repay according to each one's deeds: to those who by patiently doing good seek for glory and honor and immortality, he will give eternal life; while for those who are self-seeking and who obey not the truth but wickedness, there will be wrath and fury" (Rom. 2:5–8). When will this day of final judgment take place?

Jesus and the Last Judgment

Jesus connects the day of judgment with his return to earth. At the end of his speech about the end times, he provides an extensive description of his coming (Matt. 24:29–31) that he then connects with the last judgment: "When the Son of Man comes in his glory, and all the angels with him, then he will sit on the throne of his glory. All the nations will be gathered before him, and he will separate people one from another as a shepherd separates the sheep from the goats, and he will put the sheep at his right hand and the goats at the left" (Matt. 25:31–33). The dissolution of the cosmos coincides with the coming of the Son of Man, that is, with Jesus' second coming,[1] which triggers the gathering of the faithful and the judgment of the nations.

Jesus' Death as God's Judgment

Paul emphasizes that when Jesus died on the cross, he suffered God's wrath and judgment for the sin of humankind. In Romans 1:18–3:20, Paul explains God's wrath on rebellious, sinful humankind, and in Romans 3:21–5:21 he explains how Jesus' death on the cross (Rom. 3:25) atoned for their sin. He rescued sinners from God's wrath in taking upon himself God's judgment due all human beings.

When sinners repent and believe in Jesus as Israel's Messiah and Savior of the world, God's judgment of sin on the cross becomes judgment of *their*

---

1. The reference to the Son of Man does not speak of the arrival of a figure distinct from and greater than Jesus, but about Jesus himself. Note that the vast majority of passages in which Jesus refers to the Son of Man leave no doubt that he speaks of himself (Matt. 11:19; 16:13; Mark 8:31; Luke 6:5; John 6:53). Some of these passages mention his authority to judge (Matt. 9:6; John 5:27).

sin. As they trust in Jesus for the forgiveness of their sins, they are saved from God's wrath of judgment (Rom. 5:9) because they are "in Christ Jesus" (3:24). Paul explains that when Jesus was crucified, repentant sinners who believe in Jesus were also crucified (6:6). When Jesus died, sinners who believe in Jesus also died (6:5). When Jesus was buried, believers in Jesus were buried (6:4). This is possible because Jesus' death was a substitutionary death: he died instead of us as he took upon himself the sins of the world.

Thus, *for believers in Jesus,* the day of judgment on which God judges sin and punishes sinners took place when Jesus died on Good Friday in the year A.D. 30. Colossians 2:13–15 most clearly explains Jesus' death on the cross as God's judgment: "And when you were dead in trespasses and the uncircumcision of your flesh, God made you alive together with him, when he forgave us all our trespasses, erasing the record that stood against us with its legal demands. He set this aside, nailing it to the cross. He disarmed the rulers and authorities and made a public example of them, triumphing over them in it." Paul quotes Psalm 32:1 in order to explain the consequences of Jesus' death and resurrection for sinners: "Blessed are those whose iniquities are forgiven, and whose sins are covered; blessed is the one against whom the Lord will not reckon sin" (Rom. 4:7–8).

Paul and the Last Judgment

While Paul understands Jesus' death on the cross as God's judgment of sin, he still anticipates a future judgment. He writes, "From now on there is reserved for me the crown of righteousness, which the Lord, the righteous judge, will give me on that day, and not only to me but also to all who have longed for his appearing" (2 Tim. 4:8). Without stating this explicitly, Paul believes that when the Lord "appears," that is, when Jesus returns, he comes as the Judge who will give him and all other believers in Jesus the "crown of righteousness" as a reward (see question 37).

In 1 Thessalonians 4–5, we find the same connection, although expressed even more indirectly. Paul first describes Jesus' second coming: "For the Lord himself, with a cry of command, with the archangel's call and with the sound of God's trumpet, will descend from heaven, and the dead in Christ will rise first" (4:16). This event is "the day of the Lord" (5:2). This day will come unexpectedly. For this reason it is important to be prepared and to live like "children of the light and . . . of the day" and not "children of the night and of darkness" (5:5 NIV). Paul reminds the Thessalonian believers that "since we belong to the day, let us be sober, and put on the breastplate of faith and love, and for a helmet the hope of salvation," and gives this reason: "For God has destined us not for wrath but for obtaining salvation through our Lord Jesus Christ" (5:8, 9). This sequence of statements indicates that Paul links Jesus' second coming with the day of judgment on which he will pour out his wrath on the unrepentant.

Jesus' Second Coming and the Day of Judgment in Revelation 19:11–21

If the day of judgment coincides with Jesus' second coming, we would expect that John's description of Jesus' coming in Revelation 19:11–21 refers to the day of judgment. While this is not explicitly the case, John has left clear hints in the text that Jesus' return indeed brings judgment on the human race.

Jesus comes through the opened heavens on a white horse and is described as the One who "in righteousness judges and makes war" (19:11). This indicates that as Jesus ends the "war" that the forces of evil have waged against God and his people, he does so as God's judgment. Three descriptions of Jesus' second coming are particularly important: his eyes are like a flame of fire (v. 12), his name is "The Word of God" (v. 13), and a sharp sword is coming out of Jesus' mouth (v. 15). These expressions describe the coming of Jesus as agent of God's judgment.[2] His name "The Word of God" (v. 13) expresses the means by which he executes divine judgment. The statement that he will use the sword coming out of his mouth "to strike down the nations, and he will rule them with a rod of iron; he will tread the wine press of the fury of the wrath of God the Almighty" (v. 15) describe God's judgment.

This allusion to Isaiah 11:4 indicates that Jesus' second coming coincides with the day of judgment on which the believers will be exonerated and their oppressors will be judged.[3] In Revelation 19:11–21, John portrays God's judgment on the political-religious system of the world represented by the Beast and the false prophet, and on "all, both free and slave, both small and great" who followed them (v. 18), as a battle. The description of the complete defeat of the forces of evil (vv. 17–18, 20–21) depicts God's judgment on all who rebelled against him. While the Beast and the false prophet are consigned to the lake of fire, the eternal place of punishment (v. 20; see 20:14), all of humankind aligned with the forces of evil are killed. John's clues in the text suggest that the ungodly are not simply consigned to Hades to await resurrection and judgment, but that they are judged on the very day of Jesus' return.

At the same time, the description of Jesus' return in Revelation 19:11–21 is described as an event of salvation for believers. Jesus is accompanied by "the armies of heaven, wearing fine linen, white and pure" who "were following him on white horses" (v. 14). This is a description of the followers of the Lamb, that is, of Christian believers described earlier as "clothed with fine

---

2. See Revelation 1:14–16 and 2:16; 19:21.
3. Isaiah 11:4: "With righteousness he shall judge the poor, and decide with equity for the meek of the earth; he shall strike the earth with the rod of his mouth, and with the breath of his lips he shall kill the wicked. Righteousness shall be the belt around his waist, and faithfulness the belt around his loins." The "rod of iron" in Revelation 9:15 alludes to Psalm 2:9 where this expression is a symbol of destruction for the ungodly nations and a symbol of protection for God's people. The reference to the treading of the wine press is an allusion to Isaiah 63:2–6 where this image is a prediction of God's last act of judgment.

linen, bright and pure," to which was added the explanation that "the fine linen is the righteous deeds of the saints" (v. 8). The believers who have perse-vered in faithfulness have "proven their case" before God with their righteous deeds, "and now they are to exercise the right of bearing witness to the truth with Christ at his coming."[4] In Revelation 3:5, the white garments of the be-lievers who persevere are the garments of those whose names are written in the book of life (21:27) and whose name Jesus confesses before the Father and the angels (Matt. 10:32–33; Luke 12:8–9). Since Revelation 20:12, 15 implies that it is the names of the resurrected saints that are written in the book of life, John's readers are prompted to connect the white garments of those who accompany Jesus with the saints, whose status has been established in God's judgment: their names are written in the book of life, and they now partici-pate in God's judgment on the ungodly.

Thus, John agrees with Jesus and Paul: the day of judgment is the day when Jesus returns. John uses the imagery of a battle in Revelation 19:11–21 to describe the day of judgment, but he describes the same event when God will come to judge the ungodly. The day of Jesus' second coming is a day when the forces of evil and the people who lived in rebellion against God will be vanquished. God's judgment is executed by Jesus by means of the Word of God. And the believers in Jesus will be united with him, participating with him in God's judgment of the unrepentant.

The Final Judgment after the Millennium

The longest and best known description of the final judgment is Revelation 20:11–15. The placement of this text poses a problem for the timing of the final judgment if Revelation 19:11–21 is interpreted as the day of judgment taking place on the day of Jesus' second coming, as expected by Jesus and Paul.[5] This problem is recognized by those who realize that Revelation 20:11–15, which follows the description of Satan's eternal punishment in the lake of fire (20:10), speaks only of the judgment of Satan's followers, that is, the unrepentant, while the judgment of the saints is not mentioned.[6]

---

4. J. Webb Mealy, *After the Thousand Years: Resurrection and Judgment in Revelation 20*, JSNTSup 70 (Sheffield: JSOT Press, 1992), 80.
5. The problem disappears if the millennium is not seen as a thousand-year period between Jesus' second coming and the final judgment, but as referring to the church period. If there is no millennium, then the judgment of Revelation 19:11–21 can be seen as being recapitulated in Revelation 20:11–15. However, since the text between these two texts (Rev. 20:1–10) is more plausibly interpreted as a period between Jesus' return and the final judg-ment (see questions 33 and 34), this solution is not convincing.
6. Thus, Osborne has to "contend" that the judgment described in Revelation 20:11–14 "is more universal" than depicted by John, "beginning with the saints and then finishing with the sinners" (*Revelation*, 719). We will see that this assumption is not necessary. See the discussion in Mealy, *After the Thousand Years*, 162–86.

In Revelation 19:11–21, Jesus appears as the Judge. But in 20:11–15 it is God who sits on a great white throne as Judge (v. 11). John describes the final judgment by God as a courtroom scene: "And I saw the dead, great and small, standing before the throne, and books were opened. Also another book was opened, the book of life. And the dead were judged according to their works, as recorded in the books. And the sea gave up the dead that were in it, Death and Hades gave up the dead that were in them, and all were judged according to what they had done" (vv. 12–13).

This judgment takes place after the millennium in connection with Satan's final judgment. The final rebellion of Satan and the unrepentant at the end of the millennium (20:7–9a; see question 34) ends in the final judgment of Satan and the unrepentant (20:9b–10). Note the parallels between 20:4–10 and 20:11–15.

(1) The resurrected saints sit on thrones with delegated authority to participate in God's judgment (20:4). God sits on the great white throne, ready to judge the unrepentant after "the earth and the heaven fled from his presence," leaving the underworld exposed (20:11).

(2) The saints have been found worthy to receive resurrection as they have been faithfully following Jesus Christ and to receive the authority to participate in God's judgment over the ungodly (20:4). The followers of Satan and the Beast did not receive resurrection: they are "the dead, great and small, standing before the throne, and books were opened," and they are "judged according to their works, as recorded in the books" (20:12). These books are different from the book of life: they contain a record of the deeds of the unrepentant. They are confronted with their deeds, which explains why they had been left in Hades while the followers of Jesus had been granted a resurrection body and life in the New Jerusalem.

(3) The dead are pulled out of the underworld (the "sea," death, Hades): they are "the nations at the four corners of the earth, Gog and Magog" who are "as numerous as the sands of the sea" (20:8). This appears to be the same event described in 20:13: "And the sea gave up the dead that were in it, Death and Hades gave up the dead that were in them."

(4) The resurrected dead appear before God's great white throne to be judged "according to what they had done" (20:13). This judgment results in punishment. Fire comes down and consumes Satan and all the unrepentant who had been released from the Abyss, and Satan is thrown into the lake of fire (20:9). Death and Hades are thrown into the lake of fire, together with all the unrepentant (20:15).

John's description of the final judgment of the unrepentant in Revelation 20:4–10 and 20:11–15 are two versions of the same event (of the retrial of the unrepentant who had been vanquished and judged and denied resurrection when Jesus' had returned in 19:11–21). The unrepentant face judgment twice as they provoke a final conflict with God and his people (19:11–21; 20:7–10). In Revelation 19:11–21, God brought judgment on the unrepentant; in

19:4–10 / 11–15 the unrepentant bring judgment upon themselves. John's description of the twofold judgment of the unrepentant ensures that "two mysteries are affirmed: (1) human agency and divine sovereignty each play a crucial role in the ultimate judgment and disposition of human beings, and (2) divine judgment will be based equally on corporate (19:11–21; 20:7–10) and on individual (20:11–15) responsibility."[7]

Summary

Jesus' death on the cross constitutes God's judgment on the sin of the world. This judgment is effective for sinners who repent and believe in Jesus as Israel's Messiah and Savior of the world. The day of judgment on which God will judge all human beings will take place at Jesus' second coming. Jesus, Paul, and John agree on this "date" of the day of judgment. John's description is complex. While he leaves no doubt that Jesus' coming as Judge brings God's judgment on the unrepentant, he refers to the judgment of the righteous only in connection with Jesus' return and the one-thousand-year period in which the resurrected saints reign with Jesus Christ. John describes two judgment scenes, which are best interpreted as two different judgments: the judgment of the unrepentant on the day of judgment at Jesus' second coming (Rev. 19:11–21) and the judgment of the dead before God's great white throne at the end of the millennium (20:11–15). The unrepentant dead are judged again because they have again followed Satan into rebellion despite being locked up with him in the Abyss for a thousand years, not having learned from this experience, which unmasked the deception of Satan, who can offer nothing but death (20:7–9).

REFLECTION QUESTIONS

1. What does the Old Testament say about the day of judgment?

2. What is the link between the day of judgment and Jesus' second coming according to passages in the Gospels and in Paul's letters?

3. How does John picture the day of judgment in his vision in Revelation 19:11–21?

4. How does John picture the last judgment in his vision in Revelation 19:7–15?

5. What is the connection between these two descriptions of God's judgment on the unrepentant?

---

7. Mealy, *After the Thousand Years*, 184.

What Will Happen to Believers on the Day of Judgment?

The New Testament passages that speak about the day of judgment distinguish between what happens to believers in Jesus and what happens to the unrepentant sinners.

It should be noted at the outset that the New Testament speaks of the possibility of God's judgment on believers during their lifetime. Examples are Ananias and Sapphira who were punished with death on account of their lying to the Christian community in Jerusalem, which is declared to be tantamount to lying to God (Acts 5:1–5). Paul urged the believers in Corinth to take action against a Christian who was having an affair with his (step)mother, directing them "to hand this man over to Satan for the destruction of the flesh, so that his spirit may be saved in the day of the Lord" (1 Cor. 5:5). Paul warned the Corinthian Christians not to despise their fellow believers who are poor and who come hungry to the assembly in which the Lord's Supper is celebrated in the context of a communal meal. He reminded them that if they eat and drink while neglecting the needs of the poor in the church, they "eat and drink judgment against themselves" (1 Cor. 11:29). This is serious indeed because such judgment can result in actual death: "for this reason many of you are weak and ill, and some have died" (v. 30).

The possibility of present judgment of believers, with potentially very serious consequences, reminds us that Christians cannot dismiss the subject of the last judgment as being irrelevant, claiming that God's judgment cannot fall on them. Christians speak of the last judgment precisely because there is the possibility of judgment falling on Christians who sin while they live on this earth.

Jesus' Death as God's Judgment

As we have seen in question 36, Paul understood Jesus' death as God's judgment, an event in which the sin of repentant sinners who believe in Jesus is forgiven (Col. 2:13–15). Believers can be assured of salvation in the last judgment, of which Paul continues to speak. Because God was "for us" on the day Jesus died on the cross and on the day that he rose from the dead (Rom. 8:31), no one can take salvation from us. Paul brings this point home in a series of rhetorical questions, followed by a confident declaration:

> He who did not withhold his own Son, but gave him up for all of us, will he not with him also give us everything else? Who will bring any charge against God's elect? It is God who justifies. Who is to condemn? It is Christ Jesus, who died, yes, who was raised, who is at the right hand of God, who indeed intercedes for us. Who will separate us from the love of Christ? Will hardship, or distress, or persecution, or famine, or nakedness, or peril, or sword? . . . No, in all these things we are more than conquerors through him who loved us. For I am convinced that neither death, nor life, nor angels, nor rulers, nor things present, nor things to come, nor powers, nor height, nor depth, nor anything else in all creation, will be able to separate us from the love of God in Christ Jesus our Lord. (Rom. 8:32–39)

The Coming Last Judgment

The apostle John links the coming day of judgment with unrepentant sinners (Rev. 19:11–21) and the last judgment with rebellious sinners deceived by Satan (20:11–15). He pictures the followers of Jesus as being in the presence of Jesus at his second coming (19:14) and as reigning with Jesus as resurrected saints (20:4). They are people who evidently do not stand before the great white throne of God to be judged according to what is recorded "in the books" because their names were found written in the "book of life" (20:12, 15; 21:27).

Jesus and Paul speak of a future judgment for believers, mostly to encourage them, but also to warn them to take sin and its consequences seriously. We will review the most important of these passages in what follows.

Acceptance by Jesus

Jesus affirms that people who acknowledge him before others will be accepted "before my Father in heaven" (Matt. 10:32–33; see Luke 12:8–9). People who understand Jesus' significance, who accept his message, who acknowledge him as Lord, who are loyal to him even in the midst of opposition, will survive the encounter with God on the day of judgment because of Jesus' loyalty to them.[1]

---

1. R. T. France points out that Peter's rehabilitation after his denial of Jesus (Matt. 26:69–75) "adds a reassuring suggestion that the stark verdict of this saying may be understood to

Life

In the saying about the broad and narrow roads, Jesus describes the eternal destiny reached on the narrow road and through a narrow gate as "life" (Matt. 7:14; also 18:9). This corresponds to the Old Testament contrast between "the way of life and the way of death" (Jer. 21:8; see Ps. 1:6; Deut. 11:26–29; 30:15–20). Understood in the context of the Sermon on the Mount, Jesus makes the point here that those who follow him stand out from the majority of society in which they live (Matt. 5:3–10, 13–16). As a result they suffer discrimination and persecution (vv. 11–12, 39–47): this is why that road is "narrow," lacking space, which explains why there are only few who travel it.

Paul speaks of eternal life: "if you sow to the Spirit, you will reap eternal life from the Spirit" (Gal. 6:8). Paul connects the transfer from being owned by sin to being owned by God with eternal life: "But now that you have been freed from sin and enslaved to God, the advantage you get is sanctification. The end is eternal life" (Rom. 6:22), which is God's gracious gift: "the free gift of God is eternal life in Christ Jesus our Lord" (v. 23).

John speaks of the followers of Jesus (sometimes implicitly) as people whose names are written in the "book of life" (Rev. 3:5; 13:8; 17:8; 20:12, 15; 21:27). Here "life" is life in the presence of God; it is life in the new age of the new earth, which will never end.

Entering the Kingdom of Heaven

Jesus promises to the people whom he "knows"—people who have a relationship with him that goes beyond doing good and pursuing spiritual achievements—that they will "enter the kingdom of heaven" (Matt. 7:21–23). Understood as a reference to the outcome of the final judgment, his promise means that true believers will be present in God's kingdom in heaven, enjoying his gracious rule.

Resurrection from the Dead

When Paul looks ahead to the future, he asserts, "I want to know Christ and the power of his resurrection and the sharing of his sufferings by becoming like him in his death, if somehow I may attain the resurrection from the dead" (Phil. 3:10–11).

This is the outcome of the judgment of the followers of Jesus at his second coming: they are in his presence when he returns (Rev. 19:14), because "they came to life" in the first resurrection (20:4).

Living on the New Earth

Peter asserts that "in accordance with his promise, we wait for new

---

refer to a settled course of acknowledgment or denial rather than to every temporary lapse under pressure" (*The Gospel of Matthew*, NICNT [Grand Rapids: Eerdmans, 2007], 406).

heavens and a new earth, where righteousness is at home" (2 Peter 3:13). This expectation can be linked with John's description of a new heaven and new earth in Revelation 21:1–22:5. The new heaven and the new earth is one single reality: the New Jerusalem, the dwelling place of God among the resurrected saints (Rev. 21:1–3). Life in this new reality means that God "will dwell with them as their God; they will be his peoples, and God himself will be with them; he will wipe every tear from their eyes. Death will be no more; mourning and crying and pain will be no more, for the first things have passed away" (vv. 3–4).

Receiving Royal Authority

In Jesus' description of the last judgment, salvation is described as follows: "Come, you that are blessed by my Father, inherit the kingdom prepared for you from the foundation of the world" (Matt. 25:34). This is more than being members of God's kingdom: Jesus speaks of a "kingdom" or "kingship" (the Greek term *basileia* can be translated in both ways) prepared for those who believe in him. He promises them that they will become kings, sharing his own royal authority. This is what Jesus had promised to the Twelve (19:28). Now he clarifies that this is God's purpose for all people who follow him as the culmination of God's purpose for them "from the foundation of the world" (25:34). (For the same concept of royal authority that believers will receive on the day of judgment, see 1 Cor. 4:8; Eph. 2:6; Rev. 1:6; 5:10; 20:6; 22:5).

Presence at the Messianic Banquet

Jesus affirms that people who have faith in him (as the Roman centurion did) "will eat with Abraham and Isaac and Jacob in the kingdom of heaven" (Matt. 8:11). This image of the messianic banquet is a picture of the ultimate blessedness of God's people in the presence of the patriarchs. Jesus specifically includes many "from east and west," that is, Gentiles: they are assured membership in the true people of God, as Gentiles. All who believe will enjoy the fullness of blessings in the kingdom of heaven.

In the parable of the bridesmaids, Jesus is presented as the bridegroom whose coming to the wedding feast is delayed. Some of the bridesmaids, called "wise," had sufficient foresight to bring enough oil for their lamps as they reckoned with the possibility of a long delay of the bridegroom. When he finally arrived, they were ready and thus "went with him into the wedding banquet" (Matt. 25:10). The wedding banquet is an image for the blessings of the kingdom of heaven (see Matt. 8:11–12; 22:1–14).

Rescue from Punishment

Paul describes Jesus as the one "who rescues us from the wrath that is coming" (1 Thess. 1:10). Believers are spared the manifestation of God's anger punishing sinners with death. Because they have accepted God's offer of forgiveness, revealed in the death and resurrection of Jesus Christ, they will not experience God's wrath, that is, God's punishment in the final judgment.

Greater Responsibility

In the parable of the slaves left in charge, Jesus assures true believers who do his will in his absence that upon his return they will receive his blessing. They will also receive greater responsibility: "Truly I tell you, he will put that one in charge of all his possessions" (Matt. 24:47). This outcome entails "the challenging assumption that faithful disciples will welcome this further and heavier commitment rather than feeling that they have earned a rest."[2]

Some have suggested that there will be degrees of reward in heaven.[3] Jesus' parable of the pounds (Luke 19:12–27) seems to introduce this idea. The slave who turned the pound that he had been given by his master into ten pounds is put in charge of ten cities, and the slave who had "grown" his pound into five pounds is put in charge of five cities; and the slave who returned his pound to the master is relieved of his pound, which is given to the slave with ten pounds. However, since only three of the ten slaves of the master are mentioned, it is not plausible to interpret the parable in terms of degrees of reward. The two slaves who have increased their pound are presented as images of faithful service leading to divine commendation. The emphasis is on the lazy slave who is an image of worthless service leading to divine condemnation. The appointment of the two slaves to rule over cities should not be allegorized, for example, in terms of responsibilities during the millennium.

Essential elements of the reward that Paul speaks of are "glory and honor and peace" (Rom. 2:10), God's praise (1 Cor. 4:5), glory (2 Cor. 4:17; Rom. 8:17–18), and God's pleasure (2 Cor. 5:9). In 2 Timothy 4:8, Paul writes, "There is reserved for me the crown of righteousness, which the Lord, the righteous judge, will give me on that day, and not only to me but also to all who have longed for his appearing." The expression "crown of righteousness" means that the "crown" that believers will receive *is* righteousness itself (the Greek expression interpreted as an epexegetical genitive). These terms make it difficult to envisage that believers will each receive various rewards of differing values.

Summary

When Christians encounter Jesus at his second coming, on the day of judgment, they will be accepted by him as they have been his followers, having persevered in their loyalty to him despite opposition and persecution.

---

2. France, *Gospel of Matthew*, 944.
3. See Stephen H. Travis, *Christ and the Judgment of God: The Limits of Divine Retribution in New Testament Thought*, 2nd ed. (Peabody, MA: Hendrickson, 2009), 170–75, 248–51. On the assessment of rewards on the day of judgment, see question 40.

They will receive life in God's eternal presence on a new earth in the New Jerusalem. Believers are spared the eternal punishment of unrepentant sinners because they have been rescued from God's wrath through Jesus' death and resurrection. On the day of Jesus' second coming, believers will enter the kingdom of heaven because they live under God's reign. More than that, they receive kingship, the authority to participate in God's rule over the new earth. Believers will take part in the banquet of the Messiah, enjoying the fullness of blessings in the company of all the saints. And believers will receive a greater responsibility: while this is not specified, it certainly means the enjoyment of participating in God's rule over the new, perfect creation.

REFLECTION QUESTIONS

1. What does Jesus say will happen to his followers on the day of judgment?

2. Why are believers not punished?

3. What is eternal life?

4. What is the new earth?

5. What is the significance of being in God's presence?

What Will Happen to Unbelievers on the Day of Judgment?

Jesus, Paul, and John all speak about the fate of the unrepentant sinners on the day of judgment. The following survey presents the most important passages.

Rejection by Jesus

Jesus affirms that those who are ashamed of him and his words, that is, people who reject his message, will be rejected by him (Mark 8:38). Similarly, he asserts that people who do good and who have spiritual achievements but who have no relationship with him will be sent away: "I never knew you; go away from me, you evildoers" (Matt. 7:23). The foolish bridesmaids in Jesus' parable thought they knew the bridegroom sufficiently to be sure that he would come soon. Yet, they ran out of oil for their lamps and were excluded from the wedding feast. The door that had been shut behind the wise bridesmaids remains shut as the bridegroom declares "Truly I tell you, I do not know you" (Matt. 25:12). The judicial verdict implied in this declaration draws the conclusions from a false or nonexisting relationship. Jesus disassociates himself from the people whom he does not know because they do not belong to him.

Exclusion from the Messianic Banquet

Jesus asserts that those who do not have faith in him will be excluded from the messianic banquet, which is celebrated in the kingdom of heaven with Abraham and Isaac and Jacob (Matt. 8:12). The same point is made in the parable of the great dinner: those who reject Jesus' invitation are excluded from the messianic banquet, even if they belonged to the originally invited guests (i.e., the Jewish people; Luke 14:24).

Exclusion from the Kingdom of God

Paul asserts that "wrongdoers will not inherit the kingdom of God," specifying that "fornicators, idolaters, adulterers, male prostitutes, sodomites, thieves, the greedy, drunkards, revilers, robbers—none of these will inherit the kingdom of God" (1 Cor. 6:9–10). Unrepentant sinners will not be admitted to the realm of God's rule on the new earth. This is why John writes: "those who conquer will inherit these things, and I will be their God and they will be my children. But as for the cowardly, the faithless, the polluted, the murderers, the fornicators, the sorcerers, the idolaters, and all liars, their place will be in the lake that burns with fire and sulfur, which is the second death" (Rev. 21:7–8).

Gehenna (Hell)

Jesus asserts that sinners are thrown by God into "Gehenna" (Greek, *geenna*), a word that is usually translated as "hell."[1] The Greek word *geenna* is derived from the Hebrew term *ge hinnom*, which means "Valley of [the sons of] Hinnom." This was a valley outside of Jerusalem (to the west and south). It had once been the site of human sacrifice by fire to the pagan god Molech (2 Kings 23:10; Jer. 7:31). A later tradition links the valley with the rubbish dump of Jerusalem, which explains its connection with "the eternal fire" of eternal punishment. Jeremiah describes the Valley of Hinnom as the place of God's judgment, where the bodies of dead Judeans would be thrown by the Babylonians (Jer. 19:6–7). In Jewish apocalyptic literature, the Valley of Hinnom, or "Gehenna," was the place of divine punishment: it is described as "the cursed valley," as an abyss burning with fire, as characterized by darkness and fire (*1 En.* 27:1–2; 54:1–6; 90:24–27; 108:3–6). In the New Testament, Gehenna is the place where God's judgment is inflicted on unrepentant sinners. Jesus says that to be cast into Gehenna is a far worse fate than physical death (Matt. 10:28; Luke 12:4–5) because it evidently involves continual, eternal torment.

Destruction

In the saying about the broad and narrow roads, Jesus describes the eternal destiny obtained by those on the broad road, reached through a broad gate, as "destruction" (Matt. 7:13). In light of the Old Testament contrast between "the way of life and the way of death" (Jer. 21:8; see Ps. 1:6; Deut. 11:26–29; 30:15–20), Jesus' reference to destruction entails a reference to death.

Jesus warns his contemporaries not to damage his followers' relationship with God. The punishment for being such a stumbling block is a quick drowning with no chance of survival: "it would be better for you if a great

---

1. Matthew 5:22, 29, 30; 10:28; 18:9; 23:15, 33; Mark 9:43, 45, 47; Luke 12:5; also see James 3:6.

millstone were fastened around your neck and you were drowned in the depth of the sea" (Matt. 18:6).

Paul asserts that "if anyone destroys God's temple, God will destroy that person" (1 Cor. 3:17). Since profaning a temple in antiquity was a capital crime, often leading to execution, Paul asserts that people who destroy the church, which is described in this passage as God's temple, will be destroyed by God. Because such a person "has already in his offense rejected the possibility of salvation . . . he has rejected grace for himself; he has denied his own relation with God."[2]

John describes the destruction of the unrighteous who had followed the Beast and the false prophet, "all, both free and slave, both small and great" (Rev. 19:18) who did not follow Jesus. Their destruction is depicted in the battle scene in Revelation 19:11–21 at the end of which all were "killed by the sword of the rider on the horse, the sword that came from his mouth; and all the birds were gorged with their flesh" (v. 21).

Fire

Jesus asserts that sin leads to "eternal fire" (Matt. 18:8). Fire (Greek, *pyr*) is an image for the ultimate, final judgment: as fire destroys wood, the unrepentant sinners are destroyed in God's judgment. Jesus describes the fire as "eternal" (Greek, *aiōnios*), which means that it is the punishment of the age (Greek, *aiōn*) to come, which is forever. In the parallel passage Mark 9:43, the fire is described as being "unquenchable" (Greek, *asbeston*), that is, inextinguishable, burning forever. Some passages combine the expression "hell of fire" (Greek, *ten geennan tou pyros*), combining the concept of Gehenna with the concept of fire which destroys (Matt. 18:9; see 5:22). The reference to fire may imply conscious eternal pain. Since hell is connected both with fire and darkness, however, this is not certain.

John mentions that the unrepentant sinners will end up in the lake of fire (Rev. 20:15), together with the Beast and the false prophet (19:20), Satan (20:10), and Death and Hades itself (20:14). Some have argued that terms such as "fire" and "destruction" allow, or call for, the view that the fate of the unrepentant sinners is not eternal conscious punishment but cessation of existence (annihilation).[3] A survey of the use of these and related terms shows that they have a range of meaning that does *not* force the conclusion that those who suffer "destruction" or who are thrown into the lake of fire cease

---

2. C. K. Barrett, *The First Epistle to the Corinthians*, BNTC (London: Black, 1968), 91–92.

3. See, for example, John Stott, in David L. Edwards and John Stott, *Evangelical Essentials: A Liberal-Evangelical Dialogue* (Downers Grove, IL: InterVarsity Press, 1989), 312–20; Clark H. Pinnock, "The Conditional View," in *Four Views on Hell*, ed. William Crockett (Grand Rapids: Zondervan, 1992), 135–66; see Stephen H. Travis, *Christ and the Judgment of God: The Limits of Divine Retribution in New Testament Thought*, 2nd ed. (Peabody, MA: Hendrickson, 2009), 104–10.

to exist.[4] Passages that parallel eternal salvation and eternal punishment and that use the language of "fire" or "destruction" are important. Note Matthew 18:8: "If your hand or your foot causes you to stumble, cut it off and throw it away; it is better for you to enter life maimed or lame than to have two hands or two feet and to be thrown into the eternal fire." The fire that Jesus refers to burns forever. At the end of the parable of the sheep and goats with which Jesus illustrates what will happen in the last judgment, he asserts that "these will go away into eternal punishment, but the righteous into eternal life" (Matt. 25:46). If the Greek term *aiōn*, translated here as "eternal," refers to the unceasing existence of the righteous in God's presence, it necessarily also refers to the unceasing punishment of the unrighteous. The argument that the eternal punishment is annihilation, the cessation of existence, is not convincing. If "eternal life" is more than mere existence in the presence of God, "eternal punishment" cannot be mere lack of existence. If the "eternal fire prepared for the devil and his angels" (Matt. 25:41) is real, the "eternal punishment" of unrepentant sinners is surely real as well. Similarly important passages such as Revelation 14:10–11 and 20:10–15 speak of the conscious torment of the unrepentant sinners as well. Although we may not know exactly what terms such as "destruction" and metaphors such as "fire" and "darkness" mean for the reality of a literal hell, they certainly describe the awful existence of those who refuse to accept God's redeeming grace.

Death

Paul describes the fate of the unrepentant sinners whose sins have not been forgiven with the word *death*: "the wages of sin is death" (Rom. 6:23). The "payout" (wages) of sin, that is, the consequence of sin, is death—physical death, and then eternal death understood as irrevocable exclusion from the presence of God.

Punishment

In Jesus' parable of the slaves left in charge, the slave who was unconcerned about his master's return and indulged in selfish, irresponsible behavior at the expense of others is "cut . . . in pieces" (Matt. 24:51). This reference to brutal execution in Jesus' parable is a metaphor for severe punishment.

Paul describes the final condemnation of unrepentant sinners as God pouring out his "wrath" (1 Thess. 1:10). The term "wrath" refers to God's anger, his reaction to the rebellion of human beings against his good and gracious

---

4. See D. A. Carson, *The Gagging of God: Christianity Confronts Pluralism* (Grand Rapids: Zondervan, 1995), 520–23. For the points that follow in the text above, see ibid., 524–36. Also see Paul Helm, *The Last Things: Death, Judgment, Heaven, Hell* (Edinburgh: Banner of Truth, 1989); Kendall S. Harmon, "The Case against Conditionalism," in *Universalism and the Doctrine of Hell*, ed. Nigel M. de S. Cameron (Carlisle: Paternoster; Grand Rapids: Baker Academic, 1992), 193–224.

will and to the sins of the unrepentant who refuse his offer of forgiveness. It is thus a term that describes God's final judgment of the wicked (also see 1 Thess. 2:16; Rom. 1:18–20; 2:5, 8; 3:5; 5:9; 9:22[2x]).

Mourning and Vexation

Jesus asserts that people who are excluded from God's eternal presence engage in "weeping and gnashing of teeth" (Matt. 8:12; 24:51). This expression speaks of mourning over missed opportunities to acknowledge Jesus and over the exclusion from God's new and perfect creation. It also speaks of hostility, anger, and vexation over their place in darkness.

Suffering in Darkness

Jesus affirms that Jews who do not have faith in him (in contrast to the Roman centurion, a Gentile) "will be thrown into the outer darkness" (Matt. 8:12). The expression "thrown out" speaks of violent exclusion from the messianic banquet that is mentioned in the previous verse. The description of the place of eternal perdition as a place of darkness (despite the fire!) underlines the absence of the light of God's presence, the light that makes life possible.[5] The expression "outer" emphasizes that this place of darkness is removed as far as possible from God.

Summary

Unrepentant sinners are rejected by Jesus. This means they are excluded from the kingdom of God, from the messianic banquet, indeed from the very presence of God. The Bible describes their fate as "destruction" symbolized by both fire (which destroys) and darkness (which does not allow life). Unrepentant sinners who all end up in hell may feel sorry for their fate, but they continue to express anger and hostility, perhaps because they blame others for their fate, still unable and unwilling to accept responsibility for their actions. To be cast into Gehenna (hell) is far worse than physical death because it evidently involves eternal torment.

REFLECTION QUESTIONS

1. What does Jesus say will happen to unrepentant sinners on the day of judgment?

2. Why are unrepentant sinners punished?

---

5. See the same metaphor of darkness and fire in several Jewish texts: Wisdom of Solomon 17:21; Tobit 14:10; *1 Enoch* 63:6; 108:14; *Psalms of Solomon* 14:9; 15:10. In the New Testament, see 2 Peter 2:17; Jude 13.

3. What is eternal fire? What is darkness?

4. What is hell?

5. What is the significance of being excluded from God's presence?

PART 4

Interpreting the End Times

How Should We View
the Prophecies of Prophecy Writers?

Some Christians who have commented on what the Bible says about the end times have not only sought to interpret the prophecies of Scripture but have frequently given interpretations and made announcements that are themselves (new) prophecies. The apostle Paul had to deal with such people: "As to the coming of our Lord Jesus Christ and our being gathered together to him, we beg you, brothers and sisters, not to be quickly shaken in mind or alarmed, either by spirit or by word or by letter, as though from us, to the effect that the day of the Lord is already here" (2 Thess. 2:1–2). What should we do with end-time prophecies? And what should we do with prophecy writers who make prophetic announcements?

Constructing New Meanings of Biblical Prophecies

We have encountered several examples of end-time writers giving new meanings to biblical prophecy, despite the stated commitment to only "literal" interpretations. One example is the interpretation of texts such as Ezekiel 38–39 and Revelation 19:11–21 in terms of a literal final battle at the end of history. Expecting a literal battle, prophecy writers realize that the possibility of a battle being fought on horses and with swords, shields, and spears is not only remote but impossible (since the use of gunpowder in Western warfare in the fourteenth century; end-time writers expect a literal battle, not the reenactment of an ancient or early medieval battle). As a result, some end-time writers interpret the horses in the text via the connection of "horse power" to be tanks, arrows as missiles, and spears as cannons. Such interpretations, offered in the second half of the twentieth century, will have to be changed in the twenty-first century where tanks and cannons are becoming quickly obsolete as weaponry used in military conflicts. End-times writers insist that they are faithfully interpreting the biblical text, merely updating the instruments of war that are used. However, we are left wondering whether this interpretation constructs a new meaning that alters the nature of the prophecy. For example, in modern warfare, the battlefield is usually no longer a "field" that can be localized (cf. the "field" outside of Megiddo) and on which the decisive clash of armies takes place.

Another example is the literal interpretation of Jesus' second coming as taking place in the city of Jerusalem (an expectation that we do not find explicitly stated in the New Testament), which then must be harmonized with the literal interpretation of the expectation that all the people of the earth will see Jesus when he returns. Prophecy writers who insist on a literal interpretation on both counts argue that the only way in which this is possible is through satellite television. Without saying so, they imply that both sets of prophesies could not have been fulfilled literally in the first century. They assume that Jesus' return can be imminent only once satellite technology was invented. These interpreters fail to see that seeing Jesus' return on a television screen is not actually "seeing" Jesus—watching a sequence of pixels on a screen is *not* the same as seeing a live event in person. The Scripture promises that believers will see Jesus face to face (1 Cor. 13:12). And they fail to see that Peter, Paul, and John all reckoned with the possibility that they may live long enough to be alive at Jesus' second coming. To introduce modern technology into the interpretation of biblical prophecy as an essential requirement for fulfillment constructs new meanings of the biblical prophetic texts.[1]

Constructing New Prophecies

Sometimes prophecy writers, probably unwittingly, construct new prophecies. For example, some claim that since Revelation 18:1–19:10 announces the fall of Babylon, which at the moment lies in ruins, the city of Babylon (in modern Iraq) will be rebuilt. However, this is not an actual biblical prophecy: there is no passage that predicts that the city of Babylon will be rebuilt sometime in the future. The statement that the city of Babylon will be rebuilt is not the interpretation of a prophecy about Babylon. Rather, it is a reconstructed event that is allegedly required in the context of a literal (geographical) interpretation. The view that the city of Babylon will be rebuilt results from a particular approach to the interpretation of Revelation 18:1–19:10, an approach that interprets references to cities as referring to literal cities. This is an approach that requires a literal interpretation of the reference to Babylon. In the process, a new prophecy is constructed that ignores the genre and the context of the biblical prophecy.

The same dynamic is involved when prophecy writers state that a third temple will be built. While this is certainly possibly—nobody knows what will

---

1. Besides, if the stars are falling from the sky (literally) and the sky is being rolled up like a scroll (literally), it becomes impossible to assume that satellites would still be working.

happen in the Middle East!—it is not a biblical prophecy but a new prophecy developed by prophecy writers. Jesus announces the destruction of the temple of Jerusalem that was standing in the year A.D. 30. This prophecy was fulfilled in the summer of the year A.D. 70. Jesus did not announce the construction of a third temple. When he refers to "the desolating sacrilege standing in the holy place" (Matt. 24:15), he speaks of an event that would occur in the temple built by Zerubbabel (Ezra 5:2) and Ezra and expanded by Herod I. One may argue that what Jesus prophesied in Matthew 24:15 was not fulfilled in the events of A.D. 70, but it is not possible to argue that Jesus' prophecy of the destruction of the temple in Matthew 24:2 did not refer to the temple in front of which he and the disciples were standing.[2] Thus, to affirm that Jesus' prediction regarding the destruction of the temple in Matthew 24:2 will take place *not* in connection with the temple that existed in the first century but in connection with a future temple, means that it has to be assumed that a *third* temple will have to be built. This expectation of a third temple is tantamount to the development of a new prophecy. It assumes that one of Jesus' prophecies refers to a time *after* the destruction of the temple in A.D. 70, thus requiring a new (third) temple. While it is not impossible that Jews will build a third temple in Jerusalem, this is not what Jesus prophesied: he spoke about the second temple, the temple that existed in A.D. 30 and that was destroyed in A.D. 70.

Prophetic Announcements

We have seen in our discussion of the Antichrist (question 20) and the nearness of Jesus' second coming (question 32) that many prophecy writers are willing to make prophetic announcements. Some have claimed that they are part of the last generation of history. Hal Lindsey published in 1970 his announcement that "there will soon begin the construction of this [third] Temple."[3] Forty years later, which is an entire generation (by Lindsey's definition), the construction of a third temple has still not been initiated. Prophecy writers in the second half of the twentieth century have been particularly bold. But the setting of specific dates for the appearance of the Antichrist and Jesus' second coming is not a recent phenomenon. Sadly, it has a regrettably long history. The chronicle of Francis Gumerlock demonstrates that announcements of dates for the end of the world are found not only among quasi-Christian fringe groups but among well-meaning and serious Christians.[4]

---

2. Note the context of Jesus' prediction in Matthew 24:1–2: "As Jesus came out of the temple and was going away, his disciples came to point out to him the buildings of the temple. Then he asked them, 'You see all these, do you not? Truly I tell you, not one stone will be left here upon another; all will be thrown down.'"

3. Hal Lindsey, *The Late Great Planet Earth* (Grand Rapids: Zondervan, 1970), 57.

4. Francis X. Gumerlock, *The Day and the Hour: A Chronicle of Christianity's Perennial Fascination with Predicting the End of the World* (Atlanta: American Vision, 2009), 5–331.

Setting a date for Jesus' second coming is prophecy. Identifying historical events and developments as fulfillment of biblical prophecy is itself a prophetic act. Christian prophecy writers seem to be unaware of this; otherwise they might be more careful in their pronouncements. Since historical events and developments have multiple causes, the assertion that a particular event or series of events is the result of God fulfilling his word spoken through the prophets requires supernatural, divine insight. This is the reason why the historical books of the Old Testament—the books from Joshua to Kings—are called the "Former Prophets" who stand next to the "Latter Prophets" encompassing the books from Isaiah to Malachi (without Lamentations and Daniel, books that the Hebrew Bible locates in the third section called "Writings"). Only a prophet, inspired by God, can know for sure, for example, how the problems in the latter part of King Saul's reign are connected with the unfolding plan of God for Israel. Apart from divine revelation, the Israelites could only speculate why Saul ran into trouble and was killed in battle and replaced by King David. This means that the identification of historical events as fulfillment of prophecy that do not turn out to be correct constitutes false prophecy. Thus, when the development of European countries coming into the European Union was interpreted as fulfillment of John's statement in Revelation 17:12 about ten kings, this was a prophetic analysis and thus a prophetic statement.[5] Since the European Union today has twenty-five members, this was a prophecy that turned out to be misguided.

What Do We Do with Prophecies?

If we believe that the gift of prophecy was possible not only in the church of the first century (1 Cor. 12:10; 14:1, 6), but that it is a spiritual gift that can be exercised in the church today, the development of new prophecies is not a problem as such. The problem is that new prophecies such as mentioned above are presented as interpretations of the biblical text rather than as new prophecies. How should we handle such new prophecies?

Also see Franz Stuhlhofer, who analyzes predictions of end-time writers, some known mostly in Europe, including Wim Malgo, a Dutch prophecy writer who announced that the third world war would begin shortly after 1974 (Franz Stuhlhofer, *"Das Ende naht!" Die Irrtümer der Endzeitspezialisten* [Giessen: Brunnen, 1992], 138–212).

5. Lindsey, *Late Great Planet Earth*, 88–113. The scenario that he announced is summarized by McGinn as follows: "By about 1980 Rome will be revived in a ten-nation United States of Europe . . . to provide the power base for the coming dictator, or Antichrist. This Gentile dictator is supposed to sign a peace treaty with Israel that will allow for the rebuilding of the temple. He will be revealed as Antichrist when he is miraculously healed of a serious head wound; he will then enthrone himself as God in the rebuilt temple. Associated with him will be a Jewish False Prophet (see Apoc. 13:11–18) who will compel everyone to worship the dictator" (Bernhard McGinn, *Antichrist: Two Thousand Years of the Human Fascination with Evil* [San Francisco: HarperCollins, 1994], 236).

In the book of Deuteronomy, three prescriptions are given in which Israel was directed by God to handle prophecies. Prophets who offer omens or portents that come true but who worship pagan deities shall receive the death sentence (Deut. 13:1–5). Prophets who speak in the name of other gods also deserve the death sentence (Deut. 18:15–20). Prophets who speak on behalf of Yahweh but whose word does not come true, that is, whose prophecy is not fulfilled, speak presumptuously and should be ignored (Deut. 18:21–22: "You may say to yourself, 'How can we recognize a word that the LORD has not spoken?' If a prophet speaks in the name of the LORD but the thing does not take place or prove true, it is a word that the LORD has not spoken. The prophet has spoken it presumptuously; do not be frightened by it").

In most countries, Christians would agree with the execution of end-time "specialists" who do not speak in the name of the one true and living God. The third case, however, is the one that applies to Christian prophecy writers (1) whose interpretations construct new prophecies that are not fulfilled, (2) whose identification of historical events and developments as fulfillment of prophecy is patently false, or (3) who make prophetic announcements about dates that come and go without fulfillment.

If announcements are made about developments or dates in the future, we wait and see whether the prophecy is fulfilled, or whether events make it obvious that it was a false prophecy. Setting a date for Jesus' second coming is a prophecy. If the date passes without the second coming happening, it is a false prophecy. Such false prophecies should be ignored. If the prophecy writer tries again and adjusts his prophecy, and the new prediction does not come to pass, the end-time "specialist" is clearly neither a specialist nor a prophet. Prophecy writers who get it wrong must apologize, and they should stop writing, speaking, blogging, and tweeting about matters related to prophecy.

Making false predictions is serious. Israel had to contend with false prophets and so does the church, as Jesus predicted: "Many false prophets will arise and lead many astray" (Matt. 24:11). Jesus warns of such people: "Beware that no one leads you astray" (24:4). God conveyed to the prophet Jeremiah the following condemnation of prophets who spoke words that proved not to be true: "The prophets are prophesying lies in my name; I did not send them, nor did I command them or speak to them. They are prophesying to you a lying vision, worthless divination, and the deceit of their own minds" (Jer. 14:14).

Summary

Some interpretations of prophecy writers imply and often explicitly assert new meanings of biblical prophecies. Some construct new prophecies on the basis of how they think biblical prophecies will be (literally) fulfilled. Some have ventured to make prophetic announcements, the vast majority of which have been proven false. Some of these relate to future developments where we have to wait and see what will happen. The identification of historical events and developments as constituting fulfillment of biblical prophecy is itself a prophetic act: it takes supernatural insight to state that a particular event was caused by God's intervention. To predict what God is doing now, or will do in the (near) future, is serious indeed. Prophecy writers who get it wrong have not spoken on behalf of God. They must be criticized, they must apologize, and they should either be more careful with their interpretations and pronouncements or refrain from "explaining" the prophetic word.

REFLECTION QUESTIONS

1. What are some of the predictions of prophecy writers that have not proven to be true?

2. Why is the identification of a historical event as fulfillment of a biblical prophecy itself an act of prophecy?

3. What is a false prophecy?

4. How does the Old Testament evaluate false prophecy?

5. What does the New Testament say about false prophets?

Why Should I Care about the End Times?

The confusion surrounding the end times has caused many Christians to become cynical and many pastors to refrain from preaching from end-time texts. Are end-times questions important enough that we must have the courage to step into this minefield of debate and opinion? What is important and what is not important? Why should I care? And how should I handle disagreements? We begin with the last question.

How Should We Deal with Disagreements Concerning the End Times?

Some participants in the discussion about the end times seem to care a lot about labels and "party" affiliation. The debate about "progressive dispensationalism" is an example. While some scholars such as Darrell Bock, Craig Blaising, and Robert Saucy are interested in reading and interpreting the relevant biblical texts, allowing for the possibility of new understandings,[1] others seem more interested in establishing whether "progressive dispensationalists" should be allowed to call themselves dispensationalists.[2] Some seminaries view differences regarding end-times positions related to the timing of the rapture or the nature of the millennium as serious enough that faculty members are asked to leave if they

---

1. See Craig A. Blaising and Darrell L. Bock, *Progressive Dispensationalism* (Wheaton: Victor Books, 1993); Craig A. Blaising and Darrell L. Bock, eds., *Dispensationalism, Israel and the Church: The Search for Definition* (Grand Rapids: Zondervan, 1992); Robert L. Saucy, *The Case for Progressive Dispensationalism: The Interface between Dispensational and Non-Dispensational Theology* (Grand Rapids: Zondervan, 1993).
2. Note some of these other contributors in Ron J. Bigalke Jr., ed., *Progressive Dispensationalism: An Analysis of the Movement and Defense of Traditional Dispensationalism* (Lanham, MD: University Press of America, 2005).

change their position. Craig Blomberg has correctly noted that "the debate about the timing of the rapture is largely limited to *evangelical* Christian circles. It is limited even more because it is predominantly an intramural debate among those who subscribe to premillennialism."[3] He could have added that the discussion is largely a North American discussion. From a perspective outside of North America, particularly those countries in which there are few Christians or in which the church is being persecuted, debates about the timing of the rapture and the nature of the millennium are curious indeed. Inquisitional "are you in?" and "are you out?" confrontations on *these* questions are seen as distracting from more important things that the church and her teachers should be doing. Seen from both a global and historical perspective (beginning with the church fathers) this emphasis on "party loyalty" regarding *these* particular questions seems misplaced. The following advice should not be controversial for people who confess to be followers of Jesus.

First, we emphasize what Jesus emphasized. Jesus predicted, apart from the particular event of the destruction of the temple and of Jerusalem, that history will continue to be tragic and chaotic and filled with human suffering. And he predicted that he will return, after a potentially long delay. The early Christians prayed, *Maranatha*, "Lord, come!" as they waited for Jesus' return, which could happen quickly; so should we. Christians do not wait for the Antichrist (whatever our interpretation of the Antichrist passages of the New Testament). They do not wait for the great tribulation or for a final battle (whatever our interpretation of the Gog and Magog and the Armageddon passages in the Old and New Testament). Christians wait for Jesus' return.

Second, we take Jesus' statement seriously that "about that day and hour no one knows, neither the angels of heaven, nor the Son, but only the Father" (Matt. 24:36). True followers of Jesus refrain from calculating the nearness of the end. They are always ready because Jesus will be "coming at an unexpected hour" (v. 44), like a thief comes unexpectedly and suddenly (Matt. 24:43; Luke 12:39; 1 Thess. 5:2, 4; 2 Peter 3:10; Rev. 3:3; 16:15).

Third, we do what Jesus told us to do. He emphasized that during his absence those who belong to him should work for him. Followers of Jesus wait by doing what Jesus told them to do: taking the gospel to people who do not yet believe (Matt. 24:14; 28:18–20) and helping people who are hungry, thirsty, naked, sick, and in prison (Matt. 25:35–36).

Fourth, we emphasize truths as central that are central in Scripture. The prophecy that Jesus will return is central. The prophecy that there will be a

---

3. Craig L. Blomberg, "The Posttribulationism of the New Testament: Leaving 'Left Behind' Behind," in *A Case for Historic Premillennialism: An Alternative to "Left Behind" Eschatology,* ed. Craig L. Blomberg and Sung Wook Chung (Grand Rapids: Baker Academic, 2009), 65.

day of judgment is central. Details concerning a coming great tribulation, the potential timing and character of a rapture, the interpretation of the Beast from the sea and of the Antichrist, and the timing and character of the millennium are all clearly not central. It is legitimate to have opinions about these matters. It is illegitimate to use one's opinions about these questions to define what orthodox Christianity is, to divide churches, and to exclude Christians from ministry positions. In view of the fact that orthodox Christians have held different positions for centuries, it is foolish, even arrogant, to insist on the absolute truth of one's position on these surely minor questions.

Fifth, we continue to read and interpret Scripture, willing to consider the truth of other interpretations of biblical passages, willing to concede that we may have to adjust our understanding. Without this twofold willingness, we are not really reading Scripture in order to understand Scripture: we are merely reading Scripture in order to confirm and defend our own position. The willingness to learn is a basic characteristic of followers of Jesus, who are called "disciples" (Greek, *mathētai*, best defined as "people who are engaged in learning through instruction from another").

Sixth, Christians seek unity in faith and in understanding God's Word, while never simply accepting differing interpretations. We should not abandon the possibility that we can come to a common understanding of God's truth revealed in his Word. This was Paul's conviction: "There is one body and one Spirit, just as you were called to the one hope of your calling, one Lord, one faith, one baptism, one God and Father of all, who is above all and through all and in all" (Eph. 4:4–6). And this was Jesus' prayer: "I ask not only on behalf of these, but also on behalf of those who will believe in me through their word, that they may all be one. As you, Father, are in me and I am in you, may they also be in us, so that the world may believe that you have sent me" (John 17:20–21).

The Significance of Prophecy

Christians cannot afford *not* to be interested in questions related to the end times because biblical prophecy is important. The importance of biblical prophecy can be ascertained in its significance for the New Testament authors. As prophecy was fulfilled in the ministry, life, death, and resurrection of Jesus Christ, God proved true to his word. While this "proof from prophecy" is usually not convincing for non-Christians, it emphasizes for Christian believers several truths: God's sovereignty over the affairs of the world, his truthfulness in what he says and promises, and his mercy in saving sinners. As God fulfilled his promises in the past, he will fulfill his promises in the future.

Biblical prophecy is important because the belief in Jesus' second coming, in the millennium, and in the new creation of a new heaven and a new earth refutes the denigration of the material world. It emphasizes that God who created the world and redeemed Israelites, Jews, and Gentiles throughout history will establish his rule on a (new) earth.[4]

Biblical prophecy is important because it reminds us of Jesus' second coming, of the day of judgment, and thus of our responsibilities as Christian believers in the here and now. At the end of his discussion of Jesus' second coming and the resurrection of the believers who die before Jesus returns, Paul asserts: "But you, beloved, are not in darkness, for that day to surprise you like a thief; for you are all children of light and children of the day; we are not of the night or of darkness. So then let us not fall asleep as others do, but let us keep awake and be sober . . . . Therefore encourage one another and build up each other, as indeed you are doing" (1 Thess. 5:4–6, 11). An important example of what Paul means is found in the context of his statement "and in this way all Israel will be saved" (Rom. 11:26 NIV; NRSV translates "and so all Israel will be saved"). We can discuss with great enthusiasm and even greater disagreement the meaning of the Greek word translated here as "in this way," the meaning of "all," and the meaning of "Israel." A much more important discussion, at least for Gentile Christians, is the discussion about the meaning of Paul's assertion that it was God's plan that Israel should "stumble" over the Messiah Jesus, resulting in their rejection of Jesus, because "through their stumbling salvation has come to the Gentiles, so as to make Israel jealous" (Rom. 11:11). This is the question: do our churches make the Jewish people jealous? Is the reality of our Christian faith and our Christian community such that unbelieving Jews want what we have? This is, quite obviously, a much more significant discussion because we can actually *do* something about how we live as Christians and Christian communities, while the event that may or may not be prophesied in Romans 11:26 is a future event that we cannot influence.

The Significance of Prophecy and the Life of the Believer

As Christians, we care about biblical prophecy and about end-time questions because we want to be ready for Jesus' second coming and for our encounter with the one true and living God. The great majority of Paul's statements about the end times, Jesus' second coming, and the day of judgment are connected with his exhortation to the believers. The same is true for John: he writes Revelation not to satisfy our curiosity about God's timetable for the end times but in order to encourage believers who are suffering and to exhort believers who are in danger of compromising their faith by adapting to the

---

4. Ibid., Donald Fairbairn, "Contemporary Millennial/Tribulational Debates: Whose Side Was the Early Church On?" in *A Case for Historic Premillennialism: An Alternative to "Left Behind" Eschatology,* ed. Craig L. Blomberg and Sung Wook Chung (Grand Rapids: Baker Academic, 2009), 105–31 (see 129–30 for a focus on belief in the millennium).

secular values of Greco-Roman society. This is why we need to return to the subject of the assessment of rewards in the last judgment (see question 37).

When Paul speaks of the role of missionaries and teachers of the church, he asserts: "the one who plants and the one who waters have a common purpose, and each will receive wages according to the labor of each" (1 Cor. 3:8). Such an assessment, which is evidently assumed as taking place on the day of judgment, is mentioned in other New Testament passages as well.[5] The "reward" is not described. Paul does not emphasize in 1 Corinthians 3 the differing achievements of the apostles and the teachers of the church but the fact that the *result* of their work depends on God who gives growth. This means that neither the number of people that an evangelist has led to the Lord, nor the number of churches a missionary has established, nor the size of the church that a pastor is leading is the basis for the assessment of the reward. The reward is not based on the "success" of their work but, rather, on the "labor" of each, that is, on the personal commitment and dedication to the tasks each believer has been given.

The description of the work of "builders" in 1 Corinthians 3:12–13 has often been misunderstood. Paul writes, "if anyone builds on the foundation with gold, silver, precious stones, wood, hay, or straw, each builder's work will be plainly seen, for the Day will make it clear, because it will be revealed by fire. And the fire will test what kind of work each has done" (NET). First, it should be noted that while Paul describes various materials, what is tested is not the materials but the building. His main point in the passage is that the foundation of a church must not be altered. The only foundation that can "carry" the weight of the church, which is God's temple,[6] is the message of Jesus, the crucified and risen Messiah, a message that is nonsense for Greeks (Gentiles) and a stumbling block for Jews (1 Cor. 3:11; see 1:18–2:5). Paul argues that if teachers of the church abandon or ignore this foundation and start erecting a building that does not conform to the standard projected by the foundation the structure will collapse. Second, the materials that do not burn (gold, silver, precious stones) are not really building materials, while the materials that burn (wood, hay, straw) are indeed materials that are used in building (wood for the roof and for the doors and windows; hay and straw in the production of mats). This means that Paul's image shifts from the construction of a building on the (right) foundation to materials that either burn up or that are preserved in fire. This shift is triggered by the reference to fire, which is a symbol for judgment. Thus, Paul does not describe here the assessment of the deeds of individual Christians in terms of their moral "durability"

---

5. Matthew 16:27; Romans 2:6; 2 Corinthians 11:15; 2 Timothy 4:14; 1 Peter 1:17; Revelation 22:12.

6. A temple is a monumental building of immense weight that needs a foundation. Private houses did not usually need foundations but were erected of fieldstones.

on the day of judgment. Rather, he clarifies which message helps a congregation develop and grow and which message destroys the congregation.

At the same time Paul indeed affirms that all believers, without exception, will appear before Jesus' tribunal to be examined: "For all of us must appear before the judgment seat of Christ, so that each may receive recompense for what has been done in the body, whether good or evil" (2 Cor. 5:10). The purpose of this examination is to establish the receipt of "an exact and impartial recompense (including the receipt or deprivation of commendation) which would be based on deeds, both good and bad, performed through the earthly body."[7]

While Jesus can speak of a "great reward" (Matt. 5:12; Luke 6:35), in the parable of the workers in the vineyard all workers receive the same remuneration, even those who have worked for only one hour (Matt. 20:1–16).

Paul does not suggest that Christians will suffer punishment for every sin they commit.[8] Paul knows that believers are not perfect and thus warns of judgment,[9] but he does not warn them of a divine judgment of their individual sins. He does at least two things.

First, Paul reminds Christian believers of who they are. He challenges the Corinthians believers, who have all kinds of moral problems, to remember that they are "those who are sanctified in Christ Jesus, called to be saints" (1 Cor. 1:2). He reminds the Roman Christians that "just as sin exercised dominion in death, so grace might also exercise dominion through justification leading to eternal life through Jesus Christ our Lord" (Rom. 5:21). This "dominion" of justification is the result of Jesus' death and resurrection and that which characterizes the believers' status and life as a result of their faith in Jesus (Rom. 3:21–5:10). This "dominion" of God's grace is in fact so overwhelming that some might draw the conclusion that one can continue to sin: if God has forgiven all our sins, whether past, present, or future, then one might conclude that committing further sin is of no consequence (Rom. 6:1). Paul rejects this conclusion with vehemence (Rom. 6:2–23), explaining what it means to be a Christian, but he does not dispute the premise that God has forgiven all sin of those who repent and believe in Jesus Christ.

Second, he tells believers that they should more fully become what they are. Thus he writes in Galatians 5:16–21:

> Live by the Spirit, I say, and do not gratify the desires of the flesh. For what the flesh desires is opposed to the Spirit, and what the Spirit desires

---

7. Murray J. Harris, *The Second Epistle to the Corinthians*, NIGTC (Grand Rapids: Eerdmans, 2005), 409.

8. See Stephen H. Travis, *Christ and the Judgment of God: The Limits of Divine Retribution in New Testament Thought*, 2nd ed. (Peabody, MA: Hendrickson, 2009), 136.

9. See 1 Thessalonians 4:6; 1 Corinthians 6:9–10; Galatians 5:21; Ephesians 5:5–6.

is opposed to the flesh; for these are opposed to each other, to prevent you from doing what you want. But if you are led by the Spirit, you are not subject to the law. Now the works of the flesh are obvious: fornication, impurity, licentiousness, idolatry, sorcery, enmities, strife, jealousy, anger, quarrels, dissensions, factions, envy, drunkenness, carousing, and things like these. I am warning you, as I warned you before: those who do such things will not inherit the kingdom of God.

Biblical prophecy and end-times questions are important because, ultimately, they are related to "inheriting the kingdom of God." Followers of Jesus are people who know that their faith in Jesus and their everyday lives have consequences—in this world, and in the world to come.

Summary

Christian believers emphasize what Jesus emphasized. They accept the limited knowledge that Jesus said they have, and they do what Jesus told them to do. Christians wait for Christ's return, not for the confirmation of their views about the end times. Christians emphasize what Scripture emphasizes as central, and they refuse to let minor questions become major disagreements that only hurt and divide the church. Christians care about biblical prophecy because the expectation of Jesus' second coming and of the last judgment is a significant emphasis of Scripture. Christians care about the end times because waiting for Jesus' return, and anticipating our encounter with the true and living God, shows us who we are: sinners who have been forgiven, who look forward to seeing the almighty God face to face, and who live with joyful commitment to the will of God and to the work that Jesus Christ has entrusted to us.

REFLECTION QUESTIONS

1. Why should we care about the end times?

2. What do Jesus, Paul, and John emphasize as central elements of a Christian's hope for the future?

3. In what way is our assessment by God in the last judgment important?

4. How should we handle disagreements over questions related to biblical prophecy?

5. Why is the teaching about Jesus' second coming important for us personally?

Select Bibliography

Archer, Gleason L., ed. *Three Views on the Rapture: Pre-, Mid-, or Post-Tribulation*. Grand Rapids: Zondervan, 1996.

Blomberg, Craig L., and Sung Wook Chung, eds. *A Case for Historic Premillennialism: An Alternative to "Left Behind" Eschatology*. Grand Rapids: Baker Academic, 2009.

Bock, Darrell L., ed. *Three Views on the Millennium and Beyond*. Grand Rapids: Zondervan, 1999.

Clouse, Robert G., ed. *The Meaning of the Millennium: Four Views*. Downers Grove, IL: InterVarsity Press, 1977.

Hays, J. Daniel, J. Scott Duvall, and C. Marvin Pate. *Dictionary of Biblical Prophecy and End Times*. Grand Rapids: Zondervan, 2007.

Mounce, Robert H. *The Book of Revelation*. Revised edition. Grand Rapids: Eerdmans, 1998.

Osborne, Grant R. *Revelation*. BECNT. Grand Rapids: Baker Academic, 2002.

Walker, Peter W. L., ed. *Jerusalem Past and Present in the Purposes of God*. Grand Rapids: Baker, 1992.

Walls, Jerry L., ed. *The Oxford Handbook of Eschatology*. Oxford: Oxford University Press, 2008.

Witherington, Ben. *Jesus, Paul, and the End of the World: A Comparative Study in New Testament Eschatology*. Downers Grove, IL: InterVarsity Press, 1992.

Scripture Index

Ancient Sources Index

40 QUESTIONS SERIES